DECENTRALIZING GOVERNANCE

INNOVATIVE GOVERNANCE IN THE 21ST CENTURY

GOWHER RIZVI
Series editor

This is the first volume in a new series that will examine important issues of governance, public policy, and administration, highlighting innovative practices and original research worldwide. All titles in the series will be copublished by the Brookings Institution Press and the Ash Institute for Democratic Governance and Innovation, housed at Harvard University's John F. Kennedy School of Government.

DECENTRALIZING GOVERNANCE

Emerging Concepts and Practices

G. Shabbir Cheema

Dennis A. Rondinelli

editors

ASH INSTITUTE FOR DEMOCRATIC GOVERNANCE AND INNOVATION
John F. Kennedy School of Government
Harvard University

BROOKINGS INSTITUTION PRESS
Washington, D.C.

Copyright © 2007

ASH INSTITUTE FOR DEMOCRATIC GOVERNANCE AND INNOVATION
HARVARD UNIVERSITY

Library of Congress Cataloging-in-Publication data
Decentralizing governance : emerging concepts and practices / G. Shabbir Cheema, Dennis A. Rondinelli, editors.
    p.   cm.   — (Innovative governance in the 21st century)
  Summary: "Assesses the emerging concepts of decentralization (devolution, empowerment, capacity building, and democratic governance) in different contexts and regions. Details the factors driving the movement, including political changes such as the fall of the Iron Curtain and the ascendance of democracy; economic factors such as globalization and outsourcing; and technological advances"—Provided by publisher.
  Includes bibliographical references and index.
  ISBN-13: 978-0-8157-1389-0 (pbk. : alk. paper)
  ISBN-10: 0-8157-1389-4 (pbk. : alk. paper)
  1. Decentralization in government. 2. Comparative government. I. Cheema, G. Shabbir. II. Rondinelli, Dennis A.
  JC355.D383 2007
  352.3'67—dc22   2007015721

9 8 7 6 5 4 3 2 1
The paper used in this publication meets minimum requirements of the American National Standard for Information Sciences—Permanence of Paper for Printed Library Materials: ANSI Z39.48-1992.

Typeset in Adobe Garamond

Composition by Circle Graphics
Columbia, Maryland

Printed by R. R. Donnelley
Harrisonburg, Virginia

In memory of

PROFESSOR DENNIS A. RONDINELLI

*for his enduring contribution to the study of governance,
public administration, and international development*

Contents

Foreword

Few issues have created as much controversy over the past half century as how governments and political systems should be structured and how public policies should be made and implemented. Centralists generally believe that national political leaders and administrators know best how to provide security, promote economic growth, and maintain political stability. Those who argue for decentralization generally tend to have a more populist view. They tend to believe that the best public policies come from wide participation in public affairs and from local knowledge about how best to solve problems and meet the needs of citizens.

Globalization has brought increasing interaction among governments, private enterprise, and organizations of civil society and, with it, increasing pluralism in shaping public policies both within and among countries. All three of these entities—governments, private enterprise, and civil society organizations—have come to be seen as institutions of governance, whose participation is crucial in mobilizing the knowledge and insight necessary to take advantage of the potential benefits of globalization and to mitigate or prevent its potential threats.

As a result of changes brought about by globalization and also of changes in the concepts of governance, new forms of participation—and demands for them—have emerged in both rich and poor countries. These changes are redefining the meaning of decentralization. In the 1970s and 1980s decentralization was seen primarily as the deconcentration, delegation, or devolution of responsibility for decisionmaking and administration from the central level of government to subordinate administrative units or local governments. New concepts and practices of decentralization are emerging, however, that create new forms of participation, new dimensions of power sharing, and new sources of influence over public policymaking and implementation.

This book, the first of a series sponsored by the Ash Institute and Brookings Institution Press on "Innovative Governance in the 21st Century," will be launched at the Seventh Global Forum on Reinventing Government, hosted by the United Nations at the UN headquarters in Vienna in June 2007. The theme of the Seventh Global Forum, endorsed by the UN General Assembly, is "building trust in government." Decentralization contributes to trust in government by bringing government closer to people. The Ash Institute and the United Nations collaborated in organizing the Global Forum.

In this book, the authors seek to explore and examine the shift from decentralization of government to decentralized governance and to assess emerging principles and practices in the public, private, and civil society sectors. We thank G. Shabbir Cheema, principal adviser, United Nations, and the late Dennis A. Rondinelli, senior research scholar, Duke University, for leading the group of eminent scholars in preparing the chapters. Their earlier book on decentralization and development, published in 1983, has been widely quoted in the literature on the subject. We are grateful to them for revisiting the subject and for their leadership in providing the conceptual framework and examining decentralized governance principles and practices. It is due primarily to the authors of the chapters in this volume and to their dedication and commitment to analyzing the emerging principles and practices of decentralized governance around the world that we are able to understand better the importance of these changing concepts. All of the observations and conclusions are, of course, those of the authors and should not be attributed to the sponsoring organizations, the United Nations, or the organizations with which the authors and editors are affiliated.

Thanks are also due to our colleagues at the Ash Institute for facilitating the work of the study group, including the organization of the authors' meeting at the Kennedy School to discuss the conceptual framework and outlines of various chapters.

GOWHER RIZVI, DIRECTOR
Ash Institute for Democratic Governance
   and Innovation
John F. Kennedy School of Government
Harvard University

GUIDO BERTUCCI, DIRECTOR
Division for Public Administration
   and Development Management
Department of Economic
   and Social Affairs
United Nations

1

From Government Decentralization
to Decentralized Governance

G. SHABBIR CHEEMA AND DENNIS A. RONDINELLI

Concepts of decentralization have changed rapidly over the past quarter of a century in tandem with the evolution in thinking about governance. Until the early 1980s government and the state were generally perceived of interchangeably. Government was seen as the institutional embodiment of state sovereignty and as the dominant source of political and legal decisionmaking. In developing countries, debates over the structure, roles, and functions of government focused on the effectiveness of central power and authority in promoting economic and social progress and on the potential advantages and disadvantages of decentralizing authority to subnational units of administration, local governments, or other agents of the state. Decentralization was defined as the transfer of authority, responsibility, and resources—through deconcentration, delegation, or devolution—from the center to lower levels of administration.[1]

By the early 1980s increasing international trade and investment; growing economic, social, and political interaction across national borders; and rapidly emerging technological innovations that increased the scope and reduced the costs of communications and transportation and helped spread knowledge and information worldwide, changed perceptions of governance and of the appropriate functions of the state. The concept of governance expanded to include not only government but also other societal institutions, including the private sector and civil associations. Debates shifted from the proper allocation of responsibilities within government to how strongly the state should intervene in economic activities, whether central governments inhibited or promoted economic growth and social development, and the appropriate roles of government, the private sector, and civil society.[2]

As international economic interaction grew and as societies became more complex and interconnected, government came to be seen as only one, albeit a critically important, governance institution. The fact that people's lives were also shaped by decisions made by individual entrepreneurs, family enterprises, and private firms; by multinational corporations and international financial institutions; and by a variety of civil society organizations operating both within and outside of national territories, became more apparent.[3] As globalization pushed more countries to adopt market or quasi-market economies, and as technology drove the growth and integration of worldwide communication and transportation networks, demands for political and economic participation grew even in countries that had totalitarian, authoritarian, or dictatorial governments and in which the state traditionally played the dominant or controlling role in managing national affairs. Good governance came to be seen as transparent, representative, accountable, and participatory systems of institutions and procedures for public decisionmaking.[4]

From this broader perspective on governance new concepts of decentralization emerged as well. As the concept of governance became more inclusive, decentralization took on new meanings and new forms. In this book, we trace the transformation and evolution of concepts and practices of decentralization from the transfer of authority within government to the sharing of power, authority, and responsibilities among broader governance institutions. The contributors to this volume assess the emerging concepts of decentralization; the political, economic, social, and technological forces driving them; and new approaches to decentralizing both government and governance. The authors of each chapter explore the objectives of decentralization within this changing paradigm and the potential benefits of and difficulties in achieving them. Each of the chapters offers lessons of experience from countries around the world where attempts have been made to decentralize government or governance and the implications for public policy in the future.

Emerging Concepts of Decentralization and Governance

As the concept of decentralization evolved over the past half century, it has taken on increasingly more diverse and varied meanings, objectives, and forms.[5] The first wave of post–World War II thinking on decentralization, in the 1970s and 1980s, focused on deconcentrating hierarchical government structures and bureaucracies.[6] The second wave of decentralization, beginning in the mid-1980s, broadened the concept to include political power sharing, democratization, and market liberalization, expanding the scope for private sector decisionmaking.

During the 1990s decentralization was seen as a way of opening governance to wider public participation through organizations of civil society.

After more than two decades—that is, the 1940s and the 1950s—of increasing centralization of government power and authority in both more developed and less developed countries, governments around the world began, during the 1960s and 1970s, to decentralize their hierarchical structures in an effort to make public service delivery more efficient and to extend service coverage by giving local administrative units more responsibility. During the 1970s and 1980s, globalization forced some governments to recognize the limitations and constraints of central economic planning and management. A shift during the same period in development theories and strategies in international aid agencies away from central economic planning and trickle-down theories of economic growth toward meeting basic human needs, growth-with-equity objectives, and participatory development also led to increasing calls for decentralization.[7] International assistance organizations promoted decentralization as an essential part of a "process approach" to development that depended primarily on self-help by local communities and local governments.[8] National governments decentralized in order to accelerate development, break bureaucratic bottlenecks arising from centralized government planning and management, and participate more effectively in a globalizing economy.

Until the late 1980s governments pursued three primary forms of decentralization: deconcentration, devolution, and delegation.[9] Deconcentration sought to shift administrative responsibilities from central ministries and departments to regional and local administrative levels by establishing field offices of national departments and transferring some authority for decisionmaking to regional field staff. Devolution aimed to strengthen local governments by granting them the authority, responsibility, and resources to provide services and infrastructure, protect public health and safety, and formulate and implement local policies. Through delegation, national governments shifted management authority for specific functions to semiautonomous or parastatal organizations and state enterprises, regional planning and area development agencies, and multi- and single-purpose public authorities.

By the mid-1980s, with the continued weakening of centrally planned economies, the waning of the cold war, and the rapid growth of international trade and investment, economic and political forces reshaped conventional concepts of not only economic development but governance and decentralization as well. The fall of authoritarian regimes in Latin America during the 1980s and in Central and Eastern Europe during the early 1990s and the rapid spread of market economies and more democratic principles in East Asia brought renewed interest in decentralization. In Latin America, East Asia, and Central Europe, governments overseeing the transition from state-planned to market economies focused on strengthening the private sector, privatizing or liquidating state enterprises, downsizing large central government bureaucracies, and strengthening local governments.[10] The International Monetary Fund, the World Bank, and other international development organizations prescribed decentralization as part of the structural adjustments needed to restore markets, create or strengthen democracy, and promote good governance.

Governments were also pressured to decentralize by political, ethnic, religious, and cultural groups seeking greater autonomy in decisionmaking and stronger control over national resources. In much of Africa, calls for decentralization emanated from tribal minorities and economically peripheral ethnic groups.[11] Growing discontent with the inability of central government bureaucracies to deliver effectively almost any type of service to local areas fueled the decentralization movement in Africa.[12] Calls for devolution or autonomous rule also came from minority groups in Belgium, Quebec, Wales, Scotland, Malaysia, the Baltic countries, Mexico, the Philippines, India, Yugoslavia, and the former Soviet Union that were dissatisfied with their political representation or the allocation of national expenditures.

The "new public management" movement of the 1990s in richer countries shaped the way international development organizations and many reform-oriented public officials in developing countries began to think about what governments should do and how they should perform. In their book *Reinventing Government,* which reflected innovative reforms in the United States and influenced thinking in other countries during the 1990s, David Osborne and Ted Gaebler argue that national, state, and local government should be innovative, market oriented, decentralized, and focused on offering their "customers" the highest quality services.[13] They and advocates of new public management contended that governments should "steer rather than row" and oversee service provision rather than deliver it directly; further, governments should encourage local groups to solve their own problems by deregulating and privatizing those activities that could be carried out by the private sector or by civil society organizations more efficiently or effectively than by public agencies.

New public management focused on making government mission driven rather than rule bound, results oriented, enterprising, anticipatory, and customer driven. Government agencies should meet the needs of citizens rather than those of the bureaucracy. At the heart of this approach to government was the notion that it had to be decentralized in order to achieve all of the other goals; that is, it would be most effective working through participation and teamwork among government agencies at different levels and with groups outside of government.

Globalization and Decentralization

Little doubt remains that globalization has shaped and will continue to shape economic, political, and social conditions throughout the world. Not surprisingly, globalization has shaped not only concepts of economic growth but also perceptions of governance and the roles and functions of government. In the twenty-first century the driving forces of globalization—increasing international trade and investment, rapid progress in information, communications and transportation technology, the increasing mobility of factors of production, the rapid transmission of financial capital across national borders, the emergence of knowledge economies and electronic commerce, the spread of innovation capability, and the worldwide expansion of markets for goods and services—are creating new pressures on governments to decentralize. Globalization is deconcentrating economic activity among and within countries. It increases pressures on governments to enhance the administrative and fiscal capacity of subnational regions, cities, towns, and rural areas in order to facilitate the participation of individuals and enterprises in a global marketplace and to benefit from it.

Increasingly, foreign direct investment flows to those countries where the government not only creates a strong national business climate but where "location assets" in towns, cities, and regions are well developed and where local governments can provide the services, infrastructure, quality of life, and other forms of support for foreign-owned and domestic firms. Strengthening these location assets usually requires strong local governments and civil society organizations that can raise the revenues and provide the supporting services that both foreign investors and domestic entrepreneurs need to participate effectively in a global marketplace.[14]

The emergence of globally dispersed industrial clusters and worldwide supply chains, the global outsourcing of manufacturing and services, and the expansion of electronic commerce have simultaneously, and seemingly paradoxically, made the spread of international economic activity less dependent on specific geographical locations and made the location assets of subnational geographical areas more important in attracting international firms or incubating domestic enterprises. Successful economic zones, science and industrial parks, geographically focused industrial clusters, and emerging urban hubs of globally oriented commercial activity all have rich networks of interaction among central and local governments, the private sector, and civil society organizations.[15] Globalization and technological change not only have pressured governments in some countries to decentralize administrative and fiscal authority but also have created conditions under which regional, state, provincial, and local administrative or government units are moving toward de facto decentralization through local leadership and initiative.[16]

The global deconcentration of economic activity has not only given localities new resources but has also brought new pressures on local governments to perform their administrative tasks more effectively. National government officials sometimes use the weak performance of local governments as a reason to keep decisionmaking centralized. One of the most critical issues in implementing decentralization, therefore, is identifying those factors that facilitate strong local government performance. As they create new local structures, organizations, and procedures, governments are training employees to perform increasingly more complex tasks and introducing reforms that increase local capacity to manage fiscal resources and public services.

A Broader View of Governance

The United Nations, in the 1990s, helped to reconceptualize governance, defining it as "the exercise of political, economic and administrative authority in the management of a country's affairs."[17] The United Nations Development Program perceived of governance as those institutions and processes through which government, civil society organizations, and the private sector interact with each other in shaping public affairs and through which citizens articulate their interests, mediate their differences, and exercise their political, economic, and social rights.

This broader concept of governance viewed decisionmaking as not only the province of government but also the right and obligation of citizens as members of a free electorate mobilized through social organizations and the private sector. Democratic governance implied a mandate for governments to create or strengthen channels and mechanisms for public participation in decisionmaking, to abide by the rule of law, to increase transparency in public procedures, and to hold officials accountable.[18] The case for democratic governance was based on two arguments: first, that it provides an institutional framework for participation by all citizens in economic and political processes; and second, that it promotes core, universal human rights and values as ends in themselves. Democratic governance implied that the state would ensure free and fair elections; appropriately decentralize power and resources to local communities; protect the independence of the judiciary and access to justice; maintain an effectively functioning civil service; ensure the separation of powers; safeguard access to information and the independence of the media; protect basic human rights, freedom of enterprise, and freedom of expression; and pursue sound economic policies.[19]

As the concept of governance expanded, so did thinking about the rationale, objectives, and forms of decentralization. Decentralization now encompasses not only the transfer of power, authority, and responsibility within government but also the sharing of authority and resources for shaping public policy within society. In this expanding concept of governance decentralization practices can be categorized into at least four forms: administrative, political, fiscal, and economic.

—Administrative decentralization includes deconcentration of central government structures and bureaucracies, delegation of central government authority and responsibility to semiautonomous agents of the state, and decentralized cooperation of government agencies performing similar functions through "twinning" arrangements across national borders.

—Political decentralization includes organizations and procedures for increasing citizen participation in selecting political representatives and in making public policy; changes in the structure of the government through devolution of powers and authority to local units of government; power-sharing institutions within the state through federalism, constitutional federations, or autonomous regions; and institutions and procedures allowing freedom of association and participation of civil society organizations in public decisionmaking, in providing socially beneficial services, and in mobilizing social and financial resources to influence political decisionmaking.

—Fiscal decentralization includes the means and mechanisms for fiscal cooperation in sharing public revenues among all levels of government; for fiscal delegation in public revenue raising and expenditure allocation; and for fiscal autonomy for state, regional, or local governments.

—Economic decentralization includes market liberalization, deregulation, privatization of state enterprises, and public-private partnerships.

As the concepts and forms of decentralization became more diverse so did the objectives of its advocates. They argued that decentralization could help accelerate economic development, increase political accountability, and enhance public participation in governance; and when pursued appropriately decentralization could also help break bottlenecks in hierarchical bureaucracies and assist local officials and the private sector to cut through complex procedures and get decisions made and implemented more quickly. Decentralization could increase the financial resources of local governments and provide the flexibility to respond effectively to local needs and demands.[20]

In the broader context of governance, those who promoted decentralization saw it as a way of increasing the capacity of local governments—and also of the private sector and civil society organizations—to extend services to larger numbers of people. It could be a way of giving greater political representation to diverse political, ethnic, religious, and cultural groups without destabilizing the state. Decentralization could allow all three governance institutions—government, the private sector, and civil society organizations—to become more creative and innovative in responding to public needs. It could help governments balance regional development, empower communities, and mobilize private resources for investment in infrastructure and facilities.[21]

In addition, many proponents now see decentralization as an instrument for building institutional capacity within local governments and civil society organizations to achieve the UN's Millennium Development Goals and improve chances of successfully implementing policies for the poor that depend on local communities to take ownership of poverty-alleviation programs.

Reassessing Decentralization

In one form or another, both democratic governance and decentralized government have been adopted by many countries over the past quarter of a century. By the early 1990s, all but twelve of the seventy-five countries with populations of more than 5 million had undertaken some form of decentralization.[22] At the end of the 1990s, about 95 percent of the countries with democratic political systems had subnational units of administration or government. By the early 2000s, there were more democratic states in the world than nondemocratic ones. Freedom House ranked 89 of the 192 countries that it surveyed as "free" and 54 as "partly free" (4 billion people, or 63 percent of the world's population, live in these countries). At least 119 of those countries were deemed to be formal electoral democracies.[23]

Although many countries have moved toward democratic governance, their attempts to decentralize have not always been easy or successful. Time and again, reformers have learned that decentralization is not a panacea for all of the ills of ineffective governance. Successful experiments in decentralization have yielded many of the benefits claimed by its advocates, but skeptics also point to its limitations. In many developing countries, decentralization may increase the potential for "elite capture" of local governments or is undermined by their inability to raise sufficient financial resources to provide services efficiently. Decentralization often fails because of low levels of administrative and management capacity in local governments and in civil society organizations.[24] Decentralization has been accompanied by widening economic and social disparities among regions in some countries and increased levels of local corruption and nepotism in others.[25]

The evidence is mixed, moreover, with respect to decentralization's effects on economic growth, public participation, and service delivery.[26] Despite the allocative-efficiency arguments for decentralization, empirical relationships between decentralization and various development variables have more often than not been negative. Some studies have found no direct links between fiscal decentralization and economic growth, for example, although they identified several strong potential indirect linkages.[27] Other studies found that fiscal decentralization is associated with lower economic growth and greater fiscal imbalance.[28] Some research indicates that decentralization increases public infrastructure expenditure for those services with local benefits but with little or no economies of scale and that private provision of services and infrastructure increases only when local governments in a politically decentralized system place more weight than the central government does on infrastructure delivery.[29]

The impacts of decentralization on citizen participation also vary from country to country depending on the type of decentralization used and the political situation in the country. Local governments in Africa have often constrained local groups and limited citizen participation, especially of the poor, as strongly as central governments.[30] Studies in Latin America indicate that decentralization is one, but not necessarily the most essential, component for citizen participation and that the relationship between decentralization and citizen participation is conditioned by complex political, historical, social, and economic factors that differ in strength and importance among and within countries.[31] Questions arise in Africa as well about whether decentralization can increase efficiency in service delivery, empower local groups, and facilitate popular participation.[32] Studies of decentralization in the Middle East note that simply because central governments allow the proliferation of civil society organizations does not mean that they encourage or facilitate real empowerment.[33]

Although evidence can be found for both beneficial and negative consequences of decentralization among and within countries, many of the failures of decentralization are due less to inherent weaknesses in the concept itself than to government's ineffectiveness in implementing it. Like any prescription for fundamental change, decentralization meets resistance from those whose interests are served by the concentration of power and resources in the central government. And as with any fundamental reforms that shift the distribution of power, the successful implementation of decentralization policies depends on the creation of multiple and complex conditions that make success uncertain in any country.[34]

Andrew Parker once compared the implementation of decentralization policies to cooking a soufflé.[35] A successful soufflé requires the precisely correct combination of ingredients, the right temperature, and perhaps a persistent chef. If any of the ingredients are missing, mixed in incorrect proportions, or cooked at the wrong temperature, the soufflé will fall. Learning to cook a soufflé often requires some experimentation and a willingness to improve through trial and error.

Experience in developing countries suggests that successful decentralization always requires the right ingredients, appropriate timing, and some degree of experimentation. The ingredients are now well known. Decentralization cannot easily be enacted or sustained without strong and committed political leadership at both national and local government levels. Government officials must be willing and able to share power, authority, and financial resources. Political leaders must accept participation in planning and management by groups that are outside of the direct control of the central government or the dominant political party.[36] Support for and commitment to decentralization must also come from line agencies of the central bureaucracy. Ministry officials must be willing to transfer some of those functions that they traditionally performed to local organizations and to assist local officials in developing the capacity to perform them effectively. Experience suggests that decentralization can be implemented effectively only when policies are appropriately designed and when local public officials are honest and competent and national political leaders view local empowerment as a benefit rather than a threat.[37]

Decentralization is a critical issue to revisit after more than a quarter of a century of attempts by governments around the world to adjust to globalization and to new perceptions of governance. Decentralization remains a core prescription of international development organizations for promoting democratic governance and economic adjustment and is seen by many of its advocates as a condition for achieving sustainable economic, political, and social development and for attaining the UN's Millennium Development Goals. Reassessing decentralization in these new contexts is also important because of the continuing difficulties experienced by governments in many developing countries in implementing it effectively. Scholars, policymakers, and development professionals need to rethink why some programs have succeeded and others have not. The relationships between decentralization and economic development and between decentralization and poverty reduction need to be clarified. The efficacy of decentralization in achieving the objectives that advocates claim for it needs to be verified.

This book focuses on three aspects of decentralization as an instrument for achieving democratic governance: how political, administrative, and financial authority can be devolved most effectively; which conditions are required for effectively sharing power and authority among governance institutions; and how capacity can be developed for effective participation by local governments and community groups in democratic governance.

The contributors to this volume seek to reassess the role of decentralization in a twenty-first-century global society. They explore how processes of globalization affect decentralized governance; examine worldwide experience with devolving political and financial authority; describe local government capacity building and the use of partnerships among governments, civil society, and the private sector; assess the impacts of decentralized governance on access to services and other equity-oriented objectives; and explore the factors that influence successful implementation of decentralization policies.

Decentralized Governance

Both economic globalization and the spread of international political and military conflicts were strong forces during the twentieth century for decentralizing governance. Hybrid forms of decentralization are being tried both in advanced economies, attempting to adapt to the challenges and opportunities of economic globalization, and in poor fragile states and those recovering from conflict. As Dennis Rondinelli points out in chapter 2, governments in weak states, especially in those that that are coping with or recovering from conflicts arising from insurgencies, civil wars, or external invasions, must deal with complex economic, political, social, and development challenges. Many face the daunting tasks of providing social services, stabilizing and legitimizing governance, reviving the economy, controlling inflation, and stimulating trade and investment. Often they must also promote political participation, hold elections, and address violations of human rights in order to sustain peace accords or move toward more stable governance systems. Sometimes, governments in weak states must also heal the wounds of war by reducing existing social and political tensions.

Governments in practically all postconflict societies face the difficult tasks of demobilizing and reintegrating ex-combatants, establishing civilian control over the military, and undertaking security reforms. Unsteady governments must often carry out all of these tasks and others while restoring or extending such essential public services as health and education, extending infrastructure to larger numbers of people, and caring for returning refugees and internally displaced persons.

Conditions in weak states and postconflict societies illustrate quite clearly the necessity of viewing both governance and decentralization broadly and the need for a wide range of alternatives for building governance capacity. Performing all of the functions required of governments in weak states calls for strong administrative capacity, a resource commonly lacking in crisis or postcrisis countries. International assistance organizations seek to enhance limited public management capacity by leveraging governments' resources with private sector and civil society organizations. Frequently, in the rush to meet the needs of people in crisis, they simply bypass governments and deliver development assistance through parallel administrative structures until critical gaps in public management capacity can be filled. The parallel structures and partnership arrangements that governments and international donors use in weak states include

—externally established governance and administration structures
—build-operate-transfer arrangements and private investment arrangements
—public-private joint ventures
—public service wholesaling
—partnerships between government and civil society organizations
—independent civil society organizations.

These and other approaches are unconventional forms of decentralized governance and development administration that either attempt to enhance the limited public management capacity of weak governments through partnerships with other governance institutions or create alternative arrangements for providing social services through parallel organizations in the private sector and organizations of civil society.

Little analysis has been done of these types of parallel arrangements for decentralized administration, however, or of their potential advantages and disadvantages in weak states. Each of these parallel structures and arrangements requires appropriate policies, coordinating mechanisms, and administrative capacities within governments to work effectively. When these preconditions do not exist or cannot easily be created, parallel structures and arrangements for development administration fail.

Rondinelli identifies the types of parallel and partnership structures that international assistance organizations and governments use in weak states for development administration. He reviews the advantages and limitations of these approaches as forms of decentralized governance and government, the conditions and circumstances under which they are likely to produce effective results, and the factors that governments and donors should consider in using them. Only by understanding these conditions more clearly, Rondinelli argues, can governments and donors identify the kinds of technical and financial resources they need to make these decentralized administrative options work better in the future to attain their development objectives.

In chapter 3 Guido Bertucci and Maria Senese look at the impact of information communication technologies (ICTs) in decentralization processes. After examining trends in political trust, which highlight low confidence in government, they analyze how ICTs can play a key role in promoting and helping the decentralization process to be more effective and meaningful. They emphasize, with some evidence from case studies, how ICTs can foster decentralization and strengthen public trust in government by increasing efficiency, transparency, participation, and citizen engagement.

Political and Fiscal Devolution

Devolution of powers and resources to local governments has been a foundation for promoting sustainable decentralization in developing countries. Advocates argue that local governments with decisionmaking power, authority, and resources can play a more catalytic role in economic and social development. Citizens are more likely to participate actively in local political processes where local governments are perceived to have the capacity to make political and financial decisions affecting their economic and social welfare.

In chapter 4 Merilee Grindle analyzes the findings of her recent study of thirty randomly selected, medium-sized municipalities in Mexico to understand how local governments are coping with new responsibilities and resources and how they differ on indexes of government performance. She examines the impacts of four factors—political competition, the capacity of political leaders to mobilize resources for change, the introduction of new methods and skills for public administration, and the demands and participation of civil society—on the capacity of local governments to carry out their responsibilities efficiently, effectively, and responsively. She then analyzes their correlation with improved government performance.

Transferring power and authority from the central government to subnational administrative and local government units and opening the political process to widespread participation provide an institutional framework for local autonomy and empower communities to pursue local aspirations. Two dimensions of devolution, political and fiscal, are complementary. Political devolution provides a legal basis for the exercise of power at the local level and enables citizens to influence local policymaking and priority setting. Fiscal devolution assigns functions and revenues to subnational and local governments and the resources by which to implement local policies and programs. Too often, central governments assign functions to subnational administrative and local government units without providing adequate revenues to carry them out or the authority to raise revenues locally. Where resource deficiencies cripple local governments and undermine their ability to provide services, citizens become disillusioned with their performance and are less likely to participate actively in local political processes.

Based on experience in African countries, John-Mary Kauzya examines, in chapter 5, the extent to which political devolution has, in practice, facilitated people's participation. He discusses the driving forces of decentralization, structural arrangements and modalities devised to implement decentralization, and factors that have influenced the process of decentralization in Africa. Kauzya assesses case studies of Rwanda, South Africa, and Uganda to determine to what extent they have decentralized, the motives and objectives of decentralization, the functions and responsibilities that have been transferred, and the degree to which decentralization has promoted or facilitated broader popular participation.

Governments promoting political devolution have generally received strong support from Western donor countries and international development institutions that see the legitimacy of governance arising from the universal franchise, free and fair elections, and political pluralism. International development organizations also claim that highly participatory governance creates conditions that make governments more accountable and more efficient and effective in delivering service. In chapter 6 Ledivina Cariño examines the relationships between political devolution and the sustainability of democracy. She assesses some of the recent reforms dealing with political decentralization in the Philippines and examines their impact on improving the quality of the democratic process.

Others argue that political decentralization often fails to deliver in practice what it promises in theory. Peter Blunt and Mark Turner argue in chapter 7 that the developmental potential of administrative deconcentration tends to be overlooked by Western donors in favor of political devolution. Despite the rhetorical claims of donors to be interested primarily in poverty reduction, the alleviation of poverty often falls victim to what in practice turns out to be an overriding ideological preference for certain forms of democratic governance.

Based on experience with attempts at decentralization in postconflict or fragile states such as Cambodia, Papua New Guinea, and Indonesia, they argue that if poverty reduction rather than participatory democracy were the overriding concern of Western donors then much more development financing would be directed to promoting administrative deconcentration.

In chapter 8 Paul Smoke reviews what is known conceptually and empirically about fiscal decentralization in developing countries. He focuses on lessons derived from cases in which some progress has been made in overcoming common obstacles to decentralizing fiscal systems. He illustrates through the cases how some governments have been able to make elements of an intergovernmental fiscal system function in tandem and how to better link them to political and institutional reform.

Enrique Cabrero, in chapter 9, reviews the main theoretical arguments about the decentralization process in Latin America. He also attempts to explain how decentralization had been executed in the region and how the process has specifically affected fiscal management. He argues that Latin American reforms promote expenditure decentralization (mainly through fiscal transfers) better than revenue decentralization (broadening the fiscal attributions of subnational governments). Analyzing cases in Brazil, Chile, Peru, and Mexico, Cabrero describes how decentralization has allowed local governments to develop innovative capacities to manage the ever-growing public policy agenda and to interact with citizens.

Another challenge in implementing devolution in some developing countries is rampant corruption and misuse of authority at both national and local levels. These problems are especially serious in societies with inequitable social and economic structures and high levels of poverty and illiteracy. Even the staunchest advocates of decentralization argue, therefore, that effective devolution requires strong accountability not only by politicians and government officials but also by the private sector and representatives of civil society. In chapter 10 Shabbir Cheema examines four components of local government reform to ensure accountability: prevention, including identifying transparent local government procurement procedures; enforcement, through independent investigators, prosecutors, and adjudicators; public awareness campaigns; and institution building, including strengthening local oversight bodies. He offers examples of good practices in developing countries for each of these components and identifies factors that lead to success.

Forging Results-Oriented Partnerships

Partnerships among government, the private sector, and civil society organizations are becoming an increasingly popular form of decentralization. Partnerships and other forms of cooperation among government agencies, civil society, and the private sector are being used to develop and expand energy and utility networks and services, extend transportation systems, construct and operate water and waste treatment facilities, and provide such basic services as primary health care, education, and shelter.[38] Governments and the private sector are cooperating through a variety of mechanisms, including contracts and concessions; build-operate-transfer arrangements; and public-private joint ventures. Interest in public-private cooperation emerged for many reasons: insufficient national and local government capacity to extend services, public dissatisfaction with the quality and coverage of government-provided services, the ability of the private sector to provide some services such as transportation and housing more efficiently than government, and pressures from international assistance organizations to mobilize private investments.

Experience suggests, however, that successful partnerships between government and private or social organizations must be designed carefully and reflect the interests of those who are affected by the arrangement. An effective partnership must take advantage of the relative strengths of each partner, resulting in greater combined capacities to understand the needs and priorities of citizens, in improved quality and coverage of service provision, and in lowered costs. By increasing the ability of the state to respond to the needs of citizens, partnerships can play an important role in promoting local development.

Derick Brinkerhoff, Jennifer Brinkerhoff, and Stephanie McNulty develop in chapter 11 a framework for investigating the design parameters and decision spaces for participants in partnerships. They argue that a well-designed policy framework for decentralization expands design parameters; that is, it gives local governments more authority and leeway to negotiate and enter partnerships. It expands their ability to adapt and share power, their flexibility in ensuring accountability, their range of decentralization options, and their potential access to and application of resources. They apply this framework to decentralization reforms in Ghana and Peru to illustrate the expansion of citizen participation in local governance.

Capacity Building in Local Governments and Organizations of Civil Society

When civil society organizations such as farmers' associations, youth clubs, local branches of political parties, women's organizations, and community groups can engage in public decisionmaking, they can become powerful instruments for decentralization and democratic governance. They can increase local support and legitimacy for government intervention, safeguard the interests of local groups and citizens, and expand access to basic services.[39] Civil society organizations can increase citizens' awareness of government programs and projects and, in some cases, provide services directly to the poor. Civil society organizations can also play an important role in creating political awareness among the people at the local level and provide disadvantaged groups with a means for organizing themselves for political action.[40]

Goran Hyden argues in chapter 12 that decentralization is undermined in many African countries by central governments' dependence on external funding, clientelist politics, and limited administrative capacity in local governments and in civil society organizations. Drawing on past experiences with promoting local development in Africa, he proposes a new partnership between central and local institutions to increase the capacity to promote development and alleviate poverty. The partnership would use autonomous public funds insulated from patronage politics, and it would have the capacity to direct external funding into projects that stem from local demands rather than from the central government's supply of money. He argues that this form of parallel decentralization encouraging competition for scarce development resources among local governments and civil society organizations increases the chances of nurturing local ownership and pride and helps to build executive capacity from the bottom up. Hyden focuses on the case of the Culture Trust Fund in Tanzania to illustrate a successful application of this form of decentralization. He identifies potential roles of civil society in this process and linkages with local governments that can ensure the sustainability of local development projects.

International development organizations and bilateral donors have significantly increased their funding for decentralization in developing countries, both in response to requests from governments and to support programs for generating sustainable livelihoods. Naresh Singh examines in chapter 13 the role of decentralized governance in alleviating poverty and promoting sustainable livelihoods in poor but well-governed countries, in failed and fragile states, and in middle-income countries. He explores how these programs bring about changes in established power relations between elites and the poor, how they prevent local capture of decentralized public goods and services by the elite, and how they root out endemic corruption. Singh reconceptualizes power as a positive-sum game rather than as the usual zero-sum game and describes cases demonstrating the results.

In chapter 14, Kadmiel Wekwete discusses other cases—from Uganda, Senegal, Mali, and Ethiopia—demonstrating that rural local authorities can and do deliver services to the people when they meet key conditions of effective planning, budgeting, financing, and capacity building. He contends that the success of decentralization depends on whether political parties and political leaders identify decentralization as a serious goal and create conditions that promote successful implementation. Based on experience in these four countries, he points out that, with the right enabling environment, local communities take a more active interest in how resources are used and increase their dialogues with political representatives.

One of the enduring lessons of experience in developing countries is that local capacity building—that is, increasing the ability of an institution, organization, group, or individual to perform required functions effectively, efficiently, and in a sustainable manner—is the foundation for successful decentralization. Globalization and technological change have created a more dynamic interpretation of capacity development, one that takes into account the external policy environment, focuses more sharply on core competencies, and emphasizes the importance of cross-border communications, cooperation, and interaction. In chapter 15 Kem Lowry examines how the sharing of authority, resources, and accountability affects decentralized coastal management in countries around the world. He notes that successful implementation of decentralized environmental management programs requires not only the transfer of authority from the center to lower levels of government but also close intergovernmental coordination and shared governance. Lowry examines five models of decentralized coastal management—deconcentration, coercive devolution, cooperative devolution, devolved experimentation, and local entrepreneurship—and analyzes their characteristics and requirements.

William Ascher identifies the challenges of devolving control over renewable resources and over the proceeds from nonrenewable resources. In chapter 16 he assesses the preconditions for devolution to subnational governments and to common-pool-property communities and the roles of government and other governance institutions in facilitating devolution for successful local resource management. Ascher highlights the challenges facing government and civil society organizations in managing natural resources, including the risks of conflict over membership in the community or the controlling authority; vulnerability vis-à-vis government agencies, private encroachers, and other entities; excessive resource extraction; weaknesses in managerial or technical expertise; unproductive downstream diversification; and negative externalities for other communities that arise from resource exploitation. Guided by the premise that successful devolution depends on facilitation that avoids heavy-handed control, Ascher suggests the types of services that governments ought to divest themselves of and those they ought to retain.

Conclusion

The difficulties of finding strong and consistent evidence of direct causal relationships between decentralization and many of the benefits that its advocates claim for it may lead reasonable people to conclude that decentralization can be instrumental in promoting development and good governance but that it is not an end in itself. If decentralization is viewed as an instrument for achieving other goals, the studies in this book indicate that decentralization can be instrumental in facilitating development and democratic governance. New types and forms of decentralization are being used around the world to achieve more effective governance. The case studies and the contributors' examination of experience in various regions of the world identify the wide range of objectives that advocates of decentralization are seeking to achieve. The most successful experiments in decentralization have mobilized the support and commitment of political, governmental, and civic leaders to sustain governance reforms. The roles of governance institutions and the lessons about the most effective ways in which the administrative, financial, and political capacities of decentralized organizations can be enhanced and strengthened are still emerging. The chapters that follow explore the diversity of ways in which decentralized governance is contributing to the achievement of development objectives and assess the challenges of designing appropriate decentralization policies and programs and of implementing them effectively.

Notes

1. Dennis A. Rondinelli, "Government Decentralization in Comparative Perspective: Theory and Practice in Developing Countries," *International Review of Administrative Sciences* 47 (1981): 133–45; Dennis A. Rondinelli, John R. Nellis, and G. Shabbir Cheema, "Decentralization in Developing Countries: A Review of Recent Experience," Working Paper 581, World Bank Staff, 1983.

2. P. Drummond and A. Monsoor, "Macroeconomic Management and the Devolution of Fiscal Powers," *Emerging Markets, Finance & Trade* 39 (2003): 63–82.

3. Dennis A. Rondinelli, "Sovereignty on Line: The Challenges of Transnational Corporations and Information Technology in Asia," in *Sovereignty under Challenge: How Governments Respond,* edited by J. D. Montgomery and N. Glazer (New Brunswick, N.J.: Transaction, 2002): 345–71.

4. G. Shabbir Cheema, *Building Democratic Institutions: Governance Reform in Developing Countries* (Bloomfield, Conn.: Kumarian, 2005).

5. For a more detailed discussion of the evolution of concepts of decentralization, see Dennis A. Rondinelli, "Decentralization and Development," in *International Development Governance,* edited by A. M. Haque and M. Zafarulla (New York: Marcel Dekker, 2005).

6. Dennis A. Rondinelli and G. Shabbir Cheema, "Implementing Decentralization Policies: An Introduction," in *Decentralization and Development: Policy Implementation in Developing Countries,* edited by G. S. Cheema and D. A. Rondinelli (Beverly Hills, Calif.: Sage, 1983).

7. D. Korten and F. Alfonso, eds., *Bureaucracy and the Poor: Closing the Gap* (Singapore: McGraw-Hill, 1981).

8. Dennis A. Rondinelli, *Development Projects as Policy Experiments: An Adaptive Approach to Development Administration,* 2nd ed. (London: Routledge, 1993).

9. Rondinelli, Nellis, and Cheema, "Decentralization in Developing Countries"; D. A. Rondinelli, J. McCullough, and R. W. Johnson, "Analyzing Decentralization Policies in Developing Countries: A Political-Economy Framework," *Development and Change* 20, no. 1 (1989): 57–87.

10. R. Bird, R. Ebel, and C. Wallich, "Decentralization of the Socialist State: Intergovernmental Finance in Transition Economies," World Bank, 1995.

11. P. Mawhood, ed., *Local Government in the Third World: Experience with Decentralization in Tropical Africa,* 2nd ed. (Johannesburg: Africa Institute of South Africa, 1993).

12. Paul J. Smoke, *Local Government Finance in Developing Countries: The Case of Kenya* (Nairobi: Oxford University Press, 1994).

13. David Osborne and Ted Gaebler, *Reinventing Government* (Boston: Addison-Wesley, 1992).

14. Dennis A. Rondinelli, James H. Johnson Jr., and John D. Kasarda, "The Changing Forces of Urban Economic Development: Globalization and City Competitiveness," *Cityscape: The Journal of Policy Development and Research* 3, no. 3 (1998): 71–105.

15. Dennis A. Rondinelli, "Making Metropolitan Areas Competitive and Sustainable in the New Economy," *Journal of Urban Technology* 18, no. 1 (2001): 1–21.

16. Dennis A. Rondinelli, "Metropolitan Areas as Global Crossroads: Moving People, Goods and Information in the International Economy," in *Moving People, Goods and Information: The Cutting Edge Infrastructures of Networked Cities,* edited by Richard Hanley (London: Routledge, 2004).

17. United Nations Development Program, "Reconceptualizing Governance," Discussion Paper 2 (1997), p. 9.

18. D. Kaufmann, A. Kraay, and P. Zoido-Lobaton, "Governance Matters," Policy Research Paper 2196, World Bank, 1999.

19. Cheema, *Building Democratic Institutions.*

20. Dennis A. Rondinelli, "Financing the Decentralization of Urban Services in Developing Countries: Administrative Requirements for Fiscal Improvements," *Studies in Comparative International Development* 25, no. 2 (1990): 43–59.

21. M. Serageldin, S. Kim, and S. Wahba, "Decentralization and Urban Infrastructure Management Capacity," background paper, UNCHS/Habitat, Harvard University Graduate School of Design, 2000.

22. William Dillinger, "Decentralization and Its Implications for Urban Service Delivery," Urban Management Program Paper 16, World Bank, 1994.

23. Freedom House, *Freedom in the World* (Washington: 2005).

24. Food and Agriculture Organization of the United Nations, "Country Experiences in Decentralization in South Asia," 2004; O-H Fjeldstad, "Decentralization and Corruption: Review of the Literature" (Bergen, Norway: Chr. Michelsen Institute, 2003).

25. R. Fisman and R. Gatti, "Decentralization and Corruption: Evidence across Countries," *Journal of Public Economics* 83 (2002): 325–45.

26. A. Estache and S. Sinha, "Does Decentralization Increase Public Expenditure in Infrastructure?" Policy Research Working Paper 1457, World Bank, 1995.

27. Jorge Martinez-Vazquez and Ronald M. McNab, "Fiscal Decentralization and Economic Growth," *World Development* 31, no. 9 (2003): 1597–616.

28. H. Davoodi and H. F. Zou, "Fiscal Decentralization and Economic Growth: A Cross-Country Study," *Journal of Urban Economics* 43 (1998): 244–57; L. R. De Mello, "Fiscal Decentralization and Intergovernmental Fiscal Relations: A Cross-Country Analysis," *World Development* 28, no. 2 (2000): 365–80.

29. A. Estache and S. Sinha, "Does Decentralization Increase Public Expenditure in Infrastructure?" Policy Research Working Paper 1457, World Bank, 1995.

30. N. Devas and U. Grant, "Local Government Decision-Making—Citizen Participation and Local Accountability: Some Evidence from Kenya and Uganda," *Public Administration and Development* 23 (2003): 307–16.

31. Inter-American Development Bank, "Summary of Findings—Decentralization and Effective Citizen Participation: Six Cautionary Tales," Report RE-250, 2001.

32. P. Francis and R. James, "Balancing Rural Poverty Reduction and Citizen Participation: The Contradictions of Uganda's Decentralization Program," *World Development* 31, no. 2 (2003): 325–37.

33. Q. Wiktorowicz, "The Political Limits to Nongovernmental Organizations in Jordan," *World Development* 30, no. 1 (2002): 77–93.

34. A. Shah and T. Thompson, "Implementing Decentralized Local Governance: A Treacherous Road with Potholes, Detours and Road Closures," Policy Research Paper 3353, World Bank, 2004; H. M. G. Oeudraogo, "Decentralization and Local Governance: Experiences from Francophone West Africa," *Public Administration and Development* 23 (2003): 97–103; James S. Wunsch, "Decentralization, Local Governance and Recentralization in Africa," *Public Administration and Development* 21 (2001): 277–88.

35. Andrew Parker, "Decentralization: The Way Forward for Rural Development?" Policy Research Working Paper 1475, World Bank, 1995.

36. William Ascher and Dennis A. Rondinelli, "Restructuring the Administration of Service Delivery in Vietnam: Decentralization as Institution-Building," in *Market Reform in Vietnam,* edited by Jennie I. Litvack and Dennis A. Rondinelli (Westport, Conn.: Quorum, 1999).

37. R. Mitchinson, "Devolution in Uganda: An Experiment in Local Service Delivery," *Public Administration and Development* 23 (2003): 241–48.

38. Dennis A. Rondinelli, "Partnering for Development: Government–Private Sector Cooperation in Service Provision," in *Reinventing Government for the Twenty-First Century: State Capacity in a Globalizing Society,* edited by D. A. Rondinelli and G. S. Cheema (Bloomfield, Conn.: Kumarian, 2003): 219–39.

39. A. Krishna, "Partnerships between Local Governments and Community-Based Organizations: Exploring the Scope for Synergy," *Public Administration and Development* 23 (2003): 361–71.

40. G. Shabbir Cheema, "The Role of Voluntary Organizations," in *Decentralization and Development: Policy Implementation in Developing Countries,* edited by G. Shabbir Cheema and Dennis A. Rondinelli (Beverly Hills, Calif.: Sage, 1983).

2

Parallel and Partnership Approaches to Decentralized Governance: Experience in Weak States

DENNIS A. RONDINELLI

Globalization brings many developing countries the benefits of international trade and investment and broader access to jobs, entrepreneurial opportunities, information, education, and services. At the same time, however, it also increases access across national borders to a wide array of goods and services, including arms and weapons that have made it easier for disaffected factions in countries around the world to foment violent insurgencies, civil wars, and external invasions of weak states. The International Crisis Group counted eighty-two countries engaged in or recovering from some type of internal conflict in 2006.[1] Rebuilding postconflict countries and governments in weak states has become an increasingly important focus of Western governments' foreign aid programs and of the development assistance efforts of international organizations such as the World Bank and the United Nations. More than forty countries in Africa, Eastern Europe, Asia, Central and South America, and the Middle East during the 1990s were in or were recovering from serious conflict requiring United Nations peacekeeping forces and foreign donor reconstruction assistance.[2] By 2002 the World Bank was committing 16 percent of its total lending for postwar reconstruction in weak states.[3]

Governments in countries coping with or recovering from conflicts must deal with complex political challenges: providing security, strengthening governing authority and rule of law while restoring or extending essential public services, extending infrastructure, and caring for returning refugees and internally displaced people. Performing all of these functions requires strong governance and administrative capacities, resources often lacking in countries with weak or unstable governments.

International assistance organizations often try to enhance limited capacity in weak states by leveraging governments' resources with private sector and civil society organizations, thereby creating deconcentrated governance. Sometimes, in the rush to meet the needs of people recovering from crisis, they simply bypass governments and deliver development assistance through parallel administrative structures until public management capacity can be strengthened. Frequently, they use parallel structures and partnership arrangements to restore some semblance of government and to achieve pressing development objectives. Little analysis has been done of these parallel arrangements for decentralized development administration, however, or of their potential advantages and disadvantages in weak states. Mounting evidence suggests that in order to be effective, deconcentrated governance through parallel structures and arrangements requires appropriate policies, some degree of coordination, and basic administrative capacities within governments. When these preconditions do not exist or cannot easily be created, deconcentrated governance for development administration often fails.

In this chapter I examine the parallel and partnership structures that international assistance organizations use for deconcentrated governance in weak states. I review the advantages and limitations of these approaches as forms of decentralized development administration, the conditions and circumstances under which they are likely to produce effective results, and the factors that governments and donors should consider in using them. Only by understanding these conditions more clearly can governments and donors identify the technical and financial resources they need to make these deconcentrated governance options work better in the future to attain development objectives.

Governance Challenges in Weak States

Governments in most weak states, and especially those in postconflict countries, face similar tasks. They differ significantly, however, in their needs and the conditions under which they must perform their functions. The U.S. Department of State's Office of the Coordinator for Reconstruction and Stabilization summarizes succinctly the challenges facing governments in postconflict countries.[4] They generally must have or be able to develop quickly the administrative capacity to perform five essential functions:
—establish safety and security
—strengthen governance and participation
—stabilize the economy and provide infrastructure

—provide for emergency humanitarian needs and social welfare and
—strengthen justice and reconciliation organizations.
Not only is each of these governance functions crucial in its own right, but all
are also related and affect each other.[5]

Two decades of recent experience with recovery and reconstruction leave little
doubt that governments in postconflict countries find it difficult if not impossible
to meet these immediate and crucial challenges without effective public institutions. Yet their ability to strengthen public institutions may be limited, and in
some countries there may be no real government to develop management skills.
The World Bank pointed out that when it reengaged in Somalia in 2003, for
example, there was no fully functional national government through which to
provide the essential services needed to stimulate socioeconomic recovery and
help move the country toward sustained development and poverty reduction.
"Policies, institutions, and governance are weak or non-existent," its reengagement
report emphasized. "The security situation is difficult in many areas, making
on-the-ground visits difficult."[6] In other postconflict countries such as East
Timor, Kosovo, and Bosnia-Herzegovina international organizations had to create
a governing authority capable of carrying out basic functions until indigenous
governments could be created. Donors must often supplement a weak civil service in other postconflict countries still plagued with political fragmentation or
internal conflicts.

Although strengthening governance is a precondition for reconstructing postconflict countries, the government's ability to function effectively was often weak
before the onset of hostilities and generally became worse during the war. In the
aftermath of military conflict, governments in these countries are often called on
by internal factions and international organizations to make what, for them, seem
like traumatic administrative reforms at a time when they have limited financial
and technical capacity and weak political support. Many central governments in
crisis countries lack the administrative capacities even to carry out the minimum
responsibilities expected of a functioning state, much less to tackle the enormous
challenges of economic, social, physical, and political reconstruction.

The World Bank's assistance to East Timor, for example, "was affected from
the start by the virtual absence of any administrative capacity in the territory,
the extremely weak human resource base and its poverty."[7] Political and administrative fragmentation in Bosnia-Herzegovina resulted in a dysfunctional governance structure, further weakened by interethnic tensions. In Cambodia the
civil service performed poorly in the years following the cessation of hostilities.
It had weak capacity to deliver public services, and the services that it did deliver
were of poor quality and uneven distribution. Although the Cambodian civil
service was not extraordinarily large, it suffered from ineffective deployment
of government officials to priority sectors and rural areas and from understaffing

in social services such as health and education. Many civil servants had little or no education or training, and because of low salaries many took external employment, resulting in high levels of absenteeism from government jobs and poor job performance.[8] The civil service system was plagued by high levels of corruption, and the government had little financial management capacity.

Yet attempts by international organizations to promote public administration reforms and to strengthen central and local governments in weak states have been slow and the results have been uncertain. The World Bank's evaluation of its civil service reform assistance during the 1990s found that only about one-third of the interventions achieved satisfactory outcomes.[9] They fared little better than many of the public administration reforms proposed in Western and developing countries, where, as Charles Palidano points out, "they do not fail because, once implemented, they yield unsatisfactory outcomes. They fail because they never get past the implementation stage at all. They are blocked outright or put into effect only in tokenistic, half-hearted fashion."[10] Often, governments that do pursue reforms face conflicts among ministries and agencies with different objectives and bases of power, fear among public officials of losing personnel or budgetary resources, and widespread inertia because no organization within government has overall coordinating responsibility for implementing reforms or because they lack a sufficient number of "champions" to sustain the momentum.

Because strengthening governance in postconflict societies often requires difficult and complex changes that may take a long time to implement, donor governments and international assistance organizations often seek to bypass weak governments or create parallel structures or public-private partnerships to achieve urgent development objectives. They often use a wide array of arrangements, as depicted in figure 2-1: externally established governance and administration structures; build-operate-transfer and private investment arrangements; public-private joint ventures; public service wholesaling; government partnerships with civil society organizations; and independent civil society organizations.

Decentralized Approaches to Development Administration in Weak States

In many countries with weak governments, donors enhance administrative capacity by exploring parallel or public-private partnership approaches. As figure 2-1 illustrates, parallel approaches include bypassing weak governments altogether, at least until urgent problems can be addressed, or using civil society and private organizations to perform public functions while building the capacity of government agencies to take them over later. Public-private partnerships leverage whatever amount of administrative capacity exists in government by

Figure 2-1. *Parallel and Partnership Arrangements for Deconcentrated Governance and Decentralized Development Administration*

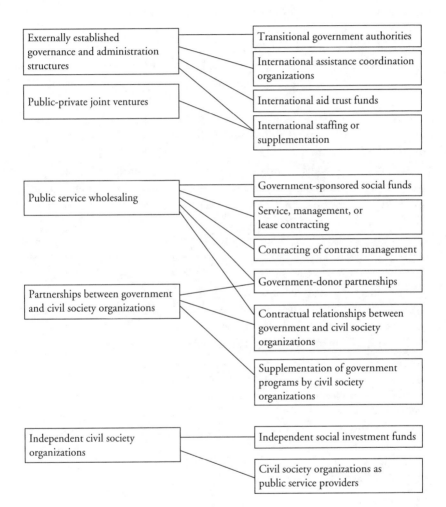

using the private sector and organizations of civil society to deliver services and infrastructure or to perform public service functions under the supervision of the government or of international organizations.

Of course, neither parallel nor partnership approaches may be as desirable for sustained recovery and development in postconflict societies as building permanent administrative capacity in central and local governments. In weak states, however, donors may have few viable choices in the absence of government's ability to quickly and effectively reform public administration other than to use alternative means.

Externally Established Governance and Administrative Structures

As figure 2-1 indicates, among the most frequently used arrangements for supplementing weak capacity in weak states are transitional governance authorities, international assistance coordination organizations, international aid trust funds, and international staffing or supplementation.

Transitional Governance Authorities. The United Nations Security Council has established transitional administrations in several postconflict states, including Kosovo, East Timor, Afghanistan, and Bosnia.[11] Following the cessation of hostilities in Kosovo, the United Nations established a parallel governance and administrative structure, the UN Interim Mission in Kosovo (UNMIK), as a political trusteeship in 1999. UNMIK was charged with performing civilian administrative functions, promoting autonomy and self-government in Kosovo, coordinating the humanitarian and disaster relief of all international agencies, supporting the reconstruction of infrastructure, promoting human rights, and ensuring the safe return of refugees and displaced persons. UNMIK also maintained civil law and order and supervised the development of a constitutional framework establishing the Provisional Institutions of Self-Government (PISG). After the creation of PISG in 2001, it and UNMIK redefined the division of responsibilities and operated as dual governing authorities.[12]

Similarly, the United Nations Transitional Administration in East Timor (UNTAET)—created to oversee the transition to an elected legitimate government in Timor-Leste—operated through a staff of 7,687 uniformed personnel, including 6,281 troops, 1,288 civilian police, and 118 military observers; 737 international civilian personnel; and 1,745 local civilian staff. UNTAET exercised overall responsibility for the administration of East Timor and all legislative and executive authority, including the administration of justice. It provided security throughout East Timor; established an indigenous public administration; helped develop civil and social services; and coordinated the delivery of humanitarian, rehabilitation, and development assistance. In addition, it supported capacity building for self-government and assisted in establishing conditions for sustainable development."[13]

International Assistance Coordination Agencies. Often, because governments in weak states are unstable or unable to extend their authority over the entire national territory, the functions of aid coordination, programming, and financial management must be performed by parallel organizations set up independent of the government or supplemental to government agencies. For example, international donors in Somalia created the Somalia Aid Coordination Body (SACB) in 1994 to coordinate international assistance because of the lack of a legitimate government and the weak capacity of temporary governments to do so. The Transitional National Government (TNG) established in Mogadishu in 2000 had only limited control over the country, and sometimes dissident administrations had strong influence if not outright control in cities and regions outside the capital.[14] Without a government counterpart with the capacity to coordinate aid, the SACB became a parallel agency for aid management.

Because of security and logistics difficulties in Somalia, SACB's secretariat was located in Nairobi, Kenya. SACB membership was voluntary and consisted of representatives of donors, UN agencies, and international civil society organizations. Representatives of organizations such as the Inter-Governmental Authority on Development (IGAD), the World Bank, the Organization of African Unity (OAU), and the Arab League served as ad hoc members and observers; they cooperated with autonomous organizations such as the International Committee of the Red Cross and Federation of the Red Crescent. The SACB provided policy guidance and technical assistance to implementing agencies and policy and operational coordination for rehabilitation and development activities, developed recommendations for the regional allocation of resources, and assisted with programs for resource allocation.[15]

The SACB took on many of the responsibilities usually associated with government. It acted as an information exchange for international organizations providing assistance; updated donors on political, security, and humanitarian conditions and needs in Somalia; and acted as a forum for debates on important development issues and as an advocacy group for expanding social and economic aid for the Somali people. Subcommittees met regularly in and outside of Somalia to coordinate aid programs for the country.[16] The SACB thus carried out many of the functions of aid coordination and programming that government ministries and agencies would ordinarily perform in countries with stronger public institutions.

International Aid Trust Funds. Countries whose governments are weak, that lack the capacity to manage large infusions of international aid, or about which donors are concerned regarding corruption or the legitimate use of revenues from externally financed projects often set up semiautonomous trust funds to manage aid and enhance public administration capacity. In countries where stable or legitimate regimes do not yet exist, trust funds may work independently of the government or as an external, parallel organization in cooperation with the national government.

For example, international donors set up the Afghanistan Reconstruction Trust Fund (ARTF) in 2001 to coordinate external assistance for the transitional government of Afghanistan. ARTF was funded and jointly managed by international aid agencies. It provided short-term emergency funding for civil servants' salaries and for projects and programs to rebuild Afghanistan and facilitated the return of skilled expatriate Afghans. ARTF promoted transparency and accountability of reconstruction assistance, supplemented the national budget for reconstruction activities, reduced the burden on limited government capacity while promoting capacity building, and helped fund the recurrent budgetary expenditures required for the government to function effectively.[17]

Donors that see strong risks of corruption or a lack of financial management capacity on the part of the government often create special trust funds that the government cannot control alone, to ensure that income from internationally financed infrastructure or other revenue-producing projects is protected from misappropriation and is allocated to development activities. Increasingly, the World Bank uses trust funds or special administrative arrangements as part of its system of safeguards to ensure that revenues from large-scale infrastructure projects that it supports are allocated to programs that reduce poverty or achieve other social objectives.

In supporting the Chad-Cameroon petroleum pipeline project, for example, the Bank insisted on creating a special revenue management program, in which 10 percent of Chad's dividends and royalties on oil were placed in the Future Generations Fund, 80 percent of royalties and 85 percent of dividends were earmarked for priority social development sectors (education, health and social services, rural development, infrastructure, and environmental and water resource management), and the remainder was allocated for regional development in the oil-producing area. Chad's revenues were deposited in an escrow account and in the Future Generations Fund at Citibank in London.

The agreement created a petroleum oversight committee—the Collège de Contrôle et de Surveillance des Ressources Pétrolières (CCSRP)—to monitor the use of petroleum revenues. The CCSRP included representatives of the government, parliament, the supreme court, and civil society organizations, who had to approve all allocations and disbursements of oil revenues.[18] Although the government of Chad eventually reneged on its trust fund commitments, the Bank was able to protect revenues for social development for a few years and to take punitive action against the government when it unilaterally changed the allocation of funds going into the general treasury.

International Staffing or Supplementation of Government Ministries or Agencies. Lack of governance capacity or weaknesses in public administration in many postconflict states require international donors to temporarily either staff government agencies and ministries or perform functions that are normally a government's responsibility. Donor staff, technical advisers, or contractors often perform public administration functions either in conjunction with government agencies or in place of them. In some cases they play such a significant role that they become, in effect, shadow governments.

In crisis states or those in postconflict recovery the United Nations peacekeeping forces or the United Nations missions, for example, play strong roles in performing police and security functions. In 2005 the United Nations Stabilization Mission in Haiti (MINUSTAH) provided more than 6,000 military personnel to carry out security functions that would ordinarily be a government responsibility. In addition, MINUSTAH mobilized 648 civilian police officers from thirty-three countries and 750 police units from four countries to supplement, supervise, and train Haiti's military and police forces.[19] Similarly, during 2004 and 2005 the United Nations Mission in Liberia (UNMIL) mobilized more than 14,000 international military troops to provide security for the weak government and provided more than 1,000 civilian police to carry out security and crime prevention functions that the government could not perform.[20]

Because of weak financial management capacity in Timor-Leste, the International Monetary Fund provided financial assistance to staff the central fiscal authority with international experts while the government was recruiting and training Timorese nationals to take over from international personnel.[21] The United Nations Mission in Support of East Timor (UNMISET), in addition to providing international military and police forces, deployed forty-five civilian advisers to the Office of the President, the National Parliament, the judiciary, and the ministries of justice, foreign affairs, planning and finance, interior, transport, communications, and others. These external experts not only provided technical advice but also participated in drafting civil service and judiciary legislation and electoral laws and procedures and in training public administrators.[22] In Burundi the United Nations staffed with foreign experts many of the government's ministries and agencies during more than a decade of civil war, "often seeming to take on more responsibility for the functioning of the country than the government did."[23]

Build-Operate-Transfer and Private Investment Arrangements

In many weak states, international donors encourage or require governments with limited administrative capacity to use private sector financing and management to build, operate, and transfer infrastructure for ministries, agencies, and state-owned enterprises. This parallel channel of providing assistance either bypasses ministries with weak administrative capacity or enhances government's limited capacity, depending on the way the arrangement is structured. The World Bank calculates that, between 1990 and 2002, private investment in infrastructure in thirty-one conflict countries totaled more than $112 billion and that $15 billion of that investment went into "nonfunctioning" conflict countries.[24] The sectors attracting private investment in postconflict countries in the period immediately after peace were usually mobile telephony and electricity, followed later by transport and water.

Build-operate-transfer arrangements have also been used extensively for telecommunications systems, highways, utilities, and water supply systems; they are operated under a concession from the government. In Afghanistan a project undertaken by TCIL of India funded by a $14-million tied-aid grant by the government of India built wireless telecommunications loop networks in eleven secondary cities.[25] Sri Lanka, even during a period of continuing conflict with the Tamil Tigers, extended cellular telephone service through Sri Lanka Telecom and the licensing of local loop mobile networks to private companies. Sri Lanka Telecom operated about 85 percent of Sri Lanka's fixed-line telecom market; the government relied on licenses to Sun Tel—a private collaboration of companies based in Sweden and Hong Kong, the Sri Lankan National Bank, and the International Finance Corporation—to provide Internet and ISDN (Integrated Services Digital Network) voice and data services. MTN Networks (a subsidiary of Telecom Malaysia) was licensed to provide cellular telecom services, along with CellTel Lanka, Mobitel, and Lanka Cellular.[26]

Donors recommend build-operate-transfer arrangements most frequently in infrastructure and service provision projects, but occasionally they use them to establish or reestablish, and to operate temporarily, government agencies and organizations. For example, because of weak public management skills in Mozambique during the late 1990s and early 2000s, and the need to improve customs management, the International Monetary Fund supported such arrangements for government capacity building. A private organization undertook customs management in Mozambique in 1997 and, as systems and procedures improved, gradually handed over operations to a Mozambican staff in the early 2000s.[27]

Public Service Wholesaling

In the immediate postconflict period in many countries, government management capacity is consumed by providing security and humanitarian assistance and establishing political stability and legitimacy. Although providing public services is a crucial need in postconflict countries, the weak administrative capacity of many ministries and agencies limits their ability to reach large portions of the population with services and facilities. In countries with scarce administrative, financial, technical, and logistics capabilities, donors try to increase capacity for service delivery by encouraging public service "wholesaling." Through this arrangement governments attempt to focus the scarce administrative capacity of civil servants on implementing broad service and infrastructure policies and supervising and coordinating service provision through what Paul Collier and Ngozi Okonjo-Iweala call "retail organizations"—civil society groups such as private firms, small-scale enterprises, ethnic organizations, religious organizations—rather than on delivering public services directly.[28]

Government-Sponsored Social Funds. International donors encourage governments in weak states to reach out to local communities by creating or sponsoring social funds. Social funds are organizations through which civil society groups channel financing to local governments and communities for services or social development. Despite their sponsorship by a government agency, these organizations usually are independent of politics. They are the intermediaries between the central government and local communities that are able to "appraise, finance, and supervise implementation of social investments identified and executed by a wide range of actors, including local governments, civil society organizations, local offices of line ministries, and community groups."[29]

The Inter-American Development Bank has invested more than $2.7 billion in more than forty social investment funds in Central and South America. Between 1987 and 2003 the World Bank alone financed nearly sixty social funds (some of which were government sponsored and others of which were independent) in weak crisis states such as Rwanda, Angola, Ethiopia, Eritrea, Sierra Leone, Kosovo, Sri Lanka, Cambodia, East Timor, the West Bank and Gaza, and Lebanon.[30] When they were funded by international donors the funds were subjected to independent audits using international standards.

For example, the World Bank supported one of the largest social funds in a postconflict country, Nicaragua. A presidential decree in 1990 created the Nicaragua Social Investment Fund (FISE) as a temporary agency, though the World Bank twice extended its funding into the early 2000s. Between 1991 and 1998 FISE accounted for about 40 percent of total public investments in social sector infrastructure, constituting about 1 percent of Nicaragua's GDP.[31] Although FISE's four-member board of directors was appointed by the president, the organization was run by an executive director and operated relatively autonomously. It was exempt from government budget, procurement, and personnel recruitment regulations. Financing for FISE came through a special account in a commercial bank approved by the World Bank Group's International Development Association and was audited by independent organizations using World Bank standards.

In a period when Nicaragua's government struggled with recovering from a long and bitter conflict and with stabilizing governance, FISE provided a parallel means of wholesaling public services and reconstructing infrastructure. Most of FISE's funds went to extremely poor communities for education and health; for environmental and municipal infrastructure; for water and sanitation projects; and for construction of low-cost housing and early childhood development centers. FISE worked with national government ministries, local governments, associations of municipalities, local civil society organizations, and international donors.

Outsourcing Public Service Provision to the Private Sector. Donors also encourage governments in weak states to outsource service provision to the private sector, another approach to public service wholesaling. International donors play an important role in providing technical assistance to government agencies and ministries for creating private sector outsourcing procurement, contracting, coordination, and management and by giving them financial assistance to cover, at least temporarily, some or all of the government's overhead costs of contracting. For services that private sector retail firms might not be able to provide at a cost that the poor can afford, international donors occasionally provide some or all of the recurrent costs or subsidies needed to make outsourced services more widely available. In countries where the private sector is weak or in disarray because of conflicts and hostilities, international donors sometimes arrange for services to be outsourced to international firms.

Generally, governments wholesale services through private organizations by using service, management, and lease contracts. In Sierra Leone, after conflicts abated, the government used service contracts with small- and medium-sized enterprises for road maintenance in order to leverage its own limited administrative capacity and to redevelop local enterprises and individual contractors.[32] Following the peace accords and elections in Nicaragua, the government privatized almost 90 percent of state enterprises and leased, with a purchase option, about 25 percent to workers or ex-soldiers.[33] Under a lease contract in Mozambique a private operator provided water to five major cities and Maputo beginning in 1999.[34]

Public-Private Joint Ventures

The weak administrative capacity of many governments in postconflict countries requires them to attract private investment to extend public services more quickly or more widely than public agencies or state-owned enterprises are able to do. The World Bank points out that in Cambodia, for example, the postconflict government had neither the financial resources nor the administrative capacity to reconstruct infrastructure and restore public services effectively and was not likely to develop sufficient capacity in time to meet urgent requirements: "The need for efficiency in service delivery is a key driver for change, given Cambodia's lack of tax revenue, its substantial reconstruction and maintenance needs, and the poor record of public provision of services."[35] World Bank analysts pointed out that the government would not be able to meet those needs without mobilizing private investment and private sector provision of the infrastructure networks through which services would reach local communities.

Donors, therefore, often recommend another means of attracting private capital investment in infrastructure reconstruction: public-private joint ventures. This parallel channel allows governments to retain some control over politically strategic service sectors while enhancing limited administrative and financial capacity. Joint ventures are often formed between domestic and multinational companies and state-owned enterprises or public agencies at both the central and local government levels.

In Afghanistan, for example, the Ministry of Communications and the American company Telecommunications Systems International formed a joint venture with the Afghan Wireless Telecommunications Company to set up a mobile network there even before the Taliban was overthrown. After a new government was installed following the U.S. invasion in 2001, the joint venture upgraded substantially Afghanistan's mobile platform. In 2003 the government of Afghanistan approved a telecommunications and Internet policy that looked to private sector investment for implemention. The government licensed two private sector operators to operate the mobile network: the joint venture Afghan Wireless and Roshan, a consortium led by the Aga Khan Foundation for Economic Development; and Monaco Telecom International and Alcatel.[36]

Partnerships between Government and Civil Society Organizations

All international donors encourage or support leveraging limited public administration capacity in weak states by directly or indirectly funding international and civil society organizations to provide services. Three types of these partnerships appear frequently in weak states: government-donor partnerships for service delivery, government-civil society contractual relationships for services provision, and supplementation of government programs and services by civil society organizations.

Often, governments in postconflict countries require a combination of all three types of arrangements to supplement or substitute for public sector provision of public services or to extend their limited capacity to reach large numbers of citizens, especially the poorest groups, those living in remote areas of the country, and those living in areas still experiencing hostilities. Hostilities in the Central African Republic made its government almost entirely dependent on civil society organizations to deliver social services. "Several organizations are involved in service delivery at the community level, including to the most needy," World Bank analysts observed. "Faith-based organizations have been active in delivering education and health services; and in several communities, Parents' Associations have taken charge of hiring teachers and the financing of education services. The UN agencies, particularly UNICEF, have also developed efficient community-based service delivery mechanisms."[37]

In postconflict Rwanda, civil society and international organizations worked together with government agencies attempting to restore agriculture. The nationwide Seeds of Hope Initiative, which provides seeds and tools for rural households in order to increase agricultural production and food security, was funded by the United Nations Children's Fund and the Food and Agriculture Organization (FAO), among other UN organizations; USAID; and several bilateral donors. Although the Rwandan Ministry of Agriculture and the FAO provided some coordination for the program, it was largely implemented by civil society organizations such as CARE, Catholic Relief Services, Lutheran World Federation, World Vision, and Action Nord-Sud.[38] CARE, for example, carried out large-scale surveys of rural households to determine needs and to better understand the problems in delivering agricultural inputs, and Caritas International in conjunction with Catholic churches delivered thousands of metric tons of vegetable seeds to farm households. World Vision provided seed and tool packages, helped rehabilitate the seed multiplication programs, and paid the salaries of some government extension agents until the government could take over the responsibility.

Independent Civil Society Organizations Providing Public Services

Over the past two decades international donors have come to see a robust network of social and civil society organizations as essential to development. In many crisis countries, international donors encourage and support government efforts to strengthen these civil society organizations, which operate as permanent, independent, and parallel providers of social services. Although they may have no formal contract or arrangement with government agencies, civil society organizations either supplement limited public administration capacity or substitute for governments in providing services. USAID's Global Development Alliance formed coalitions of civil society organizations, private foundations, and international donors to extend the scope and coverage of public services in weak states. In Guatemala and Nicaragua, for example, USAID, Visa International, and other partners funded FINCA, a civil society organization involved in providing small-scale loans to women who want to start or expand small businesses. Together with Visa and Bancafe, FINCA provided debit cards by which women entrepreneurs could draw loans of $200 or less to begin or sustain their small businesses.[39]

In most weak states the government alone simply cannot provide basic social services.[40] In Cambodia, for example, the Catholic Church provides a significant share of educational services, ranging from preschool level to university. As a civil society organization, the Catholic Church both supplements the public education system at all levels and offers a higher quality alternative to public schools. The International Crisis Group points out that the almost total focus of the government in Burundi on fighting a war for more than a decade left international civil society societies with the task of providing social services in the country, leaving them the only coordinators of international bilateral and United Nations assistance.[41]

Assessing Deconcentrated Governance and Decentralized Development Administration

For international donors seeking to help people to find ways of providing humanitarian and social services that may be beyond the capacity of the governments of weak states, parallel structures that bypass, temporarily supplement, or leverage what limited capacity exists through the private sector and civil society organizations and transitional administrations may be the only options available.

The dangers of the arrangements that donors use to bypass governments have been known for more than a quarter of a century. The tendency of the United Nations Development Program, the World Bank, regional development banks, and bilateral aid programs to create autonomous project implementation units for large-scale projects during the 1970s and 1980s in order to avoid government weaknesses often created as many problems in developing countries as they solved.[42] The independent project units usually paid higher salaries than did the civil service and were not constrained by bureaucratic regulations and procedures. They often attracted away from governments some of their most talented public administrators. Because they had large amounts of resources, many did not coordinate or integrate their work with government ministries and agencies, and some became powers unto themselves. Thus the use of autonomous project implementation units became known as "enclave" project management.[43]

One important difference between the context of aid today and that of a quarter century ago, however, is a broader perception of governance. In the 1970s governance was perceived of simply as the actions of government. Today governance is seen as the interaction of government, the private sector, and organizations of civil society; and there is a wider acceptance of the fact that the decisions and actions of all three sectors shape the modern state.[44] Moreover, many more people recognize that development in all states requires widespread administrative capacity not only in government but also in private enterprise and civil society organizations. No single sector can bring about political, economic, social, and technological change, and weaknesses in administrative capacity in any sector diminish governance capabilities in others.

Donors now use parallel structures and arrangements to achieve many of the same objectives in bypassing government as did autonomous project implementation units—and they share some of the same potential pitfalls. Parallel structures and arrangements have strong potential advantages for donors, governments with weak administrative capacity, and the people struggling to survive in weak states. They also have potential disadvantages. If they do not operate effectively they can weaken the state rather than strengthen it; or they can do harm to citizens by acting corruptly, ineffectively, or inefficiently.

Donors continue to use parallel structures and partnerships in weak states because of their potential advantages and because international organizations may have few options. If they seek to build and sustain long-term capacity in public administration, however, they must address potential adversities in using parallel structures and partnership arrangements by designing and implementing them based on an understanding of the conditions and needs in host countries.

Potential Advantages of Deconcentrated Governance

Although each of the parallel options reviewed in this chapter for enhancing administrative capacity has potential advantages and disadvantages that are specific to its structure and operation, most parallel arrangements share common ones as well. In postconflict states, parallel structures and channels, when they work effectively, can achieve at least some donor objectives and assist weak governments with immediate needs. Among the most frequently observed advantages of parallel and partnership arrangements are that they can respond rapidly to emergency situations and humanitarian crises; fill gaps in public administration capacity until governments become more stabilized and public administration reforms can be undertaken; and substitute as a governing authority where no legitimate or acceptable government exists.

Deconcentrated governance can help international assistance organizations overcome complex obstacles caused by weak administrative capacity or inefficient or ineffective civil services and leverage scarce public administration capacity, extend government's ability to perform functions or deliver services, and increase the efficiency and effectiveness of existing government services and functions.

Without United Nations trusteeships or transitional governance authorities in Kosovo, Bosnia, Timor-Leste, and Cambodia, for example, little could have been done to restore security after the cessation of hostilities. Nor could the weak or emerging central governments have coordinated the resources necessary to provide basic services and infrastructure. In Burundi, as the International Crisis Group points out, international civil society organizations "have represented the sole direct and constant point of contact between the international community and the Burundian population."[45]

Parallel approaches such as public service wholesaling allows weak governments to leverage the managerial capacity of private and civil society organizations, mobilize private and social capital, and extend access to services. Often, "retail" organizations are based in or have strong relationships with local communities and can develop stronger ties with local governments or service organizations than can civil servants in the central government. Assessments of reconstruction efforts in East Timor, for example, found that international assistance that used an appropriate balance of approaches to extending services to rural communities was essential to progress after hostilities ended. In East Timor, the World Bank reports that focusing on community-driven reconstruction and the use of the private sector and civil society organizations would "achieve rapid results on the ground while the capacity of the public administration is building up."[46]

Independent project implementation units supplement limited government administrative capacity, allow direct monitoring and accountability to international donors, and provide greater flexibility in recruiting competent personnel and in hiring, paying, and directing them.[47] These parallel organizations provide some safeguards against mismanagement, corruption, and diversion of foreign assistance funds to nonproject or unintended activities. When they are effectively designed and make provisions for training public managers and for transfer of functions to government as public administration capacity becomes stronger, they can temporarily lighten the burdens of project management on weak governments, expedite implementation of projects needed for development and stability in the host country, and help alleviate crisis conditions.

The World Bank's evaluations of social funds indicate that parallel organizations can be far more effective than government agencies in reaching the poor in funding community-level investments that best reflect community needs and priorities, in helping community groups mobilize complementary inputs, and in accessing high-quality infrastructure and services.[48] The Emergency Social Investment Fund in Nicaragua provided health centers for the rural poor that were better staffed, equipped, and supplied and attracted more clients than centers provided by the government. The Nicaraguan Social Investment Fund was also able to target the poorest groups for education and health services more effectively than the government's line ministries.[49]

Often indigenous civil society organizations can tap into and mobilize resources of the international community and of local organizations that may not be available to government. Civil society organizations in Liberia, for example, played a part not only in peace brokering but also in community development and reconstruction. They carried out small development projects in rural communities, programs for rehabilitating traumatized children soldiers, and postconflict programs for women, children, traditional leaders, and local government leaders.[50]

Public-private partnerships help mobilize private financial, managerial, technical, and knowledge resources for public service provision and extend the reach of weak governments in providing services to the poor, to remote rural areas, and to regions subject to continued fighting or hostilities. When properly designed and implemented, these approaches build public administration capability to take over functions carried out by parallel structures and to manage public-private partnerships while at the same time creating or strengthening administrative capacity in the private sector and organizations of civil society to deliver services that supplement those of the public sector.

Potential Disadvantages of Deconcentrated Governance

As with any form of international assistance, parallel and partnership structures have not only potential advantages but also potential weaknesses, which can undermine governance capacity if they are poorly designed and implemented. In some countries donors might use these approaches inappropriately or in circumstances where they prove inadequate. Often they may have negative unintended or unanticipated consequences. Sometimes the effectiveness of parallel and partnership approaches is undermined by corruption, lack of transparency, or political favoritism. The weaknesses in the administration of partnerships and private provision of services and infrastructure in Cambodia, for example, led to large numbers of nonbankable projects for which private investors could not easily obtain project financing; higher costs to consumers in Cambodia because of administrative inefficiencies in licensing, permitting, and approval of concessions; and lack of information by which to assess their costs and effectiveness and to protect the public interest in awarding concessions.[51]

Independent project implementation units set up by international donors sometimes weakened line departments, promoted job hopping by experienced administrators, lengthened the implementation time of foreign-funded projects, and undermined national ownership of the projects.[52] Although they were created as temporary organizations, project implementation units have often perpetuated their existence by seeking continued international funding for increasing numbers of new projects, competing with regular government agencies for funding. They often responded more willingly to donor criteria and objectives than to the development plans of the government. They usually had little incentive to respond to the needs of the people or the intended beneficiaries of their projects. Few autonomous project units contributed to developing administrative capacity within the government; many of their employees took jobs with the private sector, international donors, civil society organizations, or multinational corporations after gaining skills and knowledge while working on internationally funded projects.

If they are not adequately supervised and monitored by government, partnerships may not achieve their objectives of delivering public services and infrastructure more efficiently and effectively. The inability of government to manage contractual arrangements between the public sector and the private sector and also between the public sector and civil society organizations may lead to cost overruns, poor performance, and citizen dissatisfaction. Governments in weak states gain little if the administrative and financial management capacity of civil society organizations is also weak or if their technical capacity is no stronger than that of government. Although in Burundi international civil society organizations were the primary means of providing services through international assistance to the local population, most of these organizations bypassed a weak government occupied with suppressing military conflict. As critics point out, such international organizations did not always coordinate among themselves, did not build the capacity of public administration to take over these functions, and often encouraged the local populations' dependency rather than strengthening their self-sufficiency.[53]

Parallel or partnership arrangements are not always appropriate or adequate in all postconflict situations or in all weak states. Although they offer international donors a means of expanding services and infrastructure in weak states and offer the private sector commercial opportunities to expand their businesses, deconcentrated governance and decentralized development administration are complex arrangements and can create problems for both the public and the private sectors if they are not properly designed and administered.

Conclusion

Although there are well-known dangers involved when donors bypass a weak government or use parallel governance and administrative arrangements, in some circumstances deconcentrated governance may be the only feasible way of ensuring that financial assistance is directed to crucial development tasks. Experience with parallel and partnership arrangements reveals lessons that donors should consider in selecting, designing, and implementing parallel and partnership alternatives.

Experience suggests that when they are using parallel and partnership structures, international organizations providing aid to weak states should also build capacity in public administration. Although channeling aid through independent, private, or civil society organizations can be a viable means of supplementing weak public administration in postconflict countries, care must be taken to build in transition procedures whereby appropriate functions are transferred to the government as its administrative capacity becomes stronger. Donors should make provisions in their assistance programs to strengthen the capacity of the civil service and of public officials to formulate and implement supporting policies and procedures for, and maintain oversight of, partnership arrangements. Institution building and training for government officials should be an integral part of donors' implementation plans for creating independent or autonomous development organizations.

To make partnership arrangements between governments and the private sector or civil society organizations effective, donors should help build the capacity of public administrators at both the central and local government levels to design and manage contractual arrangements. Even relatively weak governments must have basic procedures for transparent contracting and procurement and strong mechanisms for preventing abuse and corruption. Experience in developing countries with outsourcing, public-private partnerships, and public–civil society organization arrangements for service delivery suggests that for these parallel channels to work effectively central and local government officials must be able to decide among competing development objectives; to define objectives for services provision; to set standards, criteria, and output targets; and to safeguard citizens' welfare.[54] National or local government agencies must have at least a minimum capacity to decide on the level of services needed and the financial resources available to pay for them; to set and monitor safety, quality, and performance standards; and to enforce those standards and the output targets.

In many countries, public-private partnerships simply will not work unless donors apply safeguards ensuring honesty, transparency, and fairness in the governments' transactions with private and civil society organizations and provide assistance for creating stronger business and investment climates. As a part of its support for the Nam Theun 2 hydropower project in the Lao People's Democratic Republic, for example, the World Bank created a decision framework in which the government of Laos had to meet major milestones for improving its financial management, for which the Bank provided extensive capacity-building assistance. The Bank identified serious weaknesses in the government's budget preparation, execution, and control systems. It supported improvements in the government's expenditure management, including fiscal planning and budget preparation, treasury, accounting and reporting, information systems, and the legislative framework for public expenditure management.[55]

Deconcentrated governance and decentralized development administration are likely to be effective only if donors also assist civil society organizations and private enterprises—both important governance institutions—in developing their administrative, technical, and financial capacity to partner with or supplement government in the provision of infrastructure and social services. Temporarily using parallel or partnership channels for assisting weak states does not obviate the need for donors to strengthen public administration capacity nor does it lessen their responsibility for helping central and local governments build the capacity to make deconcentrated governance and decentralized development administration work effectively.

Notes

1. International Crisis Group, "Crisis Watch," No. 33, May 2006.

2. Stewart Patrick, "The Donor Community and the Challenge of Post Conflict Recovery," in *Good Intentions: Pledges of Aid for Post-Conflict Recovery,* edited by Stewart Forman and Shepard Patrick (Boulder, Colo.: Lynne Rienner, 2000).

3. World Bank, "The World Bank in Conflict Prevention and Reconstruction," issue brief, World Bank, 2003.

4. Office of the Coordinator for Reconstruction and Stabilization, "Post-Conflict Reconstruction Essential Tasks," U.S. Department of State, 2005.

5. See Dennis A. Rondinelli and John D. Montgomery, "Regime Change and Nation Building: Can Donors Restore Governance in Post-Conflict States?" *Public Administration & Development* 25, no. 1 (2005): 1–9.

6. United Nations Development Program and World Bank, "Country Re-Engagement Note: UNDP/World Bank Somalia," 2003, p. 1.

7. Salvatore Schiavo-Campo, *Financing and Aid Management Arrangement in Post-Conflict Settings,* Social Development Note 12, World Bank, 2003, p. 1.

8. World Bank, "Cambodia: Enhancing Service Delivery through Improved Allocation and Institutional Reform," Report 25611-KH, 2003.

9. World Bank, "Civil Service Reform: A Review of World Bank Assistance," Operations Evaluation Department Sector Study 19599, 1999, p. 2.

10. Charles Palidano, "Why Civil Service Reforms Fail," IDPM Public Policy and Management Working Paper 16, University of Manchester, 2001, p. 1.

11. Henry H. Perritt Jr., "Structures and Standards for Political Trusteeship," *UCLA Journal of International Law and Foreign Affairs* (Fall/Winter 2003): 385–472.

12. United Nations, "United Nations Mission in Kosovo," 2001 (www.unmikonline.org/intro.htm).

13. United Nations, "East Timor—UNTAET Mandate according to Security Council Resolution 1272 of 25 October 1999," 2001 (www.un.org/peace/etimor/UntaetM.htm).

14. UNDP and World Bank, "Country Re-Engagement Note," pp. 2–3.

15. See Somalia Aid Coordination Body (www.sacb.info).

16. UNDP and World Bank, "Country Re-Engagement Note."

17. World Bank, "Afghanistan Reconstruction Trust Fund" (www.worldbank.org.af/).

18. M. Edgar Barrett, "The Chad-Cameroon Oil Project: Poverty Reduction or Recipe for Disaster," Thunderbird Case A03-04-0023, Garvin School of International Management, Glendale, Ariz., 2004.

19. United Nations Security Council, "Report of the Secretary-General on the United Nations Stabilization Mission in Haiti," S/2005/24, 2005.

20. United Nations Security Council, "Seventh Progress Report of the Secretary-General on the United Nations Mission in Liberia," S/2005/391, 2005.

21. International Monetary Fund, "Background Paper for Rebuilding Fiscal Institutions in Post-Conflict Countries," Fiscal Affairs Department, 2004.

22. United Nations Security Council, "Progress Report of the Secretary-General on the United Nations Office in Timor-Leste," S/2005/533, 2005.

23. International Crisis Group, "A Framework for Responsible Aid to Burundi," 2003, p. 8.

24. Jordan Schwartz, Shelly Hahn, and Ian Bannon, "The Private Sector's Role in the Provision of Infrastructure in Post-Conflict Countries: Patterns and Policy Options," World Bank, 2004.

25. Ken Zita, "Afghanistan Telecom Brief," Network Dynamics Associates, New York, 2004.

26. Ken Zita and Akash Kapur, "Sri Lanka Telecom Brief," Network Dynamics Associates, New York, 2004.

27. International Monetary Fund, "Background Paper for Rebuilding Fiscal Institutions in Post Conflict Countries."

28. Paul Collier and Ngozi Okonjo-Iweala, "World Bank Group Work in Low-Income Countries under Stress: A Task Force Report," World Bank, 2002.

29. Mukhmeet Bhatia, "Social Funds: A Review of Public Sector Management and Institutional Issues," Social Protection Discussion Paper 0508, World Bank, 2005, p. 1.

30. Julie Van Domelen, "Social Capital in the Operations and Impacts of Social Investment Funds," World Bank, 2003, p. 1.

31. World Bank, "Nicaragua: Ex-Post Impact Evaluation of the Emergency Social Investment Fund (FISE)," Report 20400-Nt, 2000.

32. World Bank, "Project Performance Assessment Report, Republic of Sierra Leone: Roads Rehabilitation and Maintenance Project, Freetown Infrastructure Rehabilitation Project," Report 29308, 2004.

33. Tilman Bruck, Valpy FitzGerald, and Arturo Grigsby, "Enhancing the Private Sector Contribution to Post-War Recovery in Poor Countries," QEH Working Paper QEHWKPS 45(2), Queen Elizabeth House, London, 2000, p. 24.

34. Schwartz, Hahn, and Bannon, "The Private Sector's Role in the Provision of Infrastructure in Post-Conflict Countries," pp. 18–19.

35. World Bank, "Cambodia: Seizing the Global Opportunity: Investment Climate Assessment and Reform Strategy for Cambodia," Report 237925-KH, 2004, p. 56.

36. Zita, "Afghanistan Telecom Brief."

37. World Bank, "Country Re-Engagement Note for the Central African Republic," 2004, pp. 28–29.

38. David Tardif-Douglin, "Rehabilitating Household Food Production after War: The Rwandan Experience," in *Rebuilding Societies after Civil War: Critical Roles for International Assistance,* edited by Krishna Kumar (Boulder, Colo.: Lynne Rienner, 1997).

39. USAID, *The Global Development Alliance,* 137–41.

40. World Bank, "Timor-Leste: Education since Independence, from Reconstruction to Sustainable Improvement," Report 29784-TP, 2004.

41. International Crisis Group, "A Framework for Responsible Aid to Burundi."

42. Dennis A. Rondinelli, *Development Projects as Policy Experiments: An Adaptive Approach to Development Administration,* 2nd ed. (London: Routledge, 1993).

43. Operations Evaluation Department, "Utilization of Project Implementation Units," World Bank, 2000.

44. Guido Bertucci and Adriana Alberti, "Globalization and the Role of the State: Challenges and Perspectives," in *Reinventing Government for the Twenty-First Century: State Capacity in a Globalizing Society,* edited by Dennis A. Rondinelli and G. Shabbir Cheema (Bloomfield, Conn.: Kumarian, 2003).

45. International Crisis Group, "A Framework for Responsible Aid to Burundi," p. 8.

46. Klaus Rohland and Sarah Cliffe, "The East Timor Reconstruction Program: Successes, Problems and Tradeoffs," Working Paper 2, Conflict Prevention and Reconstruction, 2002, p. ii.

47. United Nations Development Program, "The PIU Dilemma: How to Address Project Implementation Units," practice note, 2003, pp. 2–3.

48. Laura B. Rawlings, Lynne Sherburne-Benz, and Julie Van Domelen, "Evaluating Social Funds: A Cross-Country Analysis of Community Investments," World Bank, 2004.

49. World Bank, "Nicaragua: Ex-Post Impact Evaluation," pp. iii–vii.

50. United Nations Economic Commission for Africa, *Countries Emerging from Conflict: Lessons on Partnerships in Postconflict Reconstruction, Rehabilitation, and Reintegration* (2003), pp. 12–13.

51. World Bank, "Cambodia: Seizing the Global Opportunity," p. viii.

52. United Nations Development Program, "The PIU Dilemma."

53. Ibid., pp. 8–10.

54. United Kingdom, "Public Private Partnerships: The Government's Approach" (London: Her Majesty's Treasury, 2000), pp. 10–12.

55. World Bank, "Project Appraisal Document, Proposed IDA Grant to the Lao People's Democratic Republic and Proposed IDA Partial Risk Guarantee and Proposed MIGA Guarantees to the Nam Theun 2 Power Company Limited for the Nam Theun 2 Hydroelectric Project," Report 31764-LA, 2005.

3

Decentralization and Electronic Governance

GUIDO BERTUCCI AND MARIA STEFANIA SENESE

Global trends show a general decline of trust in government. Polls evidence a steady erosion of public trust in authorities and institutions. Despite a diffusion of democratic systems, citizens seem increasingly disenchanted by civic engagement. Such low confidence in government is likely related to the perception that civil society is unable to influence government activities. Furthermore, the general perception of public corruption, of a lack of public expertise in the face of complex issues, and of incompetent political structures contribute to the public's alienation from government and public affairs.

Governance is essential but not sufficient to guarantee political trust.[1] To tackle the challenge of reearning public trust, governments should enhance citizens' participation in public policy decisionmaking while also increasing government transparency and accountability. Over the last twenty years, various countries have undertaken reforms with the goal of improving the effectiveness and accountability of government through a decentralized approach. Experts and researchers have hailed decentralization as the best tool to bring government closer to the citizens, to improve public decisionmaking, and to render service delivery more effective. All over the world a wave of reforms has been aimed at transferring responsibilities and resources to local government levels so as to promote democratic values and good governance.

In other words, decentralization has emerged as a global trend aimed at empowering autonomy at the local level by facilitating citizens' participation and improving public services delivery in terms of responsiveness, effectiveness. and efficiency. Many agents trigger decentralization, although it is the purpose of government to encourage the local level's involvement in the decisionmaking process so as to promote public participation, ownership, and engagement. Such local involvement ensures that decisions reflect the needs and priorities of the local population.

Decentralization thus means a new model of state governance through re-distribution of power. From a political point of view, decentralization seeks to increase local participation, thereby achieving good governance and fostering democratic values. If decentralization promotes more involvement of stakehold-ers, efficiency and transparency will be improved through better operations man-agement planning, since local governments are equipped to support local service delivery and to respond to local needs.

However, in many developed and developing countries, a lack of civic involve-ment by public officers together with endemic institutional inefficiencies and a high potential for corruption make it difficult for decentralization to be success-ful. In the light of this scenario, can information and communication technolo-gies make decentralization and local governance more effective and meaningful?

Information and Communications Technologies, Decentralization, and Local Governance

Information and communications technologies (ICTs) can help overcome the obstacles mentioned above and make decentralization effective and responsive by increasing efficiency, transparency, participation, and citizen engagement, thus strengthening public trust in government. In fact ICTs have the potential of promoting transparency and accountability in the decisionmaking process by improving the delivery of basic services, providing new communication chan-nels, and developing capacity building and social and economic growth.

The Digital Divide

The benefits of ICTs—improving participation and civic engagement—are how-ever often hindered by incomplete access to digital technologies. Access to ICT information is often limited by the digital divide among countries. The digital divide—the gap in ICT access—is still wide between rich and poor countries, exacerbating external divisions. Inequality of participation can be overcome only through a precise strategy aimed at ensuring and implementing e-democracy val-ues. Many initiatives, projects, and programs have been developed by govern-ments to bridge the digital divide as well as empower citizens and increase their opportunities for participation.

In Dublin the problem of the digital divide was addressed by giving free web space and free web access to the local community. The city has promoted the integration of local government and local development, thus facilitating communication between local organizations and local citizens. Moreover, participation in city and community initiatives has been encouraged through the online community forum and bulletin boards.[2]

In the Solomon Islands the establishment of an e-mail network, People-First Network (PFnet), facilitates the flow of information regarding developmental activities.[3] The network has also facilitated "equitable and sustainable" rural development and peace building, after years of ethnic conflict. Based on sustainable technology, this e-mail system allows remote locations across the islands to have access to the Internet and e-mail, using a simple computer, short-wave radio, and solar power. The People-First Network also allows rural businesses to expand their customer base and facilitate their banking transactions. "In providing improved communications and access to trusted information, PFnet is helping to build peace and national unity. In particular, the popular PFnet web site is being developed into a true development portal and will be used as part of an e-Citizen Initiative aimed at encouraging participation in democratic processes and thus furthering good governance."[4]

Sharing experiences in e-access and e-participation and creating networks, partnerships, and appropriate environments to access and facilitate information and communication through the use of ICTs can bridge the gap between the connected and the isolated and strengthen local governance initiatives.

Meaningful and Effective Participation

Information, access, and participation are important for local authorities during the transition to decentralization. To this end, local authorities are equipping themselves with ICTs to facilitate information access. Internet bank accounts, databases, city websites, consultation platforms, and other venues have been introduced, all of them enabling citizens to access information and services. The Internet in particular resolves the problem of lack of citizen information. Internet use has also become an indispensable tool for streamlining public administration processes and maximizing government effectiveness. Furthermore, use of the Internet has led to better local government services.

In France, the city of Issy-les-Moulineaux resorted to e-democracy and e-government strategies after developing an effective local information plan.[5] To bridge the digital divide, Issy-les-Moulineaux opened more than 118 free Internet access points. "With approximately 70% of inhabitants connected to the Internet from their homes, and more than a half by means of a high-speed connection, Issy-les-Moulineaux has a connection rate twice that of the French national average."[6] Through the launch of the Issy interactive city council e-initiative, citizens can participate in city council meetings by phone or e-mail.[7] The development of a policy based on consultation with and participation by citizens in the decisionmaking process has always been considered a pillar of city policy.

Consultation platforms facilitate transparency in decisionmaking and citizen involvement in that process. Citizens can offer, for example, an agenda of goals accepted by the local community and can cooperate with the local government in reaching these goals. That is, the Internet offers two-way communication between local government and citizens.

E-participation is defined as "the sum total of both the government programs to encourage participation from the citizen and the willingness of the citizen to do so."[8] The goal is to increase citizens' access to information (e-information), to engage citizens in discussion (e-consultation), and to support their participation in decisionmaking (e-decisionmaking). Hence the e-participation framework includes e-information, e-consultation, and e-decisionmaking, all important features of e-democracy. Implementing e-participation initiatives could trigger a virtuous circle among the three dimensions (figure 3-1), thereby strengthening participatory democracy.

By facilitating access to information, e-consultation and subsequently e-decisionmaking are activated, and more information will enable citizens to take part in discussions and to help define the content of policies. In this way citizens can become a significant motor of public policy. In fact ICTs can empower all stakeholders and help them reach the consensus necessary for the implementation of successful and sustainable public policies. Citizens must be involved in political processes at all levels. To this end, governments around the world are starting to support and implement engagement initiatives.

The United Nations' "Global e-Government Readiness Report" includes the first-ever e-participation assessment of all countries.[9] This is an innovative e-democracy approach that facilitates civic engagement through several participation forms. Building a participatory and inclusive society requires a multistakeholder approach. Several countries are exploring ways of developing interactive mechanisms to encourage e-engagement and e-participation. However, e-participation is still in its infancy, and only a few countries have actively promoted it to date. In fact it is not easy to assess the impact of e-consultations and e-participation because there have been few dramatic policy outcomes.

An exception is the experience of the Sheffield City Council in the United Kingdom. The council, voted one of the greatest innovators in e-democracy, launched an e-voting pilot project that gives citizens the opportunity to vote through informatics tools. Voters may use the Internet, phone, text messaging public kiosks, or polling stations. Citizens are equipped with a polling card plus a voter identification number attached to a "smart" card, with an embedded electronic chip. These tools enable the holder to access a range of services, including transport, libraries, leisure activities, and bill payment.[10]

Thus the strategic and meaningful application of ICTs for the purpose of improving the efficiency, transparency, accountability, and accessibility of government is possible if the ultimate objective of e-government is to promote

Figure 3-1. *Three Dimensions of the E-Participation Circle*

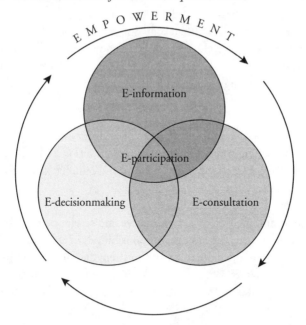

social inclusion (e-inclusion). The real challenge lies not only in ensuring that certain preconditions are met but also in enabling people to participate. Particularly in policymaking, e-participation can be inclusive, open, responsive, and deliberative. But when ICT penetration and use differ greatly among socio-economic groups, the digital divide increases. The focus should therefore be on empowerment rather than merely access. E-inclusion requires a shift in focus from technology per se to its use in promoting economic, social, and cultural opportunities for all people. E-inclusion is a holistic approach toward narrowing the digital divide and preventing new forms of exclusion from developing. The circles in figure 3-1 imply that each citizen is given the same opportunities for participation in society.

Brazil for example seeks to reduce social and digital exclusion for over 3 million people in the periphery of São Paulo through an extensive network of telecommunication centers. In addition, the project aims to increase professional training, to disseminate free software, and to encourage popular participation in administrative councils, community media, and so on.[11] Internet access is, in the case of São Paulo, a way to reach isolated and marginalized groups that lack access to technology, education, and well-paying jobs.

Particularly, ICT penetration can reduce the social divide through the provision of access to excluded communities or disadvantaged and marginalized groups. For example, an ICT-based improvement of a service of critical value for deaf, hearing-impaired, and deaf-blind people has been promoted in partnership with the deaf community by the Sign Language Interpreting Service in Glasgow, Scotland. This project has allowed deaf people to have twenty-four-hour access to the interpreting service rather than only during office hours. Furthermore, the project has provided greater choice and access to information, giving its clients the "opportunity to become part of a more e-inclusive world that gives an increased recognition to sign as a language."[12]

Empowering Local Governments

Local institutions need to promote the use of ICTs to encourage local involvement in decisionmaking, thus supporting decentralization and local governance. ICTs can overcome obstacles that otherwise would hamper successful decentralization. These obstacles are
   —lack of trained or motivated human resources
   —inadequate and inefficient administrative and service delivery system
   —inadequate resources to meet the responsibilities of the local authority.
Efforts to overcome these obstacles and to strengthen human resources can be supported by the provision of access and information skills through ICT tools. In fact information technology can reinforce the capacity of public servants by providing them with timely, efficient, and effective inputs. In Mexico, for example, an online learning program (@Campus) for public servants has been launched. Civil servants are provided with an Internet-based education portal, which offers courses and information, with the aim of improving the efficiency and accountability of Mexico's government programs. "With financial support from Institute for Connectivity in the Americas (ICA), and the expertise of the Canadian School of Public Service, Mexico instituted a pilot phase where 800 public servants have received training. The goal is for up to 47,700 public employees to have access to the e-learning platform and for the project to be a reference project for future rollout in the region."[13] @Campus aims to strengthen good governance and competence in such core areas as management and technology, areas usually associated with specific job requirements. This important project is a good example of "how e-learning can deliver training to large numbers of civil servants across vast geographical areas. It can provide the necessary e-learning elements at a lower cost, and is a strategy that is scalable to the region, yet adaptable to the needs of specific countries."[14]

A core challenge for public service is to constantly upgrade the managerial and technical competencies of public servants. High-quality public service requires a qualified, trained, and professional staff. E-learning can deliver timely training to the staff, allowing it to gain new skills and knowledge faster and at lower cost than traditional training methods. The Internet breaks down barriers of cost and time, building a mass of knowledge in a short time.

The efficient use of ICTs facilitates communication among the various structures of government and between these structures and citizens. In addition, ICTs increase the flexibility and effectiveness of staff training and strengthen staff's capacity to plan and manage. Moreover, the staff can be relocated or retrained, and processes, organizational procedures, and services can be rethought. In sum ICT systems can reengineer internal processes and implement best working practices thanks to a better flow of information, ultimately bringing a better provision of public services.

The use of ICTs creates a competitive environment for local government staff, strengthening knowledge and capacity building to support the decentralization process. In addition, ICTs can reach people in remote areas; their involvement in local government can make important contributions toward decentralized policymaking. So ICTs foster the efficiency of (significant) internal processes, minimize resources and costs, and maximize the timeliness and quality of service delivery. Faster information transfer reduces bottlenecks. These virtuous processes may facilitate the development of open procurement systems (e-procurement). Governments are testing e-procurement to see whether it streamlines purchasing and reduces administration costs. The hope is that it makes procurement easier, faster, and cheaper. In fact use of the Internet can simplify and render transparent the purchase process. In this way, government interactions and transactions between government and business are facilitated, and the public system becomes more efficient and accountable. In addition, the Internet's standard procedures allow the traceability of transactions. This leads to a decrease in corruption and also in red tape; it also enhances transparency by storing relevant information in the system.

Local administrations are testing e-procurement systems, developing online purchasing systems. This phase of developing e-procurement systems consists of analyzing spending categories and adopting an approach that fits the requirements of the administrations. The city of Jundiai, in Brazil, has for example established an Internet portal in order to improve its purchasing process in terms of transparency, efficiency, cost, and information availability. The city has experienced a significant reduction in annual expenditure and has also simplified the sellers' process. "Today 80% of the Municipality's purchase of materials is made through the portal, and the time of certain purchases has been reduced from three days to inside one day."[15]

Thus the benefits that ICTs seem able to bring to the functioning of local authorities are great, but the introduction of ICTs can also aggravate problems.

The Decentralization Challenge

Endemic problems at the local level, such as corruption, poverty, and lack of appropriate infrastructure, complicate access to and availability of resources, significantly hampering the decentralization process. Corruption is a treacherous obstacle to effective and meaningful decentralization. ICTs, however, can help reduce corruption and promote democratic values by facilitating communication and disseminating information. In fact the use of ICTs can open up administrative and financial records and transactions to control bodies and to citizens. It can lead to a more transparent and accountable system as well as improve management operations, bringing efficiency and cost savings to the government.

In India the government of Karnataka has implemented a project known as *bhoomi* ("land," in Hindi), for efficient online service delivery and accessible information for all citizens. *Bhoomi* was one of the winners of the UN Public Service Awards of 2006. With the aim of improving the quality of service delivery to the citizens, easing records administration, and ensuring the project's self-sustainability, *bhoomi* computerized land records and administers the system through its computer program. The district administration is now able to use its land records for complex planning and development activities. Also, the Indian government believed that disclosing land records to the public, thereby improving transparency, would reduce corruption and wrongdoing by government officials. By March 2002 all 177 *bhoomi* centers became operational, and citizens have been able to check land record data.[16]

ICTs can also facilitate the capacity building of local administrators and enable and support private sector development, with the ultimate goal of promoting socioeconomic growth. Partnerships among governments, the business community, and civil society are very important for the development and spread of ICTs. These partnerships can mobilize resources for the wider use of the Internet.

In Uganda the Grameen Foundation has launched, in partnership with local microfinance institutions and local operators, a project called Village Phone Direct.[17] Recognized by governments and development agencies as a sustainable development tool, the project aims to bring low-cost phone service to rural villages.[18] This project has been successfully replicated in India, the Philippines, and Rwanda. "Entrepreneurs, usually women, buy a phone and airtime with a microfinance loan and sell services by the minute. Some are also reselling information. Discount margins allow operators to repay loans. Voice calls are the most common use, but SMS [text messaging] now provides current market information for farmers to use in negotiations, link with other businesses and their clients, or stay in touch with absent family members."[19]

In countries characterized by low per capita incomes and lack of access and connection, Village Phone Direct brings telecommunications benefits to local communities and microentrepreneurs. "The Village Phone Direct microfranchise creates a win-win opportunity for both the microfinance institution and the micro-entrepreneur with a replicable, sustainable business that will stimulate community development."[20]

Mobile telephony is an innovative and cost-effective solution to e-access and e-participation and overcomes the issue of resources. Alternative tools, such as mobile phones or radios, continue to be widely used in Africa, South America, and parts of Asia.[21] These tools, too, allow citizens to be involved in local policies at relatively low cost. Access to low-cost tools can overcome lack of services, resources, and information (for example adopting local languages), addressing the isolation, marginalization, and exclusion of local communities. In India the Vijayawada municipality offers municipal services via interactive television to poor and middle-class families without home Internet connections:

> While only 5,000 homes have Internet connections, about 160,000 have phones and TV. Using the system, the citizen dials in to the municipal server and the phone pad becomes the keyboard, while the TV monitor displays the server output over the cable TV network. Users can then access all services available to the Web, including tax payments and ledgers inspection, citizen database certificate requests, complaint filing and tracking, and pending city government issues.[22]

So broadband and wireless technologies can address the digital divide. Accelerating the adoption of wireless technologies will provide "opportunities for low-cost access and bottom-up network deployment led by community needs."[23] However, they can be successful only if they are supported by government policies. "Experience has shown that up-scaling of ICTs projects is much easier in countries which have put in place an enabling ICTs environment and a national ICTs strategy."[24]

Creating an ICT institutional regulatory legal framework is an important challenge for government policies. The fast growth of ICTs and their cross-cutting nature push governments to rethink such a framework and to implement one that is effective and flexible. In fact well-planned formulation, implementation, and enforcement of the regulatory legal framework can avoid risks linked to cybercrime and lead to better management of operations (such as security for online bill payment, protection of personal and confidential data, and measures against fraud). In Japan the e-Japan strategy (which envisaged Japan's becoming the world's most advanced ICT nation) provides for several legal and technological initiatives in order to ensure a security environment. The government has established a public infrastructure reached through an encrypted code, allowing citizens to securely perform online transactions with any ministry. "They are able to obtain a digital certification that confirms their respective identity, thus reducing identity theft and fraud."[25]

Appropriate legal and regulatory measures can provide reliable and affordable access to ICTs and prompt ICT diffusion as well as increase investments and competition in the sector. It is also important for governments to equip the ICT regulatory framework with an effective communication plan to disseminate awareness on security risks among Internet users. The ICT regulatory framework must thus be structured, integrated, transparent, and accountable; it must also encourage public participation in the decisionmaking process. An effective regulatory framework "strengthens public and investor confidence and increases the stability and objectivity of the regulatory process."[26]

Paraguay has implemented a platform for a secure and trusted Internet-based mechanism. Through the platform, operators and service providers can exchange sensitive information (such as income declaration) with the national regulatory agency. This mechanism streamlines the process of issuing licenses to public telephones and also increases the efficiency in the business process of the regulator.[27]

Political, legal, economic, and social factors characterize national ICT regulatory frameworks. However, governments could address issues linked to ICT security through guidelines and good practices. Sharing good practices in ICT security and encouraging their use is surely one way to ensure confidence and security.[28]

Conclusion

By ensuring more efficiency, effectiveness, accountability, and participation, ICTs can be a powerful tool for decentralizing. Precisely, ICTs can support local governments' capacity during the transition from a centralized to a decentralized system by strengthening governance structures. ICTs can address a lack of transparency and accountability at the local level and inadequate participation by local communities in the policymaking process. Through facilitating global flows of information, ICTs can foster a broad-based involvement of communities and their representatives in local decisionmaking, breaking barriers to participation and access. In many countries, central and local governments have created connectivity points to help those not connected to connect. Building domestic ICT tools may contribute significantly to address the digital divide and give opportunities in terms of information access and social economic growth.

Furthermore, improved mechanisms for a greater involvement of citizens can build public confidence and strengthen trust in institutions. ICTs can generate a deeper awareness of public issues, and this can help form a general consensus about public policies. Decisions then would be the result of participation by all stakeholders. Reaching consensus is key to defining and implementing public policies. Consensus is important also to the achievement of the UN millennium development goals. The effective use of ICTs can, in this vein, foster sustainable development, fight poverty, develop such basic services as education and health, promote equality and empowerment, reduce mortality and disease, and develop a global partnership for development.

ICTs can, then, contribute in a meaningful way to a more responsible government and democratic governance. However, the lack of a developed infrastructure, of a market, and of skilled human resources, as well as an inefficient regulatory legal framework threaten ICT development. In many cases, these challenges can be overcome, but that would require very specific measures.

In sum ICTs can make decentralization more effective and meaningful—but not in all cases and not without certain caveats. In fact if ICTs are not implemented properly, they can increase the "imbalance between rich and poor, powerful and marginalized."[29] They can slow the pace of decentralization in service delivery, cooperation among levels of government, and decisionmaking mechanisms. In addition, the lack of a proper regulatory framework can increase cybercrime, obstructing the difficult process of building public confidence and trust in decisions and institutions. Decentralization, to be effective, needs transparent and accountable management of resources, adequate cooperation and collaboration at all levels, and a constant evaluation of service delivery to ensure the optimal utilization of resources. Moreover, the development of capacity-building activities can empower communities.[30]

For these reasons, it is important for governments to create an enabling environment for ICT diffusion. A proper national regulatory framework can promote the use of ICTs and guarantee access of information for all groups of people as well as Internet security. Government strategies should promote partnerships with the potential to mobilize resources and overcome the gap between physical infrastructure, market resources, and human capacity.

The United Nations has been working to build online partnerships to bridge gaps among stakeholders. The UN Fund for International Partnerships facilitates partnerships among UN agencies, the private sector, and foundations.[31] Such multistakeholder partnerships are an invaluable tool to address development challenges, provide initiatives, and share good practices in order to improve access and the use of ICTs and to increase global understanding of the benefits of ICTs.

Notes

1. G. Shabbir Cheema, *Building Democratic Institutions: Governance Reform in Developing Countries* (Bloomfield, Conn.: Kumarian, 2005).

2. United Nations Department of Economic and Social Affairs, *Compendium of Innovative E-Government Practices*, 2nd ed. (2006), p. 216.

3. For more information, see www.peoplefirst.net.sb/.

4. Anand Chand and others, "The Impact of ICT on Rural Development in Solomon Islands: The PFnet Case," ICT Capacity Building Project, University of the South Pacific, Fiji, 2005 (www.usp.ac.fj/jica/ict_research/documents/pdf_files/pfnet_report.pdf).

5. "With almost 70,000 jobs in a town of more than 60,000 inhabitants, Issy-les-Moulineaux offers a very dynamic economic fabric. A true Medialand, the town has based its economic development strategy on communications companies. With 1,430 businesses in the town, almost 60% of which are in the Information and Communication Technologies (ICT) sector, Issy-les-Moulineaux is focused resolutely on ambition and progress" (http://issy.com/index.php/fr/english/news/welcome_to_medialand).

6. Eric Legale, "Issy-les-Moulineaux: The Cyber City," in *Good Practice Database: eGovernment,* 2005, edited by Edgar Krassowski (www.egov-goodpractice.org/gpd_details. php?&gpdid=156).

7. United Nations Department of Economic and Social Affairs, *Compendium of Innovative E-Government Practices,* p. 202.

8. United Nations Department of Economic and Social Affairs, *Global E-Government Readiness Report 2005: From E-Government to E-Inclusion* (2006), p. 18.

9. Ibid.

10. Sheffield City Council, "E-Democracy in Sheffield, Pilot Scheme Evaluation," 2003 (www.sheffield.gov.uk/index.asp?pgid=1912).

11. City of São Paulo, "Digital Inclusion Plan" (www.telecentros.sp.gov.br).

12. Glasgow City Council, "Sign Language Interpreting Service Project" (www.glasgow. gov.uk/).

13. Icamericas, "@Campus Mexico: Public Service E-Learning Strategy Project" (www. icamericas.net/index.php?module=htmlpages&func=display&pid=747).

14. Ibid.

15. EuropeAid Cooperation Office, "eGOIA Electronic Government Innovation and Access," 2004 (http://unpan1.un.org/intradoc/groups/public/documents/Other/UNPAN02 4325.pdf).

16. United Nations, "Best Practices in Innovation: Public Service Award Winners, 2006" (http://unpan1.un.org/intradoc/groups/public/documents/UN/UNPAN023509.pdf).

17. The Village Phone equipment kit is made by Nokia and includes a Nokia mobile phone, a booster antenna, a recharging solution, and custom-designed cables to connect all of the components.

18. The development agencies are the World Bank, the United Nations, the International Finance Corporation, and USAID.

19. Grameen Foundation, "Grameen Foundation and Nokia Launch Village Phone, Pilots Planned in Four Countries," 2006 (www.grameenfoundation.org/resource_center/ news/~story=194).

20. Grameen Foundation, "Village Phone Direct: A Microfranchise Opportunity" (www. grameenfoundation.org/what_we_do/technology_programs/village_phone_direct/).

21. SDC/Panos, "Information and Communication Technologies and Large-Scale Poverty Reduction: Lessons from Asia, Africa, Latin America, and the Caribbean," 2005 (http:// 162.23.39.120/dezaweb/ressources/resource_en_25250.pdf).

22. EuropeAid Cooperation Office, "eGOIA Electronic Government Innovation and Access, Strategy Report, 2004" (http://unpan1.un.org/intradoc/groups/public/documents/ other/unpan024325.pdf).

23. Galperin Hernan and Bar François, "Research Network on International Communication, Project Proposal, Wireless Networks, and Community Development," 2003 (http://arnic.info/Papers/HG-FB_Wireless_and_Community_Development_Sep03.pdf).

24. SDC/Panos, "Information and Communication Technologies."

25. United Nations Department of Economic and Social Affairs, *Compendium of Innovative E-Government Practices,* p. 157.

26. "ICT Regulation Toolkit, infoDev and ITU" (www.ictregulationtoolkit.org/section/ legal_regulation/introduction/).

27. United Nations and ITU, "Building the Information Society: An Overview of ITU-D Mandate and Activities in Cybersecurity," 2005 (www.itu.int/itu-d/e-strategy/ cybersecurity/documents/itud%20mandate%20and%20activities%20in%20cybersecurity. pdf).

28. United Nations and ITU, "Building the Information Society: A Global Challenge in the New Millennium," 2005 (www.itu.int/dms_pub/itu-s/md/03/wsispc3/td/030915/S03-WSISPC3-030915-TD-GEN-0006!R1!PDF-E.pdf).

29. Regional Cooperation in Information and Communication Technology (www.unescap.org/pdd/publications/regcoop/ch5.pdf).

30. United Nations Secretary General, *Report of the Economic and Social Council, Public Administration and Development,* General Assembly, Fifty-Ninth Session, September 9, 2004.

31. Dossal Amir, "Digital Partnerships," UN Fund for International Partnerships, 2003 (www.un.org/unfip/docs/Digital%20Partnerships%20WSIS%202003.pdf).

4

Local Governments That Perform Well: Four Explanations

MERILEE S. GRINDLE

Throughout the world, decentralization has created new responsibilities and expectations for local governments. And while the process of decentralization has brought significant new resources and power to local decisionmakers, it has also brought new pressures and concerns. Long bereft of authority and resources by highly centralized political systems, municipalities throughout the world are now grappling with how to carry out routine administration, provide good quality public services, and plan for the economic development of their localities. Institutions for local decisionmaking, in some cases atrophied from decades of centralization, are now being revived to take on complex problems. Service-providing organizations are also being created or restructured, employees need to be trained, and new procedures have to be put into effect. Fiscal management is becoming more exacting, even as citizens become increasingly aware that local officials can be appealed to, blamed, or supported for the delivery of a range of public services.

These are among the challenges that local governments—and local public officials—face in increasingly decentralized countries. In a number of places, states and large cities were in the forefront of new efforts to insist on greater autonomy, increase local capacity to manage fiscal resources and public services, expand the level of local taxation, and challenge the central government for additional responsibilities and resources. But questions remain about smaller municipalities—those that are not regional or national capitals, for example.

Were they blundering in the wake of decentralization, bereft of capacity to handle new activities, too corrupt to manage finances effectively, and too politicized to demand greater autonomy? Or were they, like some states and larger cities, getting better governance? If the latter scenario were occurring, what factors might explain improved governance in these locations?

A study of thirty randomly selected municipalities in Mexico sought to address this question of how local governments were coping with new responsibilities and resources in an era of decentralization.[1] These municipalities shared a political history of gradual decentralization and democratization, yet they differed significantly on the index of government performance that was developed for the study. The research explored the impact of four factors on the capacity of local governments to carry out their responsibilities efficiently, effectively, and in response to citizen needs and demands. Could performance differences among the study sites, we asked, be explained by the impact of political competition; the capacity of political leaders to mobilize resources for change; the introduction of new methods and skills for public administration; or the demands and participation of civil society? This chapter presents a brief review of the findings of the study.

Decentralization in Context: The Mexican Experience

Municipalities in Mexico are equivalent to counties in the United States. They are generally composed of a town that serves as a county seat and its surrounding communities, which are often rural.[2] At the time of the research local governments were responsible for basic municipal services, including water, sewage, garbage pickup, urban transport, public markets, public lighting, roads and highways, public security, and slaughterhouses.[3] They maintained such infrastructure as school buildings, playgrounds, health clinics, and hospitals. They regulated zoning and environmental issues. They had control over property taxes and could levy other local taxes and fees. Annually, they prepared budgets for approval by state legislatures.

Local governments are composed of a mayor and councilors, who are elected for three-year terms and are legally barred from holding the same position again for three years. These officials are elected by party lists, with the first name on the ballot that of the candidate for mayor; proportional representation determines the makeup of the council.[4] In all municipal governments, mayors have extensive discretion over appointments of local administrative officials. Among the most important are heads of various departments—treasury, public works, public safety, culture and youth, public health, urban development, rural development, and so on. Mayors also appoint a chief administrative officer and the secretary of the government, who usually serves as chief of staff to the mayor. Beyond these high-level positions, the mayor usually can appoint subdepartmental officials, secretaries, office workers, laborers, and others.

Throughout most of the twentieth century municipal governments were poor and almost powerless in the Mexican political and administrative system. Highly centralized, the country boasted a powerful executive, a weak legislature and judiciary, and a dominant party (the Partido Revolucionario Institucional, PRI), which won all presidential elections between 1929 and 2000 as well as the vast majority of legislative, state, and local elections.[5] The system was held together by extensive clientelist networks, which reached from the most remote locations to the presidential office; despite injustice and inequality, this system produced decades of a relative political peace that was the envy of politicians in many less stable countries. Beginning in the early 1980s, however, dual processes of decentralization (from above) and democratization (from above and below) introduced significant changes in the way this system worked.[6]

In the days of PRI hegemony, "the exercise of municipal government followed the rationale and orthodoxy of its role as a cog in the Mexican political (that is, PRI) machine."[7] In the late 1980s this tradition of local subservience to the PRI began to change, as the Partido Acción Nacional (PAN) and the Partido de la Revolución Democrática (PRD) began to make electoral inroads at state and municipal levels.[8] In 1995 over 50 percent of the Mexican population was governed at the local level by parties other than the PRI. Although this percentage declined in subsequent elections, in 2003 about 44 percent of municipalities were governed by non-PRI mayors. As is clear in figure 4-1, opposition party victories became increasingly common in Mexico.

In addition, decentralization, initiated hesitantly in the early 1980s and evolving equally hesitantly over the next two and a half decades, gradually allowed local governments greater autonomy and more resources. In 1994 they began to receive significant amounts in grants and transfers from the federal government, by far the most important source of their revenue.[9] Figure 4-2 shows the growth in funds provided to local governments from all federal sources between 1990 and 2002. In constant pesos of 1993, municipalities received extremely little before 1994; by 2002 they were receiving almost 2 percent of GDP. In per capita terms, there was an increase from 0.14 pesos per person in 1990 to 311.58 pesos in 2002 (see table 4-1).

In the research reported here, a random sample of six states (one from each region of Mexico) served as a base for the random selection of five medium-sized municipalities (25,000 to 100,000 inhabitants), for a total of thirty municipalities in the sample.[10] During the summer and fall of 2004 researchers interviewed past and present officials in the thirty municipalities; delved into relevant documents about local fiscal conditions; explored the dynamics of changes in administrative, service, development, and participatory activities of local government, assessing the electoral history of each; generated insights into the relationship of local governments to state and federal ones; and came to know well the sites they were studying.[11] In addition, data from national election archives, socioeconomic

Figure 4-1. *Municipalities and States Governed by Parties Other than the PRI, 1985–2003*

Percent

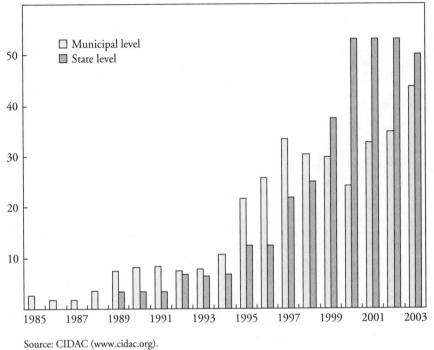

Source: CIDAC (www.cidac.org).

Figure 4-2. *Federal Transfers to All Municipal Governments, 1990–2002*

Billions of 1993 pesos

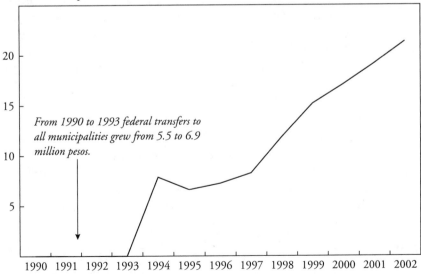

From 1990 to 1993 federal transfers to all municipalities grew from 5.5 to 6.9 million pesos.

Source: INEGI, Sistema Municipal de Base de Datos (www.inegi.gob.mx/prod_serv/contenidos/espanol/simbad/default.asp?c=73).

Table 4-1. *Funding of Municipal Governments, 1990–2002*

Year	1993 pesos	As percent of GDP	1993 pesos per capita
1990	11,493,530	0.00	0.14
1991	12,844,330	0.00	0.15
1992	13,957,728	0.00	0.16
1993	15,670,364	0.00	0.18
1994	16,627,876,932	1.27	185.69
1995	13,467,271,150	1.10	147.76
1996	13,593,322,125	1.05	146.84
1997	14,834,650,367	1.08	157.94
1998	19,041,518,428	1.31	199.91
1999	22,914,372,452	1.53	237.25
2000	24,847,462,509	1.55	253.63
2001	27,730,706,387	1.73	279.05
2002	31,412,724,549	1.98	311.58

Source: INEGI, Sistema Municipal de Base de Datos (www.inegi.gob.mx/prod_serv/contenidos/espanol/simbad/default.asp?c=73); and Banco de Mexico (www.banxico.org.mx/eInfoFinaciera/FSinfoFinanciera.html).

data, and a 2002 municipal census were used to test hypotheses related to local governance.

The project sought to understand how local governments functioned—how the business of government was carried out on a daily basis. Local performance was judged on the basis of five aspects of municipal governance: efficiency, effectiveness, responsiveness, development orientation, and change initiatives. To measure these factors, I selected conditions related to the presence or absence of administrative structures and processes, formal and informal rules that constrained public officials in the pursuit of their responsibilities, the extent of participation in public business, and the degree of effort to promote development and change. In total there were seventeen indicators; municipalities were awarded one point for the presence of each of the indicators and a zero for its absence, plus additional points equal to the number of change initiatives undertaken.[12] Scores differed significantly among the municipalities, from 3.0 to 18.0, with an average score of 9.4. Simple regression analysis indicates that there was no significant relationship between the performance of the municipality and the party in power at the municipal level, the state in which the municipality was located, or the degree of wealth or poverty of the municipality.[13] This initial testing opened the way for exploring four other hypotheses about local government performance.

Explaining Local Government Performance

The rhetoric and theory of decentralization promise better governance and deeper democracy as public officials are held more directly accountable for their actions and as citizens become more engaged in local affairs.[14] Practice over more than two decades, however, suggests that these are not the only possible outcomes of decentralization policies. For many, new experiments with decentralization have resulted in disappointed expectations and the emergence of unanticipated problems.[15] There is considerable potential for diverse outcomes in local political contexts increasingly characterized by more responsibilities and resources. Among explanations for this diversity in outcomes, the Mexico study considered four: competitive elections, public leadership, capacity building, and civil society mobilization.

Competitive Elections

The dynamics of party competition and elections are at the core of one approach to explaining variations in the performance of local government. In this view, democratization and greater competition among political parties to win local mayoral and council elections increase the pressure on incumbents to perform effectively while in office.[16] According to this perspective, where local elections are competitive and opposition parties have real opportunities to win positions of authority, incumbents will be motivated to prove their competence in the management of public affairs and will seek to find new ways of addressing important problems.

In Mexico the rationale behind the hypothesis rests on the assertion that politicians in office will try to perform well because they prefer to have their own parties rather than other parties win subsequent elections—they cannot succeed themselves, after all—or they want to do well in office because they hope to run for higher level office on the basis of their good performance. And in municipalities with less competitive elections, there will be fewer incentives for elected public officials to perform well while in office.

Nevertheless, statistical tests of electoral competitiveness and government performance failed to produce a significant correlation between these factors in the research municipalities. The relationship between the variables was found to have a low magnitude and was not statistically significant.[17] Indeed, some of the most competitive electoral sites were characterized by very low and even dysfunctional performance, while some less competitive sites had good performance; overall, no clear patterns emerged. Yet the field research suggests that there *is* a link between competitive elections and performance—although not a direct one. Greater electoral competition set in motion a number of important changes in local politics.

First, winning positions in local government became more attractive in the wake of serious efforts to decentralize responsibilities and resources. Control over those resources and the jobs and opportunities that they created increased interest in running for office as mayor and councilor. In particular, becoming a mayor was an increasingly attractive goal for the politically ambitious. It provided access to important resources to distribute to constituents and clienteles and an opportunity to use local office as a jumping-off point to higher office. As a consequence, competition increased for public office in all of the research municipalities, even where the dominant party had long been unquestioned. Often the competition began within that party, the PRI. Traditionally in the hands of local political bosses, contestation to be chosen as a candidate gave rise to initiatives to debunk old caciques and to introduce new groups into political relevance. In the wake of increased competition for office within the PRI, new local political parties emerged and provided, often for the first time, alternatives for citizen choice in elections.

Second, at least at the local level, party identities and labels of candidates were usually not reflective of ideologies, positions, or platforms. Time after time, our fieldwork indicated that new parties emerged when aspiring candidates were rejected by the locally dominant party and then defected from it in order to run for office. Thus greater competition among parties was more often a result of a changing opportunity structure than it was of the mobilization of particular perspectives and commitments—or even the diligence of party activists in recruiting and organizing new members. When locally ambitious politicians began to believe that it was possible for alternative parties to win elections, local organizations of national parties sprang up in many localities.

Increasing competition was often reflected in the turnover of power from one party to another—at times on several occasions. But even in municipalities that continued to bring PRI candidates to office, the threat of losing elections heightened. Increasingly, there were fewer "safe boroughs" for the party that had dominated political life in Mexico for so long, as is suggested in table 4-2. It was difficult, therefore, to distinguish between more or less competitive political contexts; all parties and candidates were under increased pressure to perform in ways that would win votes in subsequent elections. Moreover, parties began to pay more attention to internal mechanisms for selecting candidates, to becoming more open and transparent in terms of how they selected candidates, and to finding candidates who were popular locally. Again, this affected all parties and was not limited to the most competitive areas.

Third, when voters had real alternatives among candidates, electoral campaigns increased in meaning. They were the vehicles for bringing alternative leadership to local government. This leadership was not consistently better than the old leadership—scoundrels were elected as well as reformers—but opportunities were opened up for the greater circulation of political elites, and this in some cases resulted in the election of public officials committed to improving the performance of local government.

Fourth, as competitiveness increased, divided and contentious municipal councils became more likely. Under the principle of proportional representation, most mayors were able to count on a party majority in the council, but

Table 4-2. *PRI Strength in Municipal Elections, 1980–2004*

State and municipality	First time less than 60 percent of votes	First time less than 50 percent of votes	First time less than 10 percent away from closest opponent	Number of PRI losses	Parties in office at time of research
Guanajuato					
Abasolo	1982	1991	1991	2	PAN
Manuel Doblado	1991	2003	2003	1	PAN
San Luis de la Paz	1988	1991	1988	2	PAN
Santa Cruz de Juventino R	1991	1997	2000	1	PVEM
Yuriria	1991	1997	1997	2	PAN
Oaxaca					
Acatlán de Pérez Figueroa	1992	1992	1992	1	PRI
San Juan Guichicovi	1992	1995	1995	0	PRI
Santiago Pinotepa N.	1995	1995	1995	1	PRI
Santiago Juxtlahuaca	1995	1995	1995	0	PRI
Santo Domingo T.	1980	1995	1995	0	PRI
Puebla					
Chignahuapan	2001	2001	. . .	1	PAN
Coronango	1983	1992	1995	1	PRI
Ixtacamaxtitlan	1995	2001	2001	0	PRI
Libres	1995	1995	1995	0	PRI
San Pedro Cholula	1992	1995	1995	1	PRI
Sinaloa					
Escuinapa	1992	1992	1992	2	PAN
Mocorito	1995	1995	1995	0	PRI
Rosario	1995	1995	1998	1	PRD
Salvador Alvarado	1992	1992	1995	1	PRI
San Ignacio	1998	. . .	. . .	0	PRI
Tamaulipas					
Aldama	1995	1995	. . .	0	PRI
Gonzalez	1995	1995	1998	0	PRI
Miguel Aleman	1995	1995	1995	1	PAN
San Fernando	1995	1995	. . .	0	PRI
Tula	1995	. . .	. . .	0	PRI
Yucatan[a]					
Oxkutzcab	1993	1995	1995	3	PRI (PAN)
Progreso	1993	. . .	. . .	0	PRI (PRI)
Ticul	1993	1995	1995	2	PRI (PAN)
Uman	1990	1995	1995	1	PRI (PRI)
Valladolid	1993	2001	1995	1	PRI (PRD)

Source: Based on data from CIDAC and local electoral institutes.

a. The results of the 2004 Yucatan elections held in middle of the research period are shown in parenthesis. These are accounted for in the number of PRI losses.

the vagaries of close elections, shifting party identities after elections, and negotiations for support in the absence of strong party platforms meant that some mayors found it more difficult to act on their policy or programmatic preferences, and some even faced gridlock. Resource allocation decisions became more subject to contention as the amount of resources increased and as municipal councils became increasingly pluralist.

Thus while improved municipal performance was not a necessary outcome of increased political competition, this competition facilitated opportunities for introducing change in the way municipal business was done. Clearly, it was a dynamic underlying the second hypothesis—that state entrepreneurship is an important driver of local government performance.

Public Sector Entrepreneurship

Another explanation for variations across localities in responding to new mandates and relationships focuses on the activities of public officials who develop ideas, mobilize coalitions, and make strategic choices about how to advance new organizational or policy agendas, even in the face of political opposition, public apathy, or capacity constraints. In this view, the state, in the guise of reform leaders and their teams, identifies particular problems and promotes policy, programmatic, or organizational solutions to them, even in the absence of party support or future electoral opportunities and incentives. Ideas, leadership skills, and the strategic choices made to promote a reform agenda and acquire resources take central place in such an approach.[18] Public officials and their strategic behavior thus explain what issues are taken up and the political dynamics of promoting them, from agenda setting through decisionmaking to implementation.

In the thirty research sites, mayors and other elected and appointed officials were the most important source of change in local governments; they had the greatest opportunities to set public agendas and use public resources to achieve their objectives. Mayors and others in leadership positions were expected to find resources for projects, manage the daily business of town hall, attend to constituent needs, and resolve conflict. Mayors were almost always the primary movers and shakers of local governments, although they differed significantly in terms of their commitments and abilities. This was reflected in differences among municipalities in how well they operated.

Some of the impact of leadership on local government was explained by the extent to which local electoral campaigns avoided party platforms or programs. Instead, politicians retailed promises to fix this or that at the community level and gathered petitions from individuals and communities about things they wanted. To a remarkable degree, campaigns in a more democratic Mexico were patterned on campaigns when Mexico had a one-party dominant system: it was about the exchange of promises for votes. A consequence of this style of campaigning was that, when new administrations came to power, they generally had no program of government, no clear priorities, and no consistent goals they were committed to. In many cases, programs, priorities, and goals were selected in the aftermath of elections, in contexts in which new mayors had a major say in what was to be pursued and in which their priorities or perspectives held considerable sway.

As it turned out, mayors were particularly important because many of the resources needed to pursue public goals had to be acquired from other levels of government. Indeed, as resources available to local governments increased, so did the time needed to "bring down" these resources. Thus the commitments, personality, persistence, and political networks that mayors brought to the office were important factors in determining how much could be done in any three-year period, as were the relationships they cultivated while in office. If mayors generally set public agendas for their terms in office, it was their connections to governors, ministers, and administrators at other levels of government that helped determine whether they could carry them out. In some of the research municipalities, differences in the party affiliations of mayors and governors were overcome by the creation of close personal relationships.

In addition, elected leaders had great discretion in appointing officials to public positions in the municipalities. They used this discretion variously— some to appoint cronies, some to solidify coalitions of support on the council, some to bring new purpose to town hall. In making use of this power, they had considerable capacity to change the orientation and performance of the government. Those they appointed could introduce new policies, procedures, programs, and projects. Newly appointed officials usually did not have to deal with embedded administrative routines that constrained their activities; instead, they could create and recreate administrative processes. They directly controlled financial resources and staff, and often they were part of the entrepreneurial apparatus that brought new resources to the municipality. Their connections, as well as those of the mayor, were critical factors brought into play in change initiatives. Indeed, liberating resources and managing a large number of projects and programs funded by other levels of government were principal responsibilities of department heads in Mexico's municipalities.

Municipal councils tended to be less important players in local government, although at times individuals on the council were also able to be entrepreneurial in helping initiatives get funding and support. Councils approved plans, programs, and budgets, and individual members were usually assigned to oversee some particular function in town hall. In the former role, they usually did little to hinder the mayor and his appointees, although a significantly divided council could bring local government to a standstill. In the latter role, councilors were primarily active when they selected a particular initiative and mobilized their networks at other levels of government to promote or support it. Compared to the mayor and appointed officials, however, councilors were not usually key to promoting changes in the municipalities.

State entrepreneurship, encouraged by the opening of the electoral system to increased competition, was particularly important because of the weakness of institutional structures that could act as a constraint on what leaders were able to do. Party platforms were weak or nonexistent, so leaders were not bound to a particular program once in office. Campaigns often left them considerable discretion to determine a program of government after they were elected. In most municipalities there was no entrenched bureaucracy to resist change—mayors could recreate the administrative structure and replenish its human resources when they came into office. State and federal laws, rules, and regulations were burdensome and constraining, but it was possible to honor them in the breach.

But the very lack of institutional constraints that helped explain how much change could happen in the course of three years also systematically undermined the sustainability of change. Thus the extensive room to maneuver that local public officials had was matched by possibilities that their initiatives would be undermined by their successors and that institutional memory would be weak. In a relatively open institutional context, then, leadership success and subsequent failure were both relatively easy.

Public Sector Modernization

New ideas, new technologies, and training provide a stimulus for change in government performance, according to a third hypothesis.[19] In particular, through the introduction of modern techniques of management and improvement in the administrative and technical capacities of elected and appointed officials, the efficiency and effectiveness of local administration and service provision could be expected to improve. Moreover, this hypothesis projects that state modernization will be an important factor in reducing systematic corruption in town hall.

In the thirty research municipalities, state modernization was much in evidence. Reorganizations were common, as was improving the "profile" of those selected to hold appointive office and the extent to which new technologies were used in routine activities. Performance standards were introduced in some municipalities, and computers were functioning in all sites, although they were being put to more sophisticated use in some than in others. Indeed, the extent to which computerization was being adopted for administrative and service provision tasks was often surprising, given that some of the municipalities were significantly rural, had declining economies, and were located in regions with poor higher education and with electric and transport networks subject to interruption.

There was certainly no paucity of training courses offered for local public officials, and there seemed to be resources in almost all municipalities to allow at least some to benefit from training. Many officials were conversant with the principles of the "new public management" movement and with private sector organizational and management techniques. In some cases, capacity building to improve performance took on added importance as a way to improve the legitimacy of the long-dominant PRI.

The professionalization of appointed officials was an important aspect of state modernization in many municipalities—accountants in the comptroller's office, architects and civil engineers in charge of public works, doctors and nurses handling responsibilities in the health office. Often it was these officials who were behind the introduction of new organizational schemes and technologies for accomplishing the work of town hall. They had ideas, contacts, and staff to solve problems. And although capacity building is often viewed as a difficult initiative that requires ongoing commitment over many years, the experience of Mexico's municipalities suggests that significant changes in the capacities of local officials and the programs they managed could be made relatively quickly. The ability to appoint and dismiss administrators certainly added to the potential for relatively rapid changes in capacity.

The dynamics of state modernization were important, a process that was largely demand driven rather than supply driven. That is, municipalities introduced modernization programs when their leaders promoted it, not simply because it was on offer from other levels of government or required from above by administrative fiat. In this way the hypothesis that improvements in capacity drive changes in local performance was not a stand-alone hypothesis but rather one closely aligned to the first two hypotheses. Elections provided opportunities for new leadership to emerge in local governments, their commitments and activities were paramount in explaining how local government fared (at least for three years at a time), and they were the ones to decide on how much emphasis to put on state modernization during their tenure. Thus capacity building initiatives were a tool of effective leadership, not an independent source of change for municipalities.

Civil Society Activism

A fourth possible way to explain variations in the performance of local government is the extent to which local citizens are mobilized to participate and demand accountability.[20] According to this perspective, social groups in the local community exert pressure on the public sector to provide better services or more opportunities for participating in policy processes. Not only do these groups demand good performance, they can also provide models of how improvements can be made, how to participate in decisionmaking and implementation, and how to monitor the performance of elected and administrative officials—and sanction and reward them at election time. Through extension of this argument, localities without active civil societies are less likely to take on difficult tasks of providing better services, innovating in their activities, or being responsive to local needs.

Indeed, proponents of decentralization place great emphasis on the fact that when government is closer to people, it is easier for citizens to know what is happening, to have input into decisionmaking and management, and to hold officials accountable for their actions. More than any other factor, it is the altered relationship between citizens and the state in decentralized settings that promotes better government, or so many argue.

In the research municipalities, there was considerable evidence of organized citizen interaction with public officials, particularly for a country often viewed as having a weak or incipient civil society. Across communities, groups identified common interests, organized themselves, and adopted common strategies for finding solutions to collective problems. They were not shy in approaching public officials, and they seemed to have good knowledge about whom they needed to contact in order to acquire resources—both financial and technical—to achieve their objectives. They wrote petitions and, impressively, persisted in pressing government officials to attend to local problems. Frequently, these groups not only committed their time and energy to community problem solving, they also collected money, donated land, and took on financial commitments in order to "partner" with local government. Collective action was a fact of life in many of the municipalities in the study.

It was clear that groups in civil society were best able to organize around activities that involved extracting benefits from government. The needs they identified were largely tangible and related to works that could be accomplished in relatively short time periods—a paved road, streetlights, drainage ditches, potable water, a community center, and so on. Participation initiated from the bottom up, then, focused primarily on petitioning for resources and attention. In a country that had, through many years of authoritarian government, encouraged clientelism in the distribution of public benefits, it is perhaps not surprising that much citizen activity under more democratic conditions mimicked previous mechanisms of making connections and presenting petitions.

Extracting benefits, however, is only part of full participation in public life. Citizens also need to be actively engaged in decisionmaking and to be able to hold public officials accountable for their actions. In the research municipalities, several initiatives were undertaken to increase the involvement of citizens and citizen groups in local decisionmaking. Particularly in the initial year of a new administration, many municipal governments encouraged community-level processes of consultation and priority setting, seeking to establish plans for municipal works for the three-year period in office. Citizens were also invited to attend council meetings in some municipalities, and local opinions were sought on a variety of local services through surveys and suggestion boxes. There were also initiatives to take government to the people through mechanisms such as Citizen Wednesdays, when officials made themselves publicly available to receive requests, complaints, and suggestions. In the reorganizations put in place in a number of municipalities, new positions were created for departments of social development or social communication, and part of their responsibilities was to stimulate citizen engagement with the municipality.

These initiatives, however, were far more likely to have been initiated by government than by citizen groups. Thus while citizens seemed well able to petition government and to extract resources, it was usually government that led the way in introducing mechanisms of participation and accountability. In time, of course, citizens might become more ready or able to initiate participatory and accountability-related tasks, but at least at the time of the research, the links among decentralization, democratization, and public accountability, so often promoted as one of its clear advantages, was primarily in evidence only at election time—and then only in some locations.

Thus citizen knowledge and action about how to make local government responsive proceeded at a faster pace than knowledge about how to hold government more responsible for its actions. Citizens had good ideas for how to get problems solved, but they were limited in terms of what seemed appropriate for demanding performance from government. On the whole, the research suggests that important dynamics were encouraging municipalities to work better; it was less clear that local accountability was flourishing. A civic culture of accountability remained weak.

Of the four hypotheses, that dealing with the role of civil society proved to be the most loosely connected to the interactive dynamic of electoral competition, leadership, and capacity building. The constraints on reelection limited the extent to which public officials could be directly punished or rewarded for the job they did, and leaders, although some activities had been pressed upon them by citizen groups, most frequently set public agendas relatively autonomously. Petitioning rather than participation was the objective of most citizen action. While the research suggests that changes in the dynamics of elections, in municipal government, and in management practices can be introduced over relatively short periods of time, it may take longer to assume the full habits of citizenship and opportunities for public debate promised by decentralization in democratic contexts.

Conclusion

This chapter seeks to analyze and explain how local governments and local public officials are coping with new responsibilities and resources in the wake of decentralizing policies. The answer? In the context of Mexico, they are coping variously. Decentralization is a dynamic process, suffering setbacks as well as advances, introducing opportunities for lapses as well as improvements in performance, and calling attention to the diversity of local response to new responsibilities and resources.

More competitive elections, new opportunities for leadership, the introduction of new technologies, new spaces for citizen engagement—these factors clearly characterized changes in local governance by the mid-2000s. These changes were the result of the twin processes of ongoing decentralization and democratization—both processes being slow and halting at times, both demonstrating the potential for reversal, and both needing to be bolstered. Nevertheless, after twenty-five years of initiatives to decentralize and a decade and a half of experiences with a more open political system, Mexico's municipalities are changing. By the mid-2000s state and municipal governments clearly have more authority and resources to deal with regional and local issues than at any other time in the country's history; likewise, citizens enjoy more democratic elections and more opportunities to participate in public decisionmaking than has been true in the recent or distant past.

Why are there significant differences in performance among the research municipalities? The research project explored four distinct hypotheses about conditions under which we might expect improvement in local government performance. In fact, a central finding of the project is the dynamic interrelationship among the four hypotheses. Although the leadership of local public officials—elected and appointed—emerged as the most important factor in explaining differences among municipalities in how they were adjusting to decentralization, their leadership was made possible through competitive elections, it drove the dynamics of capacity-building initiatives, and that leadership was challenged to some extent by a mobilized local civil society.

Decentralization can mean progress toward improved governance and democracy as well as the erosion of local conditions of well-being. Clearly, decentralization in the research sites had set in motion significant changes. But local governments continued to vary in terms of their performance and in terms of the extent to which they took advantage of the opportunities offered by decentralization. Thus the benefits of decentralization are a palette of possibilities, not necessarily of realities.

Legacies of the past also continued to mark how public problems are addressed. Despite many changes, municipalities in Mexico continue to reflect the weight of seven decades of authoritarian government and an even longer tradition of centralization. These legacies are particularly evident in the choices that officials and citizens made about how to solve problems. First, local governments in Mexico were acquiring more responsibilities, resources, and autonomy in a system still characterized by considerable centralization. This legacy is most apparent in terms of the fiscal strictures on local governments, in which both federal and state governments looked with some skepticism on local control over resources and hedged resource-sharing mechanisms with restrictions. In addition, the spigots that made resources available for specific needs continued to be located in state and national capital cities and in ministries and agencies belonging to governments at those levels. Public officials spent considerable time "bringing down" resources for local initiatives. When citizens found no response to their petitions in town hall, they likewise looked to other levels of government to provide resources and assistance.

Of course, local governments could have done more to free themselves from the legacy of dependence on other levels of government. They had the right to collect property and other taxes and were no longer required to send those revenues to higher levels of government. In some municipalities, public officials took advantage of this opportunity to improve revenue collection for municipal improvements. At the same time, however, the characteristic reluctance of politicians to impose taxes on citizens was very much in evidence in most municipalities. It was not uncommon to hear local officials claim that their citizens were simply too poor to pay more local taxes or to comply with stricter tax collection. "We don't have the culture of paying taxes," was the refrain that encouraged many officials to look to other levels of government for salvation rather than to their own citizens.

Moreover, to the extent that local governments continued to be dependent on other levels of government for resources, the success of local officials in gaining access to those resources continued to lie with their knowledge of higher level government and their familiarity with public officials at those levels. The "myth of the right connection," so typical of Mexican politics in the past, seems to be as much a result of centralization as of authoritarian decisionmaking.[21] This is also true of citizen groups seeking assistance from government—the right connection is as integral to the strategy as it often is to the solution of a particular problem. Clientelism remains embedded in Mexican local politics.

Overall, the experience of decentralization in Mexico provides some good news. Elections have come to play a more important and democratizing role in local government. In the research municipalities, there is clearly greater circulation of elites—one of the classical attributes of democracy—and citizens are increasingly aware that they have options when they go to the polls. While political parties usually do not have clear programs for local government, they offer alternative lists of candidates, and increasingly, competition characterizes election campaigns as well as internal party decisionmaking processes. From the back rooms of party headquarters and the back pockets of governors and presidents in state and federal capitals, then, competition has increasingly become a public opportunity for choice.

Similar good news about increases in political competition is encouraging leaders in municipal governments to pay more attention to their constituents. In the thirty municipalities, many politicians were aware that the rules of the game have changed and that the layers of political bosses who control political power no longer do so automatically. For politicians, voters have become more important, and citizen satisfaction is an important way to enhance a political career. While some public officials are more sensitive to this than others, and the chance of losing public confidence is greater in some local contexts than in others, even politicians in traditionally entrenched PRI enclaves spend more time worrying about the competition.

In addition, many citizens have more information on the activities of government and on opportunities to become involved in municipal decisionmaking and operation. Information about the workings of government, public finance, and the allocation of resources had been elusive for generations of Mexicans. This legacy is dying slowly in some municipalities, but the trend is toward greater openness and more sources of information about what is going on, who is benefiting from local decisions and who is not, and where resources are going. To the extent that information is a vital component of a vibrant democracy, this is good news. Eventually, it might be expected that the availability of more information could strengthen public debate about issues of local importance in those same municipalities.

It is also good news that increasing numbers of officials (because of alternation in power) and citizens (because of more opportunities to participate) are developing experience with local-level problem solving. In particular, some municipalities introduced new mechanisms whereby citizens could discuss priorities and build consensus about the most important local needs for public investment and attention. Through such mechanisms more democratic communities and more democratic debate could be built.

There are, then, some signs that decentralization in some of Mexico's municipalities is serving as a school for democracy. Learning is not always positive and not always consistent, and complaints and cynicism are commonplace throughout the municipalities studied. Yet trends toward greater engagement and possibly greater accountability are in a positive direction. This is potentially good news for those who advocate decentralization as a means to greater participation and democratic decisionmaking.

Notes

1. For a full description of the research and its findings, see Merilee S. Grindle, *Going Local: Decentralization, Democratization, and the Promise of Good Governance* (Princeton University Press, 2007). The research was carried out with funding from the Ash Institute for Democratic Governance and Innovation, the David Rockefeller Center for International Development, and the Center for International Development, all of Harvard University.

2. The municipal census of 2002 reported that Mexico contained 2,429 municipalities; their size and population varied greatly. The largest municipality, in the state of Baja California, extends for almost 52,000 square kilometers; the smallest, in the state of Tlaxcala, measures just 4.3 square kilometers. Similarly, populations ranged from 1.65 million people in a municipality in the state of Jalisco to 109 people in a Oaxacan municipality.

3. On municipal service provision, see Rodolfo García del Castillo, "La política de servicios municipales en México: Casos y tendencias recientes," in *Políticas públicas municipales: Una agenda en construcción,* edited by Enrique Cabrero Mendoza (Mexico City: Miguel Angel Porrúa, 2003).

4. The number of councilors is dependent on the population of the municipality and is determined by state law. In the thirty research municipalities, councils ranged from six to twenty-two elected officials, with an average of twelve. Depending on the municipality, the council met once a week, every two weeks, once a month, or irregularly. In most municipalities, each councilor had oversight responsibility for one or more public departments. In states with significant indigenous populations, local governments can legally be governed by traditional rules, known as

usos y costumbres (traditions and customs). In such circumstances, local governments are generally constituted through large community meetings, in which participants nominate individuals for particular office and then vote by voice, show of hands, or lining up behind particular nominees. There are a few municipalities in which a council of elders determines the leadership of local government. Parties may or may not play a role in these local decisionmaking processes.

5. Opposition parties began winning elections at the local level in the 1980s. In 1989 the first governor from an opposition party won election (although earlier in the decade, a number of other opposition candidates at this level may have fallen victim to electoral fraud).

6. For a history of this process, see Tim Campbell, *The Quiet Revolution: Decentralization and the Rise of Political Participation in Latin America's Cities* (University of Pittsburgh Press, 2005), chap. 2.

7. Peter M. Ward, "Policy Making and Policy Implementation among Non-PRI Governments: The PAN in Ciudad Juárez and Chihuahua," in *Opposition Government in Mexico,* edited by Victoria Rodríguez and Peter M. Ward (University of New Mexico Press, 1995), p. 141. Local politics was controlled by party bosses, or *caciques,* who used their power in the local economy to marshal or coerce votes for their PRI patrons at state and national levels.

8. The PAN was created in 1939 and had been successful in winning a number of state and local electoral contests in the 1980s and 1990s. The PRD was established in 1989 (from its predecessor, the Frente Nacional Democrático, established in 1988); its capacity to win local elections has been less than that of the PAN, but in 1997 it won control over the government of Mexico City, one of the world's largest cities.

9. In the thirty research municipalities, locally generated resources accounted for an average of only 11 percent of total funding.

10. Kathryn Stoner-Weiss, *Local Heroes: The Political Economy of Russian Regional Governance* (Princeton University Press, 1997); Richard Snyder, "After the State Withdraws: Neoliberalism and Subnational Authoritarian Regimes in Mexico," in *Subnational Politics and Democratization in Mexico,* edited by Wayne A. Cornelius, Todd A. Eisenstadt, and Jane Hindley (Center for U.S.-Mexican Studies, University of California, San Diego, 1999), on this methodology. The states were Guanajuato, Oaxaca, Puebla, Sinaloa, Tamaulipas, and Yucatán. In 2000 municipalities of this size included 23.6 percent of all local governments in Mexico and 25.3 percent of its population; their average population was 46,516. See INEGI (Instituto Nacional de Estadísticas y Geografía), *Censo General de Población y Vivienda, 2000.* These municipalities were large enough to have substantial responsibilities and significant resources for attending to them yet small enough to facilitate understanding complex political, administrative, and fiscal interactions.

11. Collectively, 569 individuals were interviewed, including 51 current and former mayors, 113 councilors, 229 local public managers, 98 community leaders and important citizens, 26 local party officials, 48 state and federal officials, and a number of academic experts. Orazio Bellettini, Karla Breceda, Alexi Canaday-Jarrix, Elizabeth Coombs, Xochitl Leon, and Alberto Saracho-Martínez, graduates of the Kennedy School of Government at Harvard University, and Sergio Cárdenas-Denham, of the Harvard Graduate School of Education, carried out the research. In addition, Naomi Walcott, Elizabeth Gewurz Ramírez, and Emanuel Garza Fishburn assisted in the research.

12. The indicators are not weighted, reflecting considerable ambiguity about the ease or difficulty of actions needed to carry out the activity.

13. These results, of course, might be explained by the limited number of observations, a fact that also limited the ability to introduce important control variables.

14. Campbell, *The Quiet Revolution;* Archon Fung, *Empowered Participation: Reinventing Urban Democracy* (Princeton University Press, 2004); Dennis A. Rondinellli and G. Shabbir

Cheema, eds., *Reinventing Government for the Twenty-First Century: State Capacity in a Globalizing Society* (Bloomfield, Conn.: Kumarian, 2003).

15. Shahid Javed Burki, Guillermo Perry, and William Dillinger, *Beyond the Center: Decentralizing the State* (World Bank, 1999); Wayne A. Cornelius, "Subnational Politics and Democratization: Tensions between Center and Periphery in the Mexican Political System," in *Subnational Politics and Democratization in Mexico,* edited by Cornelius, Eisenstadt, and Hindley; William Dillinger and Steven B. Webb, "Fiscal Management in Federal Democracies," Policy Research Working Paper 2121, World Bank, 1999; Jonathan Fox, "Latin America's Emerging Local Politics," *Journal of Democracy* 5, no. 2 (1994): 105–16; Kiichiro Fukasaku and Ricardo Hausmann, *Democracy, Decentralization, and Deficits in Latin America* (OECD, 1998); Paul D. Hutchcroft, "Centralization and Decentralization in Administration and Politics: Assessing Territorial Dimensions of Authority and Power," *Governance: An International Journal of Policy and Administration* 14, no. 1 (2001): 23–53; Jonathan T. Hiskey and Mitchell A. Seligson, "Pitfalls of Power to the People: Decentralization, Local Government Performance, and System Support in Bolivia," *Studies in Comparative International Development* 37, no. 4 (2003): 64–88; Eduardo Wiesner, *Fiscal Federalism in Latin America: From Entitlements to Markets* (Inter-American Development Bank, 2003).

16. Victoria Rodríguez, *Decentralization in Mexico: From Reforma Municipal to Solidaridad to Nuevo Federalismo* (Boulder, Colo.: Westview, 1997; Victoria Rodríguez and Peter M. Ward, eds., *Opposition Government in Mexico* (University of New Mexico Press, 1995).

17. Ordinary least squares (OLS) regressions of municipal performance scores and four measures of threat of electoral loss failed to produce any significant correlation. On average, for every additional unit in political competitiveness there was a positive difference of 0.72932 in performance. However, political competitiveness explained only 3.26 percent of the variation found in performance, and this relationship was not statistically significant at the 90 percent level ($t = 0.97$; $p = .3395$). This result is also found by Matthew Cleary, "Electoral Competition and Government Performance in Mexico," paper prepared for the Twenty-Third International Congress of the Latin American Studies Association, Washington, September 6–8, 2001. Cleary analyzes political competition and data on services and finances for all municipal elections between 1980 and 2000. He finds a small effect of competition on performance and concludes that "elections alone are less influential on government performance than is commonly thought, and are not sufficient to induce more responsive or efficient government" (abstract).

18. See particularly Joe Wallis, "Understanding the Role of Leadership in Economic Policy Reform," *World Development* 27, no. 1 (1999): 39–53; see also Rebecca Abers, "From Clientelism to Cooperation: Local Government, Participatory Policy, and Civic Organizing in Pôrto Alegre, Brazil," *Politics and Society* 26, no. 4 (1998): 511–37; Merilee S. Grindle, *Despite the Odds: The Contentious Politics of Education Reform* (Princeton University Press, 2004); Stoner-Weiss, *Local Heroes;* Campbell, *The Quiet Revolution.*

19. See for example Elaine Ciulla Kamarck, "Globalization and Public Administration Reform," in *Governance in a Globalizing World,* edited by Joseph S. Nye Jr. and John D. Donahue (Brookings, 2000); Cheema and Rondinelli, *Reinventing Government for the Twenty-First Century.*

20. Jonathan Fox and Josefina Aranda, "Decentralization and Rural Development in Mexico: Community Participation in Oaxaca's Municipal Funds Program," Monograph 42, Center for U.S.-Mexican Studies, University of California, San Diego, 1996; Fung, *Empowered Participation.*

21. Evelyn P. Stevens, *Protest and Response in Mexico* (MIT Press, 1974).

5

Political Decentralization in Africa: Experiences of Uganda, Rwanda, and South Africa

JOHN-MARY KAUZYA

> The mere fact of opting for decentralization shall not by itself ensure that the population effectively participates in its development which is the ultimate goal of a good policy of decentralization and good governance. It is important to set up mechanisms reassuring the participation of the population.
>
> —Rwanda, Ministry of Local Government and Social Affairs

Historically, African countries have experienced fused, personalized, and at best highly centralized governance systems and practices. In precolonial times kings or traditional leaders represented basically all authority. During the colonial and immediate postcolonial periods governance was structured and practiced in a highly centralized manner. During military dictatorships, which in many countries replaced the immediate postcolonial governments, governance was practically personalized. The search for inclusive, involving, and participatory governance has taken the path of decentralization. Political and administrative reforms that have been going on in many countries in Africa, especially since the 1990s, have sought to break with the past through decentralization of powers to lower government levels.

Decentralized governance is increasingly being favored by many African countries as the most suitable mode of governance through which poverty reduction interventions can be conceived, planned, implemented, monitored, and evaluated.[1] Many hope that the process of decentralization will facilitate greater participation of communities in problem analysis, project identification, planning, implementation, and oversight, which in turn will increase ownership and the likelihood of sustainability of such initiatives. In figure 5-1 Stephen N. Ndegwa shows the extent to which different African countries have decentralized their governance.

The term *decentralization* embodies several concepts, including devolution, deconcentration, delegation, and delocalization.[2] In many instances a decentralization policy that promises success will most likely include dozens of examples of each of these. This chapter, however, looks at only political decentralization, or devolution, and attempts an assessment of how it has been designed and implemented and how successful it has been in achieving the intended objective of promoting grassroots decisionmaking. The chapter specifies a working understanding of political decentralization (devolution) and attempts to answer questions such as the following:

—What are the practical reasons and objectives for devolution?

—Through what processes, modalities, and mechanisms was devolution decided and agreed upon and how did such processes facilitate or constrain its implementation and success?

—If devolution was intended to promote participation in decisionmaking by local governments, what was introduced into the design?

—Based on the objective of promoting participatory decisionmaking in local governments, what are some of the cases that illustrate that devolution so far has worked?

The answers to these questions are based on the decentralization experiences of Uganda, Rwanda, and South Africa.

Political Decentralization: A Working Understanding

Political decentralization can be understood to refer to either or both of the following: transferring the power of selecting political leadership and representatives from central governments to local governments; and transferring the power and authority for making socio-politico-economic decisions from central governments to local governments and communities.

Understanding political decentralization only in the first sense would limit the meaning of *political* to the choice of political leadership through elections. Therefore the promotion of political decentralization in this sense would entail only putting in place structural arrangements that would allow local people to exercise their voting power with limited hindrance or intervention from the central government. Here political decentralization would refer to only electoral decentralization, and participation would be understood only in terms of elections.

Figure 5-1. *Decentralization in Africa*

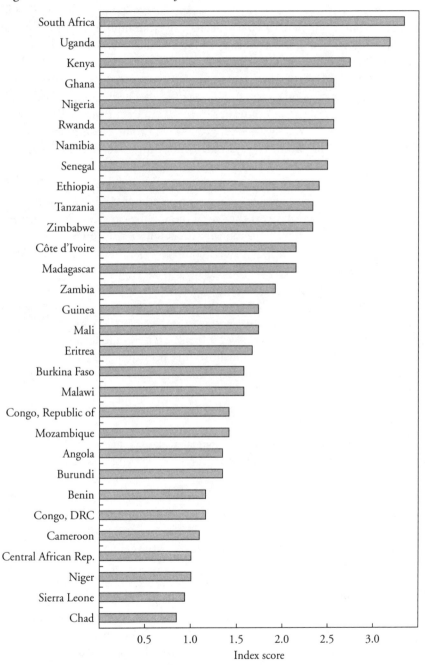

Source: Stephen N. Ndegwa, "Decentralization in Africa: A Stocktaking Survey," Africa Working Paper Series 40, World Bank, 2002.

On the other hand, promoting political decentralization in the second sense would entail putting in place structural arrangements and practices that would empower and facilitate local governments and communities to influence the making, implementation, monitoring, and evaluation of decisions that concern their socio-politico-economic well-being and to demand accountability from their local leadership. The first sense of political decentralization refers to the vote, while the second one refers to the voice. A combination of both enhances the influence of local people on the decisions that concern them.

Political decentralization is best conceived within these two frameworks so that the power and authority to decide is not limited to electing leaders or representatives but includes the full transfer of decisionmaking from the central government to local governments, authorities, or communities. This requires a structural arrangement that goes beyond putting in place local governments. It requires a process that combines vertical and horizontal decentralization.[3] Vertical decentralization transfers power and authority from the central government to local government; horizontal decentralization empowers local communities and enables them to receive and utilize the powers transferred to them, especially regarding problem analysis, priority setting, planning, and accountability by leadership and governance actors at all levels. Horizontal decentralization requires the growth of civil society as well as structuring local governments in such a way that they are legally obliged to seek and promote the participation of local communities in setting priorities and in planning and making decisions that the local governments will implement in a whole range of socio-politico-economic activities.

Objectives of Devolution

The rationale behind devolution in Uganda, Rwanda, and South Africa can be found in the countries' decentralization policy documents. Essentially, decentralization in the three countries was promoted in response to the political and economic problems in their history. In South Africa promoting local governments was aimed at "rebuilding local communities and environments, as the basis for a democratic, integrated, prosperous and truly non-racial society" following the trauma of apartheid.[4] In Rwanda decentralization was to "provide a structural arrangement for government and the people of Rwanda to fight poverty at close range, and to enhance their reconciliation via the empowerment of local populations" following the trauma of the genocide of 1994.[5] In Uganda decentralization is "a democratic reform, which seeks to transfer political, administrative, financial and planning authority from central government to local government councils and to promote popular participation, empower local people to make their own decisions and enhance accountability and responsibility" following the brutal and ineffective regime of Idi Amin (1971–79) and the Obote II regime (1981–86).[6] Political empowerment,

Box 5-1. *Uganda: Five Objectives of Decentralization*

1. The transfer of real power to local governments with the aim of reducing the load of work on remote and underresourced central officials.
2. Bringing political and administrative control over services at the point where they are actually delivered, thereby improving accountability and effectiveness, and promoting people's feeling of ownership of programs and projects executed in their local governments.
3. Freeing local managers from central constraints and enabling them to develop effective and sustainable organizational structures tailored to local circumstances in the long term.
4. Improving financial accountability and responsibility by establishing a clear link between the payment of taxes and the provision of services they finance.
5. Improving the capacity of local authorities to plan, finance, and manage the delivery of services to users.

economic development, improvements in the efficiency and effectiveness in the delivery of services, ownership of local programs by local people, participation of the people in planning and implementation of development activities as well as improvement in democracy and accountability are common terms in the decentralization policy of the three countries. Boxes 5-1, 5-2, and 5-3 summarize the stated objectives of decentralization in the three countries.

Engineering Consensus on Devolution

In decentralization parlance, devolution is about the transfer of decisionmaking powers and authority from the central government to lower entities (local governments), by whatever name they are called. Considering the objectives given in the boxes, devolution represents a radical departure from the past (the centralized systems and practices people were used to).

In the context of the three countries in question, it is tempting to arrive at an easy conclusion that the traumatic past (apartheid in the case of South Africa, genocide in the case of Rwanda, and brutal dictatorships in the case of Uganda) made agreement and consensus on devolution easy and straightforward. In reality this is not necessarily the case. There is a need to analyze and assess the processes and mechanisms through which the consensus on devolution was engineered and reached. In fact, for African countries still in the initial stages of introducing decentralization and still trying to manage resistance to decentralization, the three countries may offer lessons on how to engineer consensus on the transfer of decisionmaking powers from the central government to local governments and communities.

Box 5-2. *South Africa: Five Objectives of Decentralization*

1. Provide democratic and accountable government for local communities.
2. Ensure the provision of services to communities in a sustainable manner.
3. Promote social and economic development.
4. Promote a safe and healthy environment.
5. Encourage the involvement of communities and community organizations in the matters of local government.

Box 5-3. *Rwanda: Five Objectives of Decentralization*

1. To enable and reactivate local people to participate in initiating, making, implementing, and monitoring decisions and plans that concern them, taking into consideration their local needs, priorities, capacities, and resources by transferring power, authority, and resources from central to local government and lower levels.
2. To strengthen accountability and transparency in Rwanda by making local leaders directly accountable to the communities they serve and by establishing a clear linkage between the taxes they pay and the services that are financed by these taxes.
3. To enhance the sensitivity and responsiveness of public administration to the local environment by placing the planning, financing, management, and control of service provision at the point where services are provided and by enabling local leadership to develop organization structures and capacities that take into consideration the local environment and needs.
4. To develop sustainable economic planning and management capacity at local levels that will serve as the driving motor for planning, mobilization, and implementation of social, political and economic development to alleviate poverty.
5. To enhance effectiveness and efficiency in the planning, monitoring, and delivery of services by reducing the burden from central government officials who are distanced from the point where needs are felt and services delivered.

The stakeholders and actors in the process of decentralization are several, and their interests are rarely the same. First, the political wing of the central government must have the political will to engage in shared exercise of power and authority. Without political will, decentralization cannot succeed. Second, the bureaucracy of the central government (the civil servants) must be ready and willing to facilitate the process of transferring power, authority, functions, responsibilities, and the requisite resources. Without bureaucratic will, there will be many stumbling blocks in the way of decentralization. Third, the society at the grass roots—especially community leadership, however organized—must be capable and willing to receive and utilize the power and authority responsibly for the socioeconomic development of the people. Without civic will and capability, the functions transferred through decentralization will not be carried out effectively and the resources transferred will be wasted. In addition, local leadership is likely to behave as local dictators and jeopardize the participatory or even representative democracy that decentralization is intended to achieve. Fourth, since we are dealing with relatively poor countries mostly dependent on donor funds for implementation of decentralization, there has to be willingness on the part of donors and development partners to support decentralization. Donor support for decentralization is not always a given. It is interesting to see how these issues were handled to engineer consensus for devolution in the three cases.

Uganda. Uganda's current decentralization was born from both the exigencies of a guerrilla war and ideological conviction. In Luwero district, which was the initial area occupied by Museveni's guerilla force, resistance councils—political, local, people-based groups—were secretly organized. Despite the necessary secrecy, the councils were democratic in the sense that they were composed of democratically elected members of the villages. The councils aimed at cultivating and sustaining support for the National Resistance Army (NRA). As the councils were introduced into other captured areas, they served the purpose of educating the villagers about the importance of supporting the guerrilla war and removing the Obote II regime from power.

The first point of the ten-point program of the National Resistance Movement (a program elaborated during the guerrilla war and that became Museveni's manifesto around which he galvanized national support) emphasized democracy, especially participatory local democracy. Political decentralization was therefore a step already articulated. In addition, the National Resistance Movement (NRM) pursued decentralization right from the beginning so as to widen grassroots support. The NRM not only wanted political support from the grass roots but also wanted to plant seeds of participatory democracy for empowering the people.[7]

After the NRA capture of state power, the rhetoric of war had to be curtailed, and new methods of galvanizing support for and reaching consensus on decentralized governance had to be deployed. Essentially, several methods were used to gauge and galvanize support for the decentralization policy of the NRM. The Commission of Enquiry was established in 1987 to conduct surveys, enquiries, and consultations at all levels to establish what form of local government should be formed. The Commission of Enquiry recommended the resistance councils as democratic organs of the people.[8] In 1993 implementation of decentralization started in thirteen districts. Officially this was known as the first phase of decentralization, but technically it was viewed as a pilot exercise in decentralization. The experiences and lessons learned in the first thirteen districts to be decentralized were used to decentralize the rest of the districts. In 1993 the Local Government Transition Act was passed, providing a legal basis for resistance councils. These two methods—the Commission of Enquiry and the Local Government Statute—provided sufficient consultations, discussions, and negotiations to reach consensus on devolution. In 1995 a new national constitution was promulgated after nationwide consultations. Chapter 11 of the constitution gives a clear constitutional base for decentralized governance. Following the constitution, the Local Government Act of 1997 was enacted, cementing devolution.

The implementation of decentralization has experienced some resistance, some of which is still going on. First, some ministry bureaucrats, believing they would lose power over resources through decentralization, resisted its implementation. To counter this, the Decentralization Secretariat was established in 1992 as a semiautonomous body under the Ministry of Local Government to spearhead the implementation of decentralization.

Second, since independence there has always been a claim—especially from the Buganda region—for a federal arrangement of governance. This claim was undermined by the decentralization policy. Advocates of federalism have never given up, however, and at any given opportunity they raise the issue of establishing federalism. In a way, this has given the impression that consensus on decentralized governance has never been reached. However, the chances that federalism will be implemented are slim, because the grass roots have tasted power and authority under decentralization, and they will not easily give away any of their powers to a higher level of government.

Third, during the initial stages of implementing decentralization, donors were not completely in agreement with the government on what kind of decentralization was to be chosen. While the government was clear in its priorities (that it sought to implement devolution as a policy of participatory democracy and people's political empowerment and to decentralize up to the subcounty level), the World Bank, for example, sought to persuade the government to implement decentralization as a means of efficiency in financial management and financial accountability and to decentralize only up to the district level. The Danish International Development Agency (DANIDA) and the United Nations Development Program (UNDP) agreed with the government on the objective of democratization and people empowerment and provided funding for implementing decentralization—including the financing of the Decentralization Secretariat in the initial stages. After decentralization demonstrated success and popular support, most other donors also supported it.

But engineering support for devolution in Uganda had also to do with the substantive content, especially in terms of widening the bracket of political involvement and participation to include women, youth, and people with disabilities. Most Ugandans saw the introduction of the inclusive resistance councils as an opportunity for them to have a say in the affairs of their locality. They also took it as a chance to politically get rid of those among them who had been associated with the regimes of Idi Amin and Milton Obote. As for women and people with disabilities, their representation and participation in the resistance councils was perceived as a sign of the magnanimity of the new leadership and its commitment to the well-being of the disadvantaged.

South Africa. If in Uganda decentralization was born from the logic of searching for support for the guerrilla war and introducing grassroots participatory democracy, in South Africa it was an offspring of the struggle to dismantle the segregating local administration system of apartheid. The process was different from the one in Uganda, described above. In fact the debates on and public nature of the process of abolishing apartheid at the national level in a way masked what was going on at the local level: introducing a local government system that would correct the socio-politico-economic injustices and segregation that obtained through apartheid.

Although apartheid was abolished during the first half of the 1990s, it left a permanent mark on the local government system. For this reason a complete understanding of the process of post-apartheid devolution is only possible when one grasps the history of human settlements and the role that local governments played in establishing and sustaining separation, segregation, and inequality.[9] The history of local resistance against this system also played a big role in shaping the development of local governments. It should be noted that, while in Uganda decentralization was supply driven from above, with consultations made to confirm and galvanize support for it, in South Africa decentralized governance as it stands today was demanded from the grassroots black communities as a way of dismantling apartheid. Consultations about it were to determine what shape it would take and to solicit at least cooperation from the white communities in its decision and implementation. In a way it was a new deal reached between the aspirations of the black local communities and the status quo of white supremacy and segregation to implement the agenda of doing away with apartheid for the benefit of everyone.

The negotiations were spearheaded by both the local forums and the National Local Government Negotiating Forum, which eventually negotiated the Local Government Transition Act of 1993, forming three phases through which the postapartheid local government system would be put in place. The current decentralized governance system is part of the outcome of the negotiated national constitution.

Rwanda. After the war and the 1994 genocide in Rwanda, the leadership sought to decentralize governance and let people have a strong say in determining their socio-politico-economic destiny. The leadership had a legal basis for this in the Arusha agreements—which, without mentioning decentralization, committed government to creating a governance system that passes power to the people. In the decentralization document it is stated that one of the legal foundations of decentralization is the "principle of power sharing as expressed in the Accord de Paix d'Arusha entre le Gouvernment de la République Rwandaise et le Front Patriotique Rwandais. Up to now power sharing has only been seen among the political elite at Parliament and Executive levels. The decentralization policy will reinforce power sharing by ensuring that the Rwandese people themselves are empowered to shape their political, economic, and social destiny."[10]

The proposal for decentralization thus came from above. The government then had the hard task of convincing a traumatized population, used to being told by central government authorities what to do in almost everything, to take on the authority for local decisions. Rwanda is a typical example of decentralization from above. The formulation of the decentralization policy was done by government with assistance from consultants. The unique aspect in the formulation of the policy is that it was initially done as part of an overall governance program and strategy, which was formulated through consultations (meetings, workshops, and seminars) with all government institutions. After decentralization was adopted as one of the components of the national governance program, the decentralization policy was formulated. The policy is premised on promoting participatory democracy and reconciliation and empowering grassroots communities for socioeconomic development.

While these are noble causes to pursue, the population needed to be sensitized to them and persuaded, and enabled to embrace them. This task constituted the initial years of introducing decentralization (generally from 1997 to 2000). Seminars, field visits by the minister (and his staff) in charge of local government, study visits to other countries that had implemented decentralization, intensive sensitization of the population on their understanding and contribution to the success of the decentralization were successfully conducted, and the population came to understand and accept decentralization as a mode of governance. Political will to decentralize initiated the policy, civic will to accept decentralization was cultivated, but bureaucratic will was generally lacking. Because of the reluctance of the bureaucracy (civil servants) in 2005, six years after decentralization was implemented a number of services that had been legally decentralized—especially health, education, and agricultural services—were yet to be effectively decentralized. This prompted another bout of consultation—workshops and seminars—which culminated in a review of decentralization. Without changing the initial thrust and objectives of the policy, a formulation was reached whereby the "decentralized governance reform policy" was aimed essentially at effectively decentralizing the delivery of these services and improving the performance of local governments in this regard.[11]

With hindsight, one notices that some of the aspects of the "decentralized governance reform policy" confirm an important aspect of Rwanda's decentralization. It is supply driven and highly driven from the top. In the decentralized governance reform policy, it was possible to reduce the number of local governments (districts) from 106 to only 30.[12] This is contrary to the usual tendency, which is for local governments to strongly resist their abolishment. If the districts had gained local identity and had concern for control of their local problems and interests, they would not so easily have accepted being combined. On the contrary, lower administrative units would have been demanding local government (district) status. Either the government's persuasion was very powerful, or central government still has the strongest say even in local affairs.

Summary. In this section I illustrate that, even if devolution means transferring decisionmaking power and authority from central government to local government, its support is not always a given. It has to be engineered according to the circumstances that obtain.

In Uganda, engineering this support was in the interest of the government because, first, decentralization had to be used to galvanize support for the resistance war. Second, it had to be used to spread the ideology of participatory democracy of the National Resistance Movement. Third, it was used to dismantle the political bases of the political parties that had dominated the political landscape since independence. Sensitization workshops, consultations through a commission of enquiry, and a pilot phase were instrumental in galvanizing support.

In South Africa, support or at least collaboration had to be mobilized especially from the white communities to accept the principle of empowering local communities through shifts in the local government system to dismantle apartheid. The National Local Government Negotiation Forum as well as local forums were instrumental in these negotiations, which operated alongside negotiations for the postapartheid national constitution.

In Rwanda, the decentralization policy having been initiated and led from the top, the population had to be sensitized about its meaning and benefits so that they could support it. Workshops, seminars, and such were instrumental in this.

The next section illustrates how participation in decisionmaking, which is the real indicator of political power, has taken root and been institutionalized in the three countries.

Institutionalizing Participation

Rwanda's Ministry of Local Government says in an August 2005 publication,

> Participation does make better citizens. I believe it, but I can't prove it. And neither can anyone else. The kinds of subtle changes in character that come about, slowly, from active, powerful participation in democratic decisions cannot easily be measured with the blunt instruments of social science. Those who have actively participated in democratic governance, however, often feel that the experience has changed them. And those who observe the active participation of others often believe that they see its long-run effects on the citizens' character.[13]

Decentralization has many aspects, one of the fundamental ones being the establishment of local governments with legislative assemblies to make decisions and with executive arms to implement these decisions. Traditionally, democratic participation is understood to refer to the participation of the people in elections to choose their leaders. In this chapter I do not pay particular attention to the participation of local people in the election of their representatives in the councils but concentrate instead on the participation of the people directly in the decisions of local governments.

The participation of the people of Uganda, South Africa, and Rwanda in electing their representatives to local government councils has effectively taken root.[14] On the other hand, participatory democracy, which refers to how local communities engage in the making of the decisions that concern them, needs to be studied not only in respect to whether and how it is taking place but especially in the way institutions have been created to formalize its operation and sustainability. This is a rather lengthy subject. I present some of the prominent cases to illustrate the institutionalization of participatory decisionmaking in Africa.

Women, Youth, and the Disadvantaged. In Uganda as well as in Rwanda the policy of devolution introduced a form of direct participatory decisionmaking at the lowest level of the local government system. In Uganda the lowest level is termed the local council 1, which is composed of all members of the village eighteen years and above. They elect from among themselves a chairperson and an executive to lead the process of their decisionmaking and its implementation. In Rwanda the lowest level is the cell; all members of the cell who have reached voting age are members of the council. They elect from among themselves an executive to manage their affairs. This is direct participatory democracy. As the local government system progresses to higher levels, however, participation is through representation. Here the inclusion of representatives of groups formerly excluded (such as women, youth, and the disabled) is significant in the implementation of participatory decisionmaking.

Participation should not be generalized. Some groups need special encouragement to participate. These are mostly women, youth, the disabled, and the very minority groups. While in certain societies provisions are made to have such groups represented—in for example national legislatures and the national voting processes—such participation is very limited. The participation of these groups can be best promoted at the local community level within a framework of decentralized governance. For them to influence the development process, inputs, and outputs, they need to participate, using the vote, their voice, and their direct action.

In designing local government councils in Uganda and Rwanda, local leaders took care to legislate mandatory representation of women and youth in local government councils. In Uganda, for example, at least one-third of each local government council must be women. In Rwanda at least half of the local government council must be women. However, care should be taken not to mistake the number of women on local government councils with their participation and influence. In Uganda the former director of the Decentralization Secretariat observed that, although there was a significant improvement in the number of women serving on local government councils, this increase does not automatically guarantee that the decisions are more gender sensitive.[15]

Integrated Development Plans, South Africa. In South Africa each municipality is by law required to make an integrated development plan elaborated with the participation of the entire municipality, the community, and all the stakeholders and coordinated with the plans of all other levels of government (the district, the province, and the nation).[16] The Integrated Development Plan Representative Forum is the structural arrangement that facilitates the formulation of the plan and may be composed of the following: members of the executive committee of the council; councilors, including district councilors; traditional leaders; ward committee representatives; heads of departments and senior officials from municipal and government departments; representatives from organized stakeholder groups; people who fight for the rights of unorganized groups (such as a gender activist); and resource people or advisers, and community representatives. The main aim of the forum is to provide an opportunity for stakeholders to represent the interests of their constituencies; to provide a structure for discussion, negotiations, and joint decisionmaking; to ensure proper communication between all stakeholders and the municipality; and to monitor the planning and implementation process.

Given the history of apartheid—which left the country with racially divided businesses and residential areas; badly planned towns that left the poor lacking in service delivery; undeveloped and underserviced rural areas; dispersed settlements that made the delivery of services difficult and expensive—local municipalities have had to use integrated development planning for all areas.

The law requires that municipalities come up with integrated development plans that provide the following: a vision of the long-term development of the city; an assessment of the existing level of development in the city, which must include an identification of the need for basic municipal services; the city's development priorities and objectives for its elected term; the city's development strategies, which must be aligned with any national or provincial sectoral plans and planning requirements; a spatial development framework, which must include the provision of basic guidelines for a land use management system; the city's operational strategies: a disaster management plan; a financial plan, which must include a budget projection for at least the next three years; and key performance indicators and performance targets.[17] The process generally goes through analysis of the problems and their causes, prioritization of the problems, development of a vision for the future of the community or the municipality, development of strategies for realizing the vision, identification of projects for implementing the strategies, design of the projects, integration of the plans, and approval of the plans.

Integrated development plans have served to ensure effective use of scarce resources in local government; speed up the delivery of services; attract additional funding; strengthen participatory democracy; promote coordination between local, provincial, and national governments; and overcome the legacy of apartheid, especially in municipalities. But above all, these plans have institutionalized participatory decisionmaking in local governments and given a whole new meaning to political decentralization, going far beyond election of leaders to embrace the ultimate purpose of local government—which is economic development. South Africa's experience with integrated development plans illustrates how communities can be empowered to participate in and influence the socio-politico-economic decisions that concern them.

Community Development Committees, Rwanda. The Ministry of Local Government and Social Affairs in Rwanda points out a critical fact that is often forgotten in the design and implementation of political decentralization to foster participatory democracy:

> The mere fact of opting for decentralization shall not by itself ensure that the population effectively participates in its development, which is the ultimate goal of a good policy of decentralization and good governance. It is important to set up mechanisms reassuring the participation of the population especially in a country like Rwanda, where the community, which constitutes the base of community development, is rather skeptical because, in the past, it was not fully involved in its development.[18]

Community development in Rwanda is therefore conceived of as a dynamic process of socioeconomic activities in which members of a community analyze their environment; define their needs and problems, both individual and communal; elaborate collective and individual plans to address the problems and needs; and implement the plans using community resources, complementing them where necessary with resources provided by the central government or the private sector. Noting that people's participation in their own development is the key element of community development and the main solution on which all the other solutions rely in fighting poverty in a comprehensive way, the Community Development Policy of November 2001 set decentralization as its key objective, suggesting ways and means of ensuring actual and durable participation by the community in its own development—and focused on poverty reduction. To this end, the Community Development Policy of November 2001 called for the formation of community development committees throughout the country.

Figure 5-2. *Interrelations between the Community Development Committees and Other Organizations at the Local Level*

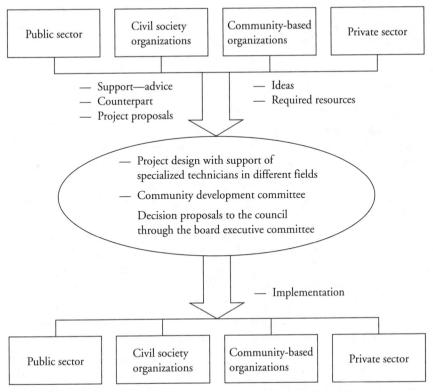

Source: Ministry of Local Government and Social Affairs, Community Development Policy, 2nd ed. (Government of Rwanda, 2001), p. 27.

A community development committee characteristically includes all actors in the community (see figure 5-2). The composition of a committee might consist of an executive committee secretary in charge of finance and economic development, who also chairs the committee; a district urban area executive secretary; a committee chair at the sector level; women representatives at the district and urban levels; youth representatives at the district level; and representatives of other actors involved in development at the district or urban levels. Even foreign development partners and donors with projects in the district are represented.

The various development actors channel their ideas, support, advice, technical assistance, project proposals, and resources to the committee, which, in collaboration with those actors, develops them and makes proposals to the council through their executive committees. The decision of the council is communicated back to those actors for purposes of implementation, and these actors implement the activities relating to their specialization and domain of operation. Monitoring, evaluation, and control of activities are coordinated by the committee with the support of the community, donors, and other development partners. By providing the structure for an institutionalized interrelationship among actors, community development committees enable the local population to own its development destiny.

Conclusion

The discussion in this chapter shows that decentralization in Africa (at least in the three countries highlighted) is an ambitious process that seeks to empower local communities to engage in their own development. This is a departure from most past decentralization efforts, which were geared only in the direction of administration. Decentralization in Uganda, Rwanda, and South Africa gives decentralized governance a development mission and calls upon local communities to shape their own destinies.

Decentralization has enhanced participation in decisionmaking, has enabled local communities to determine their local leadership through democratic elections, and has provided institutionalized structural arrangements for participatory, bottom-up development planning and for the involvement of special groups such as women, youth, and the disabled.[19]

The experience of Uganda, Rwanda, and South Africa also illustrates that whether decentralization is demanded (as in South Africa), engineered from the top through consultations and pilot programs (as in Uganda), or directly driven from the top (as in Rwanda), the process of agreeing on shared power and authority should not be taken for granted. Whichever approach is followed, support for decentralization comes through patient and sustained negotiation, sensitization, persuasion, demonstration of positive results, and when necessary, cohesion. The three cases also show that decentralization is not a one-time action but an ongoing process, which constantly engages relevant stakeholders and actors in order to produce the desired results. Finally, if decentralization is to be successful it needs to be conceived as the transfer of power and authority to the people and not only to local governments. This requires innovative ways of structuring and institutionalizing the interface between the people and their local governments.

Notes

1. John-Mary Kauzya, "Decentralization: Prospects for Peace, Democracy, and Development," paper prepared for the First Conference of the European and African Regional Assemblies on Decentralization: The New Dimension for Peace, Democracy, and Development, Florence, September 17–18, 2004.

2. *Decentralization* is a generic term, which covers a number of modes, such as the following: deconcentration, which refers to the process of administrative decentralization whereby the central government designs a structure that enables its agents to work close to

the local people in field units or agencies of central government; delegation, which is the transfer of responsibilities from the central government to semiautonomous bodies that are directly accountable to the central government; devolution, which is the process of transferring decisionmaking and implementation powers, functions, responsibilities, and resources to legally constituted local governments; and delocalization, which is the spatial distribution of central government socioeconomic development facilities and activities in peripheral regions. Discussion of these terms can be found in Gay Braibant, *Institutions Administratives Comparees: Les Controles* (Paris: Fondation nationals des Sciences politiques, Services de Polycopies, 1985–86, pp. 89–93); Jacques Chevallier, *Science Administrative* (Presse Universitaire de France, 1986), pp. 372–86. See also Charles Debbasch, *Science Administrative,* 5th ed. (Paris: Dalloz, 1989), pp. 221–37.

3. John-Mary Kauzya, "Strengthening Local Governance Capacity for Participation," in *Reinventing Government for the Twenty-First Century: State Capacity in a Globalizing Society,* edited by Dennis A. Rondinelli and G. Shabbir Cheema (Bloomfield, Conn.: Kumarian, 2003).

4. Republic of South Africa, Department of Provincial and Local Government, *White Paper on Local Government* (1998).

5. Government of Rwanda, Ministry of Local Government, *Good Governance, Community Development and Social Affairs: Decentralization Policy* (2000); also see this ministry's *Decentralization Implementation Strategy* (2000); and *Community Development Policy* (2001).

6. Government of Uganda, Ministry of Local Government, Decentralization Secretariat, *Decentralization in Uganda: The Policy and Its Implications* (1994).

7. Note that this was in the context in which politics in the country had been dominated by two parties, the Uganda People's Congress and the Democratic Party.

8. Government of Uganda, *Commission of Enquiry into the Local Government System* (1987).

9. Government of the Republic of South Africa, *White Paper.*

10. Government of Rwanda, *Good Governance, Community Development and Social Affairs.*

11. Government of Rwanda, Ministry of Local Government, *Good Governance, Community Development and Social Affairs: Decentralized Governance Reform Policy* (2005).

12. Ibid.

13. Ibid.

14. Stephen N. Ndegwa, "Decentralization in Africa: A Stocktaking Survey," Africa Region Working Paper 40, World Bank, 2002.

15. Fumihiko Saito, "Decentralization for Participatory Development in Uganda: Limitations and Prospects," *Journal of Intercultural Communication,* Ryukoku University, 2000 (www.ryukoku.ac.ip/~fumisait/en/jic2000.pdf).

16. Government of the Republic of South Africa, Department of Provincial and Local Government, *Integrated Development Planning for Local Governments* (www.etu.org.za).

17. Government of the Republic of South Africa, *The Municipal Systems Act* (2000).

18. Government of Rwanda, *Community Development Policy,* p. 20.

19. Ndahimana Emmanuel, "Rwanda Decentralization Assessment," Government of Rwanda, Ministry of Local Government and Social Affairs, 2002.

6

Devolution toward Democracy: Lessons for Theory and Practice from the Philippines

LEDIVINA V. CARIÑO

President Ferdinand E. Marcos justified putting the Philippines under martial law in 1972 by citing the primacy of bread over freedom.[1] In this he was echoing orthodox modernization theory, which states that development is the harbinger of all good things, including democracy. Fourteen years later, the still impoverished Filipinos ousted his dictatorship through the ultimate democratic weapon, "people power." One of the main accomplishments of the post-Marcos redemocratization period was enactment of the Local Government Code. The code stood orthodox theory on its head. Its principal sponsor called it "the key to development," and state policy declared democratizing local governance as the main instrument toward that goal.[2] Development would proceed from democracy.

This view is not the aberrant perspective of Filipino political leaders. Amartya Sen argues for the priority of political freedoms and democracy before economic growth, citing their direct importance in human living, their instrumental role in enhancing the attention to people's needs, and their constructive role in conceptualizing the needs themselves.[3] Even the gatekeeper of the modernization orthodoxy, the World Bank, now prescribes democracy for attaining development, albeit by using the apolitical term *governance*. This change of heart has been traced to the failed experience of structural adjustment in the 1980s, the influence of neoliberalism, the collapse of communism, and the impact of prodemocracy movements, including that of the Philippines.[4]

I trace here whether and how devolution connects to democracy in the Philippines, a frequently assumed link. Consider the following from a 2001 study: "Decentralization is considered to be a guarantee of democracy. Following the Marcos era, decentralization was envisioned by the country's leaders not only as a specific strategy to bring development to the countryside but was also considered as one of the safeguards against the return of any form of dictatorship."[5]

Dennis Rondinelli regards the decentralization-democracy connection as a hypothesis.[6] He lists four possible democratic benefits of decentralization: it could institutionalize citizen participation in development planning and management; it could allow for greater representation of nondominants for greater equity in the allocation of government resources and investments; it could increase political stability and unity by giving more groups a greater stake in maintaining the political system; and it could overcome the control of local elites who may not be sensitive to the needs of the poor.

Like him, I believe that the way decentralization would lead to those benefits requires elaboration, especially since the type spoken of is devolution, which transfers political power and is not just an administrative rearrangement. The expansion of power for any entity is never a neutral process since it can be used for self-regarding as well as for public ends. As Keith Griffin states: "It is conceivable, even likely in many countries, that power at the local level is more concentrated, more elitist and applied more ruthlessly against the poor than at the center. Thus, greater decentralization does not necessarily imply greater democracy, let alone, 'power to the people.'"[7]

This problem is not unique to local governments. James Madison said:

In every political institution, a power to advance the public happiness involves a discretion which may be misapplied and abused. . . . Therefore, in all cases where power is to be conferred, the point first to be decided is whether such a power be necessary to the public good; as the next will be, in case of an affirmative decision, to guard as effectually as possible against a perversion of the power to the public detriment.[8]

The transfer of power to levels closest to citizens seems to be universally accepted as desirable. What is then needed is to take Madison's counsel by analyzing how it would lead to the preferred goal of democracy and what it needs to deter the perverse use of power.

This chapter concentrates on the Philippine experience since the passage of the Local Government Code in 1991. That country is an appropriate example because of its leading role in the redemocratization and the decentralization waves of the last years of the twentieth century. It is also an appropriate case study because with these highs are terrible lows, such as its continued poor performance in growth and poverty reduction and its notoriety for corruption and bossism. The same society and the same laws and systems have produced both extremes. My task, then, is to study the factors and processes at work in devolution, to give a fair appraisal of their effects on democracy, and to point out how the positive effects may be strengthened.

This chapter is primarily a reanalysis and synthesis of available literature and documents. My analysis is based first on nationwide conditions and national trends related to devolution and democracy. Precisely because devolution encourages differential responses, I also studied the performance of individual local government units. I conservatively place greater value on those performing well despite difficult odds since they can serve as models of similarly placed local units, can be more easily replicated by better-off units, and thus may begin future trends.

Devolution is the transfer of power from central to local units by means, in the Philippines, of the Local Government Code and other Philippine laws. The move toward local democratization is shown by meaningful citizen participation, local governments' attention to disadvantaged sectors, their regard for the rule of law, and their accountability to the people.

Historical Background

The communities of pre-Hispanic Philippines enjoyed local autonomy, if not sovereignty. As conqueror of the Southeast Asian archipelago in the sixteenth century, Spain centralized governance from Mexico to Manila in Madrid and transformed the local elite into tax collectors for the crown. In 1893, in a "belated and half-hearted tribute to Filipino ability in self-government," a decree established municipal and provincial boards, with limited franchise granted to the *principalia,* descendants of the original elite.[9] Centralization proceeded nevertheless, marking the start of empty grants of decentralization that the Philippines experienced under its two colonizers and its own leaders after independence. The First Philippine Republic, created in 1898 by the first successful war of liberation in Asia, provided for popular elections of local officials and people's participation in governance. How far-reaching this decentralization would have been cannot be known since Spain ceded the colony—which had already declared its independence—to the United States, also in 1898.

While the Philippine Revolution continued against the new imperialists (until 1907), American colonization recentralized the government, a situation that independence from the United States in 1946, and the decentralization movement of the 1960s, hardly changed. Municipal elections were instituted in 1901, national legislative elections in 1907, and presidential elections in 1935, extending the influence of the *principalia* from their local bailiwicks to higher levels. Many parlayed their wealth in land into other enterprises. These became lucrative because their ties with central politicians—and the latter's kinship or dependence on them for votes—insulated them from both state regulation and economic competition. Local politics became an intense rivalry of clans. To maintain their power, mayors and governors supplemented rent seeking from the center with violence against local opponents.[10]

The martial law declared in 1972 promised to dismantle the oligarchy, but it established a new one instead with Marcos and his allies. When the people ousted them in 1986—setting off popular, nonviolent uprisings around the world—hopes were high for a true democratization of the country, different from both the dictatorship and the elite democracy that held it in thrall throughout most of the twentieth century.

The revolutionary transition led by President Corazon Cojuangco Aquino produced the Constitution of 1987 with provisions for social justice, human rights, and "people power" in governance. However, the first elections under that constitution saw the restoration of politicians and politics from before the martial law era; they did, however, pass the Local Government Code and other social legislation.

The Law and Practice of Devolution

The constitution called for "a more responsive and accountable local government structure."[11] The code and other laws responded by increasing the power of local units, providing for the involvement of people in governance, and altering central-local relations.

Increase in the Power of Local Units

The code devolved health, social welfare, environment, agriculture, and peace and order services. Beyond the long list of specific powers is the general welfare provision, which deserves full quotation:

> Every local government unit shall exercise the powers expressly granted, those necessarily implied therefrom, as well as powers necessary, appropriate, or incidental to its efficient and effective governance, and those which are essential to the promotion of the general welfare. Within their respective territorial jurisdictions, local government units shall ensure and support, among other things, the preservation and enrichment of culture, promote health and safety, enhance the right of the people to a balanced ecology, encourage and support the development of appropriate and self-reliant scientific and technological capabilities, improve public morals, enhance economic prosperity and social justice, promote full employment among their residents, maintain peace and order, and preserve the comfort and convenience of the inhabitants.[12]

To give life to this expansive list, the code increased local units' share of government revenues, enhanced their taxing powers, and allowed them a share in the national wealth found within their boundaries.

The constitution also provided for the creation of autonomous regions in Muslim Mindanao and in the Cordilleras to acknowledge and preserve their distinctive historical and cultural heritage.[13] Accordingly, organic acts for their regional governments were passed, with an elected executive and legislature and special courts with jurisdiction over personal, family, and property law. The organic act for the Autonomous Region of Muslim Mindanao was accepted by the people in a plebiscite, albeit by a much smaller number of cities and municipalities than envisioned, while the Cordillerans rejected the regional government proffered them.[14]

Providing for the General Welfare

Based on the number of applications to the Galing Pook awards from 1994 to 2005, 81 percent of cities, 68 percent of provinces, and 30 percent of municipalities have assessed themselves as having served their constituents well enough to withstand strict scrutiny by independent evaluators. The top five programs (out of nineteen types), all with 155 or more entries, are environmental protection, enterprise and livelihood development, health and nutrition, welfare services, and agriculture programs whose importance in the countryside cannot be gainsaid. Those awarded also converged on these services. Only 215 (8 percent of all applicants)—30 percent each of provinces and cities and 5 percent of municipalities—have won the Galing Pook awards.[15]

These awards have been historically dominated by first-class provinces and cities, but of the thirty-five awards in the 2002–05 period, twenty-five went to lower-class municipalities: thirteen to third-class municipalities, and twelve to fourth-to-sixth-class municipalities.[16] The following gives a glimpse of what the poorest towns have accomplished:

—Opol, Misamis Oriental, has become a center of ecocultural tourism and sustainable agroindustries. Its program incorporates education, people empowerment, their economic well-being, and program sustainability. Its business tax collections exceeded its target, and it was reclassified from fourth class to second class over just three years. Even before it won the award in 2004, other local governments in Mindanao had already used it as a model.

—Anao, Tarlac, was the only sixth-class municipality in prosperous Tarlac. It is now fifth class, because of its Rural Industrialization Can Happen (RICH) program. At the core of RICH are Anao's ubiquitous ylang-ylang flowers. Previous to the program, these flowers were sold only as garlands. Following tests by the New York–based International Flavors and Fragrances, ylang-ylang is now incorporated into perfumes and cosmetics. Anao has guaranteed community ownership of the trees along the roads, transferred appropriate technology, distributed seedlings, and provided market support to the cooperative implementing the program.

—Naawan, Misamis Oriental (fifth class), created an economic enterprise development office, which dramatically increased its income from water, goat breeding, and markets. The increased revenues were used to improve social service delivery.

—Linamon, Lanao del Norte (fifth class), has integrated information on solid-waste management into premarriage counseling and business licensing and has changed from the dirtiest town in the province to an example to its neighbors.

—Batad, Iloilo (fourth class), with an image of corruption and poor fiscal administration, sought to improve its accountability with a twice yearly "Pahayag sa Banwa" (Report to the People) and with popular involvement in its development and annual investment planning.[17]

Examples of such programs are found in all kinds of public services. These programs have inspired interest from other local government units, suggesting that they are the most likely to be replicated.[18] The common thread binding these municipalities seems to be a combination of visionary leadership by local chief executives and an aroused citizenry. Sometimes, external forces like civil society organizations complete the picture. These programs are low cost. None of these poor towns had foreign-funded programs (as many higher-class winning units have).

Attending to Nondominants

Beyond the participatory requirements of the Local Government Code and other laws, some local units have taken the initiative to attend to the most disadvantaged in Philippine society, the indigenous peoples. In some areas, such as in the Cordilleras and Muslim Mindanao, these people constitute a majority. But in lowland areas with many Christian settlers, their numbers are low.[19] This is where North Upi's invention of a "tripeople" governance framework is instructive. This third-class municipality in Maguindanao, Muslim Mindanao, has made the national *barangay* (village) justice system territorially and ethnically specific by utilizing traditional modes of conflict resolution for intraethnic problems and devising an arbitration system to take care of clashes between Tedurays (an indigenous people), Moros (Muslims), and Christians.[20]

Daiun, Negros Oriental, a fourth-class municipality, could not implement laws against illegal fishing (such as dynamite use) since fishers feared losing their livelihood. Assisted by the provincial government and Silliman University and with community organizing and consciousness raising, Daiun established a community-based marine protected area, now managed by the fishers' association. It has attracted divers to its marine sanctuaries and increased its income from user fees by twenty times between 2002 and 2005.[21]

Capoocan, Leyte, a fourth-class municipality, faced a poverty incidence of 90 percent, with women vulnerable to physical abuse at home or forced to work as prostitutes in the cities. Capoocan instituted consciousness-raising programs for women and men, along with services on reproductive health and counseling for victims of violence. It formulated a gender and development plan and budget, people's policy advocacy, and a coastal resource management program. By 2001 twenty-nine of its fifty-two representatives in local bodies were women.[22]

However, gender and development programs had a different fate in Angeles City. Left with 18,000 prostitutes (of 200,000 inhabitants) when the United States withdrew from Clark Air Base in 1991, the city enacted a gender and development ordinance, as advocated by a local women's action group. However, the following administration repealed practically all the gains of the women's movement.[23]

Upholding the Rule of Law

Insurgency is fed by poverty and injustice; thus programs to tackle these problems promote peace and order and lawfulness. Life in Trinidad, Bohol, was so bad that people joined the rebellion in frustration. Its Galing Pook award winner was an agricultural program with high doses of technology and empowerment that saw family incomes increase a hundredfold in five years. This fourth-class municipality thus battled both poverty and the insurgency in one stroke.

Sampaloc, Quezon, even poorer than Bohol, was a fifth-class municipality in a guerrilla-ridden area. The government conceptualized, with civil society organizations, a counterinsurgency program with health, agriculture, and livelihood components. Their efforts involved 80 percent of the inhabitants and culminated in the return of rebels to their homes, increased agricultural production, and decreased malnutrition

Similarly battling the insurgency was Ligao City, Albay (fifth class). Its main instrument was the Upland Central Economic Zone, with an access road to mountain villages, a multipurpose solar dryer, and a place to market upland produce. Peace and accessibility paved the way for improved health and nutrition services to the usually ignored mountain dwellers.[24]

Peace and order councils are special bodies required by the Local Government Code to formulate, monitor, and implement peace and order and public safety programs. The National Police Commission gives citations annually for the best peace and order councils.[25] In 2004 the municipal peace and order council of Concepcion, Iloilo, was declared the best municipal council in the fourth-to-sixth-class category. Concepcion's council had perfect attendance by the government and by representatives of civil society organizations; it also had programs on crime prevention, prosecution, and corrections; counterinsurgency and disaster management; environmental enhancement; and fire prevention. Over two years the level of crime decreased and 100 percent of crimes were solved. Local media chronicled positive public perception.

Concepcion has been singled out by Galing Pook for its integrated population, health, and environment programming; and by the League of Municipalities for its Zero Poverty 2020 program, under which it reduced poverty incidence from 87 percent in 2001 to 47 percent in 2004. Its program to reduce poverty included a great deal of participation by citizens, a strategy of achieving minimum basic needs, and alliances with local organizations, central agencies, and international funding organizations.[26]

The creation of zones of peace is a growing movement in many areas, particularly those caught between government and the Moro Islamic Liberation Front (MILF). Barira, Maguindanao (sixth class), the site of a major MILF base, managed to have town officials, military commanders, MILF rebels, the Ulama Peace Council (a Muslim group), and members of civil society organizations sign a covenant, with each villager pledging to honor the peace zone. Barira successfully prevented revenge murders and fighting within the town.[27] Similar initiatives have since been forged in other areas of Muslim Mindanao.

Where local governments cannot guarantee peace, those who expose local problems in the media live under constant threat. Between 1992 and June 2006, the fourteen years under the Local Government Code, sixty-one journalists and radio reporters (more than four a year) were killed. Four of the nineteen murders between 1992 and 2002 and six of the seven killed in 2003 seem to be due to the victims' crusades against local officials.[28] The Commission on Human Rights cited local officials and employees as the second-worst human rights violators (after the police) in 1995 to 2000.[29]

Human Rights Action Centers were started in 1995 in *barangays,* the places most vulnerable to human rights abuses. The centers are expected to provide information, education, and mobilization on human rights and to refer complaints to higher levels; each is voluntarily run by a resident elected by the *barangay* assembly. A third of the 42,000 villages had such centers by 2000. Unfortunately, few local governments have given them operating funds. The interface of local governance and human rights still takes place on an ad hoc basis, although the centers mentioned here are promising developments.

Misusing Powers

Aside from human rights violations, local executives and personnel have been accused of corruption, with the ombudsman reporting only two resolved charges every year.[30] Many more abuses of public office have been reported in local dailies, including abuses perpetrated by entrenched bosses and warlords, but most are not prosecuted.[31] The code instituted a system of recall, on grounds of loss of confidence, for local officials. Recall may be initiated by a preparatory recall assembly or by 25 percent of voters in a jurisdiction. The assembly is composed of all the elective officials of a locality and is unlikely to institute charges against one of its own. The people's initiative is therefore the more likely route to recall, but the process is tedious and has been used in only a few cases. Besides, recall can only be done in the second year of a three-year term. Thus this accountability measure has basically lain dormant.[32]

Many local governments practically live on their share of internal revenue, despite their strengthened taxing powers. The extent of dependence by local governments on central largesse was 36 percent in 1985–91 and 63 percent in 1992–2002. Dependence is also indicated by the low collection rate (55 percent) of real property taxes (the main local revenue source) for the years 1992–2000. The revenue effort of all local units as a proportion of gross national product stands at a very low 0.81 percent for 1985–91 and 1.18 percent for 1991–2002.[33]

Some local governments have no incentive to raise their own revenues because more than enough resources are transferred to them by the central government. This is a factor in the conversion of many municipalities into cities, which received a larger share of internal revenue in 2002 than in 1990. It appears that many local governments see local autonomy as a way to increase their benefits rather than to attend to their responsibilities.[34] Revenue allocation has no performance criterion. Some localities do not exercise their taxing powers because they can always blame central government for their lack of resources and accomplishments. Besides, citizens do not complain about services when they are not taxed.[35] To use their taxing powers would require both more government competence and more government accountability.

Involving the People

Under the Local Government Code the people seem to have ample powers to exact accountability through elections and recall and can direct policy through both their power of initiative and referendum and their power to elect representatives to the local legislature. However, most local governments are still waiting for a specific law on sectoral representation. Only a few standouts, like Naga City, have invoked the spirit of the code and enacted local ordinances for sectoral representation.

The code mandates representatives of civil society organizations to participate in development planning; in preparing proposals for budgetary allocations and technical and administrative standards for health and public safety; in advising on health and education; and in enforcing accountability in government contracts.[36] These mandates regard the people as truly sovereign, involved in conceptualizing, planning, implementing, and assessing state policies and programs. As of 2002 two-thirds of all local governments (55 percent of provinces, 67 percent of municipalities, and 63 percent of cities) reported creation of the code-required participatory bodies.[37] This is low compliance with the law but is an improvement over the 2001 figure of only 56 percent overall.[38] There are no sanctions for ignoring the participatory provisions.

The legal requirement for membership in local development councils forces the creation of large, unwieldy bodies. Local development councils are supposed to prepare local, multisectoral, medium-term development plans. Provincial development councils must have as members all mayors of component cities and municipalities, the chair of the provincial appropriations committee, congresspersons, and representatives of provincial civil society organizations (at least a quarter of the total membership of provincial councils). The average number of municipalities per province is nineteen, yielding a mean size of twenty-nine. Partly because of this, most provincial development councils meet only for the legal minimum number of times: first to launch the planning process and, second, to approve the plan. The actual work is left to the council's executive committee, composed of the governor, the appropriations chair, the president of the Provincial League of Mayors, and a representative of a civil society organization. The governor reportedly tends to dominate the deliberations and control fund allocations.[39]

While the code instructs that each organization choose its own representative, 33 percent are selected instead by local chief executives.[40] Preferential accreditation, through favoring the supporters of local chief executives and blacklisting their rivals', also occurs.[41] Focus group discussions in eighteen local development councils across the country found that people feel that accreditation to the councils is not handled properly. They contend that openings are not advertised widely, limiting the organizations that may join. They also complain of lack of transparency, oversight by the Department of the Interior and Local Government, and sanctions for violators.[42]

Rural field appraisals between 1992 and 1999 found that civil society organizations were invited only to attend meetings, not to offer their ideas and expertise. Local officials tend to see these organizations as implementers rather than co-planners. The appraisals found "from a hopeful beginning . . . a consistent picture of moderate disenchantment with the [local development council] and a turning to other forms of participation."[43]

The problems are not due to the local governments alone. Many civil society organizations actively opposed government during the period of martial law and find that collaborating with government is still discomfiting. Besides, many are unfamiliar with government mechanisms, have difficulty relating with local officials, lack funds to attend meetings, and do not use their membership to advance their sectoral or the public interest.[44]

Even when participation actually takes place, its effect on governance may be small. The local development council is dubbed the "mother of local special bodies," where the thrusts of government could be debated and resolved between government and civil society.[45] The provincial development council is at the top of the heap.[46] In a nationwide survey, 30 percent of the secretariat heads of these councils say that representatives of civil society organizations make important inputs to the plan, much higher than those who say that representatives of the two central regulatory agencies do so (15 percent and 19 percent). They also welcomed the large representation of civil society organizations, as it increases public awareness about the development plan. In fact, though, the performance of such organizations may be a mixed bag. In one province, these representatives supported the governor's recommendation to keep the provincial development fund rationally distributed, unlike pork barrel. But in another, their representatives were concerned with ensuring their pork barrel share.[47]

Unfortunately, how they perform hardly matters, because provincial development councils are engaged in a largely worthless exercise. While the Local Government Code explicitly provides that the provincial development fund can be allocated only to projects identified in the provincial development plan, in practice, the fund supports the annual investment plan. The annual investment plan is formulated by the governor, the mayors, and the whole provincial legislature, along with the heads of provincial offices and representatives of national offices. (As such, the group is larger than the provincial development council.) The group is thought of as political because the provincial development fund is often allocated simply by dividing "by N," to allow all participants to have a project. By contrast, the provincial development council is considered technical because the projects are data driven. However, the council is not tied to provincial resources and may list projects beyond a province's capacity to implement. The provincial development plan could have been a political plan in which local officials and civil society organizations together set directions for the province. But under present circumstances, their participation hardly counts for anything.[48]

Civil society has a different view of the results of their participation. At least forty-two provincial civil society organizations (of seventy-seven provinces) report that they sustained their development agenda through advocacy work in local special bodies.[49] They also formed interprovincial networks for coordination in similar advocacies. Civil society organizations have generally made the difficult transition from "outside" (the combative phase), to "alongside" (coordinative), to "inside" (critical-strategic and collaborative) government. Their work often starts on the *barangay* level, where participatory planning is not overrun by politicians as in the provincial development council. This grassroots work proceeds from community organizing to elections. In 1997 *barangay* elections increased voter participation from 45 to 65 percent, and a million candidates vied for elective posts. Of these, about a thousand leaders from people's organizations were elected. This is minuscule in quantitative terms, but a factor for progressives to find hope in the system instead of in the underground.[50] Participation might not necessarily be valued for its results but rather as a means of social inclusion, of deepening trust in local government, and of increasing social capital.[51]

The Local Government Code's participatory thrust has been extended by other laws requiring the involvement of nondominants, such as indigenous peoples, fishers, agrarian reform beneficiaries, and women. Farmers and farmworker beneficiaries, farmers' organizations, agricultural cooperatives, and civil society organizations are supposed to have at least four representatives in *barangay* agrarian reform councils and their counterparts at higher levels. However, the agrarian reform councils at the local level are largely unorganized or are headed by local officials and landowners. Poor farmers get to participate instead in special projects, task forces, or civil society organization initiatives.[52]

The situation may be better in the fisheries and aquatic resource management councils. Of each council's seventeen members, seven must be municipal fishers and one must be a fish worker. As of August 2006, 75 percent of coastal *barangays* and 99 percent of municipalities or cities had organized their councils.[53] The director of the National Farm Program Management Center regards representation as "a very good example of democratic processes because it focuses on the empowerment of a marginalized sector 'neglected' by the government." She also considers local governments as comanagers of fisheries with the Department of Agriculture.[54]

There are also local government units that encourage participation beyond the law's minimum requirements. Naga City has earned worldwide prominence for its Empowerment Ordinance and People's Council, which have withstood the test of time and the departure (and return) of the mayor who started it all.[55] Naga City involves the people in all of the decisionmaking boards of the city.

On the other side of the coin are examples of when participation has had the opposite of the desired effect. Pandan, Antique (fourth class), is such an example. Pandan's local government unit established marine sanctuaries as a cooperative venture with civil society organizations to regenerate its dwindling marine resources. But when the Pandan government approved the entry of a diesel-fueled power plant, these civil society groups objected, contending that the plant would destroy the sanctuaries. Civil society won this classic battle between development and the environment when the local government agreed to scrap the diesel project.[56]

Organizations sitting halfway between government and civil society are the League of Provinces, the League of Municipalities, the League of Cities, plus the league of leagues, the Union of Local Authorities of the Philippines (ULAP). Except for ULAP, they predate the Local Government Code and were actually pressure groups for its passage. The code tasked them to assist the central government in formulating policy for local governments, promoting local autonomy, encouraging people's participation in governance, and "ventilating, articulating and crystallizing issues affecting [that level of] government administration, and securing [their] solutions."[57]

The leagues have always allied themselves with the sitting executive, the better to gain concessions from the center. But beyond this partisan and opportunistic stance, each league has spearheaded programs of value to its members. For instance, the League of Municipalities has undertaken the localization of the millennium development goals, population management (not exactly aligned with the president's program), and devolution of the environment sector. It has a professional staff and is establishing a mayor's academy to build capacity for its members. It has also partnered with Galing Pook and the Local Government Support Program for peer-on-peer coaching for learning best practices. This is a step away from instituting self-regulation for local governments shorn of the recentralizing predilections of central agencies.

Elections versus Citizen Participation

Participation is usually hailed as a mechanism for upholding popular sovereignty. That begs the question of why elected representatives are deemed not adequate to play that role. The doubt about elections stems from an unequal social structure exacerbated by patronage, vote buying, intimidation, and campaigning based on personal appeal rather than platforms. Joseph Capuno found a poor correlation between the quality of governance and electoral performance in the 2001 local elections, making elections a poor instrument for extracting accountability.[58] The emphasis by civil society organizations on causes that respond to the interest of the masses seems to make their participation a corrective for these problems.

However, the legitimacy of unelected leaders of civil society organizations has also been raised.[59] They do not necessarily come from the ranks of those marginalized by elections and are frequently self-chosen. They are not subject to elections, nor are they accountable to those they claim to represent. Hence they—along with elected representatives—are imperfect vessels of the people's sovereignty. The situation is potentially conflictive, as shown by the disinclination of local legislative bodies to accept local development council plans.[60] The issue is joined now that some civil society leaders have become the elected representatives of the people. Some mayors of the innovating towns have gotten power through this route, but the process is just starting.

Altering Central-Local Relations

The Local Government Code has changed central-local relations by transferring the responsibility for the delivery of certain services from central to local units; by increasing local share of the proceeds of national taxes and national wealth derived from forests, waters, and mines in their jurisdictions; and by requiring central units to consult with local governments and organizations when operating in their locality. The president is constitutionally required to exercise general supervision over local government units. The Department of Environment and Natural Resources maintains "supervision, control and review" of devolved functions in integrated social forestry, and the Department of Health sends representatives to local health councils. Local plans are submitted to the National Economic and Development Authority for incorporation into the national plan.[61] The Department of Budget and Management must "furnish the various local development councils information on financial resources and budgetary allocations to guide them in their planning functions."[62] It would seem then that the only remaining task of central agencies is to coordinate with one another and with the local governments in their program implementation functions. They may, however, provide financial or technical assistance upon request of the local government and provide basic services when the local government is unable to do so.[63]

Devolution in the Local Government Code refers to "the act by which the national Government confers power and authority upon the various local government units to perform specific functions and responsibilities."[64] It implies a one-time action, after which it seems the central government will have little to do with the local government. However, the tasks given to the National Economic and Development Authority, the Department of Budget and Management, the Department of Environment and Natural Resources, and the Department of Health show the need for, first, the central offices' constant interest in devolution and, second, the local government units' conscious contribution to a national thrust.

The constitution provides that local governments get "a just share, as determined by law, of national taxes." The code provided that 40 percent of internal revenues be shared by local government units.[65] Successive congresses and presidents have provided, at the maximum, 17 percent of internal revenue.[66] Moreover, local governments chafe at unfunded mandates (new local functions incorporated in national laws with no corresponding funds).

The Department of the Interior and Local Government, along with local governance projects funded by bilateral organizations, has constructed indicators to assess local government performance. It belatedly created the National Monitoring and Reporting Committee in 2001, with representatives from the leagues and civil society organizations. One of these organizations is working on a benchmarking project on civil society participation in local special bodies.[67] These could be starting points for standard setting and benchmarking, which would assist interested local government units to improve their performance or seek central assistance when necessary.

While agencies like the Commission on Human Rights and the National Police Commission encourage autonomy through grassroots work and awards, other central agencies weaken the autonomy of local government through directives that require the local units to seek their permission in undertaking certain matters or by exempting some central agencies from local regulation.[68] Meanwhile, three "devolved" departments continue to increase their budget for programs and projects set from the center; these programs and projects are not in conjunction with local needs, nor are actors in the areas affected consulted.[69] Joining these culprits are congresspersons whose Countrywide Development Fund—the euphemism for pork barrel—is not subjected to oversight by the provincial development council, is not part of the annual investment plan, and has been known to be implemented despite local resistance.[70] This is not a small complaint since on the average, between 1997 and 2001, the fund was as big as the total local development fund of all local governments. In 2001 it was 116 percent.[71]

Central agencies may also be faulted for allowing violation of national laws, which eventually undercuts local political reform. I am speaking specifically of lax regulation and implementation when politicians are the rent seekers or the perpetrators. Continued elite domination in the Philippines can hardly be traced to a lack of laws. Nor is it only a continuation of the power of the landed oligarchy descended from the *principalia* of Spanish times. It can also be traced to the parlaying of local prominence into central power through relationships with regulators and dispensers of state funds.[72] Many newer political dynasties entered politics from the poor or the middle class, but they gained their wealth through manipulation of state power at the local and central levels, with industrialization being the usual justification for their chicanery. Thus did Juanito Remulla, governor of Cavite from 1979 to 1995, convert agricultural land to an export processing zone, without regard for the farmers there and with the support, or at least tolerance, of the Department of Agrarian Reform. Labor unions could not be organized in Cavite with an unsupportive Department of Labor and Employment. Remulla has openly boasted of complicity in the killing of a notorious gangster who had been nurtured by a rival politician; and he may have played a part in other murders as well—of mayors as well as labor leaders—but no investigations or indictments ever came his way.[73]

Aside from flouting national laws and getting away with it, national politicians ensure their hold on power through legislation favorable to their interests. How is this related to local governance? Around 40 percent of national legislators have relatives who are or have served as local legislators, local chief executives (governors or mayors), vice governors, or vice mayors. Political dynasties were jump-started when the Americans instituted single-member district representation in a suffrage system allowing only literate, propertied males to vote. This gave elite families control over their bailiwicks while being projected toward the national stage. Despite the deletion of the property qualification in 1935, the fortunes of these families were already set. Of the now

135 politically active clans, 45 first held office during the American regime.[74] More study would be needed to determine how many of these political clans have used state power for their enrichment and continued political prominence. However, a mere reading of their names suggests the confirmation of John Thayer Sidel's hypothesis of the use of state power as a factor in their political ascendancy.[75]

Nevertheless, some conditions are likely to change traditional politics. Within these dynasties, their scions are better educated, given more to discussion than to violence; they are modern in their social ideas and secure in their wealth and, therefore, perhaps less acquisitive than their elders. The nation itself has a growing middle class, a strong civil society, and cosmopolitan inhabitants—even among the poor, as fully a tenth of them work abroad and are exposed to cross-cultural influences. A party-list system at the central level provides for a functional equivalent of sectoral representation that, for all its shortcomings, paves the way for more ideological, not personalistic, politics.[76]

Affecting national as much as local governance is the absence of laws (and political inclination) to implement constitutional provisions against political dynasties and for reform of the electoral system, especially campaign finance. Without such laws, elections will continue to be skewed toward the already privileged, leading to greater power concentration.

What the foregoing suggests is the complicity of the central level in the lack of local democracy. Central offices quietly resist devolution to, and competition with, local government units by not conceding any power to them. Without such power—and funding and standards of performance—local governments cannot be responsive to local needs. More pernicious is the tolerance of local governments of violations of law by power holders, perhaps because of ignorance of their violations or because of the realization that their power trumps that of the local government. The Philippines has a whole slew of anticorruption and penal laws with which to charge the warlords and bosses. The misdeeds of national or local politicians have been exposed in local media, in investigative reports, and in the academic literature. However, the culprits have managed to go scot-free and even be reelected to public office.[77]

Has Devolution Led to Democracy?

The law and practice of devolution can be assessed against democratic criteria of enhancing popular power, advancing justice and equity, upholding the rule of law, and manifesting accountability to the governed. The record is mixed.

The Answer Is Yes

Devolution has certainly led to democracy in many areas. The Local Government Code and other laws have enabled stronger and more government and citizen action for the public interest. The general welfare provision especially has freed local governments from the narrow confines of what the center authorizes them to do into a local governance bounded only by their visions and capacities.

Later laws have continued the code's participatory provisions, requiring popular involvement in many more areas than were originally devolved and pinpointing specific marginalized groups as people who should have a say in decisionmaking councils. Existing laws against abuse of public office are now supplemented by local powers of initiative, recall, and referendum. In addition, the enhanced power of taxation and the transfer of more funds facilitate the practice of local autonomy.

These increased powers of local government units have thus made local governance more responsive in many areas. A majority of these units have submitted at least one program with a distinctive service, suggesting a general mood of working toward good governance. Of those whose performance has been judged outstanding, a few poor local units, some of them war torn and suffering from long years of neglect, are singled out above. These examples give but a glimpse of the possibilities of local democracy—by attending to the specific problems of their constituents, be that poverty, insurgency, or environmental degradation, with appropriate and effective programs that the people believe they own.

These examples suggest that responsive policies and programs are now within the capacity of most local governments. Their achievements, along with similar innovations by richer local government units, provide models for a nationwide movement toward democracy. Specific mention should be made of programs involving the historically excluded or marginalized, because these widen the definition of what we have called the sovereign people. The best programs not only serve them but also invite their participation in governance. The attention to peace and human rights shows an acceptance of people not only when they embrace the government but also when they disagree with it, with their freedom to dissent also a manifestation of the rule of law in that area.

While some programs seem oriented only to efficiency, the desire to reduce waste and to render service with regularity and equity shows a nascent sense of accountability that does serve democracy. It may be conceded, however, that where democracy is only a by-product of development programs rather than an explicit goal, it is possible (although I did not observe it in any program cited here) that rights may be ignored on the way to obtaining tangible results.

Civil society has also risen to the challenge. Many of its organizations have made use of the space for participation that the laws allowed, have pressured their respective local governments to take heed of their causes on behalf of the needy and marginalized, have organized themselves into networks for greater strength, and have attempted the monitoring and benchmarking that can institutionalize good practices. Their involvement shows how citizens should act in a democracy. Even where participation does not yield immediate results, the social capital it engenders becomes a building block for future collective endeavors.

The center has a stake in devolution even though only a few agencies retained functions related to local governance. The Department of the Interior and Local Government particularly can play a significant role in setting standards for local performance, which, with civil society prodding and assistance, it has now started to do. The work of central departments and oversight agencies is invaluable in encouraging local accountability even when they do not exercise control over local programs anymore.

The Answer Is No

On the other hand, devolution has not always led to democracy. There are problems in the laws themselves. Shortfalls in implementation have occurred because local governments can violate participation requirements—such as their creation, accreditation, and connection to other processes of local governance—with impunity, there being no legal sanctions, nor even social pressure, from such bodies as the Department of the Interior and Local Government or the various leagues. Attempts are rife to rig accreditation and keep participation at a token level. In the case of local development councils, the code provided for large councils without thinking through how these unwieldy bodies can accomplish their tasks. In analyzing the code, I see the old problem of the "effective" neutralizing the "formal" provisions of law.

Even as I extol some local governments for their innovations to benefit the people, power has also been misapplied in other local units. A century of seeing political positions as means for personal enrichment has not yet been reversed. Bosses and warlords still thrive and enjoy even more powers to manipulate with even less central oversight. Meanwhile, even the power to recall can be used against political rivals as a ploy to reverse elections and not as a means of exacting accountability.

Unfortunately, citizen power and programs for the public interest are more prominent than the improvement of accountability under devolution. There are some innovations—like citizen charters and reports to the people—but it is difficult to discern a trend toward greater accountability. Instead, the general situation is of local governments afraid to take the responsibilities for local autonomy, being content with relying on national transfers for their sustenance. Meanwhile, the interest in *barangay* elections is growing, with civil society activists joining in. Nevertheless, most of them are still unsuccessful, and elections as a whole are still not connected to performance.

At the same time, some civil society organizations are not ready to maximize the reason for their participation, which is to push for the demands of the poor majority they are supposed to represent. A few are lacking in capacity to deliberate in governance forums, or they may even act like the worst traditional politicians—looking out for themselves—in these participatory councils. Citizen participation that repeats the antidemocratic excesses of elected officials removes the justification for their representation.

Central-local relations also present a problem in devolution. Devolution is national policy and should play a role in the nation's advance toward both democracy and development. However, the national perspective seems to be muted in law and practice, leaving central agencies free either to compete with local units for their sectoral turf or to simply ignore them until they cry for help. Fostering a common vision, setting standards, providing assistance for disadvantaged units, and similar tasks need to be developed by central agencies in a regime of devolution. The golden mean between control and laissez-faire is a kind of effective general supervision that has not been concretely operationalized. I would comprehend democracy to be a strengthening of a nation-state toward equity and social justice, rather than leaving some local units behind because they cannot cope with the demands of devolution.

Unfortunately, instead of assisting these poor local governments, some central agencies have continued their predevolution practice of assisting, or at least not resisting, politicians, both national and local, who use state resources and regulations to keep themselves and their kin and allies in power. Since the law does not run after them, it is up to citizen groups to do so.

Conclusion

The main actors of devolution are local government units, civil society organizations, and central agencies empowered by law to bring responsive and accountable governance to the people. Our journey through this terrain shows that some actions by these participants have clearly led to democracy but that much more remains to be done.

For instance, a lot of hope has been placed on local development councils both as participatory instruments and as methods of promoting the general interest. However, even where their size is manageable, the councils cannot support strategic visioning when most members expect a political quid pro quo. Similarly, a vigilant press cannot work efficiently in a setting where a mayor's wish and private army trump nonviolent conflict resolution. Nor can legal processes thrive where state resources are manipulated in the interest of having certain national and local politicians stay and grow in power.

General changes in the economy and society—an increase in the educated sector, faster urbanization, changes in the local environment, and growth of local press and radio stations—would provide the base for changes, but these alone cannot bring about democratic change. What is most important is that local government units actively promoting local democracy increase and be strengthened and that civil society uses its participatory powers toward the same goal. Their way can be lighted by clearer standards and benchmarks of acceptable behavior, provided by self-regulation through the leagues, or as their collaborative exercise with the Department of the Interior and Local Government and civil society organizations. The connection of accountability and devolution must be made more prominent. Sanctions for erring officials must be imposed. Ordinary citizens, too, must learn how to make elections a real instrument for accountability.

Devolution is a national policy and is the responsibility not only of local units and resident citizens. It requires direct improvements in local government units and a stronger commitment by the center and all citizens to make devolution work for democracy.

Notes

1. Onofre D. Corpuz, *Liberty and Government in the New Society: An Intellectual Perspective in Contemporary Philippine Politics* (Philippine Bureau of National and Foreign Information, 1974).

2. Aquilino Pimentel Jr., *The Local Government Code of 1991: The Key to Development* (Manila: Cacho, 1993).

3. Amartya Sen, *Development as Freedom* (Oxford University Press, 1999).

4. Adrian Leftwich, "Governance, Democracy and Development in the Third World," *Third World Quarterly* 14, no. 3 (1993): 605–24.

5. Philippine Department of the Interior and Local Government in collaboration with Urban Resources and the Evelio B. Javier Foundation, Inc. (DILG-UR-EBJFI), "A Study on People's Participation in the Local Development Councils," 2001, p. 13.

6. Dennis Rondinelli, "Government Decentralization in Comparative Perspective: Theory and Practice in Developing Countries," *International Review of Administrative Sciences* 47, no. 2 (1981): 133–45.

7. Keith Griffin, "Economic Development in a Changing World," *World Development* 9, no. 3 (1981): 221–26, quotation p. 225.

8. James Madison, "General View of the Powers Proposed to Be Vested in the Union," *Federalist # 41* (www.national center.org/Federalist41.html).

9. Quotation is from Jose P. Laurel, *Local Government in the Philippine Islands* (Manila: La Pilarica, 1926), p. 290.

10. Alfred W. McCoy, *An Anarchy of Families: State and Family in the Philippines* (Ateneo de Manila University Press, 1994).

11. Constitution of 1987, article 10, section 3.

12. Republic Act 7160, Local Government Code, section 16, "General Welfare."

13. Constitution of 1987, article 10, sections 15–21. These areas were never effectively colonized by Spain or the United States and were largely neglected by successive Philippine administrations. Not surprisingly, they have sought to secede from the Republic and were the most troubled areas during the period of martial law.

14. Aside from substantial disagreements with certain provisions of the organic acts, the rejection can be traced to the large number of lowland Christians already living in the areas claimed as their own by the regions' leaders.

15. Galing Pook Foundation, "The Galing Pook Awards, an Internal Analysis of the Program," 2006. *Galing Pook,* meaning "exemplary locality," is arguably the most prestigious of the awards given for innovation and excellence in local governance in the Philippines. Galing Pook was started by the Asian Institute of Management and the Ford Foundation. Now an independent foundation, selection continues to be undertaken by an independent and well-regarded set of local government experts, officials, and academics.

16. Municipalities in the Philippines are classified by the Department of Finance according to average annual income: first class, P50 million or more, second class, between P40 million and P50 million; third class, between P30 million and P40 million; fourth class, between P20 million and P30 million; fifth class, between P10 million and P20 million; and sixth class, less than P10 million (www.nscb.gov.ph/activestats/psgc/articles/con_income.asp).

17. Philippines-Canada Local Government Support Program, *Creating Inroads in Forging Partnerships: A Practical Guide for Civil Society Organizations* (Philippine Department of the Interior and Local Government, the National Economic and Development Authority, and the Canadian International Development Agency, 2004).

18. Communication with Genielind Chavez, Galing Pook staff, August 10, 2006.

19. Soliman M. Santos Jr., "Local Government and Human Rights: A Philippine Perspective on the Feasibility of Their Interface in Policy and Practice," in *Decentralisation, Local Government and Human Rights Project 116: Stage One—Survey of the Issues* (International Council on Human Rights Policy, 2002).

20. Philippines-Canada Local Government Support Program, *Creating Inroads in Forging Partnerships.*

21. Galing Pook Foundation, 2005 (www.galingpook.org).

22. Ibid., 2001.

23. Nina T. Iszatt, "Legislation for Citizens' Participation in the Philippines, " Logolink 2002, 72 (www.ipd.ph/logolinksea/resources/SEA%20Regional%20Paper1.pdf).

24. Galing Pook Foundation, 2004 (www.galingpook.org).

25. Criteria are the quality of the community public safety plan, the efficiency and effectiveness of the peace and order council, and the outcome of plan implementation.

26. "Achieving the Millennium Development Goals—LGUs as Frontliners: Zero Poverty 2020 (Concepcion, Iloilo)," *Ang Punong Bayan* (The Mayor) 1, no. 1 (2005): 17–18.

27. Philippines-Canada Local Government Support Program, *Creating Inroads in Forging Partnerships.*

28. Information for 1944 to 2002 from "57 Journalists Killed in the Philippines," Center for Media Freedom and Responsibility (www.cmfr.com.ph/smfr-database_files/sheet01.htm.); information for 1986 to June 2006 from "Filipino Journalists Killed since 1986" (http://nujp.org/?page_id=12); for narratives in 2003, Reporters without Borders, "The 2003 Global Press Freedom World Tour" (www.rsf.org.article.php3?id_article=10089).

29. Santos, "Local Government and Human Rights."

30. Office of the Ombudsman, 2003 and 2004 (www.ombudsman.gov.ph/downloads/Annual Report 2004.zip).

31. Jose F. Lacaba, *Boss: Five Case Studies of Local Politics in the Philippines* (Pasig, Metro Manila: Philippine Center for Investigative Journalism and Institute for Popular Democracy, 1995); McCoy, *An Anarchy of Families;* John Thayer Sidel, *Capital, Coercion and Crime: Bossism in the Philippines* (Stanford University Press, 1999).

32. Local Government Code, title 2, chapter 5; Iszatt, "Legislation for Citizens' Participation in the Philippines."

33. Benjamin V. Cariño, Arturo G. Corpuz, and Rosario G. Manasan, "Preparatory Work for the Proposed Technical Assistance on Strengthening Provincial Planning and Expenditure Management," submitted to the Asian Development Bank, 2004, p. 78.

34. In this they may not have changed from the attitude of the 1960s. See Leodegario Soriano Jr., "An Exploratory Survey on Local Autonomy," *Philippine Journal of Public Administration* 10, no. 2 (1966): 214–30.

35. Cariño, Corpuz, and Manasan, "Preparatory Work," p. 78.

36. Republic Act 6657 (Comprehensive Agrarian Reform Law); Republic Act 8371 (Indigenous Peoples Rights Act); Republic Act 8550 (Fisheries Code); and Republic Act 7279 (Urban Development and Housing Act), respectively.

37. Department of the Interior and Local Government, Bureau of Local Government Supervision, "Status of Submission of Report per MC 2001-89," June 2002.

38. Iszatt, "Legislation for Citizens' Participation in the Philippines," citing M. Gabito, "Status of Compliance with DILF Memorandum Circular No. 2001-89, Appendix D, in Documentation of the 10.10.10 Celebration: CSO Conference on Participatory Local Governance, 7–9 October 2001."

39. Cariño, Corpuz, and Manasan, "Preparatory Work."

40. Iszatt, "Legislation for Citizens' Participation in the Philippines," citing Gabito, "Status of Compliance." It is interesting that a contemporaneous study found that "at least 25 percent of LGUs [local government units] were themselves selecting the NGO representatives" and found that "generally satisfactory." See Caucus of Development NGOs Network (CODE-NGO), "Sharing the Load: Looking into People's Participation in Local Governance," cited in DILG-UR-EBJFI, "A Study on People's Participation," p. 23.

41. Roel Ravanera, "Decentralizing Government in the Philippines," Food and Agriculture Organization, 2004 (www.fao.org/docrep/004/ac158e0f.htm); DILG-UR-EBJFI, "A Study on People's Participation"; Joseph J. Capuno, "Local Governance and Development," in *Dynamics of Regional Development: The Philippines in East Asia,* edited by Arsenio Balisacan and Hal Hill (Cheltenham, U.K.: Edward Elgar, 2007), forthcoming.

42. DILG-UR-EBJFI, "A Study on People's Participation."

43. Associates in Rural Development, Inc./USAID, "Synopsis of Findings of the Rapid Field Appraisal of the Status of Decentralization: The Local Perspective," Local Development Assistance Program, August 10, 1999.

44. DILG-UR-EBJFI, "A Study on People's Participation."

45. Ibid., p. 9.

46. Arguably, the top level is filled by the regional development council, which was established under martial law. However, the region is an administrative level, even though the council is headed by a provincial governor.

47. Cariño, Corpuz, and Manasan, "Preparatory Work."

48. Ibid.

49. Iszatt, "Legislation for Citizens' Participation in the Philippines," p. 62, citing Cesar Liporada, "Highlights of NGO/PO Participation in Local Governance," *Working Papers: NGO/PO Perspectives for the Local Government Code Review* (Quezon City: Institute of Politics and Governance, 1997).

50. Aya Fabros, "Civil Society Engagements in Local Governance: The Case of the Philippines," 2003 (www.ipd.ph/logolinksea/resources/SEARegionalPapers5.pdf).

51. Capuno, "Local Governance and Development."

52. Iszatt, "Legislation for Citizens' Participation in the Philippines," p. 67.

53. Republic Act 8550.

54. Gloria C. Diaz, personal communication with author, August 8, 2006.

55. Its remarkable mayor, Jesse Robredo, has won the Ramon Magsaysay Award for government service, an Asia-wide search for exemplary leaders in community and public service. He has also been invited to many conferences to present the Naga City model, including the inaugural workshop of the Ash Institute for Democratic Governance and Innovation at Harvard, our sponsor for this book.

56. Philippines-Canada Local Government Support Program, *Creating Inroads in Forging Partnerships.*

57. Local Government Code, title 6.

58. Capuno, "Local Governance and Development," p. 18.

59. Angelita Gregorio-Medel, "Development Work Is Middle-Class Oriented as Much as It Is Poverty-Oriented," *Philippine Politics and Society* (January 1993): 58–93.

60. Iszatt, "Legislation for Citizens' Participation in the Philippines;" DILG-UR-EBJFI, "A Study on People's Participation"; Cariño, Corpuz, and Manasan, "Preparatory Work."

61. Local Government Code, section 114.

62. Ibid., section 115.

63. Ibid., sections 25, 17 (f), respectively.

64. Ibid., section 17 (f).

65. Constitution of 1887, article 10, section 6; Local Government Code, section 284.

66. Department of Budget and Management, 1991 to 2006.

67. Fabros, "Civil Society Engagements in Local Governance."

68. Alex B. Brillantes Jr., *Innovations and Excellence: Understanding Local Governments in the Philippines* (Center for Local and Regional Governance, National College of Public Administration and Governance, University of the Philippines, 2003), pp. 11–12.

69. Their budgets increased at an average of 163 percent between 1993 (the year local government units absorbed the salaries of devolved personnel) and 2003. See Cariño, Corpuz, and Manasan, "Preparatory Work."

70. Iszatt, "Legislation for Citizens' Participation in the Philippines," p. 51. The Philippine version of the pork barrel is now an equitable allocation of PhP50 million and PhP200 million for House and Senate members, respectively, and is effectively released to the legislator concerned, with the only requirement that he or she identify the project involved. This is a retrenchment from the 1960s, when what was then called community development projects were part of the Public Works Act, whose inclusion in the national infrastructure plan had to be given some rational justification. These projects were released to the Department of Public Works and Highways for implementation.

71. Cariño, Corpuz, and Manasan, "Preparatory Work," p. 79.

72. See, for instance, the saga of the Lopez family in McCoy, *An Anarchy of Families.*

73. Sheila S. Coronel, "The Killing Fields of Commerce," in Lacaba, *Boss.*

74. Sheila S. Coronel and others, *The Rulemakers: How the Wealthy and Well-Born Dominate Congress* (Quezon City: Philippine Center for Investigative Journalism, 2004).

75. Sidel, *Capital, Coercion and Crime.*

76. Coronel and others, *The Rulemakers.*

77. Capuno, "Local Governance and Development."

7

Decentralization, Deconcentration, and Poverty Reduction in the Asia Pacific

PETER BLUNT AND MARK TURNER

I n the last twenty years or so political decentralization has become an integral component of the ruling paradigm of democratic governance reform in developing countries. In some countries domestic pressures for democratization and regional autonomy have constituted an imperative for central governments to promote political decentralization. In others the desire to emulate the devolutionary policies of neighbors and friends has also provided impetus for decentralization. But whatever the reason for decentralization, it appears that in all cases reformist governments have received strong support from Western donor countries and international financial institutions.

Prominent among the reasons for this support appear to be, first, that many Western donors have a strong ideological preference for government legitimacy that arises from a universal franchise, free and fair elections, and political pluralism. Second, it is also widely believed by the development community and many scholars that forms of government that are highly participatory and involve downward accountability are generally best at delivering needed services to citizens efficiently and effectively.[1] However, the empirical reality of developing countries has demonstrated that political decentralization often fails to deliver in practice the benefits it promises in theory.

On the other hand, the developmental potential of administrative decentralization through deconcentrated forms of governance tends to be overlooked by Western donors and international finance institutions, primarily because deconcentrated forms of governance rely on upward accountability and, in theory, are therefore less amenable to popular influence and less capable of delivering needed services efficiently and effectively. If it were possible to compare empirically the effects on poverty reduction, and value for money, of political decentralization versus deconcentration the likelihood is that circumstances rather than ideology would determine the relative merits of each case. It seems, however, that in too many instances the faith that donors invest in political decentralization diverts attention from more pragmatic calculations concerning the effects of political decentralization and deconcentration on poverty reduction. To this extent, and despite the rhetorical claims of donors to be interested first and foremost in poverty reduction, it (poverty reduction) frequently falls victim to what in practice turns out to be an overriding ideological preference for certain forms of democratic governance.

The tension between these twin aims—of poverty reduction and the institutionalization of democratic forms of governance—is clearly exposed in the experience with political decentralization and deconcentration in postconflict, or so-called fragile, states such as Cambodia, Afghanistan, and Timor-Leste. But this tension is not confined to postconflict states and is even evident in supposedly successful decentralization experiments. The authors argue that if poverty reduction rather than participatory democracy were the overriding concern of leading donors then much more development financing would be directed at improving and promoting systems of deconcentration than is currently the case.

Other possible explanations are also considered for the way in which governance reform (including decentralization and deconcentration) in developing countries evolves. This is reflected in what could be termed local-level politics and sociology of development practice. The "formal goals" of the rich, mainly Western donor countries may not be congruent with their "operating goals," the ones that tell us what the organization is actually trying to do.[2] One aspect of this is the character of governance reform in developing countries: Decisions are often left to local, midlevel donor officials (whom this chapter refers to as "donorcrats"), their agents (hired consultants), and a host of government officials. The widely varying capabilities, attitudes, and political interactions of such officials and consultants within and between countries help to explain the seemingly haphazard non-evidence-based and technically weak governance reform that takes place.

Decentralization and Deconcentration

Decentralization in its various manifestations has a long and unbroken history of being regarded as "a necessary condition for economic, social and political development."[3] For example, in the early 1960s the United Nations' *Handbook of Public Administration* declared decentralization's "special importance" for generating "increased understanding, co-operation and participation in the new national programmes of social and economic development."[4] But it is political, invariably democratic decentralization rather than administrative decentralization that has attracted the most attention and support. The optimistic case for democratic decentralization dates back to John Stuart Mill in the nineteenth century and rests on the twin pillars of participation and local knowledge. Successive generations have elaborated on Mill's pioneering work to identify the benefits that should accrue from democratic decentralization. Advocates of democratic decentralization in developing countries routinely stress such benefits as accountability to local populations, the participation of the poor and disadvantaged in decisionmaking, the improved coordination of governmental activities, and the accessibility of officials.[5]

These benefits have not always been realized. As B. Smith emphasizes, they should be seen not as benefits but as the promise or perhaps the burden of decentralization.[6] Experience demonstrates that many things can intervene to spoil the promise or to increase the burden. Turner lists seven problems and obstacles that have adversely affected the implementation of decentralization plans. These are parochialism, which encourages disunity; cynical shedding of functions by governments unwilling or unable to shoulder the fiscal responsibilities of service provision; the maintenance of central control through regulations; the capture of decentralization's benefits by local elites; the unpopularity of decentralization among citizens or public servants; limited capacity at the local level to undertake the required work; and the exclusion of the poor and disadvantaged by means such as manipulative or passive participation or "normal professionalism."[7]

A further problem is the assumption that accountability and transparency are enhanced by decentralization, when in fact the reverse may happen. Both theoretical and empirical literature demonstrate the increased opportunities for corruption under particular decentralization arrangements and country conditions.[8] It is the occurrence of such difficulties that leads Smith to observe that, first, there is no consensus on the costs and benefits of decentralization and, second, there is no methodology to determine the relative importance of particular costs and benefits.[9]

It is possible that we have come to expect too much from this dominant political variety of decentralization. Some political decentralization experiments offer disappointing results. In Bangladesh successive attempts to bring democracy and enhanced participation to subnational levels have been foiled by the ability of local elites to capture the benefits of decentralization.[10] In Papua New Guinea political decentralization was associated with declining levels of service provision (all provincial governments were at one time suspended for some form of malpractice).[11] A comprehensive overhaul of central-local relations has done little if anything to improve matters. It has given greater authority in local affairs to national politicians rather than local representatives or public servants and has failed to give local planning authorities the voice the legislation awards them.[12] There are still complaints from across the country about poor service delivery, lack of resources, politicization of appointments, weak managerial capacity, and lack of accountability by national politicians.[13] Surveying the African experience of decentralization, J. Wunsch concludes that none of the initiatives has worked particularly well in "encouraging development of genuine local-level authority, the transfer of resources to localities, development of a broadly based process of accountability, or building institutions that work effectively and reliably to facilitate decisions and make them realities."[14]

The record of decentralization in alleviating poverty does not bear out the belief that political decentralization brings about a reduction of poverty. For example, an OECD study advises donors who want to promote decentralization to distinguish between those countries that satisfy basic criteria in terms of their background and ability to implement policies and those countries that lack such characteristics.[15] It is recommended that to generate "pro-poor effects" such weak states should support "deconcentration as a first step towards decentralisation."[16] Similarly, J. Bossuyt and J. Gould see political decentralization as having potential for addressing poverty but note that "decentralisation has poor links with poverty objectives."[17] Their three-country study also concludes that "it is also hard to find a clear articulation between support for decentralisation and poverty reduction in donor policies and practices."[18] They too identify a number of obstacles in the way of local governments' making headway in the struggle for poverty alleviation.

R. Crook has posed the question of whether decentralized governments are more responsive than central governments to the needs of the poor in Africa.[19] He concludes that decentralization is unlikely to challenge local elites who are uninterested in pro-poor policies and who act in concert with national elites to retain the latter's power bases in the countryside. Finally, even in cases where decentralization has been hailed as a success the linkage with poverty alleviation may be difficult to make.[20] The Philippines has enjoyed sixteen years of political decentralization since the Local Government Act of 1991 and has a record of innovation and experimentation in service delivery.[21] If decentralization were pro-poor then we would expect to see a distinct diminution in the incidence of poverty over this time. However, the Asian Development Bank claims that the incidence of poverty increased slightly, to 33 percent by 2005.[22] The most recent figures in mid-2006 do reveal significant improvements, but one is left wondering whether the Philippines' sustained economic growth rate of over 5 percent for the past few years has more to do with this welcome news than the activities of local governments.

If political decentralization has often failed to reduce the incidence of poverty, then perhaps its administrative form—deconcentration—may give superior performance in this regard. It is not so much that deconcentration has intrinsic merits that make it absolutely better for poverty alleviation but rather that the experience of political decentralization has shown that assumed gains may be more wishful thinking and ideological predilections than the reality. Proponents of deconcentration can claim that the delegation of decisionmaking powers to locally based public servants could lead to welfare gains. Greater efficiency in resource utilization could be achieved, and this could result in greater effectiveness in the form of reduced poverty. In previous publications the authors argue that delegating decisionmaking authority and, if possible, additional resources could result in greater success in combating poverty.[23] The following seven requirements were posited:

—Accessibility of officials: Officials are available for consultation, advice, and complaint. As local officials can exercise decentralized authority, they make the decisions and do not need to pass them up the line to distant central offices.

—Mobilization of local resources. It is easier for locally based officials to identify local resources, both human and physical, and then mobilize them in the pursuit of locally determined developmental purposes. Officials should also be familiar with specific local constraints and the dynamics of local politics.

—Rapid response to local needs. Officials are better placed to respond rapidly to local needs as they are in the territory and aware of local conditions.

—Orientation to the specific local needs. Because the officials know the local conditions, they are well placed to make decisions and allocate resources that fit with the specific conditions prevailing in a particular territory. Each subnational territory may have some unique features, which can be taken into account when resources are planned and allocated.

—Motivation of field personnel. Appointed government officials are more motivated to perform well when they have greater responsibility for the programs they manage.

—Interoffice coordination. Coordination among offices dealing with different functions is more easily achieved at the local level, where officials are physically close together and are often familiar with each other.

—Central agencies. The decentralization of service functions relieves central agencies of routine tasks, responsibility for which has been passed to the local level. Central agencies can thus focus on improving the quality of policy. Monitoring local-level performance and providing assistance to subnational units are key elements of this reformulated government role.

Deconcentration even offers possibilities for enhanced popular participation. Consultation on planning, promotion of user groups, consumer surveys, client charters, and guaranteed minimum service standards are among the techniques that might be employed by deconcentrated governments to improve popular welfare and reduce poverty. There is, of course, no certainty that the potential benefits will be realized. As with political decentralization, deconcentration may result in undesirable consequences. The dysfunctions of distant central bureaucracies may simply be replicated by minibureaucracies at the subnational level. Controlling and directing may remain the principal concerns of local-level public servants. Participatory methods may be of little or no interest to appointed officials. Standardized central regulations, however inappropriate, may still be the prime reference point for local bureaucrats operating in diverse and changing situations. The skills and knowledge of local officials may be inadequate for the tasks confronting them, while they may be risk averse in situations that require innovation and location-specific responses to developmental problems. Poor terms and conditions of employment, especially low salaries, may demotivate public servants. Even the communities they are meant to serve can contribute to poor service delivery by maintaining low expectations of official action.

Despite these potential pitfalls, deconcentration can provide the opportunity for making significant gains in reducing poverty—but not in all places at all times. Deconcentration is particularly relevant for weak or fragile states as it can be seen as a method of increasing the strength of the state to provide its citizens with the services they are entitled to. As has been convincingly argued by P. Hutchcroft, "a strong foundation of prior centralization" is a necessary basis for successful political decentralization.[24] Deconcentration can be seen as a step in this direction. Indeed, it must be acknowledged that central government plays an essential role in decentralization. It assumes the responsibility for the design of decentralization, oversees the implementation of the laws governing decentralization, determines the financial transfers to subnational government, sets standards for service delivery, monitors the progress of decentralization, and provides advice and support for decentralization.

Political decentralization can be "strikingly undemocratic," whereas central guidance and assistance are vital for providing services to populations in subnational territories in an equitable manner.[25] The developmental potential of the central state is closely linked to its ability to bring the benefits of development to its citizens dispersed across the entire national territory. Deconcentration can be viewed as an extension of the state, a governance arrangement that has the potential to fulfil the dual objectives of increasing state control while satisfying the demands of its citizens for more and improved services in a timely manner. Investment in deconcentration could bring increased resources more rapidly and in greater quantity to the people who need them most urgently. Deconcentration may be an underused and underestimated governance device for achieving the targets of the leading Millennium Development Goal—to eradicate extreme poverty and hunger.

The Politics and Sociology of Development Practice

As with all areas of development policymaking and implementation, decisions concerning decentralization and deconcentration are subject to a variety of influences, which will vary according to, among other things, national circumstances and international interest in the country concerned. In nearly all cases, however, the technical merits of different policies will figure in policy calculations less prominently than broadly defined "political realities," both national and international.

The authors suggest elsewhere—and also in our introduction above—that policy concerning decentralization has as much or more to do with the interplay between the political interests of governments and the ideological preferences of donors for strong forms of participatory democracy as it has to do with poverty reduction.[26] But even this revisionist view, which breaks with much conventional decentralization discourse within the dominant decentralization paradigm, may be too naïve and simplistic an account of a much more complex reality.

Important also is a range of microsociological variables that exert an influence on the policy process. Often overlooked among these variables are the normal science inclinations (or otherwise) of midlevel, locally based, donor officials and their agents (consultants). "Normal" science refers to "the assumption that the scientific community knows what the world is like" and that most of its members conform in their practice to this shared view. In this case, the scientific community is the ever-changing group of midlevel donor officials whose job it is to interpret and apply their host country's policy with respect both to governance reform and to the application of whatever position has been taken on donor support modalities following the Paris Declaration on Aid Effectiveness.

The authors are drawn to this conclusion partly because, at the level of grand politics (international relations involving the major powers), it is now clearly unsafe (and naïve) to suppose that the statements of the major powers (and donors generally) about democracy or anything else should be taken at face value. There are surely few who would still doubt that the interests of the so-called coalition of the willing in Iraq had more to do with control over strategic economic resources (oil) than with the freedom or general well-being of the Iraqi people. Noam Chomsky has argued persuasively for a long time that this is so and that what, for example, the United States says about democracy and what its actions in foreign countries suggest that it really means can be very different things.[27] The evidence and argument presented by Chomsky, combined with a critical consumption of everyday accounts in the news, suggest strongly that statements about democracy and its virtues are used frequently by the major donor countries as a pretext for realizing economic and strategic interests and that it is the compliance of poor country regimes in serving these economic and strategic ends that is critical. Questions concerning the political legitimacy of regimes in poor countries only seem to arise and to matter when compliance is deemed to be insufficient to produce the desired economic and strategic results.

If what matters is political compliance that serves the largely short-term economic and political interests of rich countries, rather than political legitimacy based on democratic institutions in poor countries or poverty reduction, our understanding of local policy choices (concerning decentralization and deconcentration or anything else) should be revised accordingly. It is only in this light, it is suggested, that much of the seemingly opportunistic policymaking that surrounds decentralization becomes intelligible.

The Case of Cambodia

The authors argue elsewhere that decentralization in Cambodia involves little devolution of authority and little or no reallocation of service delivery roles.[28] From the standpoint of government, it is suggested that decentralization has been an effective method of consolidating the nationwide political control of the ruling Cambodia People's Party and a means to extend the influence and size of the Ministry of Interior. There have been some developmental benefits for local populations, but these have been limited to small-scale infrastructure projects, planned and implemented by elected commune councils, and to the maintenance of national political stability.

Evidence-based policymaking designed to optimize positive development results such as poverty reduction would want to make judgments about the relative merits of various national governance structures. For example, is it wise in circumstances in which central governance institutions are widely recognized as being weak (as in Cambodia) to embark on a difficult and costly decentralization program? Would scarce development resources be better spent initially on strengthening the state's core institutions (the legal and judicial systems, for example) or on supporting existing systems of deconcentration that are the only existing means of (weak) service delivery in crucial sectors such as health, education, and agriculture?

Service delivery problems in health and education have mainly to do with resource availability and public expenditures, low salaries for health and education workers, and inadequate infrastructure. Proposed developments in decentralization now under consideration in Cambodia, which include the possibility of elected councils at the district and provincial levels, would have little bearing on the service delivery problems just mentioned. Indeed, the bureaucratic inflation that would inevitably accompany such elaboration of subnational government may well reduce the resources available to service delivery. Yet these questions have not been the subject of much debate in Cambodia, and it is important to try to understand why this is the case.[29] This can best be done by considering the matter from the perspectives of the actors involved and of the meanings that can attach to the same empirical phenomena.

On the supply side, several perspectives must be considered. First are clearly the perspectives of government and the Cambodia People's Party (CPP). Second are the views of major donors concerning the economic and strategic significance of Cambodia. Third are the interpretations of resident and visiting midlevel donor officials of the policies of their host governments. Fourth are the views of opinion leaders in the host government—those whom some donor officials allow to set the pattern and extent of their engagement with so-called decentralization and deconcentration.

The first set of actors is the government and the political party (the CPP) that supplies the overwhelming majority of government members. The main guiding principle here is likely to be maximizing donor support to decentralization and deconcentration in a way that serves the interests of the CPP, both in terms of consolidating its position nationally and in terms of allocating rewards among the CPP elite (mainly, as suggested above, in terms of the rise of the Ministry of Interior).

The second set of actors is composed of leading decisionmakers among Cambodia's major donors. These are the people who set the strategic directions of foreign policy. While oil in significant commercial quantities has recently been discovered in Cambodia, the country is not, and is unlikely to be in the foreseeable future, a major supplier of oil or gas. The significance of Cambodia and the compliance of the current regime are diminished accordingly. Questions concerning the character of political legitimacy and the development of democratic governance and of human rights are therefore not pressed too vigorously or too persistently.

The third set of actors is composed of representatives of major donors. These donorcrats staff the offices of international financial institutions, multilateral organizations, and bilateral donors. The relative unimportance of Cambodia to the strategic and economic self-interest of major donors allows much more freedom to midlevel donorcrats, both resident and peripatetic, to determine, on the basis of their interpretations of their host countries' policies, the direction, form, and extent of donor support concerning decentralization and deconcentration. In this scenario, widely varying levels of technical capability and commitment are brought to bear on (in this case) decentralization and deconcentration through:

—First, the quality of consultants to assess what should be done and how

—Second, the quality of the written terms of reference that guide the work of such consultants

—Third, the quality of the reports written by the consultants

—Fourth, the extent to which the findings and interpretations of the consultants are transparent and are shared among interested parties

—Fifth, the existence among donorcrats of strong opinion leaders

—Sixth, the existence among donorcrats of coalitions of interest and opinion

—Seventh, conversely, the existence among donors of interinstitutional and interpersonal rivalries and animosities.

All of these considerations individually can be expected to vary among countries, resulting in a potpourri of outcomes for decentralization and deconcentration in terms of the technical merits of policies: the extent to which poverty reduction features in such policy calculations; the extent and character of support; and the maintenance of donor interest. In Cambodia these variables have combined with government interests (as described above) to produce significant and sustained donor support for a very limited form of decentralization, which is unlikely in the short term to yield sufficient benefits for poverty reduction or the institutionalization of democratic ideals to justify the expense. In a country in which 35 percent of the population live below the poverty line and 91 percent of these people live in rural areas, scarce resources would be better directed at the realization of short-term, sustainable benefits for the poor through making existing (weak) systems of deconcentrated service delivery in health, education, and agriculture work better than they do at present.[30]

The Case of Timor-Leste

Just four years after the realization of a hard-won independence, and before the recent spate of civil disturbances that resulted in a change of government, Timor-Leste experimented with a limited form of decentralization. Pilot projects were initiated—for example, in the Bobonaro district—and local council elections were held throughout the country in 442 *sucos* (subdistricts) and 2,228 *aldeias* (villages) in late 2005.

The trials involved the allocation to elected councils at the subdistrict level of grant funds to be used for local development purposes. As in Cambodia, the councils had to produce satisfactory development plans and proposals, manage tendering and contract awards (with assistance where necessary), acquit the use of funds, and supervise implementation. Unsurprisingly, the major constraints were associated with financial management and disbursement capabilities at the local level, which so far have prevented the diffusion of these trials to other areas. Nevertheless, early assessments of the results by some observers are sanguine and suggest that, providing there is genuine devolution of authority, development benefits could follow. For example, consistent with conventional development thinking, a report of the World Bank suggests that such developments could lead to greater downward accountability through local committees dealing with such matters as health, education, and agriculture.[31]

The governance context of these developments in Timor-Leste is similar to that of Cambodia and Afghanistan in that, although central institutions have been established, most do not operate according to their mandates, are subject to a variety of influences, and exhibit the symptoms of systemic corruption.[32] Again, as in Cambodia, the timing of the local elections (a general parliamentary election is due in 2007), the preponderance of just-elected local officials from the ruling Fretelin party, and opposition claims of government interference in the election outcome suggest that the primary interest of government may be in the consolidation of ruling party power rather than development benefits.

Official reports say that the elections were free and fair, but opposition parties claim that various forms of "influence" were brought to bear on the election outcome by senior cabinet ministers. Public perceptions of this and other forms of undue interference by senior members of the government in the affairs of some of the central institutions of governance are said to have been a major contributing factor to the recent disturbances and the resignations of the prime minister and the minister of interior. Evidence for such interference was found in early 2006 in the police force (which allegedly was being used by senior members of government as an instrument of political intimidation), the judiciary, the office of the prosecutor general, parliament, and the office of the inspector general.[33] These findings and the events that followed—that in the light of these findings were not unexpected—reinforce conjectures concerning the likely motivations of government at the time concerning decentralization. In particular, the premature nature of these developments implies political rather than development motivations on the part of the government

The Case of Afghanistan

Afghanistan is seen to be of enormous strategic importance by at least the United States and its allies, which have poured enormous amounts of aid into the country to shore up a most fragile state and to persuade the population of the merits of what might be loosely termed democratic capitalist development. Another U.S.$10 billion was pledged at the January 2006 London Conference on Afghanistan. In this predominantly rural and typically rugged country, the state has never been strong, its nature well captured by Gunnar Myrdal's observation on "soft states"—that they "require extraordinarily little of their citizens."[34] Indeed, for much of the twentieth century the best the rural inhabitants of Afghanistan could hope for was a distant but benign state. Efforts to centralize authority were occasionally made but invariably failed to bring the population under the control of the ministries in far-away Kabul and in their outposts in the provinces. A form of de facto decentralization prevailed, "an arrangement not made through rational planning techniques or formal government policies but by mutual agreement and perhaps even neglect."[35]

The current incumbents of state office together with their international backers are now engaged in constructing very different relationships between the state and society, boldly going where no Afghan state has gone before. The principal aim is to extend and consolidate state authority over territory and population. The government's attitude toward decentralization is clearly delineated in article 137 of the constitution: "The government while preserving the principle of centralism, shall delegate certain authorities to local administration units for the purpose of expediting and promoting economic, social and cultural affairs, and increasing the participation of people in the development of the nation." This straightforward commitment to central control is more complex in its implementation. A mixture of governance devices simultaneously promoting centralization, political decentralization, and deconcentration is in evidence. Such variety is not necessarily contradictory but can simply reflect the belief that a blend of institutional arrangements may be best suited to achieving the aim of state consolidation.

The central state has been extremely cautious in deconcentrating authority to the ministry offices located in provinces and districts. For example, the center approves appointments at senior and middle levels, determines provincial organization structures, and decides the budgets for the provinces. The provincial governor also has limited decisionmaking authority. He (they are all male) is a coordinator with no direct authority over the provincial branches of line ministries, which are responsible for the delivery of most services. Unsurprisingly, given this lack of formal authority, coordination of government activities in the provinces has been poor. To address this problem, provincial development councils were established in 2005 and include the provincial heads of all relevant line ministries. External organizations such as donors, civil society organizations, foreign military provincial reconstruction teams, and UN agencies were to participate in the provincial development council's sectoral subcommittees. In January 2006 the councils in at least three provinces were still being established and had, up until then, done little if anything to enhance the coordination of development activities.

Democratic decentralization has been promoted through provincial councils and community development councils. The former were elected in 2005 to select members for the upper house of the National Assembly. They have no legislative authority and are currently exploring their somewhat vaguely defined roles, which focus on community consultation, dispute settlement, and monitoring government activity. Community development councils are the means by which the state is attempting to penetrate village society and consolidate itself in rural Afghanistan. They are introduced from above and not in response to community demands for local democratization. They are elected bodies and receive block grants of U.S.$20,000 to undertake minor infrastructure projects under the watchful eyes of "facilitating partners," normally civil society organizations and the Ministry of Rural Rehabilitation and Development. By early 2006 approximately half of the country's villages had been covered.

Optimistic supporters among the development community see the community development councils transforming into multifunctional elected village councils, identified in article 140 of the constitution. However, it is unclear how such councils would be sustained financially. It is also likely that such councils would most probably come into conflict with traditional power holders. The use of secret ballots was contentious in the establishment of some of these councils, while the resolution of other community power issues has been judged to be "temporary."[36] Elite capture is also a potential danger. Then there is the question of how such institutions could contribute to poverty alleviation. Would more authority and resources channeled through the line ministries have a greater impact on alleviating the poverty (which affects the 70 percent of the population living on less than U.S.$2 a day)?[37] There is certainly an urgent need for additional state resources to be directed to the grass roots in order to raise the standard of living, and this should have the added benefit of reducing support for the armed opponents of the state, the "warlords" and "commanders" who have penetrated the state, and the booming illegal drugs economy. Deconcentration offers considerable possibilities for improving service delivery from the current low levels and making headway in the struggle for poverty alleviation.

Conclusion

When viewed pragmatically from the point of view of service delivery and poverty reduction, deconcentration can have at least as much to offer as decentralization—and sometimes more and at less cost. Waiting patiently to reap the promised rewards of democratic decentralization may be a risky strategy. Experience shows how even the best-intentioned experiment in democratic devolution can fail to live up to expectations and in some instances can leave people, especially the poor and disadvantaged, worse off than before. Yet despite weak central institutions of governance and high cost, development practice nearly always eschews deconcentration in favor of democratic decentralization, although this latter label is frequently in name only.

The initial supposition of the authors was that the main reason for this state of affairs in development assistance is the strong ideological preferences of donors and their midlevel agents for forms of governance that encourage downward accountability and political legitimacy based on popular participation and political pluralism. These ideological preferences entail the replication of a form of political economy—open-market democracy—that currently constitutes the ruling paradigm particularly among Western donor countries.

In this chapter, the authors take this argument a step further by suggesting that their initial supposition oversimplifies a more complex reality. Rather than taking at face value, as in 2005, the rhetorical claims by rich countries of their ideological fervor to democratize the world and eradicate poverty everywhere it is found, an analysis of recent world events leads to the conclusion that much donor interest in poor countries relies more on their political acquiescence than their political legitimacy.

State compliance is of particular importance to the United States and its allies, especially where their economic or strategic political interests are concerned. Noncompliant states are criticized severely for their undemocratic and inhumane ways, threatened first economically and then militarily and, unless they acquiesce, sometimes invaded. Commonly used pretexts include the now familiar possession of weapons of mass destruction, salvation from dictatorial and inhumane rule of an oppressed citizenry, combating terrorism, and the threat of regional or even global instability. These pretexts provide justification for "preemptive" military strikes that contravene international law or for disproportionate military action. By contrast, compliant states that are of strategic or economic importance to the U.S.-led coalition are given considerable leeway when it comes to forms of governance, weapons of mass destruction, and human rights (Israel, Saudi Arabia, and Pakistan, for example).

The implications of this for development assistance are potentially stark. If the "coalition" of the United States and its allies does not really care very much about the human rights records or accountability of governments of compliant states that have something that the coalition wants, (for example, oil), then it is possible that the coalition may care even less about these matters in countries that do not arouse its economic or strategic interest. This frequently means that the negotiation of governance reform is left to midlevel donorcrats and host governments and that the widely varying success of informed policy and development (success, that is, in terms of poverty reduction) may be explicable only with reference to this phenomenon. The above interpretation of governance reform involving decentralization in three postconflict states—Cambodia, Timor-Leste, and Afghanistan—is highly suggestive of the validity of the authors' conjectures concerning what can be referred to as the politics and sociology of development practice.

Notes

1. G. S. Cheema, *Building Democratic Institutions: Governance Reform in Developing Countries* (Bloomfield, Conn.: Kumarian, 2005).

2. C. Perrow, "The Analysis of Goals in Complex Organizations," *American Sociological Review* 48 (1961): 32854–66.

3. B. Smith, *Decentralization: The Territorial Dimension of the State* (London: Allen and Unwin, 1985), p. 85.

4. United Nations Department of Economic and Social Affairs, *A Handbook of Public Administration: Current Concepts and Practice with Special Reference to Developing Countries* (1961), p. 64.

5. P. Mawhood, ed., *Local Government in the Third World* (Chichester, U.K.: Wiley, 1983); G. S. Cheema and D. A. Rondinelli, *Implementing Decentralisation Programmes in Asia: Local Capacity for Rural Development* (Nagoya: United Nations Centre for Regional Development, 1983); H. Maddick, *Democracy, Decentralisation and Development* (Bombay: Asia Publishing House, 1963); and World Bank, *World Development Report 2000/2001* (Oxford University Press, 2000).

6. B. Smith, *Choice in the Design of Decentralisation* (London: Commonwealth Secretariat, 1993).

7. M. Turner, *Central-Local Relations in Asia-Pacific: Convergence or Divergence?* (London: Palgrave Macmillan, 1999); R. Chambers, *Challenging the Professions: Frontiers for Rural Development* (London: IT Publishers, 1993), p. 15.

8. E. Banfield, "Corruption as a Feature of Governmental Organization," in *Bureaucratic Corruption in Sub-Saharan Africa: Towards a Search for Causes and Consequences,* edited by M. Ekpo (University Press of America, 1979); J. Manor, *The Political Economy of Democratic Decentralization* (World Bank, 1999); and R. Prud'homme, "The Dangers of Decentralization," *World Bank Research Observer* 10, no. 2 (1995): 201–20.

9. Smith, *Choice in the Design of Decentralisation.*

10. G. Wood, "Prisoners and Escapees: Improving the Institutional Responsibility Square in Bangladesh," *Public Administration and Development* 20, no. 3 (2000): 221–37; D. Curtis, "Cutting the Bars: Thoughts on 'Prisoners and Escapees' in Bangladesh," *Public Administration and Development* 22, no. 2 (2002): 123–34.

11. R. May, "Decentralization in Papua New Guinea: Two Steps Forward and One Step Back," in *Central-Local Relations in Asia-Pacific: Convergence or Divergence,* edited by M. Turner (London: Macmillan, 1999); M. Turner and D. Kavanamur, "Explaining Public Sector Reform Failure: Papua New Guinea 1975–2001," paper prepared for Policymaking in Papua New Guinea workshop, Canberra, February 21–22, and Port Moresby, March 21–22, 2002.

12. World Bank, *Papua New Guinea: Delivering Public Service* (1995).

13. R. May, "District Level Governance in Papua New Guinea," SSGM Report, State Society and Governance in Melanesia Project, Australian National University, June 17, 2005.

14. J. Wunsch, "Decentralization, Local Governance and 'Recentralization' in Africa," *Public Administration and Development* 21, no. 4 (2001): 277–88, quotation p. 286.

15. J. Jütting and others, "Decentralisation and Poverty in Developing Countries: Exploring the Impact," Working Paper 236, OECD Development Center, 2004.

16. Ibid., p. 23.

17. J. Bossuyt and J. Gould, "Decentralisation and Poverty Reduction: Elaborating the Linkages," *Policy Management Brief* 12 (Institute of Development Studies, University of Helsinki, 2000), p. 3.

18. Ibid., p. 4.

19. R. Crook, "Decentralisation and Poverty Reduction in Africa: The Politics of Central-Local Relations," *Public Administration and Development* 23, no. 1 (2003): 77–88.

20. M. Turner, "From Commitment to Consequences: Comparative Experiences of Decentralization in the Philippines, Indonesia and Cambodia," *Public Management Review* 8, no. 2 (2006): 253–72.

21. A. Brillantes, *Innovation and Excellence: Understanding Local Governance in the Philippines* (Quezon City: Center for Local and Regional Governance, 2003).

22. Asian Development Bank, *Poverty in the Philippines: Income, Assets and Access* (2005).

23. M. Turner, "Whatever Happened to Deconcentration? Recent Initiatives in Cambodia," *Public Administration and Development* 22, no. 3 (2002): 353–64.

24. P. Hutchcroft, "Centralization and Decentralization in Administration and Politics: Assessing Territorial Dimensions of Authority and Power," *Governance* 14, no. 1 (2001): 25–53.

25. Ibid. p. 45.

26. P. Blunt and M. Turner, "Decentralisation, Democracy and Development in a Post-Conflict Society: Commune Councils in Cambodia," *Public Administration and Development* 25, no. 1 (2005): 75–87.

27. N. Chomsky, *Power and Terror: Post-9/11 Talks and Interviews* (New York: Seven Stories Press, 2003); N. Chomsky, *Hegemony or Survival: America's Quest for Global Dominance* (Crow's Nest, Australia: Allen and Unwin, 2001); N. Chomsky, *Powers and Prospects: Reflections on Human Nature and the Social Order* (London: Pluto Press, 1996).

28. Blunt and Turner, "Decentralisation, Democracy and Development in a Post-Conflict Society."

29. Royal Government of Cambodia, *Independent Study of Donor Support for Decentralization and Deconcentration* (2006).

30. Statistics from World Bank, *Cambodia: Halving Poverty by 2015?* (2006).

31. World Bank, "Timor-Leste: Project Performance Report," Report 36590, 2006.

32. G. S. Cheema and others, "Strengthening Accountability and Transparency in Timor-Leste," 2006.

33. Ibid.

34. Gunnar Myrdal, *Asian Drama* (1968).

35. M. Turner, "State Consolidation and Subnational Governance in Afghanistan," paper prepared for International Research Symposium on Public Management 10, Glasgow Caledonian University, April 10–11, 2006, p. 10.

36. P. Kakar, "Fine-Tuning the NSP: Discussions of Problems and Solutions with Facilitating Partners," Working Paper, Afghanistan Research and Evaluation Unit, November 2005.

37. United Nations Development Program, *Afghanistan National Human Development Report 2004: Security with a Human Face* (2004).

8

Fiscal Decentralization and Intergovernmental Fiscal Relations: Navigating a Viable Path to Reform

PAUL SMOKE

The ongoing wave of decentralization in developing countries invariably includes fiscal reforms—the assignment of expenditure and revenue responsibilities to subnational governments.[1] Many efforts, however, even those that closely follow key reform principles, are usually at best modestly successful. In this chapter I consider why this has been a difficult area of reform and argue that analysts need to think about it differently.

The concept of fiscal decentralization is somewhat artificial in the sense that it cannot be isolated from broader reforms. Subnational governments with weak political accountability and institutional capacity are unlikely to use resources well. The reverse, however, is also true. Citizens who participate in such local processes are likely to disengage if these governments have inadequate resources to deliver services. The various fiscal elements are also interrelated but too often are treated separately. Redundant subnational government revenues abound, confusing citizens about what they pay for and why. Intergovernmental transfer systems have commonly undermined subnational incentives to raise revenues through taxes, borrowing, and so forth, even if they have the capacity to do so. Thus linkages are critical in decentralization reforms.

Understanding context is another key to effective fiscal decentralization. As I illustrate below, the political and institutional characteristics of a country create both constraints on and opportunities for decentralization reform. A common failure by decentralization analysts to understand the nature and relevance of these characteristics can result in inappropriate and unworkable reform efforts.

In what follows I briefly summarize key aspects of fiscal decentralization, outline common constraints on reform, and highlight the role of context in designing it. I then selectively review a few cases in which relative progress has been made, illustrating how context matters and suggesting how to improve linkages among fiscal, political, and institutional reform. The immediate challenge is often how to initiate a viable path to sustainable reform in complex and diverse environments.

Fiscal Decentralization and Subnational Fiscal Structures

Several key elements are considered necessary for an effective intergovernmental fiscal system.[2] They have traditionally been treated in a very standardized way, with a focus on normatively desirable design. Recently there has been more explicit—although as argued below, inadequate—recognition of the need to focus more on implementation.

Role of Subnational Governments: Decentralization of Functions and Revenues

Decentralization is expected to improve efficiency in resource use because residents in each subnational government can choose the mix of public services and revenues that best meets their preferences. Thus many services, except those more efficiently provided at a larger scale or that generate externalities, should be subnational functions.[3] Countries generally follow this basic logic, but there is often vagueness in service assignment. Recent reform efforts have focused on how to work out operational details.

Principles for revenue decentralization are also well defined; for example, the revenue bases for subnational governments should be relatively immobile, should not compete with central bases, and should establish a link between payments and benefits.[4] Many developing countries do often follow these principles. Public finance specialists typically advocate a variety of own-source revenues for subnational governments, including property taxes, user charges, and various licenses and fees. But assigned revenues invariably fail to match expenditure needs, subnational governments commonly use too many unproductive revenues, and they tax bases already taxed by higher levels. In addition, some sources suffer from design flaws, such as stagnant bases, complex structures, and ineffective administration. Thus there has been a move toward consolidation, harmonization, and restructuring of subnational government revenue sources.

Offsetting Fiscal Imbalances: The Intergovernmental Transfer System

Most countries use intergovernmental transfers, which help to cover fiscal imbalances or revenue inadequacy at the subnational level. They also serve redistributional objectives, reducing fiscal capacity differences, and they can encourage expenditures on national priority services. Most transfer systems are intended, at least officially, to meet these objectives, but several design issues commonly plague developing countries.[5]

A key concern is the need for a stable transfer pool to allow medium-term planning for subnational government service delivery; however, fiscal problems can be created if a large percentage of central resources is guaranteed to these governments. Thus there is a need to balance these two concerns. Another challenge is adopting an appropriate mix—conditional transfers encourage expenditures on national priorities, while unconditional transfers are best for redistribution. Finally, transfers in developing countries have often been structured poorly. Multiple programs controlled by various ministries confuse matters at the local level, subjective allocation hinders transparency and accountability, and transfers can undermine local resource mobilization. Many countries have been simplifying and consolidating their transfer programs and adopting objective allocation formulas that improve transparency and help to maintain incentives for local revenue generation. Some countries are even introducing transfer incentives for subnational governments to adopt specific reforms, including financial management procedures, participatory mechanisms, and pro-poor expenditure.

Developmental Subnational Governments: Access to Investment Capital

Subnational governments in many developing countries get much of their capital budget from transfers, but in certain cases provinces and cities are able to borrow money.[6] A good system requires a spectrum of investment finance options, from grants and subsidized loans for poorer subnational governments and non-self-financing projects, to various types of loans for fiscally sound subnational governments and self-fincancing regimes. Where such governments are relatively strong, efforts to develop access to capital markets make sense, but the center must regulate borrowing and enforce a hard budget constraint. In more typical cases, where subnational government responsibilities are smaller and these government entities are fiscally weak, special credit institutions may be appropriate. Initial public management gives the center control over subnational government borrowing, but such institutions can be increasingly privatized as subnational governments develop creditworthiness.

Perhaps the most critical challenge in advanced fiscal decentralization is helping subnational governments move from grants and subsidized loans to greater use of credit markets, which requires coordinated development of grant and loan options.[7] It is critical to ensure that wealthy subnational governments cannot use grants for self-financing projects, thereby diverting scarce resources from subnational governments that are poor and unable to borrow. At the same time, grants and subsidized lending mechanisms need to create incentives for weak subnational governments to improve fiscal discipline and begin to borrow.

Attempts to develop borrowing mechanisms within this framework are at an early stage in many developing countries.

Alternative Mechanisms: Supplementing Revenues and Building Capacity

The above discussion focuses on standard fiscal decentralization mechanisms used in formal systems. Alternative mechanisms have also been used to support reform.[8] Donor-financed community development funds have been around in various forms for years. They generally target investments identified through community participation. Their typical separation from regular government operations somewhat insulates them from common subnational government financial problems such as resource leakages and disbursement delays. If resources are managed through separate mechanisms, however, procedures may never be integrated into their systems, and attention may be diverted from capacity building. In addition, subnational governments request resources for specific projects, so they do not learn to work within a resource envelope, the core of development planning. Finally, these funds target development projects, often neglecting operation and maintenance.

Social funds operate similarly, but they directly finance civil society organizations and community groups (sometimes subnational governments as well). Civil society organizations are effective for relief services and may help develop subnational government capacity and governance where democratic decentralization is not a priority, but critics charge that they may stagnate, perhaps hindering subnational government development. Another alternative is the Local Development Fund, which provides largely unconditional grants only to subnational governments. These funds serve as a budget, which these governments allocate to priority projects, moving the governments a step beyond the still common practice of making a wish list without guaranteed funding. The Local Development Fund planning process can be used to program other available resources (for example, from social funds), and it requires local generation of resources for operation and maintenance. Local Development Funds can provide a framework for developing a sustainable finance system in the broader reform context.

Other approaches involving public-private partnership also provide options to improve subnational government service delivery. Involving private firms in some sectors can, if proper regulatory frameworks are developed and enforced, help these governments to secure capital financing, to collect user charges, and to improve services. Similarly, contracting with community groups can improve services even in low-income areas.

Reality Check: Constraints on Fiscal Decentralization

If so much is known about fiscal decentralization and there is increasingly a sense of the need for attention to implementation, why have reform efforts had such modest success? The answer centers on the nature of these efforts and how they have emerged.[9]

Politics

Although much rhetoric about decentralization centers on improving public sector performance, it is inherently political, as is in part reflected in the common emphasis on a need for political will to decentralize.[10] This is, however, often implied to be the commitment of a benevolent central government to improving the lives of citizens by empowering them. The motives, of course, are typically far more complex and often less benign. In addition, even strong political will is not sufficient for success. Countries that have developed strong decentralization frameworks, commonly seen as a measure of political will, often have not implemented reform.

The reality is that many decentralization efforts in developing countries have been political responses to crises, hastily developed attempts—with minimal agreement among stakeholders—to hold onto or secure power. Weak consensus on the form and process of decentralization results in a poor grasp of basic principles, adoption of superficial frameworks, and apathy or outright opposition during implementation.

Beyond considerations at the center, subnational governments must also learn to act autonomously and to be accountable to a constituency for resource use; elected councilors must learn to work with civil servants. who have historically taken direction from above.[11] Local elites may drive these dynamics, and they may have strong ties with national bureaucratic and political elites. Broadening participation is often a complex challenge, as is crafting a balance among various subnational government actors and between them and higher levels.

Bureaucracy

The often complex and poorly coordinated institutional environment in which fiscal decentralization must be implemented in developing countries can impede progress.[12] Multiple central agencies—including subnational government oversight ministries, multisectoral or coordinating ministries (such as finance and planning), and sectoral ministries involved in service delivery—have roles in reform. The situation is particularly problematic when these agencies have divergent views of what decentralization means.

Even with an economic or political impetus to decentralize, central bureaucratic resistance can be strong. Ministries obstruct the decentralization of major responsibilities, which undermines their control over substantial resources. They also have few incentives to work cooperatively with each other. Indeed, there may well be direct competition for control of the decentralization agenda and resources among powerful central agencies.

Finally, managerial and technical capacity is often limited at all levels. Weak skills and inadequate training are pervasive, performance incentives are weak, and capacity building is a slow process. Skilled civil servants may also move to the private sector for better compensation after being trained with public funds.

Technocratic Orientation

Decentralization reform is often based on conceptual approaches, such as fiscal federalism, which are favored by donors and Western-educated bureaucrats.[13] These provide a useful analytical starting point, but they have a narrow fiscal focus and are somewhat culture- and institution-specific, Western constructs.[14] They also target normatively desirable outcomes with minimal consideration of context or process. Even the emerging focus on implementation has a technical orientation, listing required steps without much guidance on managing the institutional and political realities outlined above.[15] Reforms may be borrowed from dissimilar countries by technocrats inattentive to target country context.

The technocratic approach has often resulted in reforms that are unworkably comprehensive, thereby overwhelming capacity at both central and local levels and threatening bureaucratic and political tolerance at the center. Many initiatives are also led by a single central agency perceived as a rival by peer agencies whose cooperation is required for success. Some reforms focus on limited (often technical) activities, such as budgeting reform, that are not developed as part of a broader decentralization agenda.

Another design concern is that reform programs tend to assume similar capacities of all subnational governments or all of those classified according to certain characteristics (such as large urban, small urban, rural), despite often great differences among them. Treating weak subnational governments as capable invites failure, while micromanaging competent subnational governments wastes resources. Programs also tend to define performance as following common steps despite the varying circumstances under which these governments function. Standardization may undermine performance.

International Donor Behavior

The role that donors play in defining and promoting decentralization reform is noted above, but there are also other problems.[16] Despite rhetoric about institution building, immediate donor interests are not always well served by it. Such efforts are time consuming and difficult and, therefore, may delay moving funds. The pressures of expenditure schedules may keep funds flowing even when serious problems arise.

Donors often try to avoid sectoral and jurisdictional coordination by defining projects specific to a single sector or ministry or to a single region or subnational government. These entities must then adopt preferred donor procedures, perhaps working through separate implementation units. Inconsistent procedures and separate mechanisms can undermine development of a unified system. In some cases, such behavior can reinforce the interagency competition discussed above.

Some serious donor efforts have been launched in recent years to deal with these concerns, but much more needs to be done.

Country Context

The different types of decentralization (deconcentration, delegation, and devolution) are well known, as are the approaches used by different administrative traditions (for example, the French in West Africa and Indochina versus the British in East and Southern Africa and South Asia). The term *decentralization,* however, is still used generically or unclearly. Currently it is often used as a synonym for the dominant democratic devolution paradigm, which is at best a long-term goal in many developing countries.[17]

Although decentralization is often undertaken in pursuit of common stated goals, it may have diverse meanings in different contexts beyond the basic distinctions noted above. In some cases (such as Kenya), it involves revitalizing diverse, legally empowered subnational governments. In other cases (for example, Indonesia), it involves transforming a relatively capacitated deconcentrated administration into democratic subnational governments in a more devolved system. In still other cases (for example, Cambodia), decentralization involves creating entirely new subnational governments. I return below to the way fiscal decentralization has been evolving in each of these cases, but it must be recognized that they only illustrate a much broader diversity of experience.

Design and Implementation in Context

The above discussion helps explain why fiscal decentralization has been unfolding unevenly in developing countries.[18] Rapidly designed or implemented technocratic and comprehensive reforms fail to recognize that the key challenge to decentralization is changing attitudes about how the public sector works. Central officials may be used to making decisions and controlling subnational governments; subnational government officials may be comfortable with central subsidization and control, and they may not feel accountable to citizens, who may have low expectations of the subnational government and little incentive to finance them. These entrenched attitudes and behaviors cannot change without patient consultation, capacity building, improved subnational government performance, and more appropriate donor support.

Historical and contextual factors—power bases, political dynamics, and institutional identities and capacities—fundamentally govern how decentralization can unfold in a particular country. A country with no developed multilevel state architecture and little history of subnational authority, for example, is unlikely to rapidly create effective, autonomous subnational governments, no matter how severe the internal crisis or donor demands. Similarly, where a particular system and degree of autonomy are entrenched, it may be difficult to reallocate functions among levels, and moving too quickly can create a backlash that undermines reform efforts.

In some cases genuine support allows considerable action in various forms: broad-based policy development (South Africa); rapid, crisis-driven legislation and resource devolution (Indonesia); or a broad process to design and implement decentralization (Thailand).[19] Even so, resistance from central actors, pushback from civil society groups that see public sector decentralization as an infringement on their role, and lack of subnational government capacity (broadly defined) to assume new functions, among other possibilities, create natural constraints on implementation. Such forces individually or collectively may delay reform or result in the emergence of countervailing efforts that hinder the development of a subnational government system.

Political momentum may be so strong that significant decentralization steps are implemented rapidly in spite of the factors noted above. For example, Uganda quickly transferred major functions and resources to local governments.[20] Argentina and Brazil crafted frameworks that provided excessive borrowing autonomy—de jure or de facto—to subnational governments.[21] In such cases, the state has generally needed—whether willingly or reluctantly—to backtrack on previously adopted reforms in order to correct the serious problems that often ensue from such precocious decentralization.

Three Countries, Three Decentralizations

In this section I elaborate on the three cases introduced above—Kenya, as a country revitalizing an existing subnational government system; Indonesia, as a country transforming from a relatively strong deconcentrated system to one in which devolution to subnational governments is becoming dominant; and Cambodia, in which an entirely new subnational government system is being created. In each case I briefly review the reform context and nonfiscal aspects of decentralization, then turn to more detail on some noteworthy features of the design and implementation of reform. The tables in the appendix to this chapter summarize the key decentralization features of each country.

Kenya: Rebuilding Empowered Subnational Governments

Local governance has a long tradition in Kenya, both from the customs of its ethnic groups and from the formal local government system created during the British colonial era.[22] Provinces were, as today, arms of the center, but local governments had significant, semiautonomous functions and revenues as per the Local Government Act (last revised in 1986 and under review again). The power of the local governments was weakened after independence (1963), but many of them continued to provide services (water, roads, sanitation, preprimary schools). They also relied almost fully on their own revenues, particularly property taxes and user charges, and remained under elected councils. Performance, however, generally declined. The center blamed the incompetence and corruption of local governments, while these governments blamed central control and interference.

The real reasons for local government deterioration are largely historical. Tribal tensions surfaced in the ethnically fragmented country after independence, prompting a major political consolidation. This was reinforced by a 1982 coup attempt against President Moi, which resulted in restrictions on political competition, the effective creation of a one-party state, and efforts to recentralize that undermined local government accountability to its constituents. Central neglect and poor local performance intensified after that. The center came to view local governments as problematic entities to be controlled rather than developmental entities to be supported.

Evolving conditions provided openings for reform in the late 1990s. Services provided by local governments declined to a point where they were broadly considered unacceptable and even damaging to development, and an increasingly free (post-1992-democratization) press increased public awareness. Rapidly changing central fiscal conditions also focused attention on the central budget burdens created by local governments, which long failed to repay donor loans received through the center's now-defunct Local Government Loans Authority (LGLA). Perhaps most significant were shifts in the political environment in the 1990s. Scandals undermined the center's legitimacy, and the public became more aware of how the center kept local governments weak. In addition, opposition parties won local elections and parliamentary seats, creating new pressures, reinforced by donors, on the ruling party to reform. An opposition candidate won the last presidential election, and new evidence of corruption has further reinforced a climate for reform.

Unlike in the cases of Indonesia and Cambodia, discussed below, responsibility for the local government system in Kenya clearly belongs to a single central agency, the Ministry of Local Government, although some sectoral ministries control certain service roles of local governments. The Ministry of Finance had little interest in local governments since there was no transfer system from the postcolonial period until 2000. So the Ministry of Local Government was in charge officially, but it was weak and not respected. When the Ministry of Local Government (with donor support) introduced reforms in the 1980s, other central agencies paid little attention. By the early 1990s, the Ministry of Local Government began to reform its own operations and pilot local government reform. But only as the fiscal and political pressures outlined above mounted during the late 1990s did some impetus for broader reform gather momentum.

Local government reforms were initiated with a program that piloted a pragmatic, gradual, and systematic approach (as opposed to the normatively inspired, comprehensive approach discussed above). The pilot defined broad common goals, but the exact steps and the pace of implementation varied. A mobile Ministry of Local Government team worked with each local government to design unique reforms to match its needs and capacity, placing some responsibility on local government officials for what they agreed to. In addition, the team helped local governments to implement negotiated reforms and, as necessary, to modify them. Citizen participation was introduced, and some task-specific training was provided. Local governments that met agreed goals were rewarded with, for example, more funding and less Ministry of Local Government control. The performance of most participating local governments—in terms of reform adoption, revenue collection, and service delivery—improved considerably.

After the successful pilot, the Ministry of Local Government received support to extend the new approach through the Kenya Local Government Reform Program, which is managed by an interministerial body. The Ministry of Finance took notice of these efforts and began larger fiscal system reforms, initially taking small steps to ensure that delinquent central payments to local governments would be made on time. The Ministry of Finance then began harmonizing duplicative central and subnational revenue sources.[23] Perhaps most significantly, intergovernmental transfers were reestablished. The Local Authority Transfer Fund is capitalized by law with 5 percent of income tax revenues. In addition, a special account was established to protect the fund, and a broad-based advisory committee was formed to ensure some degree of independence in transfer management.

The Ministry of Finance also began to assist the Ministry of Local Government with efforts to enhance local government revenue generation and financial management. Initial efforts have focused on property rates, the uniquely local source with the greatest unmet potential. An integrated financial management system is being developed, efforts to improve internal auditing and staff management are being designed and tested, and steps are being taken to deal with the local government borrowing crisis.

Finally, reform components are being integrated. For example, property tax reform is being carried out in conjunction with broader financial management reforms. The Local Authority Transfer Fund is replacing the contentious, administratively difficult, and politically unpopular local authority service charge, improving the overall structure of local government finances. The fund's formula also provides incentives for local government adoption of key reforms. All activities are embedded in a program designed to build local government capacity (governance and technical) gradually and systematically in a series of manageable, mutually reinforcing, coordinated steps. Kenya's political situation remains problematic, and it is unclear how reform will evolve, but relative to previous efforts, there has been productive progress.

Indonesia: Transforming Deconcentration to Devolution

Indonesia had an element of decentralization during its Dutch colonial period.[24] As in many ethnically diverse countries colonized by European powers, building national unity through centralization was adopted after independence, laying a base for the authoritarian Suharto regime. Various decentralization attempts in the 1970s and 1980s, often donor promoted, never had political traction and largely involved deconcentration. The 1997 Asian economic crisis hastened Suharto's fall, followed by secession of the former province of East Timor and growing protests from resource-rich provinces over their limited revenue autonomy. The post-Suharto government adopted decentralization as a strategy to hold the diverse and weakly unified country together. Reform, however, primarily empowered local governments, largely due to central concerns that strong provinces could fuel regional conflicts, separatism, or federalism.

Indonesia has a relatively advanced decentralization framework. Law 22 (1999) eliminated hierarchical relationships between local governments and higher levels and defined their responsibilities. Law 25 (1999) modified fiscal transfers and outlined own revenues. Law 34 (2000) modestly enhanced subnational government revenues, and constitutional amendments in 2000 consolidated subnational government reforms. In 2004, however, new laws weakened subnational government budgeting and civil service control, partly in reaction to problematic performance.

In terms of the political and civil society landscape, Indonesia was effectively run by the Golkar Party until Suharto's collapse. Golkar is still important, but other parties have been successful in national and subnational elections, changing the political dynamics. Constitutional revisions and an anticorruption law guarantee freedom of information and transparency, but bureaucratic and capacity barriers complicate the exercise of these civic rights. Thousands of civil society organizations have been established after decades of state repression, but the Internal Security Law has limited their development, and the social movement that helped overthrow Suharto dissipated to some extent. Civil society organizations, however, have engaged in advocacy on key policy issues, including decentralization.

On the fiscal side, the legislation devolves many functions, with only defense, foreign affairs, justice, monetary policy, finance, police, development planning, and religion reserved for the center. Subnational governments must provide health, education, environmental, and infrastructure services and may provide others not reserved for the center or provinces. Provinces were strengthened by the 2004 legislative reforms mentioned above.

Revenue decentralization is weak relative to subnational government responsibilities. These governments enjoy a share of selected central taxes (property, natural resources, and income). Provinces have motor vehicles, fuel, and ground water taxes, but rates are uniform and portions must be shared with lower levels.

Local governments exercise limited control only over taxes on hotels, restaurants, entertainment, advertisement, street lighting, parking, and mineral exploitation. All subnational governments may collect user charges. Many of these revenues are prereform holdovers—subnational governments have not been granted significant new revenue autonomy. The 2000 law noted above did allow local governments to adopt additional sources of revenue, but extensive abuse of this authority resulted in its curtailment by 2004 legislative reforms.

Indonesia's decentralization significantly altered intergovernmental transfers. Formerly fragmented, recurrent transfers were combined into the Dana Alokasi Umum, a revenue-sharing fund capitalized by a minimum of 25 percent of national domestic revenues and largely targeted to the subprovincial level. The fund is allocated by a transparent formula that considers expenditure needs and revenue capacity. The formula needs work, but it improves on the previous system. There is also a provision for special-purpose transfers, which have seen limited use to date.

Indonesian subnational governments once borrowed extensively, but much of this was done through the Regional Development Account and other mechanisms controlled by the Ministry of Finance. When the account was created in 1987, it was an improvement over the fragmented system it replaced, and it provided a common window for donors to channel capital to subnational governments. Its performance deteriorated over time, however, with both poor loan allocation and poor repayment, and it is now barely functioning. Reform has been slow, largely due to disputes between Ministry of Finance departments over resource control. Developing a subnational government lending framework is an urgent fiscal decentralization challenge for Indonesia, where these governments have major unmet infrastructure development responsibilities.

There has been debate about whether Indonesia's "big bang" decentralization was positive or negative, but it may simply have been an inevitable political response to crisis. Its fiscal effects were probably relatively neutral, as a substantial portion of staff transferred from the deconcentrated bureaucracy, and own-source revenues are limited. Thus some design features, whether intentionally or not, constrain subnational government autonomy, limiting problems sometimes experienced with extensive decentralization. Still much work remains. Operational details on many legally devolved functions still need to be specified. Other outstanding problems include the lack of local revenue autonomy, the dysfunctional lending framework, and limited capacity building efforts.

Two broad issues underlie these weaknesses. First, Indonesia never established a coherent strategy or coordination mechanism to operationalize or implement aspects of its fiscal decentralization framework. A ministerial-level Regional Autonomy Review Board was empowered to design policy, but subsequent leadership has been problematic. The Ministry of Home Affairs has the strongest official role, but other central agencies, such as the Ministry of Finance, Bappenas (the national planning agency), and sectoral ministries, are important. Overall, there is no empowered leader, so coordination remains weak and progress is ad hoc and erratic rather than strategic and progressive.

Second, the development of mechanisms for subnational government accountability is complex and difficult. Subnational civil servants used to looking to parent ministries are learning to pay more attention to their local elected councils, the councils are learning to deal with civil servants and citizens, and citizens are learning how to hold councils and service providers accountable. There has been inadequate attention to fostering these accountability relationships, which are critical to securing the potential benefits of decentralization and to creating an environment conducive to further relaxation of central control over local government fiscal activities. How Indonesia will deal with the need to more strategically develop decentralization, coordinate the central actors involved in it, and improve horizontal and downward accountability and technical capacity at the subnational level remains to be seen.

Cambodia: Creating Local Government

In what might be seen as an improbable development, the highly centralized Royal Government of Cambodia recently began to decentralize.[25] This includes deconcentration to provinces and municipalities, which are arms of the center, and modest devolution to newly created commune-elected governments (including those in urban communes known as *sangkats*). Communes have existed as administrative levels since the French colonial era but were largely vehicles for the provinces and municipalities to communicate with local people. The entire system deteriorated during the protracted conflicts of the Khmer Rouge era, Vietnamese occupation, and civil war.

The United Nations negotiated a peace agreement in Paris in 1991 providing for 1993 elections, which were contested by the Cambodian People's Party (CPP) under Hun Sen and the royalist Funcinpec Party. Hun Sen lost, but he controlled the military and refused to yield power. Rather than risk new hostilities, a power-sharing agreement was brokered. This fragile arrangement, which resulted in frequent paralysis of the Royal Government, collapsed in a 1997 power grab engineered by Hun Sen. The CPP narrowly won the 1998 and 2003 elections. Consolidation of CPP power in a more stable political environment ended up enhancing the climate for decentralization. Facing greater expectations, the Royal Government began to focus on developmental concerns. The center's inability to deliver services in much of the country led it to see subnational governments as a means to help fill this gap.

The groundwork for decentralization was laid by donor relief efforts in the postconflict period. The UN Cambodia Resettlement and Reintegration

(Carere) project provided basic services to returned refugees displaced during conflict. Over time Carere became active in local institutional development and capacity building, and it was adopted as a Royal Government program named Seila.[26] The Royal Government was barely involved in the early stages—the United Nations worked directly with officials of the provinces in project areas. Over time the center took notice. When Carere ended in 2000, the Royal Government assumed full responsibility for Seila, with donor support. By 2002 Seila systems and procedures provided the basis to develop communes into elected subnational governments.

How did such an unusual path emerge? United Nations success in brokering elections (and perhaps the decision not to challenge Hun Sen's post-1993 election behavior) gave it enough credibility to bypass the weak Royal Government in experimenting with subnational institutions and processes. Some key central ministry officials and provincial governors must have also seen opportunities in Seila for greater influence and resources. Also relevant is the fact that Seila started in provinces that benefited from the return of Cambodian exiles educated by international donors in border refugee camps. These areas experienced a growth of civil society organizations funded by post-1993 international contributions and skilled in community organization and service delivery. Initially, many of these organizations viewed Seila as unwelcome competition, but they learned to cooperate with it and to integrate themselves into it and, later, into the commune system.

These realities explain why Seila was able to establish itself and operate effectively but not why the Royal Government decided to create elected commune councils. First, Seila delivered much local infrastructure, an achievement noted by the Royal Government when making its postconflict shift to development. Second, Seila developed subnational capacity and awareness, creating internal pressures on the Royal Government to institutionalize the experiment. Third, donors favor democratic participation, and Royal Government leaders were undoubtedly aware that they would receive substantial support to develop subnational governments. Finally, the CPP must have seen opportunities after its 1998 electoral victory to consolidate power at the grassroots level.

It is important to note that fiscal decentralization in Cambodia has been relatively limited. Provinces and municipalities remain almost fully dependent on and integrated into the Royal Government budget. What is happening at the commune system level cannot be considered true devolution. *Sangkats* have few formal functions and own resources—the system is based on small transfers made through the Commune/Sangkat Fund. Yet the achievements are real. The fund has been institutionalized in the Royal Government budget with consolidated funds from donors and a growing share of Royal Government resources. The funds are allocated with an objective formula, and although transfers are unconditional, legal controls on commune planning, governance, budgeting, service delivery, and financial management help to ensure responsible resource use. In addition, the system is linked to a substantial capacity-building, technical assistance program based at the provincial and municipal level. There are critics of and problems with this approach, but it may have been the most appropriate way to begin reform in a postconflict environment, where citizens' trust of government is very low. The process of building subnational government credibility and capacity has been put into motion by strategically providing subnational governments with limited resources to provide new services prioritized through local participation.

Clearly the commune system has a long way to go. At the broadest level, Royal Government structures, systems, and procedures pose great challenges to further reform. These include, first, poor revenue generation, dependence on aid and technical expertise, a weak civil service, and primitive budgeting and financial management, all of which are influenced by an extensive system of Royal Government patronage from which the local system has been protected to date. Second, coordination problems similar to Indonesia's are relevant here, with the Ministry of Interior playing a lead role (and contested by other key ministries). Third, the Commune/Sangkat Fund is small, and the need to finance many new commune after the 2002 elections diluted resources flowing to each one. The current level limits incentives and opportunities for capacity building and citizen engagement. Fourth, many communes are too small and poor to be viable planning and budgeting entities. Consolidation is desirable, but after the second round of commune elections held in 2007, it will be politically difficult. Perhaps most fundamentally, communes ultimately need formal service and revenue assignments if stronger accountability is to emerge.

Further commune development cannot be divorced from the development of province and municipality systems. The 2005 Royal Government's decentralization strategy indicates that provinces and municipalities are to evolve into something more than just arms of the center, but the Royal Government has not released details. As the structure evolves, district administrative subdivisions are likely to become service delivery agents. These could partner or compete with commune councils, or they could emerge as the planning and budgeting tier of a two-tier subnational government system. These various scenarios have multiple implications for accountability and service delivery.

The political motivations for rapidly transforming Seila into an official local government system have clearly produced positive effects, but poor attention to details and coordination in framing the system has left gaps, inconsistencies, and questions about what comes next. Decentralization could provide a window for developing and institutionalizing productive governance reforms that influence the center. Or the commune system could be overtaken by the problematic patronage practices that plague the Royal Government. The evolution of the decentralization strategy will determine the fate of subnational governments and their eventual effects on governance and public resource allocation.

Conclusion

It is increasingly recognized that a major cause of weak fiscal decentralization performance is a relatively formulaic reliance by the development community on mainstream intergovernmental fiscal principles. These provide a useful analytical entry point, but they use a discipline-bound perspective, focus on normatively desirable outcomes without guidance on how to attain them, and are based on often implicit assumptions derived from advanced systems. In developing countries, the conventional approach is often applied in a piecemeal manner, with inadequate links to political and institutional reform and with insufficient attention to cross-country heterogeneity in history and context. The great challenges of implementation have been inadequately emphasized by many policy analysts and practitioners, who focus heavily on design.

The importance of thinking differently about fiscal decentralization is well illustrated by the diverse country cases summarized above. All three countries have developed decentralization frameworks to empower subnational governments but under different conditions and with dissimilar approaches. Some progress has been made in each, but flaws remain in content and implementation.

Broad assignment of functions and revenues is generally clear in Kenya, but the problematic political dynamics reviewed above long undermined subnational government performance. In recent years, Kenya has gone the furthest of the three countries in improving own-source revenues, and the recent adoption of formula- and performance-based fiscal transfers also provides incentives to adopt reforms. More attention is needed to accountability and revitalizing the once strong subnational government lending mechanism, which will be most useful after other reforms increase subnational government fiscal responsibility and creditworthiness. Kenya has approached reform relatively strategically and gradually, directly dealing with some of the major obstacles outlined above by coordinating and sequencing intergovernmental fiscal reforms and by experimenting with an asymmetric, integrative, progressive approach to reform that tailors specific steps and capacity-building efforts to individual subnational governments.

Indonesia's basic fiscal system is also fairly well defined in broad terms, but as noted above it was developed hastily in response to crisis, with little initial thought given to implementation. The complex details of functional decentralization in each sector are still being developed, but this is now proceeding in a way that could provide a model for other countries. The transfer system has been massively reformed following many key recommendations of international best practice, although there are still problems to be worked out. The overall system, however, is jeopardized by weak own-source subnational government revenues, lack of attention to restructuring subnational government lending, and inadequate efforts to broaden and nurture accountability. Reforms in these areas are hindered by bureaucratic politics, which have yet to be overcome. Of the three countries, Indonesia has been least able to manage the challenges of coordination and strategic implementation.

The situation in Cambodia, where the subnational government sector has been created from nothing, is quite different. The sector still remains very small, and it has been implemented in a highly unusual way—initially assigning no major functions or own-source revenues but providing newly elected subnational government councils with small unconditional transfers that allow them to implement projects identified through a participatory process. Although it will be some time before subnational governments are major service providers and revenue generators, this strategic approach is allowing the nascent councils to build credibility with their constituents and to develop some implementation capacity without placing excessive expectations on them. How reform will proceed is unclear, but the evolution of the subnational government system seems to be having some broader influence on public accountability.

Three main conclusions may be drawn from this selective, tentative comparative analysis. First, the diverse institutional and political histories of Kenya, Indonesia, and Cambodia have conditioned the way in which fiscal decentralization has been defined and how it is unfolding in each country. This is neither a good nor a bad thing—it is simply a reality that decentralization policymakers must recognize. This is not to say that they should passively watch politics dominate fiscal decentralization principles; rather, they should be creatively thinking about how to look for openings that will allow progress toward meeting key principles within the political and institutional constraints that are too often ignored in policy design and implementation.

Second, although serious problems remain in all three countries, each has taken positive steps that have to some extent allowed demonstrable progress with fiscal decentralization. These measures are often only the first of many that will need to be taken, but they represent tangible movement in the right direction. These specific steps may not be directly replicable in other developing countries, but some of their characteristics—gradual, limited, asymmetric, progressive, integrated—may inform fiscal decentralization analysts and help them proceed with reform even in contextually dissimilar cases.

Third, the first two points collectively suggest that fiscal decentralization analysts and policymakers need a more structured way to help them think about what can be achieved in a particular country. Analysts fall back on normative principles because they can be easily understood and form a basis for providing clear reform advice. Such recommendations, however, are almost always about the ideal system that might eventually be in place rather than what can be achieved in the near term. A more developed analytical tool—a fiscal decentralization diagnostic that goes beyond conventional public finance concerns and strives to be suggestive and strategic rather than prescriptive—would assist analysts and policymakers in laying foundations to create more fully developed subnational government systems as part of a productive and sustainable public sector.

Appendix 8A: Subnational Government Fiscal System Profiles

Table 8A-1. *Kenya*

Reform	Basic ingredients of reform	Comments
Framework	The Local Government Act empowers elected municipal, county, and town councils; provinces and districts administer central government affairs.	Local governments are important in some respects, but their overall role (about 5 percent of public spending) is small compared to the province-district system.
Services	Local services and infrastructure are important; assignment in some sectors is subject to approval by relevant central line ministry.	Municipal roles are clearer than those of counties, which to some extent compete with the central government's districts.
Revenues	Property rates, business licenses, user charges, and agricultural access are assigned to local governments.	Assigned sources are potentially revenue productive but administration is weak and equity is unclear.
Intergovernmental transfers	A local authority transfer fund block grant is funded by 5 percent of income tax revenues and managed by a broad-based board.	The formula is not explicitly poverty sensitive, but reform conditions for disbursement provide incentives for good fiscal behavior.
Borrowing	The central-government-managed Local Government Loans Authority once underwrote substantial local borrowing, but is now dormant due to poor performance.	Borrowing is much needed in larger cities to finance infrastructure, but reforms are also needed to increase local creditworthiness and develop new lending mechanisms.
Alternative finance	Some special poverty-targeted funds exist, but most are for districts, not local governments; service boards and private partners are increasingly common; civil society organizations provide basic services in some areas.	In some areas there is considerable unrealized potential for private and community partnerships in service delivery and for improved district-local government cooperation.

Table 8A-1. *Kenya (continued)*

Reform	Basic ingredients of reform	Comments
Governance	There are local multiparty elections, newly instituted participatory local service delivery plans, and improving transparency conditions.	Local governance has been weak for years, but new participatory mechanisms and a more active civil society in some areas are increasing citizen engagement.
Capacity	Capacity varies greatly across urban and rural jurisdictions.	Training is provided by government training institutes and donor programs.
Implementation	There is no explicit strategy for this, although some care is evident in the gradual and strategic introduction of certain fiscal reforms.	A local government reform program has existed for years, but implementation has been slow and sporadic until recently.
Role of donors	This role has varied over the years; assistance during tense periods under former president was reduced; support is growing under the current president.	Fiscal reform, governance, and poverty alleviation have been key targets of donor interventions; coordination is not strong but is improving.

Table 8A-2. *Indonesia*

Reform	Basic ingredients of reform	Comments
Framework	The decentralization laws of 1999 and 2004 amendments focus on the local rather than the provincial level.	Immediate crises drove what was called the big bang reform rapidly, but, there were constraints on some reforms.
Services	Substantial legal functional assignments were made, including most basic services.	Heavy central influence remains in many areas, as detailed sector-specific assignments are being defined.
Revenues	There is limited local revenue autonomy, except for taxes on hotels and restaurants, entertainment, advertisement, street lighting, limited mineral exploitation, and parking; user charges are allowed.	Central government commitment to develop productive own-source revenues is lacking; even property tax, though heavily shared with local governments, is a central tax.
Intergovernmental transfers	Property and resource taxes, among others, are shared on an origin basis; formula-driven revenue sharing is at least 26 percent of domestic revenues; special-purpose transfers are allowed.	General revenue sharing in part targets the gap between standardized expenditure needs and fiscal capacity, but problems remain in measurement; special-purpose transfers are being developed.

(continued)

Table 8A-2. *Indonesia (continued)*

Reform	Basic ingredients of reform	Comments
Borrowing	Once substantial through the Regional Development Account in the Ministry of Finance, borrowing is now weak; local governments are allowed to borrow, but many are not eligible.	Local borrowing for infrastructure is imperative, and some large cities could be creditworthy; donors are pushing for reform, but the government has not been very responsive.
Alternative finance	Substantial community-driven development funds go to sublocal government communities; in some areas, private firms and civil society organizations are involved in service delivery.	Considerable potential exists for private and community partners in service delivery; some efforts are emerging to coordinate community-driven development mechanisms with local government operations.
Governance	Local multiparty elections occur regularly; public reporting is required, but in practice it is weak; participation is encouraged (and often required by donors), but there is no official mechanism.	Accountability relationships are complex because former central civil servants were transferred to elected local governments; civil society is emerging but faces varoious challenges and constraints.
Capacity	Capacity varies greatly; it is generally better in urban areas; technical capacity is often better than governance capacity.	Local capacity was enhanced by transfer of staff from higher levels; capacity building is mostly driven by the center, although some demand comes from lower levels.
Implementation	No formal implementation strategy exists; some attention has been paid to key reforms since the big bang, such as defining functions more clearly, but the approach remains fragmented and irregular.	Fragmentation and competition among central agencies have prevented smooth and consistent implementation of decentralization; there is even departmental competition within key ministries.
Role of donors	Before the 1999 big bang the many donor projects were fragmented; even heavier support continues under current reforms but remains fragmented.	Governance and poverty alleviation have been key targets; a coordination mechanism exists but remains inadequate; some donors are identified with specific ministries.

Table 8A-3. *Cambodia*

Reform	Basic ingredients of reform	Comments
Framework	The 2001 laws decentralize to the local (commune) level, but the provincial system remains an arm of central administration.	A decentralization strategy was issued in 2005 to develop an overall system; a legislative follow-up is in process.
Services	Commune functions are modest due to the newness of the system and weak capacity. No major services are mandatory.	An early focus on building local government credibility allowed local citizens to allocate their limited resources for local priority services.
Revenues	At present there is almost complete reliance on revenue transfers; some local contribution schemes exist but are not formalized.	Pilot programs are being developed to test how to share provincial revenues with communes and how to develop some own sources.
Intergovernmental transfers	The commune transfer fund, largely unconditional, combines a growing percentage of central budgetary resources plus donor contributions.	A poverty measure is an important element in the transfer formula, but resource levels remain low, and there is no incentive for raising local revenue.
Borrowing	There is no borrowing at present.	Borrowing is not likely to be relevant for some time except in a few large cities.
Alternative finance	Decentralization evolved from a local development fund; other special funds also provice local resources; there is little private sector involvement beyond service contracting; in some areas civil society organizations are highly involved.	Altnernative mechanisms are heavily pro-poor in design, although uneven development of governance mechanisms may undermine pro-poor outcomes in some areas; combination of local government and alternative finances is a concern.
Governance	Local multiparty elections are required; citizen engagement is also encouraged through participatory planning, public information boards, and citizen roles in monitoring, operation, and maintenance.	One party dominates commune councils; there are concerns about elite capture and lack of involvement of poorer residents, but this is improving in some areas; there are also concerns about corruption.
Capacity	Capacity is generally weak but is stronger in areas with more donors and heavy presence of civil society organizations.	The central government provides substantial training of commune councils and some training of citizens and civil society organizations.

(continued)

Table 8A-3. *Cambodia (continued)*

Reform	Basic ingredients of reform	Comments
Implementation	An implementation strategy is not fully developed, but there are strategic elements in system development.	New efforts are under way to move decentralization forward more strategically and consistently.
Role of donors	Donors provide substantial resources and technical assistance; the government increasingly funds commune transfers, but donors still supply considerable off-budget support.	Programmatic coordination has been a serious problem, but a donor coordination group was formed in 2004 that is beginning to improve the situation.

Notes

1. A more comprehensive review of fiscal decentralization and related literature is provided in Paul Smoke, *Fiscal Decentralization in Developing Countries: A Review of Current Concepts and Practice* (United Nations Research Institute for Social Development, 2001); and Paul Smoke, "Fiscal Decentralization Policy in Developing Countries: Bridging Theory and Reality," in *Public Sector Reform in Developing Countries,* edited by Yusuf Bangura and George Larbi (London: Palgrave-Macmillan, 2006).

2. Fiscal federalism was introduced in Wallace Oates, *Fiscal Federalism* (New York: Harcourt, Brace, Jovanovich, 1972); and reconsidered in Wallace Oates, "An Essay on Fiscal Federalism," *Journal of Economic Literature* 37 (1999): 1120–49. More detailed treatment of fiscal systems is provided in Jennie Litvack, Junaid Ahmad, and Richard Bird, *Rethinking Decentralization in Developing Countries* (World Bank, 1998); Roy Bahl, "How to Design a Fiscal Decentralization Program," in *Local Dynamics in an Era of Globalization,* edited by Shahid Yusuf, Weiping Wu, and Simon Evenett (Oxford University Press, 2000); and Smoke, *Fiscal Decentralization in Developing Countries.*

3. The application of expenditure assignment principles is discussed in Roy Bahl and Johannes Linn, *Urban Public Finance in Developing Countries* (Oxford University Press, 1992); Anwar Shah, *The Reform of Intergovernmental Fiscal Relations in Developing and Emerging Market Economies,* Policy and Research Series 23 (World Bank, 1994); World Bank, *Entering the 21st Century: 1999–2000 World Development Report* (1999); and Matt Andrews and Larry Schroeder, "Sectoral Decentralization and Intergovernmental Arrangements in Africa," *Public Administration and Development* 23, no. 1 (2003): 29–40.

4. Literature on subnational revenues is reviewed in Bahl and Linn, *Urban Public Finance in Developing Countries;* Shah, *The Reform of Intergovernmental Fiscal Relations;* Richard Bird and Francois Vaillancourt, eds., *Fiscal Decentralization in Developing Countries* (Cambridge University Press, 1998); Richard Bird, "Rethinking Tax Assignment: The Need for Better Sub-National Taxes," World Bank, 1999; and Remy Prud'homme, "Fiscal Decentralization in Africa: A Framework for Considering Reform," *Public Administration and Development* 23, no. 1 (2003): 17–27.

5. Literature on intergovernmental transfers is reviewed in Bahl and Linn, *Urban Public Finance in Developing Countries;* Shah, *The Reform of Intergovernmental Fiscal Relations;* Theresa

Ter-Minassian, ed., *Fiscal Federalism in Theory and Practice* (International Monetary Fund, 1970); Richard Bird and Michael Smart, "Intergovernmental Fiscal Transfers: International Lessons for Developing Countries," *World Development* 30, no. 6 (2002): 899–912; and Larry Schroeder and Paul Smoke, "Intergovernmental Transfers in Developing Countries: Concepts, International Practices and Policy Issues," in *Intergovernmental Transfers in Asia: Current Practice and Challenges for the Future,* edited by Yun-Hwan Kim and Paul Smoke (Asian Development Bank, 2003).

6. Subnational credit markets are discussed in Paul Smoke, "Improving Infrastructure Finance in Developing Countries through Grant-Loan Linkages," *International Journal of Public Administration* 22, no. 12 (1999); George Peterson, "Building Local Credit Institutions," World Bank, 2002; John Peterson, "Linkages between Local Governments and Financial Markets: A Tool Kit for Developing Subsovereign Credit Markets in Emerging Economies," World Bank, 2000; and Mila Friere and John Peterson, eds., *Subnational Capital Markets in Developing Countries: From Theory to Practice* (Oxford University Press, 2004).

7. Smoke, "Improving Infrastructure Finance in Developing Countries"; and Friere and Peterson, *Subnational Capital Markets in Developing Countries,* for a discussion of grant-loan linkages.

8. Alternative donor mechanisms to support decentralization are summarized and critiqued in Leonardo Romeo, "The Role of External Assistance in Supporting Decentralization Reform," *Public Administration and Development* 23, no. 1 (2003): 89–96.

9. More detailed discussion of decentralization constraints is provided in James Wunsch and Dele Olowu, *The Failure of the Centralized State: Institutions and Self-Governance in Africa* (Boulder, Colo.: Westview, 1990); Judith Tendler, *Good Government in the Tropics* (Johns Hopkins University Press, 1997); John Cohen and Stephen Peterson, *Administrative Decentralization in Developing Countries* (Boulder, Colo.: Lynne Rienner, 1999); Paul Smoke, "Strategic Fiscal Decentralization in Developing Countries: Learning from Recent Innovations," in *Local Dynamics in an Era of Globalization,* edited by Shahid Yusuf, Weiping Wu, and Simon Evenett (Oxford University Press, 2000); and James Wunsch and Dele Olowu, eds., *Local Governance in Africa: The Challenge of Democratic Decentralization* (Boulder, Colo.: Lynne Rienner, 2003).

10. For a discussion of this issue, see Paul Smoke, "Fiscal Decentralization in Africa: Goals, Dimensions, Myths and Challenges," *Public Administration and Development* 23, no. 1 (2003): 7–16.

11. Good discussions of democratic decentralization and accountability are provided in James Manor, *Political Economy of Democratic Decentralization* (World Bank, 1998); Harry Blair, "Participation and Power at the Periphery: Democratic Local Governance in Six Countries," *World Development* 28, no. 1 (2000): 21–40; and Dele Olowu, "Local Institutional and Political Structures and Processes: Recent Experience in Africa," *Public Administration and Development* 23, no. 1 (2003): 41–52.

12. These weaknesses are elaborated in David K. Leonard, "The Political Realities of African Management," *World Development* 15, no. 7 (1987): 899–910; Tendler, *Good Government in the Tropics;* Litvack, Ahmad, and Bird, *Rethinking Decentralization in Developing Countries;* Cohen and Peterson, *Administrative Decentralization in Developing Countries;* and Smoke, *Fiscal Decentralization in Developing Countries.*

13. The seminal work is the book by Oates, *Fiscal Federalism.*

14. Critiques of the application of fiscal federalism in developing countries include Paul Smoke, "Is Local Public Finance Theory Relevant for Developing Countries?" Development Discussion Paper 316, Harvard Institute for International Development, 1989; Remy Prud'homme, "The Dangers of Decentralization," *World Bank Research Observer* 10, no. 2

(1995): 201–20; Bird and Vaillancourt, *Fiscal Decentralization in Developing Countries;* Litvack, Ahmad, and Bird, *Rethinking Decentralization in Developing Countries;* and Smoke, "Strategic Fiscal Decentralization in Developing Countries."

15. Roy Bahl and Jorge Martinez-Vazquez, "Sequencing Decentralization," World Bank, 2005.

16. Romeo, "The Role of External Assistance in Supporting Decentralization Reform," for a discussion of these issues.

17. Cohen and Peterson, *Administrative Decentralization in Developing Countries,* for more extensive discussions.

18. For an extended discussion, see Paul Smoke, Eduardo Gomez, and George Peterson, eds., *Decentralization in Asia and Latin America: Towards a Comparative Interdisciplinary Perspective* (Cheltenham, U.K.: Edward Elgar, 2007).

19. The South Africa case is discussed in Roy Bahl and Paul Smoke, eds., *Restructuring Local Government in Developing Countries: Lessons from South Africa* (Cheltenham, U.K.: Edward Elgar, 2003). The Indonesia case is discussed below. The Thailand case is discussed in World Bank, *East Asia Decentralizes: Making Local Government Work* (2005).

20. The Uganda case is discussed in Martin Onyach-Olaa, "The Challenges of Implementing Decentralization: Recent Experiences in Uganda," *Public Administration and Development* 23, no. 1 (2003): 105–13; and Paul Frances and Robert James, "Balancing Rural Poverty Reduction and Citizen Participation: The Contradictions of Uganda's Decentralization Program," *World Development* 31, no. 2 (2003): 325–37.

21. The experience of Argentina and Brazil is discussed in Kent Eaton and Tyler Dickovich, "Decentralization and Recentralization in Argentina and Brazil," in *Decentralization in Asia and Latin America: Towards a Comparative Interdisciplinary Perspective,* edited by Paul Smoke, Eduardo Gomez, and George Peterson (Cheltenham, U.K.: Edward Elgar, 2007).

22. For a more detailed discussion of the evolution of decentralization and local government reform in Kenya, see Paul Smoke, "Local Government Fiscal Reform in Developing Countries: Lessons from Kenya," *World Development* 21, no. 6 (1993); Paul Smoke, *Local Government Finance in Developing Countries: The Case of Kenya* (Oxford University Press, 1994); Paul Smoke, "Erosion and Reform from the Center in Kenya," in *Local Governance in Africa: The Challenge of Democratic Decentralization,* edited by James Wunsch and Dele Olowu (Boulder, Colo.: Lynne Rienner, 2003).

23. Nick Devas and Roy Kelly, "Regulation or Revenues: Analysis of Local Business Licenses, with a Case Study of the Single Business Permit in Kenya," *Public Administration and Development* 21, no. 5 (2001): 381–91.

24. For more detailed discussion of decentralization in Indonesia, see Paul Smoke and Blane Lewis, "Fiscal Decentralization in Indonesia: A New Approach to an Old Idea," *World Development* 24, no. 8 (1996): 1281–99; Bert Hofman and Kai Kaiser, "The Making of the Big Bang and Its Aftermath: A Political Economy Perspective," in *Reforming Intergovernmental Fiscal Relations and the Rebuilding of Indonesia,* edited by James Alm, Jorge Martinez-Vazquez, and Sri Mulyani Indrawati (Cheltenham, U.K.: Edward Elgar, 2004); World Bank, *East Asia Decentralizes;* Kai Kaiser, Daan Pattinasarany, and Günther Schulze, "Decentralization, Governance and Public Services in Indonesia," in *Decentralization in Asia and Latin America: Towards a Comparative Interdisciplinary Perspective,* edited by Paul Smoke, Eduardo Gomez, and George Peterson (Cheltenham, U.K.: Edward Elgar, 2007); and Blane D. Lewis, "Indonesian Local Government Spending, Taxing and Saving: An Explanation of Pre- and Post-Decentralization Fiscal Outcomes," *Asian Economic Journal* 19, no. 3 (2005): 291–317.

25. Much of the analysis of Cambodia's recent experiences is based on interviews and observations by the author. Limited available literature includes Mark Turner, "Whatever Happened

to Deconcentration? Recent Initiatives in Cambodia," *Public Administration and Development* 22, no. 3 (2002): 353–64; World Bank, *Cambodia Integrated Fiduciary Assessment and Public Expenditure Review* (2003); Peter Blunt and Mark Turner, "Decentralization, Democracy and Development in a Post-Conflict Society: Commune Councils in Cambodia," *Public Administration and Development* 25, no. 1 (2005): 77–85.

26. For more information, see "Cambodia's Recent History: CARERE 1," and "The Seila Initiative," United Nations Capital Development Fund (www.uncdf.org).

9

Government Decentralization and Decentralized Governance in Latin America: The Silent Revolution of the Local Level?

ENRIQUE CABRERO

During much of the twentieth century, Latin American governments maintained strong tendencies toward centralization. This was partly due to the need to take actions to control violent or revolutionary processes earlier in the century and to the need, later, for strong policies to overcome regional inequality and heterogeneity. In addition, a centralized political and administrative system had been strongly rooted in Latin American culture since pre-Hispanic times.

However, in the last quarter of the twentieth century, the Latin American centralized model began to be seen as an obstacle to development. The world economy began to transform itself at an accelerated speed, forcing Latin American states to join a new world dynamic. At the same time, most of the region's countries underwent important political changes that brought a transition toward more pluralistic democracy and the redistribution of power, ushering in a new era of decentralization. Governments in different countries, at different paces, began to transfer resources and responsibilities for policymaking and implementation to subnational regions and localities. Subnational governments also began to develop their own political agendas, and all levels of government began to integrate organizations of civil society into public policymaking.

The author thanks José Antonio Peña and Miguel Guajardo for their invaluable help in gathering data.

Figure 9-1. *Subnational Public Expenditure in Latin America, 1987–2003*

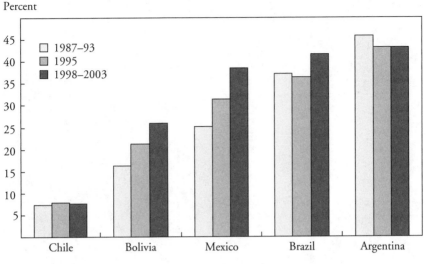

Percent

Source: Compiled by author.

This chapter describes the emergence of decentralization in Latin America, looking first at aspects of government decentralization in some Latin American countries such as Argentina, Brazil, Chile, and Mexico from the top-down approach. A second objective is to analyze the dynamics created by local governments (bottom up) as well as the impact of decentralized governance that is deeply transforming public participation in Latin American countries. Third, this chapter examines some of the challenges currently facing Latin American countries in relation to advances in decentralization.

Three Decades of Government Decentralization in Latin America: The Top-Down Approach

How much has decentralization advanced in Latin America? One way to answer this question is to examine progress with fiscal decentralization in four countries: Chile, Argentina, Mexico, and Brazil. With the exception of Chile, these countries have each in their own way decentralized to subnational governments both public expenditures and public revenues. Argentina and Brazil have high levels of subnational fiscal decentralization for both expenditure and revenue, Bolivia is advancing in that direction, and Mexico has decentralized public expenditure but not public revenue. Chile maintains a high level of fiscal centralization (see figures 9-1 and 9-2).[1]

In addition to the fiscal aspect, decentralization has also progressed in health, education, social welfare, and antipoverty policies.

Figure 9-2. *Subnational Revenue in Latin America, 1987–2003*

Percent

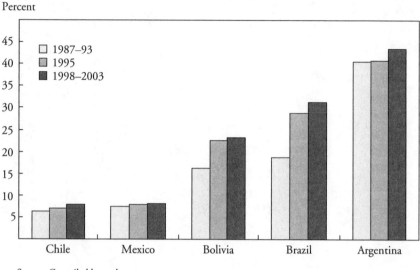

Source: Compiled by author.

Decentralization of Health Policy

Although policies decentralizing health services began in the 1970s and 1980s (with the exception of Argentina, with antecedents going back to 1957), they were only carried out more intensively in the 1990s. In general national governments decentralized—to a greater or lesser extent in each country—operational and administrative functions to subnational governments while withholding control over the formulation of policies and regulations and over some aspects of financing.[2]

In Brazil, for example, the government decentralized health services to state and municipal governments. In Argentina and Mexico, the states received most of the powers transferred from the center, although in Argentina municipalities participated in health services in some provinces. In Chile, a unitary state with only two levels of government (the regional level of administration consists of deconcentrated national government agencies), health services were transferred from the central government to the municipalities.

In Brazil and Argentina the decentralization process resulted in a new intergovernmental balance of services. Subnational governments received not only operating responsibilities but also decisionmaking powers, giving them a greater degree of autonomy. In Brazil three levels of government were involved in health policies. The federal government is in charge of formulating national health policies, designing health standards, and evaluating general directives. The states are responsible for designing policies for and controlling health service delivery in their jurisdictions. The municipalities are in charge of the formulation, administration, and execution of the programs for local health services. All three levels participate in financing, but those responsibilities decentralized to subnational governments come with no specific directives, implying a large amount of autonomy for the states and municipalities in using these resources.

In Argentina the provinces received broad operational, legislative, and programmatic powers and functions that minimized the federal government's role in health policies and reduced its specific powers over planning, regulation, and control.[3] Financial resources come mainly from the federal government with supplements from the provinces, which have a great deal of flexibility in using them.[4]

In Mexico and Chile the government transferred new responsibilities to subnational governments but withheld powers over health policymaking. In Mexico the federal government retained responsibility for developing health policies and standards and for monitoring, evaluating, and coordinating services. The states remained directly in charge of managing and operating health services.[5] Financing is completely in the hands of the federal government, which provides financial transfers to the states for current expense, medical infrastructure, workforce, and complementary contributions. The states are only responsible for administering these resources, which they distribute at their discretion according to local needs and priorities.[6]

In Chile the central government—through the Ministry of Health—is in charge of formulating the sector's policies, of supervising their implementation, and of adjusting policies to the needs of regions through the regional governments. The central government also provides second- and third-level services, while the municipalities are in charge of providing primary health care (consultation offices and first aid posts), for which they have no programmatic autonomy nor management flexibility but only the ability to hire staff.[7] The financing of the health services, including primary health care, still depends primarily on the central government through per capita subventions transferred to the municipality based on the amount of services provided.

All of the countries, with the exception of Chile, have the means—for example, through the Federal Health Council in Argentina, the intermanagement commissions in Brazil, and the National Health Council in Mexico—of coordinating health services among the levels of government involved. It is in the health sector that intergovernmental coordination has been most effective in Latin America, although there is still much room for improvement.

Decentralization of Education Policy

Unlike in the health sector, the beginning of decentralization in the education sector was not simultaneous or homogeneous in the four countries under study.

In Argentina this process began in 1978 and ended in 1992. In Brazil and Chile the decentralization of education began in the 1980s and concluded during the following decade. In Mexico this process began and concluded during the 1990s.[8] The government decentralized responsibilities to states and municipalities in Brazil and Mexico (although in the latter the local governments play a minor role), exclusively to states in Argentina, and to municipalities in Chile. Similar to what occurred in the health sector, education decentralization resulted in different arrangements in these four countries.

In Brazil three levels of government shared responsibilities because the federal government withheld many powers of regulation. State and municipal levels were given authority to establish their own education systems and to legislate on the most important aspects of basic education such as curricula, length and duration of school days, recruiting and training of teachers, professional career development, and teachers' remuneration. Financing of education was shared, and the constitution called for 18 percent of national tax revenues and 25 percent of state and municipal revenues (including transfers) to be allocated to the development and maintenance of basic education.

In Argentina the new governmental balance favored the provinces even though the federal government withheld important powers such as the regulation and administration of the university and technical systems. The government decentralized the leading roles in spending for and in managing elementary, secondary, and higher education facilities and implementing education plans and policies to the provincial level. Financing is a shared responsibility, because the provinces, in addition to contributing their own resources, receive funding from the central level to cover part of the expenses, and they use these resources with a good deal of autonomy.

In Chile, after decentralization, the distribution of responsibilities in education included a primary role for the central government in designing and evaluating educational and cultural policies, assigning resources, and granting official certification to education establishments. The central government also controlled, inspected, and supervised several aspects of administration through its regional secretaries. On the other hand, the municipalities and private schools provided basic and middle education with state subsidies for specific services.[9] The central government develops the financial plans and distributes and assigns funds among the municipalities and subsidized private schools according to enrollment and attendance. However, in special situations—such as rural schools, schools in secluded areas, and schools with high socioeconomic vulnerability—the municipalities transfer resources of their own.

In Mexico decentralization resulted in a new institutional scheme of formal concurrence among the three levels of government, the decentralized organizations, and private schools. In this concurrence, the federal government centralizes the essential functions and decentralizes those that are operational. The federal government is in charge of determining study plans and programs for primary, secondary, and normal education for the entire republic. It regulates, evaluates, and determines the sector's general characteristics, including study plans and programs, the school calendar, and the national system for teacher training. It determines the resources that the local authorities assign to the sector's development. The states are in charge of providing basic education and teacher training as well as proposing to the federal government regional components to include in study plans. The local level, as mentioned earlier, has highly restricted powers with regard to the maintenance of education centers. The federal government maintains responsibility for most of the education financing and transfers to the subnational levels funds for recurrent expenditures for salaries, services, and operational costs. The previously established criteria for assigning resources include the common school register and workforce per state, leaving little room for maneuver in the management of transferred resources.

In general, the processes of education decentralization did not provide for much flexibility in formulation, negotiation, and monitoring of policies between the central and subnational levels, except for Argentina and for some attempts in Brazil and Mexico. It is clear that there has been little intergovernmental coordination in this sector; it is simply assumed that the formal distribution of functions among the levels of government automatically resolves the coordination problem. In Mexico, for example, the absence of coordination mechanisms has created very few state initiatives in education. The municipalities occasionally come up with educational improvement activities that are completely disconnected from the other levels of government. The federal government simply does not acknowledge them and even tries to inhibit them.[10]

Decentralization of Social Welfare and Antipoverty Policies

The decentralization of social welfare and antipoverty policies in the analyzed countries (with the exception of Argentina) evolved through two periods. The first, in the late 1980s and early 1990s, was characterized by the intensive use of programs focused on community development. At least theoretically, subnational governments and civil society organizations played a strategic role in the operation of these programs. In general, these were programs with strong components for the generation of capital, citizen empowerment, and community participation in decisionmaking. This is where the intervention of the subnational governments became strategic for the adaptation of the national guidelines to the particular needs of their jurisdictions. This is the case with programs such as Comunidad Solidaria in Brazil, and Entre todos (Fosis) in Chile, which required a strong connection with the subnational governments for their operation (states and municipalities in Brazil and municipalities in Chile). A special case is the Programa Nacional de Solidaridad (Pronasol) in Mexico. It theoretically could fit into this type of initiative but, in practice, remained a highly centralized program. It reduced the power of subnational governments, contributed to the tightening of relations between the organized citizens (Comités de Solidaridad) and the federal agencies (Program Delegates), making it possible to establish a direct relationship between the federal authority and the local organized groups.[11]

The second period, which began in the mid-1990s and early 2000s, was characterized by a recentralization of control over policy by the national governments, adopting strategies of focused assistance that weakened the role of community development organizations, although these programs continued to operate with a few modifications in Brazil, Chile, and Mexico.[12] The new type of program directly transferred a financial subsidy to families living in extreme poverty. The participation of other government levels, therefore, was not required to adapt the policy to local conditions. In this sense, in many of these programs, the municipalities and state governments actually play the role of operators with little or no influence on the formulation of policy.

Among the programs using this strategy were Plan Jefes y Jefas de Hogar Desocupados in Argentina, Hambre Cero in Brazil, Sistema Chile Solidario in Chile, and Oportunidades in Mexico. Subnational governments play a bigger role in antipoverty policy in Brazil's Hambre Cero program, the main objective of which is to fight hunger, poverty, and inequality by transferring a monetary bonus associated with access to basic social rights (health, education, social assistance, and food security). Even though decentralization is not the main objective of this initiative, the three levels of government are jointly responsible for the program's implementation and for selecting the beneficiary families.[13] While the federal government is in charge of design, monitoring, and control and of directly intervening in the program's implementation, the states and municipalities are exclusively responsible for the program's operations. The federal government transfers money to poor families, but the states and municipalities can increase the resources for the families from their own budgets.

In the case of Plan Jefes y Jefas de Hogar Desocupados, in Argentina, the objective was to offer economic support to unemployed parents, guaranteeing access to health care and school for the children and work training for the parents, as well as involving the parents in productive projects. The federal government, through the Ministry of Labor, formulates standards and regulations, issues support, and participates directly in implementation. The municipalities are in charge of execution, in cooperation with a municipal advisory council; their main work is assigning the activities that the beneficiaries of the program must perform as repayment for the monetary subsidy. The federal funds are assigned to each jurisdiction, which is responsible for distributing the subsidies according to productive or social projects designated by the province, the municipality, or the civil society organizations.

Sistema de Proteccion Social Chile Solidario is, as are the other programs, an assistance-oriented strategy that focuses its resources and activities on families living in extreme poverty. The central government is responsible for the entire process: designing, planning, financing, and evaluating the program. The municipalities, on the other hand, identify the families eligible for support, connect them with the programs that make up the system, and coordinate the execution of the programs, although without affecting the way in which the program is managed.[14]

Finally, the Oportunidades program in Mexico involves a direct transfer of subsidies to families living in poverty, and social participation is not a central element. The program considers conditional transfers in the form of nutritional subsistence allowances, scholarships, minimum health care, and monetary support to elders. The federal levels have normative, regulatory, operational, and administrative powers, while the state and municipal governments have operational and administrative powers. The federal government assigns resources directly to the benefited families based on a national census.

In general, in the four countries, intergovernmental coordination in social protection policy and antipoverty programs remains incipient, although some attempts have been made to allow for negotiation through organizations such as the Federal Council for Social Development in Argentina, the National Commission for Social Development in Mexico, and regulatory councils in Brazil. In Chile, which is a unitary state, social development policy is coordinated in a hierarchical manner by a central ministry.

Government Decentralization under the Top-Down Model

In summary, top-down government decentralization in most Latin American countries is a process that remains incomplete. With a few exceptions, decentralization has generally consisted of the transfer of responsibilities and resources to subnational governments but with the national governments withholding the most important powers in the political decisionmaking process. Perhaps one of the most advanced cases is Brazil, where the experience of decentralization has been special because, to some degree, the central government has granted subnational governments more autonomy in the management of resources and more administrative responsibilities.[15] In addition, one can see an effort to share more responsibility among the three levels of government.

However, even in Brazil this process has faced difficulties because in many cases the municipalities and states did not have sufficient institutional capacities to perform the new tasks, resulting occasionally in inappropriate and irresponsible management of finances. In Argentina, even though the process consisted of an extensive transfer of responsibilities to subnational governments, the delimitation of the functions and roles that each level must perform is unclear, especially in the fiscal area.[16] In Mexico several studies agree that the process basically consisted of a transfer of resources and obligations to the states without the corresponding transfer of the powers of decisionmaking. As a result, after decentralization the balance of power among the three levels of government still favors the center.[17] Finally, in Chile, the central government transferred responsibilities but not decisionmaking power to the municipalities.[18] Subnational regions, on the other hand, continue to be deconcentrated units of the central government. Municipalities remain dependent to a great extent on the resources and decisions of the central government.

The fact that decentralization remains incomplete does not mean that there have not been serious problems of intergovernmental coordination. In fact one reason for the resistance of central governments to further decentralization is the perceived danger in dispersing responsibilities to other levels of government. In addition, lags in creating stronger managerial capacity in subnational governments also inhibit more progress in decentralization.

Last, it is worth mentioning that the top-down decentralizing effort, being erratic and incomplete, has led to frustration on the part of local governments, whose leaders are not willing to wait any longer to develop their own public policy agendas. Local governments, facing day-to-day growing citizen demands, new challenges of economic and social development, and complex challenges of local administration, are forced to react with their own initiatives, develop new forms of management, create new mechanisms for dialogue with citizens, and build public-private alliances. This process generates de facto decentralization, a bottom-up process that characterizes the new setting of decentralization in Latin America.

Decentralized Governance on a Local Level: The Bottom-Up Approach

To determine how local Latin American governments have been intervening more in affairs in which they traditionally had limited powers, a sample of local management experiences in the countries under study were analyzed. A sample of successful programs was also selected. In Brazil, Chile, and Mexico the database consisted of municipal programs in each of these countries so as to identify the best practices of local management.[19] Data on successful local experiences in Argentina were compiled by two academic institutions.[20] The first level of analysis involved 7,848 programs.

An analysis of the complete sample is shown in table 9-1. The analysis indicates clearly the tendency of municipalities to carry out more activities than they are traditionally and formally obliged to perform and thus to be engaged in de facto decentralization from the bottom up. The results of the follow-up analysis of a small sample of programs evaluated as successful are shown in table 9-2.

Table 9-1. *Number of Successful Innovative Municipal Programs, Argentina, Brazil, Chile, Mexico*

Country	Programs	Programs not formally municipal	Programs evaluated as successful[a]
Argentina	136	87	87
Brazil	4,778	2,527	72
Chile	730	613	48
Mexico	2,204	1,070	85

a. These include programs for education, health, housing, social development, poverty, employment, vulnerable groups, culture, sports, economic development, and environment.

Table 9-2. *Number of Innovative Municipal Programs, by Public Policy Aim, Argentina, Brazil, Chile, Mexico*

Country	Social and community development	Assistance to vulnerable groups	Education	Health	Economic development	Environment
Argentina	11	5	14	7	35	11
Brazil	17	12	11	12	14	6
Chile	13	4	11	9	4	7
Mexico	15	15	14	7	20	14

A breakdown of the six broad program categories shown in table 9-2 follows:

—Economic development includes the creation of funds to support rural productive projects, credit for microenterprises, development of regional productive clusters, investment promotion centers and microenterprise incubators.

—Social and community development includes community organization programs for the construction of houses and social infrastructure, citizens' participation in local management and prioritization of community projects, a participatory budget, municipal programs to promote employment and productive associations in underserved areas, and credit programs for family microenterprises.

—Educational promotion includes scholarship programs, excellence awards to teachers and students, diffusion and promotion of cultural and sports-related activities, and building and equipping education centers and libraries.

—Assistance to vulnerable groups focuses on such groups as natives and other racial minorities, indigents, abused women, elders, marginalized youth, and children.

—Environmental protection includes the promotion of environmental care practices, development of ecotourism programs, creation of centers for the treatment of solid waste, creation of protected ecological areas, and rescue and rehabilitation of natural resources.

Table 9-3. *Number of Innovative Municipal Programs, by Management, Argentina, Brazil, Chile, Mexico*

Country	Municipality	Citizens and municipality	Inter-governmental	Citizens, municipality, and other government levels	Civil society organization
Argentina	38	15	7	6	...
Brazil	33	18	13	0	...
Chile	12	17	2	5	12
Mexico	40	25	14	6	...

—Health promotion includes fights against infectious diseases, promotion of good health habits, improvement and equipping of health centers, and the integration of groups with no access to health services.

In both Brazil and Chile, municipal programs of social and community development were more frequently reported, while in Mexico and Argentina economic development programs are the most representative.

The lion's share (47 percent) of the management of these programs is at the municipal level (table 9-3). This means that the municipalities design and implement them endogenously and with resources that they can obtain autonomously. In those carried out under the comanagement of local government and citizens (29 percent), the latter participate in at least one stage of policy formulation, design, operation, or evaluation. Intergovernmental programs involving national and state governments and coordinated with the local government (14 percent) include those in which two or more municipalities agree to provide a service or to carry out jointly activities that would benefit their communities. In about 5 percent of the sample (all of which are in Chile), the initiatives came from civil society organizations. In the remaining 6 percent of the sample were programs that could be considered part of a network of public policies in which the municipal as well as other levels of government and civil society intervene.

Decentralized Governance under the Bottom-Up Model

The municipal programs in the sample indicate the vigor and drive that local communities have exhibited in Latin American countries for more than a decade. These are public policy initiatives that are often less robust technically and institutionally than those of the central government but are more spontaneous and are carried out with greater participation of citizens.[21] In fact in many cases it is hard to identify whether the program originated from the community, from municipal officials, from some civil society organization, or even from private groups that also participate actively in some cases. They are often the result of innovative alliances that emerge from local public actions of "high intensity."[22]

Particularly in the field of social policy, there has been a significant increase in the participation of municipalities, indicating their innovative capacity for the design of new policies.[23]

Despite the occasionally marginal or sometimes indefinite role that top-down decentralization has given them in Latin American countries, many local governments have performed—often with their own resources—activities promoting social well-being, economic development, and environmental protection. Local governments, without necessarily being required to do so by the central government, are obliged to react to local demands and to display democratic governance.

Even though this dynamism and innovation in local governments is not yet dominant in Latin America, it has grown surprisingly over the past decade and seems to be transforming democratic practices and public policymaking. However, this innovative tendency coexists with the tradition of local government lacking management capacities and of the central government dominating local programs. It is a setting in which tradition and change coexist. Many local governments manifest, at the same time, practices of good governance and the worst examples of authoritarianism and incompetence in government affairs. In any event, this analysis seems to indicate that the innovative spirit of local governments may spread more rapidly in years to come.

Conclusion

In much of Latin America progress on decentralization is caught between two forces. On the one hand is an attempt to advance decentralization by imposing the vision of the central government; this vision seeks to expand decentralization in an orderly way with central government resources and standards and sees local governments as not having the institutional and administrative capacities for broad control and direction, leaving those in the hands of the central government. From this point of view, it seems that decentralization must progress through top-down policies.

On the other hand, decentralized governance is also emerging from the bottom, advancing with another logic and vision. In this vision, local governments make public policy jointly with citizens. Those acting under this vision see central government initiatives as slow, lacking an understanding of local conditions, and not allowing for appropriate attention to local problems. The bottom-up approach to decentralization recognizes that local governments, due to their proximity to the problems and to the citizens, should prevail and believes that central and state governments should be supportive of local initiatives.

Sometimes these visions coincide and generate efficient policymaking through complementary actions among levels of government. However, in most of Latin America this occurs more because of a fortuitous encounter than by intergovernmental coordination. Although central governments in Latin America have transferred functions and resources to subnational governments, the slowness and uncertainty of the process has also stimulated local governments to develop innovative programs for management and for interaction with citizens.

Yet the unfinished agenda of decentralization poses challenges for Latin American countries. One is how central governments can develop new capacities for regulation and incentives without imposing rigid controls on local governments. A second challenge is to encourage local governments to pursue innovative local policies while cooperating with other levels of government. For decentralization to succeed, it is necessary for local governments to become professional quickly and to channel their dynamism and innovativeness through stable institutional channels.

Depending on how governments address these challenges, we will see in Latin America either the consolidation of decentralizing processes or institutional and political crises that will push toward recentralization because of the lack of order and efficiency in local government.

Notes

1. For a broader analysis of fiscal decentralization in Latin America, see Enrique Cabrero, "Los retos institucionales de la descentralización fiscal en América Latina," *Reforma y Democracia* 34 (February 2006): 185–216; International Monetary Fund, *Government Finance Statistics, Yearbook 2004* (2004).

2. According to Serrano and Fernández, the federation executes the powers of regulation and control indirectly, through autonomous regulatory agencies. The Ministry of Health, on the other hand, remains an institution in charge of indicative planning and of monitoring the fulfillment of international agreements on the subject. See C. Serrano and I. Fernández, *Estudio Comparativo: Descentralizacion de las Politicas y Programas de Reduccion de la Pobreza en América Latina,* Diálogo Regional de Política (Interamerican Development Bank, 2005).

3. Emanuela Di Gropello and Rossella Cominetti, *La Descentralización de la Educación y La Salud: Un Análisis Comparativo de la Experiencia Latinoamericana* (Economic Commission for Latin America and the Caribbean, 1998).

4. Tulia Faletti, "Federalism and Decentralization in Argentina: Historical Background and New Intergovernmental Relations," in *Decentralization and Democratic Governance in Latin America,* edited by Joseph S. Tulchin and Andrew D. Selee (Woodrow Wilson International Center, 2004).

5. As indicated earlier, the receptor of decentralization in Mexico was the state. However, some federal initiatives seek to incorporate the municipalities more actively in health policies. An example of this is the Municipios Saludables program, under which the federation transfers resources directly to the municipalities as compensation for commitments established by the municipal authorities and the civil society, with the objective of adopting diverse preventive health activities recommended by the federal government.

6. Serrano and Fernández, *Estudio Comparativo.*

7. The Health Services are decentralized organizations of the central government; they are autonomous, with legal personality and their own patrimony. See Di Gropello and Cominetti, *La Descentralización de la Educación y La Salud.*

8. Serrano and Fernández, *Estudio Comparativo.*

9. Each municipality is obliged to submit its Annual Plan of Education Development, proposing objectives, the year's action programs, and the budget for income, expenses, and investment.

10. Enrique Cabrero, "Descentralización de la Política Social y Nuevo Papel de los Gobiernos Locales ¿Políticas Multinivel o Múltiples Políticas? El Caso de México," in *Descentralización y Política Social en América Latina,* edited by R. Goma and J. Jordana (Fundacion CIDOB, 2004).

11. Enrique Cabrero, "La ola Descentralizadora: Un Análisis de Tendencias y Obstáculos de las Políticas Descentralizadoras en el Ámbito Internacional," in *Las Políticas Descentralizadoras en México (1983–1993),* edited by E. Cabrero (Center for International and Development Education, 1998).

12. The Comunidad Solidaria program in Brazil transformed its institutional design in such a way that it is no longer directly attached to the governmental system but is under the coordination of a civil society organization (Comunitas) that receives public and private financing (Serrano and Fernández, *Estudio Comparativo*). In the case of Pronasol, it was disintegrated in 1995, and the funds that established it were decentralized to states and municipalities through what, since 1998, was called the Social Infrastructure Fund (a fund of the branch budget called Ramo 33). Under this scheme, the federation maintained a normative function in regard to the fields in which the resources could be spent and the distribution criteria, whereas the municipalities had to promote the creation of citizen councils in order to make decisions together regarding the assignment of funds and the prioritizing and supervision of investments.

13. See Serrano and Fernández, *Estudio Comparativo.*

14. Ibid.

15. Marcus Melo and Flavio Rezende, "Decentralization and Governance in Brazil," in *Decentralization and Democratic Governance in Latin America,* edited by Tulchin and Selee.

16. Faletti, "Federalism and Decentralization in Argentina."

17. Cabrero, "Descentralización de la Política Social y Nuevo Papel"; Yemile Mizrahi, "Twenty Years of Decentralization in Mexico: A Top-Down Process," in *Democratization, Democratic Governance and Civil Society in Comparative Perspective,* edited by F. Oxhorn, J. S. Tulchin, and A. Selee (Woodrow Wilson International Center, 2004).

18. Serrano and Fernández, *Estudio Comparativo.*

19. The results were compiled from *Gestao Publica e Cidadania,* carried out by Fundação Getulio Vargas in Brazil; *Ciudadania y Gestion Local* program, carried out by Fundacion para la Superacion de la Pobreza in Chile; and *Gobierno y Gestion Local* program, carried out by the Center for International and Development Education in Mexico. The studies were supported by the Ford Foundation and have similar evaluation methodologies. The analyzed experiences are those registered from 2001 to 2005 in the three countries.

20. The Argentinean programs were taken from *Banco de Experiencias Locales* organized by Universidad de Quilmes and Universidad Nacional General Sarmiento. This bank has records for successful government programs from 1997 to 2004.

21. For more on this subject, see Enrique Cabrero, "La Agenda de Políticas Públicas en el Ámbito Municipal: Una Visión Introductoria," in *Políticas Públicas Municipales. Una Agenda en Construcción,* edited by Enrique Cabrero (Center for International and Development Education, 2003).

22. A reflection on the nature of new local alliances is presented in Gonzalo Delamaza, *Tan Lejos Tan Cerca: Políticas Públicas y Sociedad Civil en Chile* (Santiago: LOM Ediciones Chile, 2005).

23. For more on this subject, see I. Camarotti and P. Spink, *Reducto da Pobreza e Dinamicas Locais* (São Paulo: Fundação Getulio Vargas, 2001).

10

Devolution with Accountability: Learning from Good Practices

G. SHABBIR CHEEMA

The devolution of powers and resources to local governments is essential to promote sustainable decentralization in developing countries. Local governments with decisionmaking powers and ability to raise resources through their own mechanisms are able to play a catalytic role in the development process. Furthermore, citizens are more likely to actively participate in the local political process where local government is perceived to be sufficiently autonomous in making political decisions affecting them. This improves the quality of the local democratic process.

One of the challenges in promoting devolution in developing countries, however, is that frequently the local elite captures services and facilities provided through local governments or field offices of central government. Also corruption and misuse of authority are sometimes more rampant at the local than at the national level. These problems are more serious in societies that are characterized by highly inequitable social and economic structures and high incidence of poverty and illiteracy. Even the strongest advocates of decentralization argue, therefore, that effective devolution requires corresponding mechanisms to ensure accountability of local actors—politicians, government officials, representatives of civil society, and others involved in allocating resources and influencing local political decisions.

This chapter examines the relationship between decentralization and democratic governance, devolution as an essential ingredient of decentralization, and the significance of accountability and anticorruption strategies at the local level to promote the legitimacy and effectiveness of devolution. The chapter then identifies and discusses six mechanisms and instruments to enhance the accountability and transparency of local governments.

Decentralization and Democratic Governance

Democratic governance is characterized by such fundamental principles as participation, transparency, accountability, access, subsidiarity, representation, separation of powers, and an independent judiciary. Decentralization is conducive to achievement of these principles.[1] It provides an institutional framework at the subnational, local, and community levels through which groups and citizens can organize themselves and participate in political and economic decisions affecting them. Decentralization thus provides avenues and opportunities for representation by political, religious, and ethnic groups and the participation of the opposition groups in the political process (in the case of South Africa and Uganda, the latter has promoted national unity).

Democratic governance is thus achieved through a decentralization policy that

—Promotes accountability and transparency of central government officials. Because of their day-to-day interaction with local political leaders, central government officials are more likely to be held accountable for their actions than in situations where decisions are made by the central government—in many cases far away from local areas. Decentralization also improves closer monitoring by the beneficiary population of projects intended to serve them.

—Promotes the institutionalization of democratic culture by providing opportunities to groups and individuals to make political and financial decisions affecting their jurisdiction, by ongoing dialogue among local actors, and by utilizing the knowledge and expertise of communities. This creates an environment of local ownership of programs and projects.

—Helps create checks and balances among the center, the subnational level, and the local level (one of the key ingredients of democratic governance). Decentralization thus promotes a political environment of accommodation and negotiation.

—Facilitates the growth of civil society organizations and networks by providing for the establishment of civil society organizations to address local issues that directly affect the lives of the people.

Decentralization to municipalities and towns is especially important for two reasons. First, the urban population of the world has expanded from 30 percent in 1950 to 47 percent to 2000 and is projected to increase to 60 percent by 2030. Second, cities and towns are the principal drivers of social and economic development and technological transformation.[2] Cities mean an increase in productivity and improved quality of goods and services; they are also centers of ideas, innovations, and learning. Decentralization allows the emergence of an "inclusive city," or one that facilitates full utilization of energies and resources of all groups in the community, including civil society organizations.

Decentralization is not a substitute, however, for developing democratic governance. Many dangers and pitfalls associated with decentralization can impede the design and implementation of elements of liberal democracy. In some cases, authoritarian local leaders get elected and rule undemocratically.[3] In countries such as Colombia, members of opposition parties are subjected to violence. In some democracies with a federal system of government, such as Brazil, there are serious tensions between human rights agendas and the policies of the federal and state—and even local—governments. For example, political decentralization in Estonia and Latvia led to the exclusion of Russians—almost 40 percent of the population in Estonia—through language and citizenships laws. Other dangers of decentralization are that it can increase geographic inequalities due to the different resource bases of subnational units; it may lead to redundancy and inefficiency because of the lack of clear delineation of authority and responsibilities; and it may lead to more divisions among the society based on ethnicity.[4]

Devolution to the Local Level

Decentralization is a broad concept. As a means, it can improve efficiency and effectiveness of public services. As an end in itself, it can promote the basic principles of democratic governance. It can take one or more of four forms:
—Deconcentration of responsibilities from central government ministries and departments to subnational and local levels
—Delegation of powers to semiautonomous bodies to perform specific tasks
—Devolution of powers and resources to local governments
—Transfer of responsibilities to nongovernmental organizations.

In practice, all countries have a combination of these forms, ranging from a focus on deconcentration and delegation with limited devolution to much more focus on devolution of political, financial, and administrative authority to directly elected local governments. To varying degrees, each form of decentralization contributes to democratic governance. Deconcentration in these forms brings government officials—and administrative decisionmaking—closer to the people, giving citizens opportunities to monitor government programs. Delegation, though it brings decisionmaking about specific activities closer to the people who are affected, does not provide direct channels for local political control as in the case of devolution.

Decentralization through transfer to nongovernmental organizations often involves contracting out partial service provision, administration functions, and deregulation or full privatization. Public functions could be transferred to trade associations, professional organizations, farmers' cooperatives, and women's and youth associations. This form of decentralization also positively affects the promotion of democratic processes because it allows decisions to be made through processes that involve a large number of political interests.

While each of the above forms of decentralization indirectly contributes to achieving the goals of democratic governance, devolution of powers and resources to elected local governments is the key ingredient of democracy and good governance. Devolution is aimed at creating or strengthening independent units of government by devolving functions and authority. Its fundamental characteristics are the autonomous nature of local units of government, legally recognized geographical boundaries within which they exercise their authority, and the power of local governments to mobilize resources to perform their tasks. This form of decentralization also implies that local governments are seen as institutions that provide services to local citizens who have control over their functioning. Local governments are one level of the national political system, each with mutually beneficial and legally recognized roles and responsibilities.[5]

The global trends toward devolution of political and financial authority are visible in many recent country-level decentralization initiatives. In India, with two amendments to the constitution in 1992 including reservation of one-third of the seats for women, local governments have been strengthened. In 1999 about 238,000 local councils were elected across the country.

In Ghana the restructuring of local governments has provided more authority and resources to local governments. Within the guidelines provided by the National Development Planning Commission, districts have considerable autonomy to decide on their own development needs and priorities and have more control over resources. They can raise some of their own resources and can negotiate directly with donors for district-level projects. In addition, 5 percent of the national budget is allocated to districts specifically for development purposes.[6]

Yemen's experience with decentralized governance dates back to its local development associations of the late 1960s. These groups were able to mobilize most of their resources from local communities to build schools and local health clinics. Regional development initiatives, piloted in five governorates, emphasize community self-reliance and microcredit and technical assistance. The number of civil society organizations in Yemen has been growing rapidly.[7]

Uganda has one of the most comprehensive decentralization programs in Africa. The constitution adopted in 1995 calls for the devolution of power to local governments. The Local Government Act of 1997 grants local councils the powers to raise revenues and initiate their own development programs. Local councilors were elected in 1998.[8]

South Africa's local councils elected in 1995 are an example of a genuine attempt at empowerment. These councils were aimed at extending democratic processes to local areas and creating institutional mechanisms for the delivery of goods and services.

The Local Government Plan 2000 introduced by the military-led government of Pakistan is one of the most comprehensive local government reforms in the country's history in terms of local government control over local resources and financial autonomy, district and subdistrict planning systems, and local-level information and monitoring systems. The Local Government Plan integrates rural and urban local governments as well as government departments at the local level into one coherent structure, in which district administration and police are accountable to the elected chief executive of the district.[9]

There are many constraints on the devolution of financial and political authority to local governments. Both supporters and opponents of devolution agree that, without adequate mechanisms for accountability and for combating corruption at the local level, devolution could lead to inefficiencies, misuse of resources, and loss of citizens' trust in the local political process.

Accountability and Anticorruption at the Local Level

Accountability of elected local governments and effective anticorruption strategies at the local level are essential to promote and sustain political and economic devolution. These can serve as strategic entry points for improving the effectiveness of local governance through devolution. Effective financial, political, and administrative accountability mechanisms at the local government level compel local officials to focus on results, seek clear objectives, develop effective strategies, and monitor and report on performance. Lack of accountability leads to corruption, which negatively affects the legitimacy of local governments. Frequently, central government officials who are opposed to devolution point to corruption at the local level as an excuse to delay and sometimes sabotage transfer of powers and resources.

Even though in theory corrupt local politicians can be voted out of power in a democratically elected local government, in practice local political leaders in feudal societies and in societies with great economic disparities hold a monopoly on local political power. In countries where political corruption is pervasive, local elections are characterized by electoral fraud and voter intimidation. The need to make elections free and fair has been on the national agenda of many countries, but corrupt influences on the outcome of elections have become widespread. In many developing countries, local elections are marked by violence, massive fraud, vote buying, and electioneering under government auspices. In Pakistan, for example, the opposition raised questions about the fairness of local elections. In Bangladesh successive elections have led to serious disputes between the ruling and opposition parties about the outcome, leading to a constitutional amendment that provides for an interim government three months before a national election is held to ensure that the ruling party does not misuse its power during the election.

Furthermore, elections in developing countries—including those at the local level—have become expensive. Because money invested in elections has to be paid back, and because most candidates use their own funds, the incentives for corruption can be seen in two scenarios, that of being elected and that of staying in power. As the case of the Philippines shows, rising election campaign expenses result from massive spending on media, advertisements, transport, public relations, and a semisecret kitty to buy votes.[10] Elections therefore have been increasingly understood in terms of the spoils system, which in practice opens the way for elected representatives to tap into public money, in many cases without safeguards against the abuse.

In the absence of organized and disciplined political parties, local elected councils in developing countries tend to be weak and unable to use their constitutionally guaranteed powers. The executive branch of local government, with the support of civil servants, monopolizes power. In the absence of an adequate system of checks and balances, disincentives for the diversion of public funds are not enforced. Political parties tend to become personal clubs through which politicians gain power rather than arenas for debate on local policies and programs. A common trend among citizens is to join the winning party after the election in the hope of gaining favor.

Political corruption can be entrenched in the democratic systems of both developing and developed countries. When campaign finance rules are not enforced and the judiciary is too weak to hold corrupt politicians accountable, politically well-connected middlemen collect bribes in return for misuse of political patronage by those in power; some serve as specialized party "cashiers" to collect money from sources, such as the construction industry, for the party coffers.

The reasons behind corruption at the local government level are almost identical to those at the national level: to obtain goods and services from the government below market price, to persuade officials to undertake certain tasks, to avoid the costs of government regulations and taxes, and to obtain contracts and concessions from the local government.

A 2004 United Nations study emphasizes the need to promote accountability and transparency in local governance and identifies four strategies to promote transparency and accountability in local governance: monitoring of transparency; access to information and public participation; promotion of ethics, professionalism, and integrity; and institutional reform.[11] Over the past few decades subnational governments, cities and towns, and other local governments have tried various instruments of accountability and transparency to promote and sustain devolution and to strengthen trust between citizens and local governments. These include

—Local leadership commitment to accountability and transparency

—Effective anticorruption bodies

—Transparent and accountable systems of public procurement

—Participatory budgeting and auditing
—Engagement of civil society in local decisionmaking
—Promotion of ethics and integrity among local public officials.

Local Leadership

The commitment of local leaders to local accountability and anticorruption strategies is essential for preventive measures, enforcement of existing regulations, public education and awareness, and institution building. Experience suggests that similar local institutional structures and designs produce different outcomes due largely to the quality of local leadership. The promotion of accountability and combating corruption at the local level is a long-term and ongoing process in which various groups try to protect their own interests.

Leadership needs to commit to the reform agenda and to a consistent pursuit of the agenda even in the face of short-term setbacks. Effective local government leaders forge partnerships among diverse groups, mediate differences, consult with various interest groups, and are committed to social justice. Trisectoral partnerships (between governments, the private sector, and civil society) have also become increasingly vital to improve basic service delivery. There are many good-practices models of leadership that promote accountability and anticorruption strategies.

In La Paz, Bolivia, Maclean-Abaroa, the first elected mayor in almost forty years, was sworn in during September 1985. He simplified the procedure for applying for construction permits and published these procedures to make people aware of the legal requirements. The Urban Development Department's monopoly on construction permits was thus broken. The city government worked with the professional association of architects to certify members of the association to grant construction permits on behalf of the city government, provided that the requests met set regulations. Architects' fees were determined by competition in the market.

The city government undertook random checks to ensure compliance with construction regulations. To avoid extortion on the part of the investigating committee, the architects' association had the right to advocate on their behalf in case of baseless allegations. Other simplifications reduced the number of taxes from 126 to 6 and procurement steps from 26 to 7.[12] The anticorruption process paid off in terms of increased government revenues and a tenfold increase in public works investment. Mayor Maclean-Abaroa was reelected for his fourth term.

In the municipality of Jinja, Uganda, the Markets Act of 1964 delegated authority and control over the central market to the district administration and to either municipal or town councils, depending on the location of the market. Market administrators were responsible, inter alia, for regulating the use of the market and its buildings; for keeping order, issuing permits, and collecting auction fees and stalls' rents; and for making decisions as to the type of goods to be sold. Because market administration had been suffering from red tape, corruption, and inefficiency, it was privatized. Through a comanagement system, a private contractor collected dues and maintained the market according to government rules. The role of the municipality was only that of setting numbers of licenses, setting license fees and rents, and setting standards for overall supervision. A vendors association was established to defend the interests of vendors and traders.

Surveys provided positive feedback about improvement in market management and service delivery as a result of privatization and the devolution of the administrative system; in addition, 74 percent of respondents expressed more willingness to pay their dues as compared to the past.[13] After privatization, market revenues to the municipality increased by 27 percent.[14] The municipality and district boards guarantee transparency through a tendering system managed by a "tender board" composed of council members and the community. A chairman of the board is elected. Tenders are advertised in the newspapers as well as the notice boards of district and municipal councils in both local and English languages.

Curitiba, the capital of Parana state in South Eastern Brazil, became an international reference for integrated and holistic planning, being recognized by the international media, experts, and development institutions as an example of how local elected officials can mobilize stakeholders and communities to tackle development challenges and create an environment of accountability and transparency of local governance.[15]

The most critical factor was the leadership of Jaime Lerner, who as mayor introduced reforms. Mayor Lerner had to balance immediate physical expansion challenges and the growth of slum areas with the tremendous pressure for public transport, water, sanitation, and other basic services. He initiated institutional reform, including the creation of the Curitiba Research and Urban Planning Institute, the Curitiba Industrial City, and a plan for the revitalization of the historic center. During his subsequent terms of office, Mayor Lerner focused on environmental preservation, waste management programs, social services (including a network of day care centers), consolidation of the public transport system, and creation of the rapid transit system.

Various segments of society were engaged in the approval of a master plan for Curitiba, which was a blueprint for urban development based on consensus among the various communities. The plan was shared with the population and widely disseminated. It defined medium- and long-term development by outlining a growth structure based on public transport facilities going from the city center to the periphery, where the poor live; land use legislation; and the hierarchy of the road system. The plan also addressed the need to promote social services while sustaining economic growth. Dissemination of the plan helped to avoid land speculation and, by defining "equations of co-responsibility" through partnerships, helped engage various groups representing civil society and the private sector.

Mayor Lerner is widely known in Brazil and worldwide as an example of credibility and competence. The population saw results and saw the mayor leading by example. The mayor was never accused of any type of malfeasance and did not use his power to make exceptions to the rules defined to guide the development of Curitiba. The population never saw any signs of "unexplained wealth" on the part of the mayor, who has always lived in the same house and kept the same standard of living throughout his terms of office as the mayor. The mayor gained the trust of financial institutions, based on the seriousness of his administration. Banks underwrote public transport–private sector operations, and big companies such as Volvo, Bosch, and Siemens trusted the municipal administration enough to move to the Curitiba Industrial City.

Anticorruption Commissions

Over the past few years, central and local governments have established anticorruption bodies to serve as watchdogs for local governments and to combat corruption through enforcement of existing regulations, punishment of violators, and raising the awareness of citizens. Various models of institutional reform have emerged and from various entities—some from the executive branch, some from offices outside the executive branch, and some from state and local governments. The key characteristics of effective anticorruption bodies are financial independence, administrative autonomy, a wide scope for action, linkages with political leaders and government ministries and departments, and internal capacity to perform their assigned tasks.

Though there are different approaches to designing anticorruption bodies, a 2004 United Nations study shows that the key determinants of their effectiveness are independent and nonpartisan commissioners, strong educational and training units in the commissions, a proactive community outreach program, and representation of a variety of communities among the commissioners and staff. Other elements of effective anticorruption commissions are adequacy of resources and staff and legal advisory units.[16]

Devolution of financial and political authority to local governments leads to the performance by local governments of many complex functions, such as land allocation, business licensing, and recruitment and promotion of staff. The need therefore is to have clear administrative procedures that are impartially enforced. Institutional reform at the local government level that promotes accountability and transparency and effective anticorruption strategies takes many forms. One of the most important is the creation of independent anticorruption agencies. Others are the establishment of a complaints and ombudsman office, a one-stop shop, oversight committees, an independent audit function, and participatory budgeting.

Hong Kong established an Independent Commission against Corruption in 1974 to deal with corruption. It follows a multidimensional approach that includes prevention, education, and enlistment of support.[17] As a preventive measure, the commission organized corruption prevention studies for public bodies and private sector companies. Also, to educate the public, it conducted mass media and public education campaigns against corruption. To enforce its strategy, the commission recruited investigators from the police, civil servants, engineers, accountants, and media experts to undertake investigations regarding enforcement of laws pertinent to corruption. The commission increased its enforcement efforts in the private sector, resulting in the prosecution of high-profile figures of the business community, including the chairman of the stock exchange. The efforts of the commission have led to enhanced public trust in public services and the business sector.

In Ecuador municipalities are responsible for public services such as water, garbage collection, sewage disposal, and road construction.[18] They also have authority over taxation and legal codes. Pedro Moncayo is one of the 219 municipalities of Ecuador. In this municipality and another three, the United Nations Development Program and the Civic Counter Corruption Commission implemented a transparency pilot project through participatory budgeting. The project designed transparency tools to improve service delivery and public oversight and opened the way for citizens to participate in public oversight of planning, budgeting, spending, and service delivery. Workshops helped citizens diagnose and identify risk areas in the municipal finance process and a way to take action in risk areas. The workshops covered participatory budgeting and accounts oversight, participatory public audits, and opening access to information to enhance municipality transparency. The municipalities were provided with manuals: "Transparent Municipal Management" and "Transparent Fiscal Management and Oversight."

The case of Pedro Moncayo shows the need for partnership between the national anticorruption body and the municipal and local levels to design and implement accountability and anticorruption mechanisms at the local level. At the local level, as at the national level, attention should be paid to such issues as sufficient resources, qualified staff, supportive legal framework, an independent judiciary, and a competent local administration.

The city of Windhoek in Namibia established the Office of the Chief Internal Auditor to undertake audit functions of the city's nine major departments, reporting directly to the chief executive officer of the city. Since the city's visioning process in 2000, the office has been helping the departments of the city to improve their procedures and practices to enhance accountability and transparency and thus strengthen trust in the local government.

Public Procurement

Critics of political and financial devolution from the central government argue that often the systems of public procurement at the subnational and local levels are rampant with misuse of authority and corruption. Where local governments have established mechanisms and procedures for accountability and transparency in public procurement, citizen trust in and support for local decision-making is enhanced. In view of this, countries such as India and the Republic of Korea not only have devolved power and resources to municipalities and local governments but also have initiated mechanisms to hold local officials accountable for their actions, improve efficiency, and reduce corruption in the procurement system.

The government of Andhra Pradesh in India, for example, established an electronic system to offer tenders online and to handle the procedures electronically, so as to provide bidders with an equal opportunity to access tenders in a timely manner.[19] The system reduces the human interface and subjectivity in the bidding and evaluation processes; eliminates cartels and the physical threat they pose, since bidders can submit their bids from anywhere without being physically vulnerable to mafia groups; and minimizes or eliminates tampering with bids, because the information is available to all who have access to the system and does not include physical transfer by humans.

The system is implemented through a public-private partnership model in which technology investment and operation are undertaken by the private sector in return for fees collected from the government departments involved. After two and a half years, the system is being used in processing the procurement of eight government departments, thirteen public sector units, fifty-one municipalities, and five universities. The average number of participating suppliers increased from three per tender to four and a half. Quotations decreased by 16 percent in the first year of using the system (2003–04), compared to the previous year, when the system was manual. Procurement cost to the departments dropped by 20 percent as a result of the competition. The website helped tender advertising costs to shrink by 25 percent in a year.

The government of Seoul City adopted the Integrity Pact, in which the city government and companies submitting bids vow neither to offer nor to accept briber.[20] All bidders for the city's construction projects, technical services, and procurement are required to sign the pact. During the bidding stage, the pact is explained to bidders, and only those who take a bidder's oath to sign the pact are qualified to register their submissions. A government official also signs a principal's oath. During the contract's concluding execution stage, both parties must sign a "special condition for contract."[21] Provisions are made to protect and reward those reporting inside corruption. Specific guidelines have been issued for the bidder's submissions, employees of bidders, a company code of conduct, and the principal's oath.

Violators of the pact may face termination of contracts and are banned from bidding for other contracts for six months to two years. The pact is being implemented in two stages: the first stage is for projects at the head office and project offices, and the second stage is for projects in the twenty-five autonomous district offices in Seoul. The ombudsmen are a team of five persons appointed by the mayor of Seoul, one of them being the chief. The ombudsmen monitor implementation. Ombudsmen are not allowed to hold a concurrent job at the National Assembly, a political party, or any company participating in the bids for public projects.

The Public Record of Operations and Finance (PROOF) was launched in Bangalore, India, in 2002 to monitor the financial performance of the City Corporation in Bangalore. The purpose of PROOF is to build trust between local government and citizens by improving the responsiveness and accountability of the City Corporation. The City Corporation has been providing quarterly financial performance statements in a user-friendly format to the general public.

In Serbia a program titled "Towards More Transparent Budgeting and Public Procurement in Municipalities" consists of the following components: a public opinion poll in selected municipalities, workshops for public officials to introduce new software and standards of public procurements, polls about the quality of services in selected municipalities, and the creation of new project proposals. As a result, the municipalities now have new tools and technologies and training.[22]

Participatory Budgeting and Auditing

Two effective and interrelated mechanisms for ensuring accountability of local governments and combating corruption at this level are participatory budgeting and auditing. It is widely recognized that in most local governments budgets are not adequately discussed among local actors before presentation to local elected councils. In some cases there are too many donor-driven proposals. Time allowed for discussions among local councilors is too limited. Often, local budgets are written in a technical language that many citizens find difficult to understand in terms of their implications.

In some countries, local governments have initiated mechanisms to facilitate the participation of citizens in economic policymaking and, specifically, in engaging them in the process of budgeting and auditing. Porto Alegre in Brazil and Abra in the Philippines are two examples.

Porto Alegre is recognized for its successful experiment with participatory budgeting and decentralized decisionmaking.[23] The city has considerable control over revenues and taxes at the local level. The experiment started in 1989 when the Brazilian Workers Party won the municipal elections. The process of participatory budgeting provided for the active engagement of local neighborhood associations, nongovernmental organizations, labor union officials, and city government officials. The Workers Party organized two community gatherings during which the people selected regional delegates to represent them during debates about the allocation and spending of the municipal investment budget. The delegates advocate areas of need with the technical staff of the municipality.

According to World Bank reports of the Porto Alegre program, remarkable achievements have been realized. Over the period 1989–96, the number of households with access to water services increased by 18 percent, the municipal sewage system was expanded by 39 percent, and the number of children enrolled in public schools doubled. Every year thirty more kilometers of roads were paved in poor neighborhoods. These outcomes increased the trust of the people in their government. Such accountability motivated people to pay their taxes, leading to a 50 percent rise in government revenues. The successful model in Porto Alegre encouraged its emulation in another 140 of Brazil's 5,500 municipalities. It has also affected participatory budgeting in the state of Rio Grande do Sul, the capital of which is Porto Alegre.

In Abra, the Philippines, the Concerned Citizens of Abra for Good Governance (CCAGG), an NGO, was established in 1986.[24] The CCAGG was established as a result of the participatory development policy of President Corazon Aquino. The CCAGG signed a memorandum of understanding with the National Economic Development Authority and was trained by it to undertake project monitoring. The CCAGG is active in informing the public about the quality of projects, using community meetings and the media. Its members include students, professionals, housewives, priests, and government employees. Despite taking risks and receiving threats, the organization has maintained its momentum to investigate projects and fight corruption.

The spark for their action and publicity started when the group challenged a government media report claiming the successful completion of twenty-seven projects in the Abra province by the Ministry of Public Works and Highways. The CCAGG gathered information, photographed and documented the incomplete status of the projects, and submitted all of it to the national government. A government investigation was launched, and the CCAGG findings were verified. Mild reprimands for the government officials in charge of the projects set the CCAGG into action again, to hold the corrupt officials accountable through punishment. Their efforts paid off, with eleven engineers being suspended for dishonesty and misconduct.

The CCAGG investigates projects for substandard materials, poor construction techniques, and fraudulent contracting procedures. Given the effectiveness and efficiency of the CCAGG in monitoring and fighting corruption in public works projects, combined with the expertise it has acquired, the National Audit Commission entered into partnership with the CCAGG to undertake participatory audits in the Abra region. The experience of the CCAGG is a good example of participatory public audits, wherein citizens engage in fighting corruption and ensuring high-quality projects.

Civil Society Organizations

Civil society engagement and an ongoing dialogue among local actors provide other mechanisms to ensure accountability and transparency, which in turn enhances citizens' trust in political and economic devolution to local governments. Where citizens do not trust local governments and corruption is rampant, central government officials are likely to impose more conditions on local government bodies.

In Bangalore, India, the first report card on public agencies in 1994 covered municipal services, including water supply, electricity, telecommunications, and transport. Since then the Public Affairs Center, which was set up in Bangalore by a small group of citizens, has published its "Citizens Report Cards" on several other cities, rural services, and health care. The findings of the first report card on Bangalore are striking. Almost all public service providers received low ratings from the people. The agencies were rated and compared in terms of public satisfaction, corruption, and responsiveness. The media publicity that the findings received and the public discussions that followed made people aware of the magnitude of the problem. In response to increasing demands from civil society groups for better performance, public agencies began to respond to people's demands and took concrete steps to improve their performance.

The second report card on Bangalore, in 1999, showed better ratings for some government agencies but not a significant overall improvement in the performance of public sector agencies. The third report, in 2003, however, showed major improvements in citizens' rating of all public agencies. The incidence of corruption in routine transactions between citizens and public officials declined. Building on the above demand-side efforts, the chief minister established the Bangalore Agenda Task Force to serve as a body for public-private partnerships to work through to improve the quality of services. The task force is monitored by civil society groups and the media.

In Tanzania relationships between local governments, civil society organizations, and the private sector are characterized by conflict, competition over resources, and sometimes hostility. To deal with these challenges, Pajoma, a local civil society organization, developed joint action schemes to encourage cooperation in such fields as governance, education, and solid waste management. In 1998 Pajoma established the first District Advisory Committee as the multistakeholder platform to identify common development objectives. The objectives of the committee are to increase the effectiveness of service delivery, create trust among partners, coordinate development efforts, and promote collaboration and consensus. As a forum for dialogue, it has now been extended to three districts.

In the Philippines, civil society organizations and community groups have taken critical initiatives to bring about successful reform in service provision. The primary health care service delivery in Surigao City was implemented through women's clubs. A midwife from the city's health office, along with local area (*barangay*) health workers, organized mothers in neighborhoods and trained them in nutrition education and sanitation. This effort facilitated the delivery of primary health care services, including immunization, family planning, and nutrition education.

The Philippine Center for Investigative Journalism is an independent, non-profit media agency specializing in investigative journalism. It was founded in 1989 by nine journalists who recognized the need for newspapers and broadcast agencies to go beyond day-to-day reporting. The center is founded on the belief that the media play a crucial role in scrutinizing and strengthening democratic institutions and should thus be a catalyst for social debate and consensus for public welfare, trusting that well-researched information communicated to citizens leads to informed public opinions and public decisions. The center aims at providing training for investigative reporting to full-time reporters, free-lance journalists, and academics. In addition to training, it uses information technology to optimize research and investigation as well as to systematize access to data. It has been conducting ten-day training seminars on investigating corruption at both national and regional levels.

Because the reports prepared by the center are well researched and well documented, they have contributed to a deeper understanding of issues and, thus, have had an impact on outcomes. The reports have resulted in government actions dealing with corruption, public accountability, and environmental protection. The factors that have led to the success of the center are the professional expertise available among its members and its focus on capacity building and training. Its self-sustaining operations and high-quality output have attracted the attention of development partners nationally and regionally.

The power of civil society monitoring is shown by the effectiveness of an independent civil ombudsman in the city of Sendai, Japan, in exposing corruption in public agencies in Japan. In the mid-1990s a group of attorneys established the civil ombudsman to examine payments made for official entertainment. Several corruption cases were exposed, including nonexistent public travel.[25]

The Philippines Report Card on Pro-Poor Services, a pilot project, was supported by the World Bank to get feedback of citizens concerning the performance of government services, including basic health, elementary education, housing, potable water, and food distribution. Periodic Report Card Surveys provide pressure and incentives for public agencies to make concrete improvements in public services, which in turn enhance political legitimacy and effective political devolution to local governments.[26]

Equitable and mutually beneficial partnerships among local actors—government, civil society, the private sector, and community groups—are instrumental in both exerting pressure from below for devolution of power and resources and implementing existing decentralization policies and programs.

In large metropolitan areas such as Bombay, Mexico City, and Karachi, local government structures can be remote from the day-to-day needs of the people. However, representatives of the metropolitan government along with municipal government employees can forge partnerships with the representatives of civil society, the private sector, and community organizations. These partnerships enable the municipal government to elicit the participation of citizens in municipal government initiatives and also to provide a mechanism for other local actors to hold municipal government functionaries accountable to the people. More important, such local-local partnerships tap into the full complement of human energy in the city.

An interesting example of local partnerships in support of local initiatives is the Local Initiative Facility for the Urban Environment (Life) program supported by the United Nations Development Program in twelve countries.[27] The design of the Life program is two pronged. The first prong is the creation of mechanisms for promoting dialogue among local actors at the community, municipal, and national levels. These mechanisms include national or city consultation to map priorities, a program selection committee to review local initiatives to promote learning, and community groups to suggest local initiatives that have potential for learning and replication at the municipal or national level, or both. A national program coordinator is appointed to promote interaction among actors. The second prong includes providing grants for those community initiatives that respond to local environmental problems, such as waste management, environmental education, water supply, and sanitation. Other initiatives with priority are those that promote primary health care and income generation.

The Life program operates in three stages: upstream, catalyzing national dialogue, developing strategies, and gathering support; downstream, ensuring effective and collaborative small projects; and again upstream, disseminating and exchanging information nationally and internationally.

The Life program promotes democracy at the grass roots by empowering local actors and by increasing dialogue among them about their local problems and responsibilities. The result in most cases has been an increased level of local and community organization and the ability of local actors to build on their own local initiatives as well as benefit from national resources. The program also provides a mechanism for civil society organizations and community groups to interact with other local and municipal leaders and representatives of national government in the area. Through the networks created through the program, local leaders are more likely to influence the process of resource allocation at the municipal level. In addition the program provides an effective mechanism for the participation of people in the development process. In most government-initiated programs the concept of participation tends to be limited to the involvement of beneficiaries. However, the Life program provides a decentralized structure through which decisions concerning local environmental problems can be made locally.

The Life program shows the need for pro-poor local governance, in which civil society, urban government, the business sector, and representatives of the central government at the local level build partnerships to respond to problems that affect the poor. The pillars of effective pro-poor local governance include elected and autonomous local government with an adequate capacity and information base, strong developmentally oriented civil society organizations, a socially responsible business sector, and partnerships that include these various actors.

Public Ethics and Integrity

Appropriate laws and regulations and their proper enforcement are essential but not sufficient to promote accountability and transparency and anticorruption strategies. Equally important is the need to strengthen ethics and professionalism among local officials. Those without ethical standards and personal integrity usually find loopholes in laws. Some of the mechanisms used to promote ethics and integrity at the local government level are conflict-of-interest laws, disclosure of income and assets, lobbyist registration, whistle-blower protection, codes of conduct, and ethics training.[28] The focus of a code of conduct can be inspirational (including stated values) or disciplinary (containing minimum standards) or both. Usually the code includes elements of human resource development policies.

In New York City, the Conflict of Interest Board—consisting of five members appointed by the mayor—is the legal entity that enforces the conflict-of-interest laws of New York. To ensure their independence and impartiality, the members are not allowed to hold public or political party office or work as lobbyists before the city. The board examines financial disclosures, informs local officials about the provisions of the conflict-of-interest laws, and provides training and advisory opinions.[29]

The city and county of San Francisco enacted the San Francisco Lobbyist Ordinance requiring lobbyists to register, to report quarterly any compensation they received, and to report their political contributions to local officials; the ordinance also prohibits gifts to local officials with a value of more than $50. The purpose of the law is to promote public confidence in the elected local government.[30]

Conclusion

The devolution of powers and resources to local governments is the most critical component of democratic governance. However, devolution without effective mechanisms and instruments to promote accountability, transparency, and anticorruption at the local level undermines the political legitimacy and effectiveness of local governments. The case studies of good practices in this chapter suggest that devolution with accountability can be promoted through local leadership committed to accountability, anticorruption commissions, transparent procedures for public procurement, participatory budgeting and auditing, the engagement of civil society, and the promotion of ethics and integrity among local officials. These mechanisms and instruments of accountability and transparency in turn promote and sustain political and financial devolution.

Notes

1. G. Shabbir Cheema, *Building Democratic Institutions: Governance Reform in Developing Countries* (Bloomfield, Conn.: Kumarian Press, 2005).

2. United Nations Human Settlements Program (UN-Habitat), "Tools to Support Transparency in Local Governance," 2004, p. 4.

3. Ibid., 132–38.

4. Larry Diamond, *Developing Democracy: Toward Consolidation* (Johns Hopkins University Press, 1999), pp. 133–38.

5. G. Shabbir Cheema and Dennis A. Rondinelli, eds., *Decentralization and Development* (Beverly Hills, Calif.: Sage, 1983), pp. 22–24.

6. United Nations Development Program, "Ghana Case Study," in *Overcoming Human Poverty* (2000).

7. "Yemen Case Study," in ibid.

8. "Uganda Case Study," in ibid.

9. Government of Pakistan, National Reconstruction Bureau, *Local Government Plan 2000* (2000), p. 1.

10. Isgani de Castro, "Campaign Kitty," in *Pork and Other Perks: Corruption and Governance in the Philippines,* edited by Sheila S. Coronel (Metro Manila: Philippine Centre for Investigative Journalism, 1988), p. 218.

11. UN-Habitat, "Tools to Support Transparency in Local Governance," pp. 3–25.

12. World Bank, *Fighting Corruption in La Paz, Bolivia: A Case Study* (http://info.worldbank.org/etools/mdfdb/docs/WP_Janette6.pdf).

13. Ibid.

14. Ibid.

15. Jonas Rabinovitch and Josef Leitman, "Urban Planning in Curitiba," *Scientific American,* March 1996, pp. 26–33; Jonas Rabinovitch, "Urban Public Transport Management in Curitiba, Brazil," *Industry and Environment* 16, no. 1-2 (January-June 1993); Jonas Rabinovitch, "Curitiba: Towards Sustainable Urban Development," *Environment and Urbanization* 4, no. 2 (October 1992); John Mayer Jr., "Curitiba, The Little Cidade That Could," *Time* (Latin American ed.), October 14, 1991, p. 19.

16. UN-Habitat, "Tools to Support Transparency in Local Governance,"pp. 136–40.

17. United Nations Development Program, *Corruption and Integrity Improvement Initiatives in Developing Countries* (1998), p. 52.

18. UN-Habitat, "Toolkit on Participatory Budgeting: A Collection of Resources to Facilitate Interregional Transfers, Nairobi," United Nations, 2004.

19. World Bank, "E-Procurement in Government of Andhra Pradesh, India" (http://web.worldbank.org).

20. Ibid.

21. UN-Habitat, "Tools to Support Transparency in Local Governance," p. 52.

22. Ibid.

23. The case is based on a United Nations publication by its Department of Economic and Social Affairs, *Citizen Participation and Pro-Poor Budgeting* (2005), pp. 41–42.

24. This case is based on Transparency International (www1.transparency.org/pressreleases_archive/2000/2000.09.28.i_award_portraits.html) and www.worldbank.org/participation/web/webfiles/philipreport.htm.

25. See www.nbr.org.

26. UN-Habitat, "Tools to Support Transparency in Local Governance."

27. United Nations Development Program, *Participatory Local Governance* (1997).

28. UN-Habitat, "Tools to Support Transparency in Local Governance"; United Nations Department of Economic and Social Affairs, *Public Sector Transparency and Accountability in Selected Arab Countries* (2004), p. 83.

29. See www.nyc.gov/html/conflicts/home/home.shtml.

30. See www.ci.sf.us/ethics.

11

Decentralization and Participatory Local Governance: A Decision Space Analysis and Application to Peru

DERICK W. BRINKERHOFF, JENNIFER M. BRINKERHOFF, AND STEPHANIE McNULTY

Analyses of decentralization take a variety of perspectives on the concept. From an initial concentration on decentralization as a state-centered enterprise by which central government allocates resources and authorities to lower levels to improve administrative and service delivery effectiveness, this focus has expanded to look beyond the state to government's relationship with citizens. Democratic decentralization involves citizen participation and responsiveness to citizens' needs and preferences as important components of state-society restructuring to enact democratic governance throughout a society.

So in addition to expected improvements in efficient and effective public service delivery, decentralizers seek improved democratic governance outcomes through the enhanced responsiveness to, accountability to, and participation of citizens and civil society. There is an inherent tension in the democratic decentralization project: while the devolution of responsibility, resources, and authority to local government expands the possibilities of reaching these expected results, the discretion that accompanies devolution opens the door to local government capture by special interests and elites. These actors may not be interested in the objectives and tasks that the central government would like to see local authorities pursue, and further, their interests are unlikely to align with those of the poor and marginalized in local communities.

Thus devolved discretion needs to be joined by some degree of control over that discretion. In democratic decentralized governance systems, this control comes from two sources: higher levels of government and civil society. Central government, through the legal framework and institutional checks and balances, can discipline subnational governments. Civil society can exert checks as well. The classic democratic mechanism of elections is one source of such power, but there are other mechanisms besides the ballot box, such as conducting service satisfaction surveys or undertaking watchdog monitoring of local officials regarding corruption, human rights, and so on.

The examination of opportunities for discretion in analyzing decentralization becomes important to understanding the incentives and behaviors of local officials and the civil society actors engaged with them. This understanding can help to improve reform design and performance. In this chapter we apply a variant of what is called decision space analysis by Thomas Bossert and Joel Beauvais, and opportunity space assessment by the World Bank, to decentralization reform in Peru to explore the range of discretion at the local government level for local officials and civil society to engage in participatory governance.[1] We seek to illuminate the pressures and possibilities that local actors experience in decentralizing governance systems.

Decentralizers often lack knowledge of the specifics of local contexts that may or may not be subject to influence by reform designs. As described by Bossert and Beauvais, "In many cases, local agents are simply thought of as 'black boxes'; resources are transferred to them and controls exerted over them, but it is not clear exactly what factors influence their choices."[2] Moving beyond an emphasis on the design features of Peru's decentralization reforms related to citizen participation, the chapter examines progress on implementation, based on fieldwork and interview data collected in 2003–05.[3] It highlights the role and implications of actors' incentives and behaviors. Together, policy design and the incentives facing key actors determine the de facto decision space for interaction between local governments and civil society.

Decentralization and Citizen Participation

Decentralization deals with the allocation between center and periphery of power, authority, and responsibility for political, economic, fiscal, and administrative systems. The most common definitions of decentralization distinguish variants along a continuum where at one end the center maintains strong control with limited power and discretion at lower levels to progressively decreasing central control and increasing local discretion at the other end. Decentralization has a spatial aspect in that authority and responsibility are moved to organizations and jurisdictions in different physical locations, from the center to the local level. And it has an institutional aspect in that these transfers involve reallocating roles and functions both *within* government, from one central government agency to lower-level jurisdictions and agencies; and *between* government and civil society, through service coproduction and partnerships as well as joint policymaking and feedback mechanisms.[4] It is in regard to this latter institutional aspect that decentralization is intimately connected to citizen participation, democratic governance, and the revised role of the state.[5]

The institutional arrangements for decentralization create new technical, social, and political relations. Anirudh Krishna, for example, emphasizes that institutions of decentralization need to be designed with attention to both technical proficiency and local legitimacy.[6] Hazel Johnson and Gordon Wilson highlight the need to deal with power differentials.[7] For these reasons local participation, community empowerment, and partnership with civil society organizations are emphasized in many decentralization reforms. The literature suggests a range of potential outcomes from community participation and partnership:[8]

—Pressure on local governments to be more participatory and responsive

—Generation of social capital (trust, norms, networks, communication), bridging, and bonding

—Increased capacity for local collective action

—Improved beneficiary targeting of services (for example, focused on the poor, disadvantaged, and marginalized)

—Improved matches between services and beneficiary preferences

—Enhanced potential for scaling up of service delivery.

Of course, community participation and partnership are not panaceas for poor local government performance or democratic deficits. The record on achieving these positive outcomes has been mixed. For example, John Gaventa acknowledges that participation can lead to some positive democracy outcomes; however, pro-poor service delivery is not necessarily one of them.[9] In her review of participatory budgeting, Deborah Bräutigam reaches similar conclusions.[10] The desired outcomes of decentralization with civil society partnership are far from automatic, regardless of technical design and good intentions. In her study of local government performance in Mexico, Merilee Grindle confirms that in many cases, decentralization does not increase accountability.[11] Nick Devas and Ursula Grant review the experience of participation at the municipal level in Kenya and Uganda.[12] They find that while the scope for participation is greater in Uganda, the problems of accountability remain similar to those found in Kenya. They conclude that committed local leadership, high-capacity local government, central monitoring of performance, articulate civil society organizations, and information availability are critical to enhancing government accountability.

Frederick Golooba-Mutebi's historical review of Uganda's experience with citizen councils reveals that, over time, participants began to suffer from participation fatigue and interest waned due to unrealistic expectations about the potential for such participation as an effective administrative and policymaking mechanism.[13] In Uganda, as elsewhere, the introduction of participatory processes is often built upon assumptions of interest and capacity on the part of citizens and their representatives. He argues that participation often makes "unrealistic and often intolerable demands on the time and lives of already overworked people trying to construct and maintain livelihoods in difficult circumstances."[14]

Jennifer Brinkerhoff makes a related point regarding expectations for partnerships, noting that the anticipated outcomes of partnerships between local government and civil society are far from automatic.[15] Effective partnerships depend upon a power balance and joint accountability between the partners (mutuality), which ensures that partners are able to contribute their distinctive competencies to service delivery and democratic outcomes under decentralization. Among the considerations for partnership design are actors' motivations and capacities, which include a tolerance for sharing power, a willingness to be flexible in the interest of maximizing partnership efficiency and effectiveness, and trust and confidence. Regarding these latter elements, trust is voluntary, is linked to shared values, and is distinct from confidence. It often develops through relationship building over time. Confidence, however, is based on rational expectations rather than shared values and is typically grounded in institutional arrangements, such as contracts, regulations, and standard operating procedures.

These motivations and capacities may be in short supply, both in local government and in civil society. Ghazala Mansuri and Vijayendra Rao argue that the need for a responsive state apparatus increases when government and civil society actors partner in participatory community projects.[16] Research and experience with participation confirm that participation can add complexity and time delays, often requiring far greater resources than standard top-down approaches. However, the costs associated with citizen participation can be offset by the benefits. A frequently cited example of success is participatory budgeting, where the positive experience of the Brazilian municipality of Porto Alegre, which put in place an intensive consultation process on priorities and spending, has inspired numerous other local governments to adopt this innovation.[17]

Effective decentralization requires proaction and commitment on the part of all implementing actors. Institutional approaches confirm the challenges of any reform effort, as role perceptions and patterns are embedded in existing institutions and are rarely open to change.[18] In his review of Dutch governance reform, Jurian Edelenbos recounts the evolution of parallel formal and informal roles and argues that, when reforms are not adequately embedded in local institutions, reform processes often lead to "'cherry-picking' behavior on the part of decision makers," as they are not committed to the full range of new roles indicated by the reforms.[19] These findings highlight the role of discretionary space at the local level for actors to engage in behaviors that may or may not lead to intended decentralization outcomes. They also point to one of the characteristics of decentralization experience in many developing countries:

decentralization is often only partially implemented. There is frequently a wide gap between the legal mandate of decentralization and how that mandate is translated into practice.[20]

Decentralization and Decision Space

Decentralizations vary in the degree to which they enable or constrain local government and civil society. The purpose of decision-opportunity space analysis is to map the contours of discretion for decisionmaking and action. This mapping can aid in understanding how and under what circumstances decentralization reform designs achieve their intended outcomes.[21] Decision space analysis enables an assessment of decentralization in terms of the range of choices available to local decisionmakers, with wider ranges being associated with higher degrees of decentralization.[22] The decision space approach acknowledges the varied preferences and priorities of local actors and recognizes the context—legal, political, resources, and capacity—in which those actors operate. It incorporates a principal-agent perspective, noting the limits of a centralized principal to ensure compliance with reforms by local agents. That is, local agents—local governments and civil society actors alike—have "some margin within which to 'shirk' centrally defined responsibilities and pursue their own agendas."[23] This potential shirking necessitates the incorporation of incentives and sanctions into decentralization reform design in order to guide local agent behavior in support of reform objectives.

Bossert and Beauvais restrict their analysis to the decision space available to government officials and service providers.[24] We adapt their approach by adding the civil society dimension, drawing upon work at the World Bank, to highlight the interaction between local government and citizens.[25] The framework is presented in table 11-1.

Decentralization Reform and Civil Society Participation in Peru

Peru has traveled a rocky road to democratization and decentralization.[26] Historically, the country has been highly centralized and has experienced long periods of authoritarian rule. Decentralization has caused abrupt shifts in policy, largely as a function of national political battles.[27] Central authorities over the years established a variety of semiautonomous service delivery and economic development entities with regional and local mandates; the intention was to extend the reach of the center to the local level.[28] Weak governments elected during the 1980s were largely ineffective in confronting moribund economic growth, regional and social inequities, hyperinflation, and the violence of the leftist guerilla movement, the Shining Path.

President Fujimori was elected in 1990 on an outsider's reformist platform that blamed the political parties in power for Peru's ills. The outgoing President

Table 11-1. *Model of Decentralization Decision-Opportunity Space Matrix*

Decentralization dimension	Local government space	Civil society space
Legal, policy, or regulatory framework		
Political		
Resources: fiscal, financial		
Administrative capacity		

Garcia, with no national consultation, had established elected regional councils and transferred policy and service delivery functions to them. Two years later, as part of what came to be called his self-coup, Fujimori dissolved the national congress, replaced the elected councils with "transitional" regional councils with appointed members, and called for a new constituent assembly to rewrite the constitution. This reorganization of government gave the president nearly complete control of all policy, revenue, and expenditure decisions. Through a strengthened cabinet and the powerful Ministry of the Presidency, Fujimori reduced municipalities' budgets and control over their finances and, through centrally controlled financing and social development organizations, sought to build local constituencies and bypass regional and local authorities.

With the collapse of the Fujimori administration in 2000–01 in the wake of opposition to his third term and the emergence of political scandal, the fortunes of decentralization took another, more positive turn. In 2002 the Toledo government initiated an ambitious decentralization reform. The reform agenda included elections for regional officials, held in November 2002; new central institutions, such as the National Decentralization Council; new subnational entities, such as the Regional Coordination Council; and a revised legal framework that establishes the rules and responsibilities for decentralization, including fiscal controls.

The decentralization law specifies as a key objective the strengthening of the mechanisms of citizen participation, including involvement in public budgeting. Our analysis focuses on two participatory mechanisms: the Regional Coordination Council, which brings together elected civil society representatives and provincial or district mayors to coordinate regional development efforts and discuss the annual budget; and a participatory budget process.[29]

Regional Coordination Council

In addition to the general mandate of coordinating regional development and discussing the annual budget, the Regional Coordination Council is to be consulted regarding private investment projects, and the regional government is legally required to consult the council on regional integration plans. While the council is to approve regional annual plans and budgets, its decisions are not binding. The council is composed of 60 percent mayors and 40 percent civil society representatives. At least one-third of civil society participants are intended to represent the region's most important economic actors (business and agriculture); otherwise, the only requirement is legal registration and demonstration of at least a three-year existence. Legally accredited delegates register and then elect civil society representatives for two-year terms. The council meets twice a year for ordinary sessions and additionally as called by the regional president. Members do not receive payments, daily fees, or other types of remuneration.

A review of 2003–05 data from watchdog groups, along with interviews of council members and regional government officials, suggests that regional presidents formed the council to comply with the law but that there was not enough interest on the part of both governments and civil society in the regions to actively promote the council.[30] While all twenty-five regions held council elections in mid-2003 and representatives from civil society were elected for two-year terms, by 2005 more than a quarter of the regions (28 percent) had not complied with the basic requirement of holding new elections.[31] The legally required meetings were called only half of the time in 2004.[32] In addition, attendance was a problem, often preventing a quorum; it was especially hard to get mayors to attend.[33] According to Grupo Propuesta Ciudadana, this was because "they do not consider that it is an important space for decision-making."[34] In other words, mayors were not convinced that the meetings were worth their time, given that they are purely consultative. Also the traditional governing style in Peru has historically been based on clientelism, not mass participation.

Civil society participation has also proved challenging. Data on the 2003–04 Regional Coordination Councils demonstrate a lack of widespread participation, particularly with underrepresentation of rural organizations (39 percent of the regional provinces did not register civil society organizations) and of women (only 5 percent of civil society representatives were women).[35] Interviews revealed several explanations. First, civil society organizations did not fully understand the mechanism, and the process was not well publicized. Second, many civil society organizations are informal; they do not have a legal representative, nor do they register (a requirement for participation in Regional Coordination Council elections), which involves a fee. Finally, some organizations did not consider it necessary to participate since they had existing channels to regional officials, especially business organizations. Once civil society organization members are elected to the Regional Coordination Council, there are no legal means to ensure their participation, in contrast to mayors, who are subject to such means of accountability as recalls and elections. The cost of attending meetings has also proven prohibitive for some. As one interviewee noted, "Participation can make you poor!" In some regions, traveling to the capital can take days and the costs are high.

Two of the regions with successful Regional Coordination Councils provide additional insight into how to implement this reform; these are Lambeyeque (on the coast) and Cusco (in the southern highlands).[36] In both regions, their coordination councils held two meetings, saw their recommendations accepted, and experienced active civil society participation. In Lambeyeque, citizen activism seems to be growing. In 2001 the regional roundtable against poverty began actively organizing civil society and worked with the regional government on the development plan and the budget process. Cusco also has a very active civil society, as a region with a long history of leftist activism and several experiences with participatory governance. In one city participatory methods to develop the municipal budget have been implemented since 1993.

In an effort to garner stronger public support to counter partisan opposition, Lambeyeque's regional president, Yehude Simon, has been open to and encouraging of civil society participation. Interview data suggest that this openness is also due to his personality, leadership skills, and ideology, his having been a member of the radical left in the 1980s. On the other hand, Simon has been criticized by supporters and detractors alike for his tendency to use participation to garner votes and to seek publicity. Simon himself notes as constraints to deeper participation the lack of money, restrictions from central government, and people's inherent distrust of government. Beyond Simon, his administration supports citizen and civil society participation. For example, the citizen participation office tried to be flexible regarding legal requirements for the 2003 Regional Coordination Council elections in order to encourage broader participation.

Lambeyeque's Regional Coordination Council is emerging as a dynamic opportunity space for civil society participation. Civil society representatives play an active role in meetings. For example, when asked to approve the 2003 development plan, civil society representatives consulted other civil society organizations and presented formal recommendations—later accepted by the regional government—on gender inclusion, on improving the conditions of marginalized populations, on promoting youth development, and on institutionalizing spaces of civil society participation.[37] The civil society organizations took it upon themselves to ensure that at least one woman would serve as a representative. The 2003 registrants also created the Civil Society Assembly, which is consulted by the designated civil society organization representatives ahead of Regional Coordination Council meetings or decisions. Interest in civil society organization participation has increased over time. In 2003 only 34 of these organizations registered to participate; in 2005, 105 of them registered, and these were groups with broad geographic and grassroots participation.

The regional government has been responsive to the demands of civil society organizations. The organizations successfully lobbied for office space in the regional government's building and were granted permission to elect the Regional

Coordination Council president, even though by law the head of the council is the regional president. Due to the small size of the region, only two civil society representatives were elected to the Regional Coordination Council. When one of these members proved problematic—participating haphazardly and leaving the organization that he represented—the regional government called for another election and added two more civil society representatives, with voice but no vote. To maintain the forty-to-sixty proportion, expanded membership was also opened to district mayors.

Unlike Simon, Cusco's regional president, Carlos Cuaresma, was not personally committed to participatory processes. Rather, interviews suggest he slowly became convinced that they served his political goals. In 2002 he attempted to submit his own regional development plans, ignoring those that already existed; and in 2003 he developed new plans without civil society participation. The Regional Coordination Council, led by civil society representatives, refused to approve the new plans. To secure subsequent approval, Cuaresma agreed to a participatory consultative process using regional workshops. During these workshops, according to interviewees, Cuaresma realized that the process served his political interests by helping him to legitimate his government, justify his decisions, and seek support for future votes. He now regularly consults the Regional Coordination Council and personally leads the participatory budgeting process.

While considered successful, the council process has not been implemented according to the letter of the law. New elections were not held in 2005, as the 2003–04 civil society representatives requested an extension of their service in order to institutionalize some of their projects. Several problems emerged following the 2003 elections. Women, youth, and neighborhood organizations were placed in one category, resulting in the absence of a gender representative despite the regional government's mandated gender quota. In response, the elected male representative from the Lion's Club worked with the women's organizations and appointed corepresentatives to attend meetings. According to council representatives, they now work together as a team.

Regional Coordination Council members who are representatives of civil society organizations are well organized and call their own meetings as needed. One of their suggested additions to the regional development plan—a strategic objective on the environment—was accepted and integrated into the final document. These members tend to be urban-biased and highly professional. While these characteristics lend themselves to effective activism and an ability to commit resources and time to the council, the result may be an underrepresentation of rural and grassroots interests.

Participatory Budgeting

Participatory budgeting builds upon the famous case of Porto Alegre in Brazil as well as a Peruvian experiment in the port town of Ilo. The stated goal of the process is to strengthen relations between civil society and the state and to promote the just, rational, efficient, and transparent use of resources. Only capital investment costs are debated, and no salary or fees are provided to participants. The process is regulated through annual instructions developed by the Ministry of Economics and Finance, which include an eight-phase structure, beginning with preparation and information dissemination on the process and legal requirements; a public call, registration, and training of participating agents; and workshops to review the regional development plan and evaluate submitted project proposals (for example, from regional government teams, provincial or district mayors, and civil society). Public meetings are also mandated to report on funded projects and expenditures.

Proposals are to include a statement on how the project relates to the region's development plan, results indicators, and a basic budget. The final list of approved projects is forwarded to the Regional Coordination Council for review and to the elected Regional Council (whose decision is binding). The final budget is then sent to the ministry, Congress, and the General Accounting Office. Approval by the Ministry of Economics and Finance requires a feasibility study for each project, and the regional government must demonstrate minimum compliance with the eight steps in order to receive funds.

According to data sources and interviewees, the regional budget process has problems but is considered more successful overall than the Regional Coordination Council.[38] All regional governments complied with the minimum requirements to hold a participatory process in 2003 and 2004.[39] All governments undertake the process annually—a requirement for receiving funds for their budgets. However, not all regions are following the methodology laid down by the Ministry of Economics and Finance, though compliance with the eight steps has improved over time. In 2003, 36 percent of the regions tracked by the Grupo Propuesta Ciudadana did not follow all of the steps, and no region complied with the eighth step: setting up a functioning oversight committee. According to the ministry, however, by 2004 seven regions (or 28 percent) had complied with the eighth step. To date, only a small proportion of local budgets are under local control: approximately 15 percent at the regional level and 5–7 percent at the local level.[40]

Public meetings—required at least twice a year—are a key component to enhancing the accountability of local government expenditures. During these meetings, regional governments are required to supply information on the programs that have been funded and on expenditures. The budget process is not tied directly to the public meetings, but this is an important aspect of ensuring citizen oversight of the budget process. In 2003 four regions failed to hold the two obligatory meetings. In 2004 only one region did not comply. However, the quality of the meetings is also a concern. About the 2003 meetings, the Grupo Propuesta Ciudadana writes: "The majority of these meetings took place with problems in the call for participation (with short time frames) and without norms approved by the [Regional Council] that regulates them. In general, the speeches by the Presidents were limited to listing the public works that had been undertaken during the year without a balanced focus that would permit a contrast of the achievements and difficulties of his management."[41]

In 2004 many of these problems continued. The Grupo Propuesta Ciudadana found that the information presented during the meetings was not adequate for real oversight and that the meetings tended to take on a tone of marketing the regional governments' accomplishments.[42]

As with the Regional Coordination Council, the participatory budget process in Lambeyeque and Cusco was considered among the most successful of Peru's twenty-five regions. It included implementation of at least seven of the eight steps required by the Ministry of Economics and Finance. The process shows improvement over time, with the participation of civil society on the technical team and final plans linked to the regional development plan.

Decentralization and Decision Space for Civil Society Participation

Despite the ambitiousness of the Toledo government's decentralization reform on paper, its provisions for citizen participation are relatively modest. Its scope, while seemingly broad (encompassing as it does all of the regions of Peru and the creation of new administrative levels), is actually quite narrow. For example, although the new consultative body, the Regional Coordination Council, provides a forum for joint deliberation, its decisions are not binding. Similarly, although participatory budgeting opens the door to civil society engagement in resource decisions, only very small proportions of subnational budgets are implicated. As Ehtisham Ahmad and Mercedes Garcia-Escribano note, "In 2004, local governments carried out [only] 13 percent of total primary expenditures of general government."[43] Political will for decentralization remains subject to the societal forces that drive national, rather than local, politics.[44]

Table 11-2 considers the decision space related to the Regional Coordination Council. By design, the decision space provided by the legal framework seeks to limit local discretion. The process is mandated by national legislation, leaving local government little recourse on paper; however, there is no enforcement of the specific requirements, thus providing room for local officials to interpret the legislation selectively, as the above discussion illustrates. In practice, then, the decision-opportunity space created for local government by the legal framework is only moderate. For civil society, the decentralization policy framework opens up new opportunity space. It specifies parameters for participation by civil society organizations, sets mild requirements for engagement, and allows registered civil society representatives to elect their own delegates. A limiting factor for the possibility of civil society to engage local government in joint governance is the mandate that the Regional Coordination Council meet only twice a year. This

Table 11-2. *Decentralization Decision-Opportunity Space Matrix:*
Regional Coordination Councils

Decentralization dimension	Local government space	Civil society space
Legal, policy, or regulatory framework	Moderate	Moderate
Political	Moderate to wide	Moderate to wide
Resources: fiscal, financial	Narrow	Narrow
Administrative capacity	Narrow to moderate	Narrow to moderate

leaves the possibility of a deeper and continuous relationship with civil society to the discretion of those local government leaders who perceive incentives to extend the process beyond the minimum legal requirements. More complete compliance with the policy as intended would have seen a potential reduction in the decision space available to local governments and an increase in that available to local civil society.

Political factors create a mixed picture regarding the Regional Coordination Council's decision space in support of participatory governance. On the one hand, heightened citizen awareness of decentralization and the role of local government creates pressures for participation and responsiveness that suggest limitations on local governments' discretion and the presence of accountability. On the other hand, the Regional Coordination Council mechanism inspires only a mild perceived benefit, given the time and other resources that may be required and the fact that it is only consultative, not binding. Incentives for civil society participation are further narrowed by the registration fee and lack of travel support or remuneration. It is not surprising, then, that in some regions elected civil society representatives do not attend the two required annual meetings. There is no legal recourse or accountability mechanism within civil society to ensure that they do.

However, the Regional Coordination Council is not the only participatory mechanism available to civil society. Citizen roundtables (*mesas de concertación*), established over ten years ago for local development planning, exist throughout the country, as do a variety of national networks with local nodes that focus on particular issues (for example, women, the poor, indigenous peoples). Thus the political context contains more opportunity space for civil society participation than what the Regional Coordination Council itself creates. Further, beyond these various formal participatory mechanisms, Peru's traditional clientelist politics creates informal opportunities for mutually beneficial relationships between local officials and those citizens with connections.

The reform offers only narrow decision-opportunity space in the resource dimension. As noted above, the amount of resources that local governments have autonomous authority to program and expend, with or without citizen participation, is relatively small. Further, resources devoted to making the Regional Coordination Council operational are few. No additional financial support is available to local governments from the center, and civil society members may receive no payments, fees, or other remuneration for their participation, not even to defray participation costs. Civil society organizations also must pay a registration fee to be eligible for representation on the Regional Coordination Council.

In the administrative capacity dimension, the reform does little to enhance existing decision-opportunity space for local actors. The space available is largely dependent on the existing capacities of these actors in their context. Various observers note the capacity weaknesses both of subnational governments and of civil society, although capacity building for both decentralization and democratization has been an ongoing international donor focus.[45] Capacity deficits clearly limit opportunity space for effective decentralization and effective Regional Coordination Councils.

Table 11-3 summarizes the Regional Coordination Council decision space assessment in greater detail for the two regions, highlighting the manner in which the evolving implementation of decentralization reform led to a relative widening of the decision space in the political and administrative capacity dimensions in Lambeyeque and Cusco. Actors in Lambeyeque shared a complementary values orientation that helped to advance decentralized citizen participation. President Simon's personal affinity with leftist activism encouraged civil society engagement. This, coupled with his perceived self-interest in using the Regional Coordination Council as a means to counter partisan opposition, led to a more robust opening than that specified in the legal framework.

Civil society actors enhanced the cohesiveness of their representation on the Regional Coordination Council by creating and consulting with the Civil Society Assembly before all meetings and decisions of the Regional Coordination Council. Their established commitment to and previous mobilization around combating poverty provided both the capacity for interest aggregation and the commitment to inclusion. This orientation also combined with self-interest to inspire the sector to organize and draft formal recommendations beyond the mandates of the Regional Coordination Council. Civil society engaged despite or possibly because of people's inherent distrust of government. Its formal proposals to the local government could have been perceived as testing the commitment of both state and civil society actors. These actions on the part of civil society demonstrate its adaptability and commitment to sharing power within the sector.

Despite his statements about the policy's restrictions, President Simon shared more power than was mandated with the Regional Coordination Council and supported broad civil society participation, including ceding his role as president of the council to allow civil society to elect its own leadership. This power

Table 11-3. *Decentralization Decision-Opportunity Space Matrix: Regional Coordination Councils in Detail*

Decentralization dimension	*Local government space*	*Civil society space*
Legal, policy, and regulatory framework: moderate space	—Consultation is required; composition of regional coordination councils is legally specified. —Additional sessions can be called. —Mandates not enforced nor is composition specified. —Regional president is designated president of regional coordination council.	—Some requirements on overall composition, but primary requirement is legal regulation and three-year track record. —No enforcement of specifications. —Can elect own representatives from among legally accredited delegates. —Required to meet only twice a year.
Political dimension, Lambeyeque and Cusco	*Lambeyeque: moderate to wide* —Perceived need to counter partisan opposition. —Personal affinity with leftist activism. —Regional administration supports citizen and civil society participation. *Cusco: moderate to wide* —Regional President Cuaresma initially pushes own development plans, undermining his government's legitimacy.	*Lambeyeque: moderate* —Inherent distrust of government. —Some perceptions of President Simon's disingenuousness. *Cusco: moderate to wide* —Ability to reject initial development plans that do not reflect participatory processes, challenging the legitimacy of the Cuaresma government.

	—President Cuaresma discovers that the regional coordination councils and other participatory processes are in his political interest for building legitimacy and support for his government.	—Strong legitimacy gained through history and tradition of leftist activism and continues emphasis on inclusion.
Resources: fiscal, financial dimension, narrow space	—No additional financial support from the center.	—No payments, fees, or other remuneration. —Registration requires a fee. *Cusco: narrow to moderate* —Urban, professional base affords resources and time for the process.
Administrative capacity dimension, Lambeyeque and Cusco	*Lambeyeque: moderate* —Regional administration supports citizen and civil society participation.	*Lambeyeque: moderate* —Regional roundtable mobilization. *Cusco: moderate* —History of leftist activism.

sharing was driven both by President Simon's personal commitment and self-interest and by the inclination of the local government administration to support citizen and civil society participation.

While not as dramatic as in Lambeyeque, the Cusco experience eventually led to a similar broadening of the local government–civil society relationship, though this outcome evolved from an initially narrow decision space. President Cuaresma tried to maximize his available decision space by ignoring the policy and usurping the space intended for civil society. However, he discovered that his decision space was narrower than he anticipated, when the Regional Coordination Council rejected his proposed development plans. More out of self-interest than any mandate or belief in the process, President Cuaresma realized that the council and civil society participation more generally could help him establish his legitimacy and enable him to effectively promote and implement his own agenda. He thus chose to expand the local government–civil society relationship beyond the formal requirements of the policy.

Given the lack of enforcement in the policy framework, civil society groups in Cusco were able to request deviations from the legal framework to better operationalize the opened relationship, building on their history of leftist activism and associated social capital. These groups successfully postponed the 2005 elections in order to institutionalize projects that were under way, ensuring continuity in the representation in joint governance and possibly enhancing the trust and mutual benefit between these specific representatives and President Cuaresma. President Cuaresma may have viewed these representatives as important political constituents, given their urban and professional base, which also may have facilitated the participation of civil society organizations, given the required resource commitments. Like their counterparts in Lambeyeque, civil society representatives in Cusco were able to adapt and share power with other civil society representatives to improve inclusion in the process, particularly with respect to a female representative. As the process has evolved, civil society has also benefited from the capability of the Regional Coordination Council and its extended relationship with local government of providing a forum for creating change.

Both regions experienced a widening of the decision space available in part because local actors developed relationships that built trust. The policy framework outlines specific mandates, which could in principle support accountability based on confidence that mandates will be implemented as specified. However, with little specification of sanctions or recourse in the event that these mandates are not followed, civil society actors could not rely on enforcement of the provisions for the Regional Coordination Council. Unless additional rules are developed at the regional level, operational accountability in the relationship between local government and civil society will necessarily rely on building trust. Generally, incentives for both actors may be weak given the perceived powerlessness of the Regional Coordination Council as a purely consultative body and the fact that most regional civil society sectors are not sufficiently organized to have developed procedures or a culture of collective action. In Lambeyeque and Cusco the existing and evolving organizational capacity of civil society, coupled with the recognized political self-interest of regional presidents, contributed to an experimental orientation toward the decentralization reform that, with evolving experience, led both sets of actors to invest in and expect more from the process.

Despite what may appear to be a rather negative picture of the potential for meaningful local government–civil society interaction through the Regional Coordination Councils, the experience of Lambeyeque and Cusco suggests otherwise. Table 11-4 gives examples of the way local governments and civil societies in the two regions managed, within the decision space available to them, to engage in participatory local governance. In both regions, the policy framework did not keep local governments from extending the process in depth or breadth in response to perceived incentives and civil society demands.

The participatory budgeting component of Peru's decentralization reform is a top-down mandate that yields only a narrow-to-moderate decision space for local actors (see table 11-5). Local government experiences a narrowing of its discretion, both in the legal framework, as it is mandated to include citizen participation as a requirement for capital investment funding, and also in the political dimension, where it may now face additional pressures from civil society to be responsive to a wider range of constituents. On the other hand, as with the Regional Coordination Council, participatory budgeting may become attractive to local governments for the same reasons. For example, in Cusco the regional president chose to oversee the entire participatory budgeting process as a means to enhance his legitimacy.

Local civil society, on the other hand, has a moderate degree of decision space created through the legal framework, as it now has a right to participate, with some enforcement incentive from the center (the withholding of central funding), though for relatively small amounts of resources. Its decision-opportunity space in the political dimension is also potentially widened due to its sanctioned role as participant in and watchdog over local government capital expenditures. However, this widened space is only potential. As reported by the Grupo Propuesta Ciudadana, the quality of public meetings may take on a pro forma or regional government marketing orientation at the expense of more meaningful accountability exchanges.[46]

From a resource perspective, local governments see their decision space narrowed as funds that were once primarily under their own discretion are now subject to citizen input and a somewhat onerous process of planning and evaluation imposed from the center. On its part, civil society experiences a moder-

Table 11-4. *Discretionary Use of Decision-Opportunity Space: Examples*

Region	Local government space	Civil society space
Lambeyeque	—Provision of office space for civil society organization representatives. —Accepts formal recommendations from civil society organizations beyond mandates of the regional coordination councils. —Allows civil society organization representatives to elect their own regional coordination council president. —When one of the two civil society organization members proves problematic, calls for a new election; adds two more civil society organization representatives with voice but no vote.	—Creates the Civil Society Assembly to regularly consult other civil society organizations before all regional coordination council meetings and decisions. —Presents formal recommendations. —Coordinates to ensure inclusion of a woman representative.
Cusco	—Broadens process through consultative regional workshops. —Cuaresma calls on regional coordination council for consultation whenever he perceives an interest to do so. —Accepts additional regional coordination council meetings as called. —In response to civil society organization representatives' request, no new elections are called in 2005.	—Appoints a corepresentative to ensure a woman representative. —Civil society organization representatives call for their own regional coordination council meetings as needed. —Civil society organizations request waivers to formal requirement, such as postponing 2005 elections.

ately expanded decision space in the resource dimension, as it has for the first time an opportunity to influence the application of (limited) resources allocated from the center. As with the Regional Coordination Council, in the administrative capacity dimension, decision-opportunity space is dependent on the existing capacities of local actors. The reform itself narrows local governments' discretion as it requires an intensive participatory planning process, potentially taxing the capacity of the local administration. These requirements also hold for citizens, though the process arguably may enhance their capacity through experience in planning and oversight.

Table 11-5. *Decentralization Decision-Opportunity Space Matrix: Participatory Budgeting*

Decentralization dimension	Local government space	Civil society space
Legal, policy, and regulatory framework	Narrow	Narrow to moderate
Political	Narrow	Moderate to wide
Resources: fiscal, financial	Narrow	Moderate
Administrative capacity	Narrow to moderate	Narrow to moderate

Conclusion

This latest Peruvian decentralization effort has been only partially implemented. The gap between what exists on paper and what happens in practice varies widely across Peru's regions. Though modestly, the two regions assessed in this chapter have narrowed that gap, with beneficial effects on civil society participation in local governance. Consistent with the findings of Nick Devas and Ursula Grant, the relative success in Lambeyeque and Cusco regarding enhanced democratic relationships between local government and civil society can be credited to a committed local leadership and articulate civil society organizations.[47] This conclusion suggests that democratic decentralization is most likely to work where such local political will and capacity already exist, implying a relatively narrow potential for effective top-down-designed decentralization reform. On the other hand, the experience of participatory budgeting—generally believed to have more potential to enhance democratic accountability at the local level—is consistent with the literature emphasizing the need for central monitoring of local performance in order for decentralization to work effectively.

The two civil society mechanisms specified in the decentralization legal framework imply alternative approaches to decision space and the design of incentives. On the one hand, local decision space can be intentionally narrowed for government actors, with a heavy reliance on bureaucratic enforcement and accountability mechanisms when local incentives are clear and recourse for noncompliance is also specified. This was the case for participatory budgeting, despite the small proportion of local budgets that was implicated. On the other hand, the concept of the Regional Coordination Council is a more flexible approach, allowing wider decision space for local actors, enabling them to experiment with accountability through evolving relationships, experience, and trust building. Clearly the latter option depends on the perceived incentives of participating actors, especially local government. Local government actors may choose to cherry-pick, deciding which pieces of the reform to act upon, or to ignore reforms without enforcement mechanisms, as President Cuaresma in Cusco originally tried to do. An organized civil society, cognizant of its rights, was however able to counter this move, forcing President Cuaresma to consider the potential merits of compliance—at his discretion.

The Regional Coordination Council experience demonstrates how a policy framework, whose moderate decision-opportunity space and limited incentives expanded during implementation, led to an enhanced potential for a more democratic local government–civil society relationship, which was not necessarily supported in the policy's design. In contrast, the participatory budgeting policy framework represents a much narrower decision space approach, with a highly specified mandated process with teeth: capital investment resources subject to compliance. The result is a relatively more complete implementation of the policy as designed, with compliance with the full process evolving with experience.

Our analysis of the decision-opportunity space in the Toledo decentralization reform in Peru confirms the tension between centrally designed measures to constrain space locally in the interests of achieving democratic decentralization outcomes and the potential benefits of discretion. The argument is often made that constraints and sanctions are necessary to combat elite capture of local government. Our analysis indicates that such a conclusion is incomplete. While elite capture is indeed a danger, when incentives are aligned such that local officials see that engaging and empowering civil society is in their interests, then allowing them the space to act on those interests may serve the aims of democratic decentralization. This approach proved somewhat effective in the two regions where civil society is relatively organized and inclusive. Better-off and better-endowed actors will have an advantage in exploiting the decision-opportunity space that decentralization opens up. However, from a design perspective, it may be worthwhile to pay the price of a bit of elite capture in order to provide opportunities and incentives for less well-resourced civil society members to become engaged and to develop skills, while seeking to ensure that a supportive legal and institutional framework—with accountability and checks and balances—is in place or can be built.

An important driver of the effectiveness of civil society participation with local government lies with civil society members themselves. Local communities need the capacities and resources to engage in collective action for participatory mechanisms to achieve their intended effects. These capacities take time to develop and evolve from learning from both success and failure. Incentives for citizens to engage with the state are critical.

As the regional cases assessed here show, civil society groups' limited interest in a Regional Coordination Council demonstrates an astute assessment of this mechanism's ability to further their interests. However, this assessment was not universal across regions, nor was it static. In Lambeyeque, civil society organizations could be seen to have tested the commitment, and hence the salience, of the reform by offering more formal recommendations than the legal framework specified. Upon acceptance of their recommendations, the Civil Society Assembly continued to press for its process preferences and saw an inclusive and responsive relationship emerge. In Cusco, only when the assembly's refusal to approve Cuaresma's development plan yielded a more participatory response from the regional president did a more democratic relationship between local government and civil society evolve, wherein civil society representatives saw an interest not only in participating but also in extending their terms on the Regional Coordination Council.

Decentralization is fundamentally a political process, rearranging the classic political calculus of who gets what. The ebb and flow of decentralization in Peru reflects the calculations of the national actors in power regarding how best to remain there; as a function of those national decisions, a similar dynamic plays out among local government actors. Only when local citizens can exert counter-vailing power regarding those calculations can participatory and democratic decentralization be said to have succeeded. The concepts of the Regional Coordination Council and of participatory budgeting are small steps in the direction of empowered citizen participation in local governance.

Notes

1. Thomas J. Bossert and Joel C. Beauvais, "Decentralization of Health Systems in Ghana, Zambia, Uganda and the Philippines: A Comparative Analysis of Decision Space," *Health Policy and Planning* 17, no. 1 (2002): 14–31; World Bank, "Exploring Partnerships between Communities and Local Governments in Community Driven Development: A Framework," Report 32709-GLB, 2005.

2. Bossert and Beauvais, "Decentralization of Health Systems in Ghana, Zambia, Uganda and the Philippines," p. 29.

3. Stephanie McNulty, "Empowering CSOs: Exploring Peru's Efforts to Decentralize the State and Increase Civil Society's Participation in Regional Politics," Ph.D. dissertation, George Washington University, 2006.

4. Elinor Ostrom, "Crossing the Great Divide: Coproduction, Synergy, and Development," *World Development* 24, no. 6 (1996): 1073–87; Jennifer M. Brinkerhoff, *Partnership for International Development: Rhetoric or Results?* (Boulder, Colo.: Lynne Rienner, 2002); World Bank, *World Development Report 2004: Making Services Work for the Poor* (2004).

5. Archon Fung and Erik O. Wright, eds., *Deepening Democracy: Institutional Innovations in Empowered Participatory Governance* (London: Verso, 2003).

6. Anirudh Krishna, "Partnerships between Local Governments and Community-Based Organizations: Exploring the Scope for Synergy," *Public Administration and Development* 23, no. 4 (2003): 361–71.

7. Hazel Johnson and Gordon Wilson, "Biting the Bullet: Civil Society, Social Learning, and the Transformation of Local Governance," *World Development* 28, no. 11 (2000): 1891–906.

8. Ghazala Mansuri and Vijayendra Rao, "Community-Based and -Driven Development: A Critical Review," *World Bank Research Observer* 19, no. 1 (2004): 1–39; Krishna, "Partnerships between Local Governments and Community-Based Organizations"; Anirudh Krishna, *Active Social Capital: Tracing the Roots of Development and Democracy* (Columbia University Press, 2002); Sue Goss, *Making Local Governance Work: Networks, Relationships, and Management of Change* (New York: Palgrave, 2001); and Christian Grootaert, "Social

Capital, Household Welfare and Poverty in Indonesia," Policy Research Working Paper 2148, World Bank, 1999.

9. John Gaventa, "Towards Participatory Local Governance: Six Propositions," paper based on a presentation made for Ford Foundation, LOGO Program Officer's Retreat, June 2001, Institute for Development Studies, University of Sussex, 2001; John Gaventa, "Exploring Citizenship, Participation and Accountability," *IDS Bulletin* 33, no. 2 (2002): 1–11.

10. Deborah Bräutigam, "The People's Budget? Politics, Participation and Pro-Poor Policy," *Development Policy Review* 22, no. 6 (2004): 653–68.

11. Merilee Grindle, *Going Local: Decentralization, Democratization, and the Promise of Good Governance* (Princeton University Press, forthcoming, 2007).

12. Nick Devas and Ursula Grant, "Local Government Decision-Making—Citizen Participation and Local Accountability: Some Evidence from Kenya and Uganda," *Public Administration and Development* 23, no. 4 (2003): 307–16.

13. Frederick Golooba-Mutebi, "Devolution and Outsourcing of Municipal Services in Kampala City, Uganda: An Early Assessment," *Public Administration and Development* 23, no. 5 (2003): 405–18.

14. Frederick Golooba-Mutebi, "Reassessing Popular Participation in Uganda," *Public Administration and Development* 24, no. 4 (2004): 302.

15. Brinkerhoff, *Partnership for International Development: Rhetoric or Results?*

16. Mansuri and Rao, "Community-Based and -Driven Development."

17. Rebecca Abers, "From Clientelism to Cooperation: Local Government, Participatory Policy, and Civic Organizing in Porto Alegre, Brazil," *Politics and Society* 26, no. 4 (1998): 511–37; Peter Heller, "Moving the State: The Politics of Democratic Decentralisation in Kerala, South Africa, and Porto Alegre," *Politics and Society* 29, no. 1 (2001): 131–63.

18. Avener Greif, *Institutions, Theory and History: Comparative and Institutional Analysis* (Cambridge University Press, 2006).

19. Jurian Edelenbos, "Institutional Implications of Interactive Governance: Insights from Dutch Practice," *Governance* 18, no. 1 (2005): 126.

20. Richard C. Crook, "Decentralization and Poverty Reduction in Africa: The Politics of Local-Central Relations," *Public Administration and Development* 23, no. 1 (2003): 77–89.

21. John Gaventa, "Triumph, Deficit or Contestation? Deepening the 'Deepening Democracy' Debate" (Sussex, U.K.: Institute for Development Studies, 2005).

22. Derick W. Brinkerhoff and Charlotte Leighton, "Decentralization and Health System Reform: Issue in Brief," *Insights for Implementers* 1 (Partners for Health Reform Project, U.S. Agency for International Development, 2002).

23. Bossert and Beauvais, "Decentralization of Health Systems in Ghana, Zambia, Uganda and the Philippines," p. 16.

24. Ibid.

25. World Bank, "Exploring Partnerships."

26. In addition to the sources cited, the data presented here on Regional Coordination Councils and participatory budgeting derive from interviews and observations conducted by Stephanie McNulty during her fieldwork in Peru in 2003–05.

27. Kathleen O'Neill, *Decentralizing the State: Elections, Parties, and Local Power in the Andes* (Cambridge University Press, 2005).

28. Gregory D. Schmidt, "Political Variables and Governmental Decentralization in Peru, 1949–1988," *Journal of Interamerican Studies and World Affairs* 31, nos. 1, 2 (1989): 193–232.

29. As of this writing the left-leaning Alan García, Peruvian president from 1985 to 1990 (who narrowly lost to Alejandro Toledo in 2001), was elected president in a second-round

runoff in June 2006. It is too early to predict what impact the new administration will have on prospects for decentralization and local governance.

30. The watchdog groups include the Defensoría del Pueblo (Human Rights Ombudsman), a governmental office tasked with tracking progress on human rights and democracy in general; and Grupo Propuesta Ciudadana (Citizen's Proposal Group), a consortium of civil society organizations in Lima and around the country that monitors progress in the regions through its partner organizations that form the Vigila Perú network (this monitoring is partially funded by the U.S. Agency for International Development).

31. Defensoría del Pueblo, "Actores para el buen gobierno. Reporte del proceso de constitución de los Consejos de Coordinación Regional a nivel nacional" (Lima: 2003); Defensoría del Pueblo, "Recomendaciones para la elección de representantes sociales en los Consejos de Coordinación Regional correspondiente al año 2005" (Lima: 2005).

32. Grupo Propuesta Ciudadana, "Sistema Vigila Perú: Balance del primer año de la descentrealización," Reporte nacional 3 (Lima: 2004); Grupo Propuesta Ciudadana, "Vigilancia del proceso de descentralización," Reporte nacional 7 (Lima: 2005); McNulty, "Empowering CSOs."

33. Grupo Propuesta Ciudadana, "Sistema Vigila Perú: Balance anual 2004," Reporte nacional 6 (Lima: 2005).

34. Ibid., p. 37.

35. On rural underrepresentation, see Defensoría del Pueblo, "Análisis y aportes sobre el presupuesto participativo" (Lima: 2005).

36. Of the six regions studied, these were the only two that McNulty deemed successful in terms of complying with most of the implementation features of the reform; McNulty, "Empowering CSOs."

37. Centro de Estudios Sociales Solidaridad, "Reporte de vigilancia ciudadana al Gobierno Regional de Lambeyeque (GRL): Balance anual 2003" (Chiclayo, Peru: 2004).

38. Data sources include the ombudsman and two USAID-sponsored programs, Grupo Propuesta Ciudadana and Pro-Descentralización, which evaluated the process in 2003, 2004, and 2005.

39. Irma Del Aguila Peralta, "Procesos de planeamiento concertado y presupuesto participativo 2005" (Lima: Mesa de Concertación para la Lucha Contra La Pobreza, 2004); José Lopéz Ricci, "Planeamento y presupuesto participativo: Tendencias generales analizadas a partir del portal MEF," Cuadernos Descentralistas 14 (Lima: 2005).

40. José López Ricci and Elisa Wiener, "Lecciones y tensiones de una historia que recién empieza: Balance de los procesos de planteamiento y presupuesto participativo regional 2003–2004 en 11 regiones del Perú," Working Paper, Grupo Propuesta Ciudadana, 2004.

41. Grupo Propuesta Ciudadana, "Vigila Perú: Reporte nacional" (Lima: 2003), p. 43.

42. Grupo Propuesta Ciudadana, "Nuevo instructivo del presupuesto participativo en consulta," 2005 (www.participaperu.org.pe [February 15, 2005]).

43. Ehtisham Ahmad and Mercedes Garcia-Escribano, "Fiscal Decentralization and Public Subnational Financial Management in Peru," Working Paper 06 120, Fiscal Affairs Department, International Monetary Fund, 2006, p. 3.

44. Kathleen O'Neill, Decentralizing the State: Elections, Parties, and Local Power in the Andes (Cambridge University Press, 2005).

45. World Bank, "Peru Institutional Governance Review," 2001.

46. Grupo Propuesta Ciudadana, "Vigila Perú."

47. Devas and Grant, "Local Government Decision-Making."

12

Challenges to Decentralized Governance in Weak States

GORAN HYDEN

Within the international development community the Scandinavian countries are among the most ardent advocates of decentralization. They have their own long history of how decentralization has helped foster democracy. To this day, local governments in those countries raise and retain more public tax revenue than elsewhere. A great number of core government functions are controlled and managed by local authorities.

To understand the challenges that exist in trying to foster decentralized forms of governance in weak states, it is instructive to look at the factors that explain the success of the Scandinavian countries. Decentralized governance was not concocted and imposed from above by a central authority (or a group of international agencies). It evolved over time from the bottom up and was largely shaped by a social and economic transition that brought people together in urbanized communities and social movements.[1] It was a struggle between civil society and the state, in which the victory of the former eliminated the state patronage system that had been in place in previous periods of political rule. It led not to the German version of a bureaucratic Rechtstaat but to a form of governance in which officials were democratically accountable. As another observer concludes: "The process toward democratic decentralisation became messy and complex, not uniform and straightforward."[2]

In the contemporary discourse on governance, decentralization is often elevated into an end in itself. Many factors have contributed to this new situation.

Development discourse itself has shifted. As Amartya Sen argues, freedom is not a product of development; it is development.[3] Another reason is the strong emphasis on poverty reduction. This orientation puts a premium on creating conditions in which underprivileged groups do not just benefit from these policies but have an opportunity, as legitimate stakeholders, to shape them. A third factor is the significant role that the United Nations' Millennium Development Goals play in international development circles. The fifteen-year time schedule for realizing these ambitious goals exerts extra pressure on all actors, donors as well as recipients.

In this situation—in which historical context is ignored in favor of the transfer of current best practices—international development assistance for decentralized governance easily becomes a hit-or-miss exercise. Its record is hardly encouraging. As Shabbir Cheema and Dennis Rondinelli demonstrate in chapter 1 of this volume, although many countries have moved toward more democratic forms of governance, their attempts to decentralize have not always been easy and successful. This is particularly true of the countries in Africa, with their weak states. While the introduction of such democratic institutions as free and fair elections shows some success, reforming ingrained features of centralized governance has proved more challenging.[4] It is no coincidence that the international development community, as Cheema and Rondinelli also discuss, has in frustration moved from one approach to another over the past four decades.

This continuous flux—one roughly every decade—is a response partly to the changing conditions on the international scene, partly to the lessons learned from actual efforts to put various decentralization schemes into practice. It is becoming increasingly clear that, after several concerted attempts by agencies in the international development community to sponsor decentralization as a means of enhancing the prospects for improved development performance, there is a need to identify not only the contextual constraints to success but also the particular institutional models that apply to specific historical circumstances. This chapter tries to do this with reference to the weak states in sub-Saharan Africa. There are good reasons for such a focus. It is the most obvious graveyard of misconceived development programs carried out under the banner of decentralization. It is furthest away from attaining the millennium development goals. And most influential donors have recently decided that the best way of helping these countries is to provide them with budget rather than program or project aid. Ignoring everything that has been written about the nature of the state in Africa and its inability to serve the public, especially the poor, through direct policy interventions, these agencies are set to feed the centrally controlled state treasuries in these countries with a bloated augmentation of financial resources. What are the chances of decentralized governance in these circumstances? How can the interests of the poor be enhanced? These are the two main questions that this chapter addresses.

It begins with a brief review of the shifting approaches to decentralization and how they have affected development in Africa. It continues to analyze the constraints to decentralized governance before presenting an approach to funding development in countries with a weak state that turns the process away from being driven by donors rather than local stakeholders. It concludes with implications for relevant actors.

Shifting Approaches

The independent states in Africa are the creation of European colonizers with different perceptions of governance. While the French and the Portuguese introduced a state machinery that reflected a Napoleonic model of central control, the Belgians and the British favored a more decentralized way of running their colonies. This difference is often expressed in terms of direct versus indirect rule.[5] Students of government administration, like Brian Smith, call the former approach an "integrated prefectoral" model, the latter an "unintegrated prefectoral" model.[6]

These differences are less evident today, as they have been gradually erased by two processes. First is the need that African government leaders have felt to centralize power in the name of political stability and national development. Because these states are generally multiethnic and too culturally fragmented to warrant a federal solution (Nigeria being an exception), the overwhelming tendency has been to favor centralization over decentralization (Botswana being an exception). Thus states in the region have become increasingly similar, with a preference for the integrated prefectoral model of governance. The other process is the integration of the African states into the international development community after independence and their growing dependence on external funding sources. This has created a preference for adopting approaches designed by foreign consultants and funded by donor agencies. These approaches reflect what is fashionable in global professional and political circles rather than what is suitable for countries with variable socioeconomic and political circumstances. The blueprint approach to governance and development has been an integral part of Africa's interaction with the international development community over the years.

This blueprint approach began in the 1960s under the auspices of modernization theory. Defined largely in technocratic terms, development was operationalized with little or no attention to context. The principal task was to ensure that institutions and techniques that had proved successful in modernizing the Western world could be replicated. Policy efforts were concentrated in two directions. One was to produce comprehensive national development plans as guides for sectoral policies. Second was to design specific projects that would form the relevant implementation mechanisms of these plans. Project design was the prerogative of technical experts carried out on behalf of potential beneficiaries without their input. Central government institutions carried the primary responsibility for allocating resources and overseeing the implementation of the projects. In this initial period after independence in African countries, there was no consideration of decentralization, even less so the idea that people should have a stake in the projects.

It did not take long for policy analysts and practitioners to recognize that national development plans require a different organizing principle than projects require. Whereas the plans call for comprehensiveness, projects only create enclaves with few or no forward and backward linkages. Analysts concluded that the project approach failed to realize improvements, especially in the conditions of the poor. Convinced that something else had to be done, development assistance agencies decided that a sectoral approach would be more effective. This placed the emphasis on integrated programs focused on satisfying the basic needs of people in a given area. A particularly popular model was the integrated rural development program. This helped bring about the first phase of decentralization in Africa. It entailed deconcentrating authority to lower levels of government administration. The integrated prefectoral model was reinforced as more authority to lead and coordinate development activities was given to local governors. Despite the reallocation of senior administrators to the field, the new sectoral or area program approach became too cumbersome, requiring a level of bureaucratization that proved counterproductive. The public service sector grew in an almost uncontrolled fashion. Decisions were often hampered by red tape and lack of attention to technical issues. As several studies from those days demonstrate, this form of administrative decentralization did little or nothing to help the poor.[7]

It was out of frustration with trying to promote development using the state as the sole engine that the reforms in the 1980s turned in another direction, bringing in the market as a complementary resource allocation mechanism. The assumption was that the market would reduce red tape and enhance efficiency. It would also give local citizens, notably rural producers, a chance to participate more actively in the development process. As analysts went back to their drawing boards, the challenge was no longer managing or administering development as much as it was identifying incentives that would facilitate development. This implied reform at the policy level, as emphasized in a World Bank report on African development that became the new lead document.[8]

The new approach called for a look at decentralization that transcended conventional notions. Instead of treating it merely as a shift of authority or power within a government system, it required a holistic look at all institutions in society, private and voluntary included.[9] It entailed delegation of authority to newly formed independent executive agencies, privatization of public services, and establishment of new public-private partnerships.[10] These reforms also formed part of policy packages that were issued by the international finance institutions under the rubric structural adjustment. The problem with these efforts to reform the state by placing greater reliance on the market is that not only did most people in the region have at best only one foot in the marketplace, but also market institutions themselves were very weak. As a result, corruption increased rather than decreased. The expected benefits from these reforms in Africa only partly materialized. Many governments managed to get their public finances in order, but the national economy was very slow in producing benefits and better services to the public. The poor were often further marginalized and relegated to the insecurity of the informal sector.[11]

Economic reforms paved the way for what Cheema and Rondinelli call the transition from government decentralization to decentralized governance. This trend has continued from the 1990s to date (see table 12-1). There has been a growing recognition that development is not only about projects, programs, and policies but also about politics. Getting politics right is as important as getting prices right. Underlying this most recent shift toward creating a politically enabling environment is the assumption that development, after all, is the product of what people decide to do themselves to improve their livelihoods. People, not governments (especially those run by autocrats), constitute the principal force of development. They must be given the right incentives and opportunities not only in the economic but also in the political arena; hence the emphasis on decentralized governance. Development is no longer a benevolent, top-down, exercise, not even a charitable act by civil society organizations, but instead a bottom-up process in which people have the chance to create institutions that respond to their own needs and priorities.[12] The problem with this new good governance approach is that it is being promoted in a context in which civic consciousness and civic organizations are weak or nonexistent.

In 2006 it looked as though all these efforts by the international development community to shape Africa's development policy had run their course. The enthusiasm that donors showed in the 1990s for the strengthening of civil society was being abandoned. A new aid architecture that had been evolving was confirmed in 2005 by the Paris Declaration on Aid Effectiveness, signed by ministers of developed and developing countries. The declaration emphasizes in particular the fact that recipient governments have prime responsibility for formulating and implementing national development strategies. Donors agree to harmonize their own activities with each other and recipient governments.

It is too early to say whether this new approach represents anything other than rhetoric, but it is worth discussing possible implications if it is going to be pursued by the donors. It seems to imply that if African governments only get ownership of their policies and the international development community keeps channeling funds to their treasuries, the problems that have hampered policy implementation in past decades will go away. Donors appear ready to abrogate their right to intervene in the way their funds are being used; they expect that annual consultations conducted by diplomatic representatives will suffice to

Table 12-1. *Summary of Trends toward Decentralized Governance in Africa*

Decade	Development policy	Decentralization focus	Main problem
1960s	Modernization	None	Overcentralization
1970s	Basic needs	Deconcentration	Bureaucratization
1980s	Structural adjustment	Delegation, privatization	Corruption
1990s	Good governance	Decentralized governance	Civic deficit

ensure honest and concerted implementation of the policies that have been officially agreed upon by the partners. In countries in which public institutions, after four decades of political independence, remain as fragile as ever, this approach must be described as a great leap of faith by the international development community. This retreat by donors into partnerships may also have the effect of reducing their readiness to accept that the way their funds are channeled to African countries through their government treasuries is not necessarily the solution to reducing poverty but rather a growing obstacle in doing so.

Constraints to Decentralized Governance

In countries like those in Africa where dependence on foreign aid remains extensive and is likely to be so for the foreseeable future, especially in the light of pledges of more money from donors, constraints to making partnership a political reality for the poor are not just domestic but are also nested in the relationship with the donor community. Discussing decentralized governance merely in terms of policy reforms by national government agencies is not enough. By virtue of their money, donors remain agenda setters. Their concepts, their language, and their preferences tend to prevail not only in framing the agenda but also in setting policy, especially public finance policy. When it comes to implementation, however, national agencies dominate, usually in ways that diverge from official policy. This discrepancy between intent and result is not going to be resolved by the new aid architecture. In fact there is reason to assume that it will increase. The political realities of these countries are such that, when it comes to both the ends and means of national development, especially poverty reduction, donor and recipient countries, despite the new commitment to partnership, are on a collision course. Let me elaborate.

The Paris Declaration on Aid Effectiveness, like previous political statements about development assistance, assumes that everything good will come together in a harmonious manner. Fiscal reforms and decentralized governance will be in harmony; strengthening government capacity will mean more partnerships with private and voluntary sector organizations; increased alignment of aid with national policy goals will reduce poverty; and so on. There are many reasons why little, if anything, of this will happen by 2010 (the time frame set for assessing the results of the declaration). It begins with the structural realities of the African economies. First, these economies are dominated by actors who see themselves as having little need for government assistance. Farming households in rural areas are becoming more rather than less subsistence oriented, as males migrate to urban areas for work.[13] The vast majority of Africa's rapidly increasing urban population operates in the informal sector, where avoiding contact with authorities is the preferred strategy. This means that society is not organized into interest groups that demand certain services or goods in order to do a better job. Making sense of decentralized governance in these circumstances calls for approaches other than those that mainstream agencies typically prescribe.

Second, this population prefers informal, face-to-face exchanges over formal ones. Policy analysts have great difficulty in incorporating such informal institutions into their analysis because they are nested in cultural practices that transcend conventional notions of costs and benefits or cost effectiveness. The inclination of these analysts to treat this preference as a constraint that must be removed for development to take place compromises the significance of the needs of these local actors and stakeholders. Conventional policy analysts fail to see, for instance, that in Africa's rudimentary political economy there are fewer transaction costs associated with relying on a powerful relative or friend—a patron—than those associated with organizing with others to pursue a common good. Similarly, these analysts exaggerate the free rider problem in African societies, where patrons interested in building political power for themselves are more than ready to provide a common or public good even if others do not contribute.[14]

Third is the relatively high degree of political instability and the uncertainty that follows in the wake of political reforms aimed at enhancing political competitiveness. This is the case not only in multiethnic states with a record of fragility, like Sierra Leone, Liberia, and the Democratic Republic of Congo. The political order is generally quite fragile in Africa because the social order is in rapid flux. Bringing about the rule of law in these conditions is fraught with particular difficulties. Policy analysts and practitioners forget that the prevailing notion of justice in Africa is based on reciprocity, not impartiality. It stems from customary forms of justice that existed in precolonial society and that have been perpetuated to this day. This notion colors not only civil relations but also actors in the public realm. Justice as reciprocity is understood as the right of one actor—individual, group, community, or state—to pursue its ideal interest in competition with others on a common understanding of the moral limits of these pursuits.

When Africans lived and worked in local rural communities before and under colonial tutelage, these limits were well known and respected; the common good was, therefore, easy to defend and pursue. As a result of urbanization and more recently of globalization, these parochial boundaries have weakened.

What is right and wrong to contemporary Africans has become much more difficult to agree upon. It is this moral crisis in society, rather than quality of governance, that worries most Africans. Increased instances of popular justice, outbreaks of civil violence, and harsher measures by the police and security forces to deal with what the state identifies as criminal or illicit behavior are evidence of this moral crisis.

Fourth, African governments operate on the basis of patronage rather than policy. To be sure, policy pronouncements are made in public and often agreed upon in the presence of donors. These pronouncements, however, are aimed at obtaining funds from donors rather than serving as guides for what individual government institutions are expected to do. The latter functions in the context of personal networks rather than bureaucratic rules. Policy objectives, therefore, are constantly modified by these personal interactions within ministries or by clientele forms of politics. Public administration in Africa suffers from a Weberian deficit: that is, there is not enough respect for the rules—and roles—that are meant to turn a public organization into a policy implementing machine. This phenomenon has been described by a number of scholars analyzing African politics.[15]

Fifth, even in a context of political devolution of power to local government bodies, their ability to operate autonomously is severely constrained by both economic and political factors. The revenue basis in African countries is very limited. Collecting revenue in predominantly rural districts often costs more than what is being obtained. These local government institutions, therefore, can operate only with grants in aid from central government. These grants typically make up between 75 and 90 percent of their revenue. This means that the terms for how to use the funds are set by central government actors with no direct accountability to the electorate of the local councils. This dependence on central government is exacerbated by political patronage relations. National leaders rely on local politicians for support, and vice versa.

Sixth is the prevalence of standardized policy packages that make little or no consideration of national variations. Much of this stems from the reliance of African governments on foreign donors. Not only do the latter fund the majority of national development initiatives in African countries, they also design them. With due respect for the professional expertise that these advisers and consultants bring to the table, they typically have limited knowledge of the social and political circumstances in which particular policy packages are meant to be implemented. They often take solutions "from the shelf," such as best practices from other country experiences, and recommend their application with little attention to the feasibility and relevance in the new context. Given the limited backward and forward linkages that characterize economic activities in African countries, these policy prescriptions are often wide of the mark in the context of local government operations. Substantive policy outcomes fall far short of expectations. Attempts at strengthening local governance are hampered.

This list could be further extended but suffice it here to conclude that the constraints to realizing decentralized forms of governance are particularly severe in African countries. Their problems call for solutions adapted to and built on African realities rather than standardized measures imposed from the top, with the blessing and support of donors. How can this possibly be done in the context of the new aid architecture that stresses partnership, budget support, and structural lending?

A Possible Step Forward

A weak state, as defined in this chapter, is one characterized by the prevalence of informal over formal rules and patronage over policy. Based on the experience of other countries, the argument is that decentralization—and decentralized governance, for that matter—are hard to institutionalize in such circumstances. Public institutions in the United States suffered from the spoils system, which in the late nineteenth century caused a reaction that led scholars, notably Woodrow Wilson, to call for a "scientific" approach to public administration and—later— politicians, under the banner of the Progressive Party, to call for a delegation of responsibility for implementing government policy to independent executive agencies run by experts, not politicians. As suggested in the introduction of this chapter, the Scandinavians completed the transformation to a modern—and strong—state by also ensuring that it was decentralized and politically accountable to the public. They cleared their Weberian deficit and boosted their democratic qualities in a single historic leap.

The international development community is not going to sit around waiting for these conditions to emerge in Africa. Because this community wishes to accelerate the process with the help of best practices from other parts of the world, it set these weak states up for perennial failure. The best that can be achieved in these circumstances is a bogus form of fiscal decentralization, which involves retention of control by the central government treasury and, indirectly, by the donors. Left out of this equation are all the ingredients with any prospect of enhancing genuine decentralized governance: larger local revenue collection, politically more accountable local authorities, the growth of social movements, and a civil society that enhances such public accountability.

The argument here is not that these important ingredients of decentralized governance can be brought about by donors alone (certainly not within the time horizons that they operate). What is argued, however, is that donors can contribute to establishing the institutional conditions in which a move in that direction can be meaningfully initiated. The step being recommended for consideration here builds on an expert consultation that took place in Kampala, Uganda, in 1995, in which a model of autonomous development funds was discussed and adopted as a means of dealing with the problems of financing development projects in weak states.[16]

A few such funds have been established with the help of select donors, the Cultural Development Fund of Tanzania (Mfuku wa Utamaduni Tanzania) being the most prominent example.[17] The problem has not been how to get the African governmental and civil society actors to consider this complementary mode of channeling funds for development, but rather how to get donors interested in adopting it. Because donors tend to be too wedded to the Weberian model of bureaucracy, they find it hard to think outside the box. Their policy of achieving coordination, as reaffirmed in the Paris Declaration, only makes the consideration of alternatives more difficult. What donors have shown themselves incapable of doing to date is creating the conditions under which, one, a respect for public policy—and indirectly, therefore, public institutions—is strengthened; and two, policy space (possibilities for a broader range of actors) is generated. The latter is similar to the call for decision space in partnerships argued in chapter 11 of this volume (by Derick Brinkerhoff, Jennifer Brinkerhoff, and Stephanie McNulty).

The remainder of the chapter spells out in greater detail what can be done with the original autonomous development fund. It is important to point out that the proposal here is a revised version of the original model. It considers changes in African and international conditions as well as ideas about how the model can fit into donor preferences for budget rather than project support, not as an alternative but as a complement. As will become clear, the emphasis is on retaining autonomy while still achieving an adequate measure of public accountability in the context of a decentralized form of governance.

The Development Fund Model

Development funds are not new to donors. They have been used for a variety of purposes in the past: rural development, small-scale project financing, social action, and poverty reduction. The experience with the vast majority of these funds has been negative. Resources have been wasted, money has been misappropriated, and allocations have been controlled by political patrons. The image of the fund model, therefore, is not necessarily positive.

The reason that the model has a questionable reputation, however, is not because it cannot work but because it has been implemented with little attention to what enhances success. Funds have been approved by donors in the past in order to politically placate a recipient government, head of state, or (in recent years) a first lady serving as chair of a presidential fund aimed at enhancing the living conditions of women, children, and other underrepresented groups. Because such funds are controlled by the office of the head of state or one of his nearest advisers, donors have found it impolitic to raise issues of accountability and performance. If donors and recipients now label themselves development partners, it is not clear whether their dialogue will enhance or reduce the prospect for a new look at the development fund model. This chapter is written on the assumption that this dialogue is going to be frank enough to allow for a consideration of the ideas contained in the model.

Six Features of the Development Fund Model

The presentation below provide a comprehensive understanding of the underlying features of the development fund model: legal status, ownership, management, responsibility, accountability, and rules of access.

Legal Status. The legal system of countries in Africa varies according to their colonial legacy. English-speaking countries have laws that allow for the establishment of public trusts. By contrast, in French- and Portuguese-speaking countries the introduction of funds with a measure of autonomy would require new legislation. The important thing is to enable the creation of funds that are not directly subsumed under the authority of a particular ministry or minister but are one step removed from such direct control. This model is in line with the policy of introducing independent executive agencies that operate as public institutions yet are not part of the regular civil service and thus not subject to the same bureaucratic restrictions.

One possibility, therefore, is to have these funds established under separate acts of parliament, like those guiding, for example, the tax revenue authorities created in many African states under the auspices of what is called new public management. Such separation of policy management and public administration has been an integral part of governance in the Scandinavian countries and has served the transition to democratic and decentralized governance in the late nineteenth century well. Given current trends of thinking about public sector management in weak states, the fund model is a valuable complement that, legally speaking, fits into current reforms and can be introduced without appearing like a major alternative. It must not be viewed as a parallel mechanism but as a complementary means of enhancing good governance and, thus, a better use of public funds.

Ownership. These funds should be open for any one to place money into. They can be treated as public investment funds in which the main beneficiaries are not shareholders but citizens. As social development funds, it is important that they are not owned and managed solely by the investors but also by representatives of prospective beneficiaries. In the ideal setup, the board of directors would be equally divided into three sets of representatives, one from government, one from civil society, and one from resource providers. Government is there because it is the official representative of the public. Civil society is there because it articulates the opinions of crucial interests in society. Resource providers are there because they provide the money and are interested in the effective use of this money for development.

It is important that those who are appointed to the boards of directors are individuals who do not have a conflict of interest. They should be trusted public figures who are not currently employed by government or civil society organizations, do not hold a diplomatic position, and are not employed by a donor agency. If the position on a fund's board of directors is held ex officio, it will not only cause a potential conflict of interest but also may reduce the commitment that the person has toward its success. The trusted individuals who are appointed to these boards are there in their personal capacity (that is, not speaking for a particular organization) but are at the same time expected to generally represent the interests of the sector by which they have been appointed. They hold a public trust—but do so without being tied to specific organizational interests. This model is common in many countries around the world but has not yet attracted sufficient interest among donors for consideration in Africa.

Management. With boards representing government, civil society, and resource providers in equal number (say, three from each making up a board of nine), the management of these funds creates a fresh game-theoretic situation. Bilateral agreements often lead to cat-and-mouse games, in which one party tries to hide from the other what he is up to; or they lead to bitter confrontations over different interpretations of specific contractual issues. Donors are excessively interested in the cost-benefit aspects of their assistance and leave out of consideration the issue of how they can create conditions for negotiations that are not just diplomatically or administratively convenient but also constructive for the use of their funds.

A management game involving three parties rather than two creates a new dynamic, which has the potential of making decisionmaking more effective. For instance, in the (not so unlikely) case in which money is not accounted for as agreed upon, there is greater probability that someone will blow the whistle. Such an act may be politically sensitive, but it is much more likely to occur in a three-party than in a two-party game situation. With individuals acting in their personal capacity, their stands will be less rigid and possibilities for compromises that work in the interest of the organizations will be more plausible. Individual board members may of course pursue their own agenda, including the possibility of using their position for political career ambitions, but on a nine-member board, where positions are not tied to specific organizational interests, there will be enough players to reduce such tendencies—because these tendencies will be viewed as breaches of both protocol and etiquette.

This is how a good governance culture can be fostered in partnership and can tie competing actors into acceptance of a rule-of-law notion that serves the public interest. Such respect for civic rules is largely missing in weak states. It does not come about from rhetorical persuasion or the application of conditions but from practical experiences, in which the rules are applied on a regular basis by different sets of actors. Management of these funds becomes a tutelary exercise in governance, with potential benefit for overcoming the weaknesses of the state.

Responsibility. Two issues arise with regard to the scope of responsibility of these funds: should they be national or regional and should they be thematic or sector based? Experts at the gathering in Kampala in 1995 favored the idea that these funds be national rather than regional, the argument being that in many of these multiethnic countries, organizing funding on a district or regional basis has three potentially detrimental effects. One is that regional funding generates a sense that some areas are favored over others if funds are not established in every region. The second is that, if all regions are to be treated equally and get one fund, resources would be spread too thin. The third is that, instead of being driven by demands from the public, funds would be set up from above and driven instead by supply. The latter has proven to be the way that central government and donors have funded local government in weak states to date—only to find that this method does not generate sustainable local institutions.

National funds are easier to establish because they are less likely to be captured by particular individuals or interests. The smaller the scale of its operation, the more probable the threat of the fund's being hijacked by certain individuals for patronage purposes. Control of funds at the local level makes sense in a situation in which donors are bringing to an end their own direct support of programs or projects. By increasing the potential number of applicants, there is also a greater likelihood of an adequate turnover, even in countries in which local authorities and civil society are weak.

Funds may be established to cater to the needs within a particular sector, but there is the same potential risk here that such a focus would increase rivalry among representatives of particular sectoral interests. Because most developmental problems facing countries in Africa cut across political or administrative jurisdictions, there is merit in considering these funds as thematically oriented. Thus even if the funds are directed at such needs as public education or public health, their mandate should be spelled out in thematic rather than sectoral terms. It is important that the fund mandate is not too broad and that its more specific funding purposes are adequately stated to the public. It is better to establish more than one such public development fund than casting the net too wide in any given country.

Accountability. Because these are public funds, they need to be accountable to a branch of government. The choice is between the executive and the legislature. The preference of donors interacting with governments in African countries has been to place such monetary assistance at the disposal of the executive. Development funds are channeled through the national treasury or—in the case of program and project aid—directly, via sector-oriented ministries. Funds for public sector reforms have been targeted on the civil service. Little if any money has been given for the purpose of strengthening the legislature. It remains secondary to the executive in the minds of African leaders and donors alike. That this has detrimental consequences not only for decentralized governance but also for the emergence of other important qualities associated with democracy has been highlighted by others.[18]

There are good reasons, therefore, to recommend that those in charge of these funds have a responsibility to report directly to parliament. Such an arrangement would be especially appropriate if each fund is established by an act of parliament. Such a reporting responsibility not only would invite parliament to take a more active interest in scrutinizing the use of public funds but also would enhance the interest of individual members of parliament in national as opposed to constituency issues. It is one of the shortcomings of most African legislatures that they focus more on pork barrel issues than on engaging in broader national policy debates.[19] This is where donors can make a significant contribution to the emergence of good governance in African countries—by being creative and courageous enough to engage in a political dialogue aimed at providing the conditions under which parliament may be strengthened. Taking members of parliament on a study tour to Europe or North America or providing them with computers does not change the asymmetrical relations of power between the executive and the legislature in these countries; allocating responsibility for overseeing development funds does.

Rules of Access. Rules of access refer to the right to apply for money from these funds. The original model refers to the possibility of funds operating through three separate windows: grants, soft loans, and commercial loans. Depending on the overall goal of any particular fund, the actual constellation may vary. For instance, having a commercial loan window makes sense if the goal is support of business development, but this is not appropriate if the purpose is to improve public health. Soft loans, such as subsidized credit—although controversial in some policy circles—may be relevant in certain situations (for example, in facilitating the transition of informal sector entrepreneurs into formal sector operations). Rules of access, therefore, would vary and should be set with each fund's objectives in mind.

Another issue concerns the extent to which government institutions should have access to these funds. In the Kampala deliberations there were voices both for and against allowing central government institutions access to the funds. Some argued that, as public institutions, the funds should be available to every organization—public, private, or voluntary. Others pointed to the risk of conflict of interest and, above all, the exercise of power that a ministry or government department could exercise in terms of obtaining access to funds. Circumstances may vary sufficiently from one country in Africa to another such that who should have access to a particular fund is best decided on an individual case basis.

For the purpose of enhancing decentralized governance, however, it may be preferable to restrict access to local government authorities and civil society organizations. Because the amounts made available through these funds would not be large, the scale of funding also better suits such a limit. The typical clients of these funds, therefore, would be local government bodies, civil society organizations and community organizations. They could bolster their own resources by applying for development project money from the funds. Financing of such projects would be advertised publicly on an annual or semiannual basis. Resources would be allocated on a competitive basis, giving priority to the proposals that demonstrate the most persuasive indicators of desirability, feasibility, and efficiency. Those that fail to meet the standards set by the fund would be informed by the fund's staff of their shortcomings and invited to reapply once they have been adequately addressed.

From the perspective of decentralized governance, the most important aspect is the competition that the funds generate not just among local government bodies but also between them and civil society organizations. Donors tend to treat local governments and civil society organizations as two separate sectors. The funds would engage them in competition not only for extra funds but also for enhancing their management capacity. The funds would help generate an institution-building program with potentially positive consequences for decentralized governance.

Conclusion

This chapter argues that there is no shortcut to decentralized governance. Nor is there a one-size-fits-all or a business-as-usual approach to achieving it in the weak states of Africa. There is a need for a historical perspective and a contextual understanding of the political realities of these countries. The limits of conventional policy analysis centered on cost-benefit ratios or cost effectiveness must be transcended. Donors must do what African governments have done for about fifty years: think politically about their interrelations in not just prescriptive but also analytical terms. Promoting a prescriptive good governance agenda makes little sense without an accompanying political analysis.

A strong state based on the Weberian ideal type of rational-legal authority is not necessarily associated with decentralization alone, but as the example of the Scandinavian countries suggests it does provide an opening in that direction, especially if the state is under pressure from a well-organized civil society. A weak state (as defined by these Weberian criteria) is less likely to possess the qualities under which decentralization—or decentralized governance—can be effectively pursued. The African experience since the 1970s confirms that, above all, it lacks the operational autonomy that historical institutionalists consider necessary for adequate development performance.[20]

In these countries, it makes sense to encourage a bottom-up or demand-driven approach to development that is based on creating policy and decision space for local actors. The more they have an opportunity to take responsibility for raising their own funds, the sooner some steps will be taken in the right direction of strengthening state institutions that make decentralized governance a reality. Because fundraising or taxation locally is limited in these poor countries, the only fundraising alternative is from central government or international donor agencies. As long as the latter insist on direct control of the funds that they provide, there is no room for decentralization other than in fiscal terms, a gesture that does not even amount to a half measure.

Development funds, however, would operate within the legal and procedural framework of the African state and as such would not complicate reporting and accounting measures. This is in line with the proclamations of the Paris Declaration. Donors may have an initial reluctance to place their money in funds over which they have only limited control. Given the experience that they have had with governments and the tricky business of expenditure tracking, support of these funds, however, would not be riskier. First of all, expenditure tracking would be done by the funds through their staffs, and donors would not have to engage in such time-consuming and administration-intensive exercises. Second, by being represented on the board of the funds, they would have a more direct insight into what is going on than they have when trying to gauge it from the window of a diplomatic mission or the general reports at midterm expenditure review meetings.

With the prospect that Africa will receive more money in the near future from the international development community, the idea of development funds has become even more imperative. There is no way that weak states will be able to absorb additional funds without doing themselves more harm than good. Governments in many of these countries already find it difficult to spend funds allocated by donors, one reason being that these governments are reluctant to share donor money with other actors. Another reason is that funds are set aside for large programs that often prove to be white elephants. With more money being channeled to Africa, the risk is that the number of such white elephants will increase.

Development funds, though, can serve not only as depositories of donor and government money but also as mechanisms for allocating these resources in ways that are disaggregated to suit the very often small-scale projects and activities that need support in order to improve local livelihoods and stimulate demands for a decentralized form of governance. This would be a first small step in that direction, but it would be more sustainable than allocating spending from the top down.

Notes

1. Harald Baldersheim and Krister Ståhlberg, eds., *Towards the Self-Regulating Municipality: Free Communes and Administrative Modernization in Scandinavia* (Aldershot, U.K.: Ashgate, 1994).

2. Trond Vedeld, "Democratic Decentralisation and Poverty Reduction: Exploring the Linkages," *Forum for Development Studies* 30, no. 2 (2003): 159–204, quotation p. 176.

3. Amartya Sen, *Development as Freedom* (New York: Alfred Knopf, 1999).

4. Staffan Lindberg, *Democracy and Elections in Africa* (Johns Hopkins University Press, 2006).

5. Crawford T. Young, *The African Colonial State in Comparative Perspective* (Yale University Press, 1994).

6. Brian C. Smith, *Field Administration: An Aspect of Decentralization* (London: Routledge and Kegan Paul, 1967).

7. Michael Ståhl, *Ethiopia: Political Contradictions in Agricultural Development* (Stockholm: Rabén and Sjögren, 1974); Uma Lele, *The Design of Rural Development: Lessons from Africa* (Johns Hopkins University Press, 1975); and David K. Leonard, *Reaching the Peasant Farmer: Organization Theory and Practice in Kenya* (University of Chicago Press, 1977).

8. World Bank, *Accelerated Development in Sub-Saharan Africa* (1981).

9. Michael Bratton, "Beyond the State: Civil Society and Associational Life in Africa," *World Politics* 41, no. 3 (1989): 407–30.

10. Jide M. Balogun and Gelase Mutahaba, eds., *Economic Restructuring and African Public Administration: Issues, Action, and Future Choice* (West Hartford, Conn.: Kumarian, 1991).

11. Deepa Narayan with others, *Voices of the Poor: Can Anyone Hear Us?* (Oxford University Press, 2000).

12. Goran Hyden, Julius Court, and Kenneth Mease, *Making Sense of Governance: Empirical Evidence from Sixteen Developing Countries* (Boulder, Colo.: Lynne Rienner, 2004).

13. Tony Waters, "The Persistence of Subsistence and the Limits to Development Studies: The Challenge of Tanzania," *Africa* 70, no. 4 (2000): 615–52; and Deborah Fahy Bryceson, "The Scramble for Africa: Reorienting Rural Livelihoods," *World Development* 30, no. 5 (2002): 847–69.

14. Goran Hyden, *African Politics in Comparative Perspective* (Cambridge University Press, 2006).

15. Richard Joseph, *Democracy and Prebendalism in Nigeria* (Cambridge University Press, 1987); Jeffrey Herbst, *States and Power in Africa: Comparative Lessons in Authority and Control* (Princeton University Press, 2000); Thomas Callaghy, *The State-Society Struggle: Zaire in Comparative Perspective* (Columbia University Press, 1984); and Leonardo A. Villalon and Phillip A. Huxtable, eds., *The African State at a Critical Juncture: Between Disintegration and Reconfiguration* (Boulder, Colo.: Lynne Rienner, 1998).

16. Hammarskjöld Foundation, *Autonomous Development Funds in Africa: Report from an Expert Consultation in Kampala, Uganda 4–6 April 1995* (Uppsala: 1995).

17. Goran Hyden, "Making Public Sector Reform Work for Africa: Back to the Drawing-Board," Economic Research Working Paper 76 (African Development Bank, 2005).

18. Mick Moore, "Death without Taxes: Democracy, State Capacity and Aid Dependence in the Fourth World," in *Towards a Democratic Developmental State,* edited by Gordon White and Mark Robinson (Oxford University Press, 1997); and Mette Kjaer, *Governance* (Cambridge, U.K.: Polity Press, 2004).

19. Joel D. Barkan, Ladipo Adamolekun, and Yongmei Zhou, with others, "Emerging Legislatures: Institutions of Horizontal Accountability," in *Public Service Reform and Parliaments: A Guide to Public Sector Reforms for Political Representatives* (World Bank Institute, 2000).

20. Peter Evans, *Embedded Autonomy* (Princeton University Press, 1995); Atul Kohli, *State-Directed Development: Political Power and Industrialization in the Global Periphery* (Cambridge University Press, 2004).

13

Decentralization and Legal Empowerment of the Poor

NARESH SINGH

The past twenty-five years have seen significant shifts in geopolitics, the global environment, globalization, security, poverty, and economic inequality. These shifts create both new challenges and new opportunities for action. The 1980s, for example, witnessed a new wave in environmental consciousness, culminating in the United Nations Conference on Environment and Development—the Rio Summit—in 1992. In 1989, the end of the cold war ushered in a new era of geopolitics that brought the rethinking of development cooperation. *Governance* entered the development cooperation lexicon as a means of examining and better understanding how politics and power affect development opportunities and outcomes. The concept of sustainable livelihoods was introduced soon after that and received international political attention at the Rio Summit.[1] The 1990s witnessed many UN summits on various themes of development cooperation with accompanying high-level political commitment to take action, change behaviors, and increase resource flows to poor countries. This culminated with the publication, in 1996, of *Shaping the 21st Century,* by the Organization for Economic Cooperation and Development's Development Assistance Committee, outlining the ways

I am indebted to Deborah Harris and Farzana Ramzan, who provided outstanding research assistance during the preparation of this manuscript. The vision and direction, as well as any errors or deficiencies, are, however, my own.

in which donor behavior should change. The UN Millennium Summit in 2000 and the subsequent publication of its Millennium Development Goals offered a set of internationally agreed upon development targets and shared responsibilities to improve aid effectiveness.

This chapter focuses on the role of decentralized governance (meaning decentralized government characterized by effective local interaction with civil society organizations) in developing countries in this new era of development cooperation. It argues that decentralized governance can help create an enabling environment for people to transform their lives by reconceptualizing power through an expansion of the rule of law. It examines the constitutive aspects of decentralized governance, and the ways that the latter can strengthen the assets and adaptive strategies that men and women use to make a living. A reexamination of the legal frameworks that govern the allocation and protection of property and labor rights and business opportunities for the poor can help them to take greater control of their livelihoods. Coupled with decentralized governance, these legal frameworks provide useful entry points for changing power relations so that the poor can benefit without doing so at the expense of others. This chapter also examines the linkages between decentralization, power, and poverty; the opportunities that decentralization creates for power sharing; and specific actions that can be taken to make the reallocation of power a positive-sum game through decentralized governance.

Decentralization, Power, and Poverty

Decentralization, defined as the "transfer of political, financial, administrative, and legal authority from central government to regional/sub-national and local governments," plays an important role in changing power dynamics and in addressing local poverty reduction issues.[2] Successful decentralization allows for increased participation of the poor in community planning, project development and implementation, and problem solving, and increases the prospects for sustainability and local ownership.[3] Theoretically, it allows local people to become more engaged in the development process and to strengthen their capacity for decisionmaking by having greater access to local political participation.

For decentralization to effectively assist the poor in getting themselves out of poverty, it must be accompanied by fundamental structural changes in those decisionmaking processes that maintain asymmetric power relations and by changes that bring government nearer to the people. Bringing government closer to the people can be achieved in many ways. One entails giving a voice to the poor, offering greater opportunities for participation in political decisionmaking, and enhancing livelihood opportunities via government investment in pro-poor development projects. Although these changes should have positive outcomes on the livelihoods of the poor, the reality is visibly different. Unintended outcomes arise from skewed power relations between the poor and local elites that allow the latter to capture control over local provision of goods and services. The typical response to "elite capture" has been the advocacy of empowerment programs that are, because of skewed power relationships, usually doomed from the outset.

The relationship between poverty and power is rarely discussed in studies of development cooperation. Power is defined as "not just something one holds, but rather something one has or does not have in relation to others."[4] Poverty is a symptom of power inequalities because those who lack power often lack access to basic resources. Poverty is created, maintained, and often exacerbated by power relationships in society because it is these social relationships that determine how resources are distributed among people. Thus, poverty is created when the powerful limit other people's access to the resources they need to meet their basic needs. As a result, power becomes defined as material control.

In addition, poverty can be attributed to "overt bigotry against the poor and against low-power groups who are associated with poverty" as dominant groups continue to blame poverty on the "character deficits of poor people."[5] The strong prejudice against the poor (or powerless) by the rich (or powerful) further restricts poor people's power and increases poverty.[6] Therefore, we can define power as the capacity of the poor to control the factors that affect their livelihoods.

Although power is often discussed as a zero-sum game, it is possible to perceive of power as a positive-sum game in which everyone benefits. A positive-sum outcome "becomes possible when the size of the pie is somehow enlarged so that there is more wealth to distribute between the parties than there was originally, or some other way is devised so everyone gets what they want or need."[7] Those who have power, however, never willingly give it up. Development initiatives that help the poor survive at a subsistence level through income generation projects and basic health and education programs are, of course, often welcomed, but they are allowed to succeed because they maintain and even reinforce existing skewed power relations.

If real empowerment of the poor appears to be succeeding, the establishment (those who hold formal power) is likely to crush such a process in its incipient stage. Think of a plantation owner losing cheap labor because his employees can become union members. He would use his "connections" to prevent any such thing. Yash Tandon also expresses this point of view when he writes that "power is not there for the giving but the taking. Those who 'give' power condition it; power has to be taken."[8] Thus, it appears that power relations are changed through processes of *self*-empowerment. To achieve this change in power relations, power must be reconceptualized as a positive-sum game based on mechanisms that help the poor empower themselves and at the same time create benefits for "the establishment."

Negotiation can be seen as either a zero-sum game or a positive-sum game. It is a zero-sum game when actors attempt to divide a fixed amount of something, since they can only increase their share at the expense of another. Negotiations can also be conceived of as a positive-sum game when actors work to "make the pie larger, so that all actors can have a bigger share."[9] To ensure that negotiations are a positive-sum game, actors must perceive themselves as partners rather than adversaries so that they can work together to "try to negotiate mutually beneficial outcomes."[10] Actors need to "search for innovative and original win-win solutions" so that they can address "problem[s] of mutual concern, invent options for collective gain and use objective criteria to decide outcomes."[11] Expansion of the rule of law can offer greater access to legal benefits and protections to the poor and new opportunities for reducing poverty through decentralized governance.

Government decentralization can increase the likelihood of positive-sum outcomes by bringing power closer to local people. Theoretically, decentralization allows local governments to create a space where people can exercise greater political power by enabling them "to express their views and participate in local decision-making processes."[12] Although decentralization can bring about positive-sum results, this does not always happen. People may participate at the local government level but may still feel disconnected from and skeptical about higher levels of government. For example, research conducted on decentralization in Uganda found that although people felt that decision-making at local levels of government was a positive-sum game, at higher levels of government they felt that the situation was closer to a zero-sum game.[13] Further, they believed that higher-level leaders were constantly benefiting at their expense.[14] This implies that for decentralization to create a positive-sum situation, there is a need for greater transparency within all levels of government. Leaders at the higher levels also need to ensure that there is adequate communication with local people so that the latter feel that their views and ideas are being listened to and acted upon.

Empowerment implies a change in power relations between the powerful and the powerless. It is not a neutral process because it can create social problems and resistance. Furthermore, empowerment can be both a zero-sum game and a positive-sum game. For example, empowerment that requires the redistribution of land or wealth from the powerful to the powerless may result in some people losing their assets and others benefiting from this. However, if empowerment increases productivity and income it may not lead to a zero-sum game. Empowerment that brings about a growth in self-confidence and personal abilities in addition to material benefits is a positive-sum game as well, since someone does not have to lose in order for someone else to gain.[15]

For societies to become self-empowered, actions need to be taken to confront "the multidimensional nature of poverty." Actions that can effectively combat poverty include changing power relations within the community and the household.[16] Social movements are important because they focus on the roots of poverty and disempowerment and work to challenge and improve the status quo. The problem with this approach is that social movements are more susceptible to resistance and opposition from those in power and may provoke violence.[17]

Mobilizing marginalized people to organize themselves can strengthen their cause and increase their power. Organization helps to overcome the weaknesses arising from the isolation of the poor and enables them to gain the power they need to effectively deal with issues related to poverty. Community-based organizations seeking to alleviate poverty are also more effective when membership is restricted to the poor. When all members of the community are included, the organization tends "to be dominated by the minority of elite interests who will turn the activities of the organizations in their own favor."[18] A community organization as such cannot fully provide the means to enable the poor to improve their situation; organizations for the poor need to be led by the poor themselves.

Although in some countries organizations can be legally recognized if they form cooperatives under a cooperative law, many organizations continue to work informally in order to avoid bureaucracy and possible state interference.[19] The main reason for this is that the organization of marginalized people can lead to "a diffusion of power," and organizing can prove to be difficult as it meets resistance from politicians at higher levels who believe that some of their current power would be redistributed to the poor.[20] Even if they are organized, the poor are often prevented from fully participating in the growth of their communities.

Decentralized governance is inextricably linked to broader conceptual challenges and opportunities. Decentralization has many forms. Deconcentration—the shifting of administrative responsibilities from central ministries and departments to regional and local levels of government—allows the least amount of power to be transferred to the local community. Devolution, on the other hand, which is "aimed at creating or strengthening independent units of government by devolving functions and authority," provides the best opportunity for local-level participation.[21] Devolution can play a major role in promoting self-empowerment and changing power relations between the haves and have-nots. Political decentralization (another term for devolution) is a transfer of political power that gives local populations increased decision-making power in political, social, and economic issues.[22] Successful decentralization promotes "the well-being of all people" and creates a situation in which the central government and the local governments share power.[23]

Decentralization helps promote democracy by allowing people at different levels of government to have a say in political decisions while allowing "for greater representation of various political, religious, social and ethnic groups."[24] It can also support democratic reforms by encouraging greater accountability and legitimacy from the central government. In a decentralized system of governance, local communities become increasingly visible to the central government and thus are in a better position to monitor the actions of government officials and hold them accountable for the decisions they make. Decentralization "strengthens the capacity of local governments" by allowing them to take on functions that used to be filled by the central government and giving citizens the opportunity to participate in decisions affecting their community.[25] Decentralization allows the poor to voice their opinions and ideas about community concerns, so that they can participate in creating solutions to local development problems.[26]

However, decentralization may not succeed in achieving these goals if local elites capture power. Although decentralization can increase local decision-making power and control, it can also redistribute power from central government officials to local elites.[27] To prevent this, decentralization should be accompanied by stronger government accountability. One way to achieve greater accountability is to create local community organizations comprising members of the general public and of opposition parties and civil society groups that work to hold the government accountable for its actions and decisions.[28]

Decentralization is most successful if a state has a strong and legitimate central government and if local people are empowered—"otherwise it contains no intrinsic value for being a natural promoter of peaceful development and democracy."[29] Decentralization should be viewed "as part of a framework for state and public administration reform aimed at empowering local governments and communities legally, technically and financially to cater [to] their interests" while the central government remains responsible for higher state issues.[30] The participation of local people in governance is important for successful decentralization because it allows "local-level services to be tailored according to local preferences" and local knowledge and ideas to be applied in order to deal with community problems more effectively.[31] With decentralization, local resources can also be employed more efficiently to meet local needs. Some local people may even be more willing to pay their taxes if they feel that they have increased control over the use of public revenues.[32]

Decentralization and Power Sharing

As is evident from the foregoing discussion, decentralization is linked to a shift of power.[33] Indeed, decentralization may lead to good governance and poverty reduction only if it expands power through the rule of law. By changing power relationships, decentralization can enable the poor to secure sustainable livelihoods. Decentralization, as a transfer of functional responsibilities from central governments to local authorities, alters social relationships and power structures that affect people's access to and ownership of resources. To promote power sharing, a basic conceptual shift is needed in development assistance from the focus on needs to a focus on assets. The former emphasizes opportunities for donor activity, and the challenges of making aid more effective. The latter begins with what the poor already have or could have, and focuses on how to help them build their own prosperity, and in doing so addresses their needs. The needs of the poor are indeed great, but so is their potential to help themselves.

Enhanced local participation in decisionmaking designed to mobilize communities toward self-empowerment serves to improve the livelihoods of the poor. This can be done through articulation of common problems, followed by mobilization, the creation of political space, and, finally, the use of the law to confirm and protect newly recognized rights. Donors will do well to recognize this potential and work with it by designing development projects that begin with an assessment of the assets of the poor rather than an assessment of their needs.[34] The common assumption that the poor have no assets needs to be discarded.

Decentralization, accompanied by an expansion of legal rights for the poor, produces the conditions necessary to facilitate power sharing, which in turn enables them to transform opportunities into sustainable livelihoods, become self-empowered, and contribute to poverty reduction. Sustainability implies the capacity to cope with and recover from shocks and stresses, and to benefit from economic effectiveness, ecological integrity, and social equity. The sustainable livelihoods approach demands a self-empowering model of development cooperation in which the poor seek to take power over their own destinies, rather than a model of cooperation essentially between donor and recipient governments. This is not to minimize the roles of these entities but to rethink them in some rather fundamental ways.

Implicit in the notion of decentralized governance as power sharing is conceiving of decentralization not as a centrifugal phenomenon that assumes a transfer of power away from the center, such as from national to local governments or from local elites to the poor, but as a structure for expansive, and therefore inclusive, decisionmaking. Decentralization can help to reverse exclusionary trends through targeted interventions from the bottom up. Thus, a feasible strategy must be in place for the poor to participate in processes that identify existing assets and barriers toward upward mobility. Expanding the rule of law establishes an enabling environment in which opportunities for decentralized power sharing are conceived of as a positive-sum game, leading to self-empowerment. It is in this context that we draw on the lessons learned in decentralized governance, described elsewhere in this book, to examine its role in promoting sustainable livelihoods in poor but well-governed countries, failed and fragile states, and middle-income countries.

Making Power a Positive-Sum Game

Decentralized governance supports the expansion of sustainable livelihoods; both are associated with ownership and self-empowerment from the bottom up. Specifically, pro-poor policies that protect property and labor rights, expand access to justice and the law, and create business opportunities help reverse trends in developing countries that force the majority of the poor to operate outside formal legal and economic systems.

Property Rights

Attaining sustainable livelihoods requires that the poor have legal rights that protect the value of their property and labor and that enhance their opportunities for upward mobility. It is estimated that land and buildings account for up to three-fourths of a country's wealth in most economies,[35] but in many developing countries property is not formally registered. Further, in many countries, such as India, income derived from "commons" resources such as forests, fisheries, and agricultural lands accounts for 15 to 25 percent of household incomes.[36]

The concept of property is broadened in scope when it is linked to land tenure, buildings, tools, equipment, and natural resources and is redefined to include both formal and informal property holdings of the poor. To assist the millions of poor around the world who informally claim these assets yet lack the legal capacity to capitalize on them requires a process of decentralization that expands these rights at the local level and provides greater opportunity for the poor to participate in securing sustainable livelihoods.

One form of property is land, which not only is an economic asset but also is linked to social, political, and cultural sources of power. Although land itself is an easily identifiable asset, millions of the poor who depend on land for their livelihoods lack formal access to rights that recognize and protect this asset. For example, it is estimated that in West Africa, only 2 percent of land ownership is formally documented. The fact that the majority of the poor do not legally register their property is attributed to the complex and costly systems that currently regulate property rights in most developing countries. These systems deter the poor from registering property because the benefits of doing so often do not justify the cost and effort.

Formal registration systems provide local and national governments with the tools necessary to identify and protect the assets of the poor while generating economic growth. Land registration enables the poor who depend on land for their livelihood to enhance the economic opportunities of this asset.

According to the World Bank publication *Doing Business in 2006,* simplifying property registration procedures can potentially spur economic growth, reduce corruption, and enhance property rights. In Thailand, for example, the reduction of barriers to acquiring titles for land resulted in the issuance of 8.5 million property titles, almost doubling land value and investment.[37]

Simplifying the process of registering property through recording and titling, however, is only a part of the process of empowering the poor. Ultimately this measure must be accompanied by policies that ensure that the poor are able to benefit from property to which they are rightfully entitled. This is essential to the expansion of property rights. Property registration reduces the vulnerability of the poor by preventing those in power from buying and selling land that is considered unclaimed. For property rights to result in the empowerment of the poor, rights associated with property must not benefit elites at the expense of the poor. The restoration of security through acquiring ownership of fungible property facilitates the transition of the poor from the informal to the formal economy and reduces their vulnerability.

It is likely that the process of registering property and the rights associated with registration would minimally affect poverty reduction if they were driven primarily by the central government. Historically, top-down approaches to property rights have resulted in the concentration of financial advantages among existing power holders. This is why the majority of the world's poor continue to be pushed into the informal sector. The lack of real economic, social, or political incentives reduces the faith of the poor in formal institutions, particularly national governments. The notion that pro-poor property rights can in fact reduce poverty and generate economic growth has been gaining widespread acceptance, most prominently through the work of the Peruvian economist Hernando de Soto.[38] Simultaneously there is growing acceptance that local customs and systems of tenure have to be incorporated into the formal legal framework for the latter to offer an environment for sustainable livelihoods. The process of integrating these dual themes associated with enhanced property rights requires the identification of these local systems and the ways in which they can contribute to poverty reduction.

Decentralized governance can contribute to the creation of effective property rights by localizing efforts to integrate existing systems of land tenure into a formal legal framework by building on local knowledge and practices that informally govern existing systems of tenure. Decentralized governance can establish the institutional environment necessary to alleviate poverty— one in which property rights are inclusive, locally legitimate, and legally defined and protected.

Labor Rights

Labor, as an income-generating activity, also improves the well-being of the poor because the majority of the world's poor find that securing a job is the main way to get out of poverty.[39] Workers in developing countries, however, face many constraints that force them to operate outside the formal economy. These constraints stem from laws that directly affect workers' rights and determine their capacity to collectively organize. Consequently decentralization must deal with two key components broadly associated with labor rights: constraints faced by workers in the formal sector that force the poor to operate outside it, and rights that protect workers once they enter the formal economy.

At the same time the expansion of labor rights should ensure that entrepreneurs are not driven out of business. Protection of workers' rights should lead to a positive-sum outcome, in which businesses continue to profit and profit-seeking activities do not infringe on the rights of workers. The expansion of labor rights should increase productivity and be seen by business leaders as a source of increased profit. The convergence of formal and informal systems should result in a situation where power can be shared by the expansion of rights and protection of the poor. A positive-sum convergence requires a thorough reexamination of economic institutions and a better understanding of the economic contributions of informal workers.

Three conditions are necessary for labor rights and business viability to reinforce each other: first, the capacity of workers to collectively organize must be enhanced; second, local governments must help businesses and informal workers to assess their economic contributions; and third, local governments must become more responsive to the needs of businesses in facilitating the movement of workers from the informal sector into the formal economy.

The poor cannot be forced into the formal economy, nor can the formal economy be drastically altered to accommodate informal activities. However, decentralization provides the means of gradually integrating the two. Opportunities must be widespread, from access to strengthened labor rights for the poor to increased productivity and economic gains for businesses. This situation is indicative of what a positive-sum outcome would look like. Consultative processes as a means of engaging the poor and businesses in negotiations will necessarily take place at the local level, and can facilitate national processes that, when operating in conjunction, will reinforce each other and create a stronger enabling environment.

Expanding Legal Business Opportunities

Many factors contribute to an unstable economy and have significant impacts on the livelihoods of the poor. Inefficient markets, distorted macroeconomic policies, weak institutions, and high inflation rates all weaken economic performance in developing countries and deter the poor from participating fully in the economy. For the poor to become empowered, the expansion of legal business opportunities and the expansion of property and labor rights need to occur simultaneously. Regulatory limitations can exclude the poor from access to savings accounts, mortgages, consumer credit, insurance, and money transfers and restrict their ability to leverage their assets, safely store possessions, or fund entrepreneurial activity.

What type of environment is necessary for the poor to start profitable businesses in the formal market that build on the innovations, productivity, and profits that they experience in the informal sector? For the poor to access financial services, the regulatory environment has to be conducive to the needs of small businesses. Decentralized governance can make it easier to simplify local regulations and encourage the poor to participate in entrepreneurial activities. Increased accountability, accessibility, and transparency all contribute to greater trust in formal systems.

Of equal importance is the ability of the poor to access credit. Microfinance programs give the poor (and especially poor women) more access to credit and loans to fund entrepreneurial activity. Because of regulatory constraints, however, few microfinance programs have become sustainable, efficient, and part of the mainstream economy. The complexity and inefficiency of business regulations or the lack of business laws can result in exorbitant interest rates, forcing the poor to operate in the black market or be exploited if they choose to get access to credit via unregulated microfinance schemes. Simple, supportive, and enforceable local regulations, along with adequate financial services such as savings accounts, can help to make microfinance institutions more sustainable. Effective local institutions can stimulate increased economic activity with savings and investment programs that benefit the poor, a crucial factor in transforming the assets of the poor into sustainable livelihoods. Thus, decentralization is key to ensuring the success of microfinance programs.

Access to Justice and the Rule of Law

For decentralized governance to have a positive impact on the capacity of the poor to attain sustainable livelihoods, the poor must have access to the legal justice system. Perceptions that the law benefits the few have significant impacts on the decisions made by the poor to operate outside the legal and regulatory system. A justice system that encourages fair dispute resolution and that borrows from customary legal practices is the foundation for the acquisition of sustainable livelihoods. Public faith in political institutions and economic processes cannot grow unless the public has access to social justice. This is particularly true for women, who are among the most vulnerable members of society in both their productive and their reproductive roles.

The recognition and integration of customary legal systems into formal legal frameworks requires extensive dialogue among diverse groups. In a country such as Tanzania, with more than a hundred ethnic groups, central government policies are not likely to be either inclusive or sustainable. Although there is potential for conflict whether customary, formal, and informal legal systems operate independently or in association with each other, participatory processes that engage local communities can result in negotiations and compromise. Decentralized governance requires participation and interaction at all levels, linking stakeholders with each other in contributing to a culture of fairness, equity, and the rule of law.

Conclusion

This chapter analyzes the relationship between power and poverty and examines the potential for decentralization to change power relations in assisting the poor to achieve sustainable livelihoods. It argues for a shift in development assistance that focuses on the assets of the poor and on the use of a more inclusive legal system to help the poor use local assets to overcome poverty and create wealth. It describes some specific ways to expand legal inclusiveness in the areas of property and labor rights, to improve business organization, and to promote a pro-poor justice system. Decentralization is considered pivotal in helping to establish such an inclusive legal system—one where the poor can help create prosperity through legal recognition of their assets, entitlements, and the activities on which their livelihoods are based.

Notes

1. Robert Chambers and Gordan Conway, "Sustainable Rural Livelihoods: Practical Concepts for the 21st Century," Institute of Development Studies Discussion Paper 296 (University of Sussex, 1991).

2. Shabbir Cheema, *Building Democratic Institutions: Governance Reform in Developing Countries* (Bloomfield, Conn.: Kumarian Press, 2005), p. 122.

3. John-Mary Kauzya, "Decentralization: Prospects for Peace, Democracy and Development," Discussion Paper, United Nations Department of Economic and Social Affairs, Division for Public Administration and Development Management, 2005, p. 2.

4. Anthony F. Lemieux and Felicia Pratto, "Poverty and Prejudice," in *Poverty and Psychology: From Global Perspective to Local Practice,* edited by Stuart C. Carr and Tod S. Sloan (Springer, 2003), p. 149.

5. Ibid., p. 148.

6. Ibid., p. 149.

7. Brad Spangler, "Positive-Sum, Zero-Sum, and Negative-Sum Situations," in *Beyond Intractability,* edited by Guy Burgess and Heidi Burgess (University of Colorado, Conflict Research Consortium, 2003).

8. Yash Tandon, "Poverty, Processes of Impoverishment and Empowerment," in *Empowerment Towards Sustainability,* edited by Naresh Singh and Vangile Titi (Winnipeg: International Institute for Sustainable Development, 1995), p. 33.

9. David Humphreys, "Forest Negotiations at the United Nations: Explaining Cooperation and Discord," *Forest Policy and Economics* 3 (2001): 126.

10. Ibid.

11. Ibid.

12. Fumihiko Saito, "Decentralization in Uganda: Challenges for the 21st Century," Ryukoku University, Japan, 2000.

13. Ibid., p. 17.

14. Ibid.

15. Gita Sen, "Empowerment as an Approach to Poverty," Working Paper 97-07, Background Paper for the Human Development Report, Harvard University, Global Reproductive Health Forum (December 1997), p. 4.

16. Ibid., p. 8.

17. Ibid., p. 9.

18. Ibid., p. 5.

19. Ibid., p. 4.

20. Ibid.

21. Cheema, *Building Democratic Institutions,* p. 122.

22. Kauzya, "Decentralization: Prospects for Peace, Democracy and Development," p. 5.

23. Ibid., p. 12.

24. Cheema, *Building Democratic Institutions,* p. 120.

25. Ibid.

26. Ibid., p. 121.

27. Sen, "Empowerment as an Approach to Poverty," p. 5.

28. Pranab Bardhan, "Decentralization of Governance Reform in Developing Countries," *Journal of Economic Perspectives* 16, no. 4 (2002): 19.

29. Kauzya, "Decentralization: Prospects for Peace, Democracy and Development," p. 3.

30. Ibid., p. 4.

31. S. R. Osmani, "Participatory Governance, People's Empowerment and Poverty Reduction," SEPED Conference Paper Series 7, United Nations Development Programme, Social Development and Poverty Elimination Division, 2000, p. 6.

32. Ibid., p. 9.

33. For further reading on decentralization, see Alex B. Brillantes Jr. and others, eds., *Decentralization and Power Shift: An Imperative for Good Governance,* vol. 2, University of the Philippines, National College of Public Administration and Governance, 2003.

34. Kristin Helmore and Naresh Singh, *Sustainable Livelihoods: Building on the Wealth of the Poor* (Bloomfield, Conn.: Kumarian Press, 2001).

35. World Bank and International Finance Corporation, *Doing Business in 2005* (World Bank, International Finance Corporation, and Oxford University Press, 2005), p. 33.

36. World Resources Institute, United Nations Development Programme, United Nations Environment Programme, and World Bank, *World Resources 2005: The Wealth of the Poor—Managing Ecosystems to Fight Poverty* (Washington, D.C., 2005), p. 39.

37. World Bank and International Finance Corporation, *Doing Business in 2006* (World Bank and International Finance Corporation, 2006), p. 31.

38. For a more detailed analysis of property rights, see Hernando de Soto, *The Mystery of Capital* (New York: Basic Books, 2000).

39. Deepa Narayan and others, *Voices of the Poor: Crying Out for Change,* prepared for the World Bank (Oxford University Press, 2000).

14

Decentralization to Promote Effective and Efficient Pro-Poor Infrastructure and Service Delivery in the Least-Developed Countries

KADMIEL H. WEKWETE

What does it take to have decentralization programs that promote effective and efficient infrastructure and services? What does it take to have decentralization that is pro-poor and that addresses the needs of the excluded and marginalized citizens? What systems need to be put in place at local levels to ensure long-term sustainability of local programs? The answers to all these critical questions are very complex and require careful understanding of the historical, social, administrative, and political systems prevailing in countries that seek to promote decentralization. This chapter examines some of the practical consequences of decentralization and highlights some examples of the practical challenges faced by governments and their support partners in making it a reality.

Decentralization is viewed in many countries as a vehicle to promote participatory decisionmaking, local infrastructure development, and service delivery. The concept of decentralization broadly includes devolution, deconcentration, and delegation of powers and responsibilities from the center to subnational and other lower-level political and administrative entities. The ideal that many developing countries strive to attain is devolution of political and administrative powers, which reinforces the democratic culture, promotes local decisionmaking, and reinforces the local planning and implementation processes.

Many of the least developed countries are undergoing major political and economic transformations as they seek to build their fragile economies and establish modern political institutions. Most have embraced decentralization as an important pillar of the democratic governance processes, arguing for significant transfers of political and administrative powers to local authorities and governments. There are fifty least developed countries globally, and thirty-four of them are in sub-Saharan Africa. They are classified as least developed countries according to the following criteria:[1]

—Low income, meaning under $750 per capita, based on a three-year average estimate of the gross national income (GNI). Above $900 per capita for graduation out of the LDC category and becoming a developing country.

—Human-resource weakness based on a composite human assets index score including indicators of nutrition, health, education, and adult literacy.

—Economic vulnerability, based on indicators, making up the Economic Vulnerability Index (EVI), of the instability of agricultural production, the instability of exports of goods and services, the economic importance of nontraditional activities (the share of manufacturing and modern services in the GDP), merchandise export concentration, the handicap of economic smallness typical of small island nations, and the percentage of the population displaced by natural disasters.

Some of the common characteristics of all the least developed countries are low per capita income, slow growth, underdeveloped infrastructure in both the urban and rural economies, weak political and administrative structures and a high degree of centralization of government authority, and the primacy of one or two urban centers in a predominantly rural economy.

Thus least developed countries find themselves not only trying to achieve basic economic growth and development, but also simultaneously grappling with political and administrative reform processes. Many of these countries have experienced significant social and political turmoil (civil war and political turbulence) since attaining political independence and have had to deal with colonial legacies that marginalized the majority of their indigenous populations. The development process they are pursuing therefore requires them to build institutions to reduce conflict, and to establish administrative and political building blocks for long-term development. This involves a range of political and public sector reforms, including a basic reorientation of public service delivery from a purely sectoral to more territory-based approach, which emphasizes the central importance of local governments and local institutions. This discourse of local development has also projected the importance of a pro-poor focus and the achievement of the millennium development goals.

The delivery of infrastructure and services, which is a key goal of local and national development, is a multifaceted and multiactor task, one that includes central governments, local governments, nongovernmental organizations, civil society organizations, and bilateral and multilateral donors and local communities. In most cases, however, there is no exclusive group responsible for the production and delivery of services, because partnerships are needed to accomplish the different tasks. In most of the least developed countries, different levels of government play a critical role in the production and delivery of infrastructure and services, and it is common to have coproduction and codelivery of specific services and infrastructure at national, subnational, and local levels. Decentralization does not eliminate the need for other actors but simply sharpens the need for defining the comparative advantages of each of the different actors. The role of central government remains fundamental in terms of policy, planning, managing, and delivery of "bulky" infrastructure and services such as providing national electricity, bulk water supplies, and national road networks. Local governments, nongovernmental organizations, and the private sector complement this central role of government by targeting more specific geographic areas and clients with their programs.

The concept of infrastructure and services is a broad one that encompasses many of the obvious physical features of civilization such as roads, bridges, and highways; transportation infrastructure and ports; basic utilities such as power, water supply, and sanitation; schools, health-care facilities, and public buildings. The nature of infrastructure and services varies according to communities' different needs, from large metropolitan regions down to small villages, a factor with major implications for institutional arrangements. At the national level, sector ministries carry the responsibility for specific infrastructure and services; they define the policies, and they receive public sector funding to provide, manage, and maintain the infrastructure and services in their purview. In most cases these responsibilities cascade to lower levels of the subnational systems, giving powers and responsibilities to different lower-level institutions. The process of decentralizing powers and responsibilities begins through this basic deconcentration and is further consolidated through territorial devolution, which includes linking administrative and political entities at subnational levels.

Infrastructure growth and services also play a critical role in economic growth and poverty reduction and enhance human security, particularly for the poor, by contributing to their food security, job security, community security, personal security, and environmental security. The big question in many countries is, "How can we ensure that infrastructure and services are provided, especially to the poor, in a timely manner to have an impact on poverty and to spur economic growth?" There is also widespread concern about the generally acknowledged skewedness in infrastructure and service delivery between rural and urban areas, and between core and peripheral regions. More recently, with the global concern for achieving the Millennium Development Goals (MDGs), there has been a very significant focus on making the infrastructure work for the poor. The 2006 progress chart clearly shows limited progress in achieving the millennium development goals in sub-Saharan Africa and in Asia, and these limitations are even more significant on the local level, where they are amplified, than on the national level.

In particular, there has been a concern to ensure that the provision of small, community-level infrastructure achieves the desired results and that local institutions have the necessary capacity and know-how to deliver. In many countries, there has been concern about harmonizing top-down delivery mechanisms with the more bottom-up approaches that involve local communities. This harmonization has been considered a key to unlocking the potential of integrating infrastructure, economic growth, and poverty reduction, ensuring that there are positive infrastructure-capabilities linkages; infrastructure, education, and health linkages; and infrastructure and services-empowerment linkages. These challenges—highlighting the limitations of subnational governments— have been identified in both rural and urban local environments.

This chapter examines critically the issue of decentralized delivery of services and infrastructure, using the evidence emerging from United Nations Capital Development Fund (UNCDF) case studies in several least developed countries in Africa and Asia.[2] The general evidence emerging from these experiences is that decentralization through local governments is more likely to promote cost-effective and efficient infrastructure and service delivery at local levels than top-down sector delivery or other isolated community-based delivery mechanisms. Although there are no conclusive data on the impact of decentralization on service delivery, these case studies have highlighted qualitative and some quantitative assessments that point toward a positive impact, particularly for the poor and for marginalized groups. It is, however, important to recognize the overall context in which decentralization functions in order to avoid the risk of atomizing the cases studies.

Institutional Framework for Decentralization, Infrastructure, and Service Delivery in Least Developed Countries

The key challenge many countries face is to establish an institutional framework that promotes decentralization and is empowered to deliver infrastructure and services. In many countries political and administrative structures exist, but usually these structures lack the resources and capacities to make infrastructure and service delivery a reality. In some cases decentralization is overshadowed by the continued dominance of sector-based services, which are delivered from the center (top-down).

Thus the first real challenge is to understand the subnational structures of government, and the powers that are bestowed on them in both federal and unitary systems of government. Usually the true nature of local government is blurred because of overlapping responsibilities, and the lack of clarity concerning local entities' powers and functions undermines the overall function of the system—whether it operates through deconcentration, devolution, delegation, or through a combination of these.

The second challenge is to understand the resource framework and the linkages between decentralized functions and funding. This is the area of fiscal decentralization and financial management that determines how resources are transferred from the center to local levels, the roles that local governments play in generating their own revenues locally, and the systems of financial management.

The third challenge is to understand the nature of the different infrastructures and services to be delivered: Who provides them? How are they planned, funded, and maintained? What are the different mechanisms and partnerships for their delivery? There is a hierarchy of services, which relates to the different administrative, spatial, and political levels of organization. Decentralization does not mean uniformity across the country and across sectors. In most cases each sector is configured differently and calls on different technical and administrative capacities, which vary among the subnational authorities.

The fourth challenge is to understand the needs of poor households for infrastructure and services and measure services' adequacy, particularly in least developed countries' rural areas, and to examine the measures that must be taken to address the deficits where they exist. This issue is closely linked to the broader question of the achievement of the millennium development goals, and the real issue surrounding decentralization boils down to whether it is justified because it can make a difference in the lives of the poor—whether local organizations are able to do things that central organizations are unable to do and whether the former can complement the latter effectively.

Finally, there is a need to critically examine some empirical evidence of how decentralized operations through local governments and communities have made a difference, and how they compare with standard delivery mechanisms from sector ministries and other quasi-governmental agencies. This is a very difficult proposition because most of the comparisons are between donor-funded initiatives and public-sector organizations (sector or line ministries, and other quasi-government bodies), whose incentive structures are different. Where a donor-funded decentralization activity might provide living wages to its staff, this might not be the case with public-sector wage structures, and therefore the level of motivation in the latter becomes problematic.

Institutional Frameworks for Decentralization and Local Governments

In many countries the institution of local government is not "new." It has always existed as an integral part of the state, and has been shaped by the circumstances of the historical and political experiences of different political regimes. During the colonial period, local governments in Anglophone, Francophone, and Lusophone countries were instruments of colonial repression and were tools for the control of native peoples. This changed dramatically with political independence, when local governments were redefined, as "development agents" of the state; in some cases they became progressive instruments for change. In many countries, however, they were soon trapped in the era of "one-party" political systems. This political environment completely undermined the basis of local government and the devolution of political and administrative authority, as the hegemonic political parties simply engulfed their roles. Soon there were no elected bodies at local levels, and many of the local-government functionaries became political appointees.

In the 1980s and 1990s a new era emerged, as many of the developing countries underwent economic structural adjustments, which also coincided with a new era of democratization and multiparty politics. The role of local governments was once again redefined, particularly as the new paradigm called for a "shrinking" state and less intervention from central governments. Local governments, NGOs, and community organizations gained new importance, reinforced by support from donors who were clamoring for change.

The roles of existing local governments were redefined within the context of the emerging decentralization policies that grew out of both national and international consensus to devolve political and administrative powers. This commitment to decentralization has been encouraged by multilateral and bilateral donors, who have become a major funding source, and it has become normal and expected that countries define their decentralization frameworks as part of the widely accepted Poverty Reduction Strategy Papers needed to access international assistance.

In many cases the same structures that have always been there before have been reinforced, and in others, new innovative arrangements have been put in place. Ethiopia is an example of a country where a new ethnically based federal system was put in place after a very prolonged civil war, thereby redefining the nature and functions of the former highly centralized state. Uganda and Ghana have been at the forefront of redefining the nature and structure of local government within the framework of a unitary system of government based on existing arrangements, but putting strong emphasis on participatory development. Significant revival and reform of local government systems has also taken place in Senegal, Mali, Tanzania, Malawi, and South Africa.

In all cases the main issue has been restructuring and refocusing the roles of local governments within the framework of a decentralized policy environment. The delineation of functions for each level is a key challenge, along with obtaining needed manpower capacities and finance. In the majority of the developing countries, the emerging systems combine deconcentrated, devolved, and delegated authority. Central-government sector ministries are still the main policy and operational agencies for delivery of services and infrastructure, and they are the dominant public-sector frameworks for national-resource allocation. They create broad policy direction, statutory and legal frameworks, regulatory frameworks, and the operational norms for these frameworks—prescribed systems, procedures, guidelines, and practices.[3] Local governments that derive their functions from national legislation focus on the parameters for local decisionmaking, planning and budgeting, implementation and delivery, management and monitoring, and financing. Sometimes local governments emerge as mere agents of central governments with delegated, devolved, and deconcentrated functions, but in some cases they represent autonomous territorial organizations with devolved political and administrative authority.

Tables 14-1 and 14-2, based on research in Zimbabwe at the end of the 1980s, depict a typical sharing of functions among the different levels of government and the share of funding generated between the center and local levels. There is significant evidence of coproduction, codelivery, and comanagement of services. There are also major distinctions in terms of powers and levels of responsibility between the urban and the rural, given stronger urban economies and, hence, the ability of urban authorities to generate their own revenues. The level of transfer from central government ranges from 8 percent for the large city authorities to up to 97 percent for the rural authorities that have a very minimal local revenue base. This is a typical problem for most rural authorities: the revenues they generate are very low and stagnant and they can never cope with more than a fraction of the mandated service-delivery costs. This creates a vertical gap that the central government always has to fill—a universal problem whereby local governments worldwide can never be expected to generate enough revenue to meet their costs, because central governments levy and retain all the buoyant taxes (income taxes, excise duties, company taxes) that contribute to the national fiscus.

From table 14-1 it is clear that central and local governments have to work together to provide infrastructure and services, and the difference comes in terms of how much decisionmaking authority, funding, and what level of discretion is given to local authorities. Typically, central government retains the overall policymaking responsibility in education and health and provides resources to pay for teachers' salaries and education supervisors. The day-to-day running of schools, however, falls to parent and teacher associations, which work closely with local governments in the areas of maintenance, acquisition of teaching materials, and supervision. Different models exist in different countries, and the role of nongovernmental actors is very significant in education provision in most African countries.

Local authorities are required to provide certain services by the legislation that created them or by the constitution, and specific funding arrangements have to be put in place to ensure that both the capital and recurrent costs are met. The protective, amenities, and environmental functions (see table 14-1) are key mandatory functions for most urban local authorities. The rural authorities

Table 14-1. *Local Services Provided by Local and Central Governments*

Functions	City councils	Municipal councils	Other urban	Rural councils (commercial areas)	Rural district councils
Protective					
Police	l, C	l, C	C	C	C
Firefighting services	L	L	l	L	...
Street lighting	L	L	L	L	...
Pest control	L	L	L	l, C	c
Environmental					
Planning	L, c	L, c	C	c	c
Refuse collection	L	L	L	L	l
Sewerage	L	L	l	l	...
Pollution control	L	L	...	...	...
Sanitation	L	L	L	L	l
Public health	L	L	L	L	c
Roads	L	L	L	L	C
Utilities					
Transportation regulation	l, C	l, C	l, C	l, C	c
Electricity	l, C	l, C	C	C	c
Water supply	L	L	L	l	c
Social services					
Clinic and maternity	L	L	L	L	l
Ambulances	L, c	L, c	C	L, c	c
Hospitals	l, C	C	C	L, c	c
Primary education	l, C	l, C	l, C	L	L
Secondary education	C	C	l, C	L	l
Vocational education	l, C	l, C	C	...	...
Social housing	L	L	L	l	...
Amenities					
Parks and playgrounds	L	L	L	l	...
Community amenities	L	L	l	l	l
Community aesthetics	L	L	I	...	...
Trading					
Liquor (traditional beer)	L	L	L	L	L

Source: Government of Zimbabwe, *Tax Commission Report,* 1986.

L = local government, major provision.

l = local government, minor provision.

c = central government, minor provision.

C = central government, major provision.

Table 14-2. *Structure of Revenue Income of Local Authorities, 1982*
Percent

Revenue source	City and municipal councils	Town councils	Town boards	Rural councils	Rural district councils
Local taxes					
Rates, unit, poll	9.3	6.6	23.9	24.6	0.1
Nontax revenue	82.6	87.9	70.5	28.1	2.8
Fees	7.2	5.5	6.8	14.4	1
Licenses	6.7	1.3	1.1	1	0.4
Rents and charges	6.7	42.8	44.9	9.9	. . .
Water charges	0.1	23.4	. . .	0.7	. . .
Beer trading	42.9	13.5	14.8	0.1	1.4
Interest	13.6	. . .	2.9	1.9	. . .
Other	5.4	1.4	. . .	0.1	. . .
Total local revenue	91.9	94.5	93.9	52.7	2.9
Transfers	8.1	5.5	5.6	47.3	97.1
General	0.3	4.4	1.7	6.2	6.3
Specific					
Health	3.4	. . .	. . .	2.2	3.2
Roads	. . .	. . .	. . .	13	0.1
Education	. . .	. . .	. . .	14.4	87.2
Tax sharing					
Vehicle tax	4.4	1.1	3.9	11.5	0.3
Grand total	100	100	100	100	100

Source: Derived from Government of Zimbabwe, *Tax Commission Report,* 1986, table 17.11.

play a key role in maintaining social infrastructure and services, and in ensuring that critical infrastructure such as rural feeder roads are provided for the farmers. There are many other permissive functions that they might undertake, including local economic development and natural-resource management, and usually the local authorities have discretion to fulfill these functions, depending on the local resources that they generate or other funding arrangements that are put in place.

An examination of revenues shows the limitations of local taxes as a source of revenue, though they show potential when there are unit taxes on land given its growing potential value (commercial and other forms). The nontax revenues are very significant for the urban local authorities because these authorities can charge rents and fees for property, water supply, and a variety of licenses. Transfers to the rural local authorities, which have significant deficits in terms of available infrastructure and services, are very significant for the key services—health, roads, education, and other national priorities. In many countries there is a need to account for large donor transfers—including those from the World Bank Social Funds, a wide range of bilateral donor funds, international NGO funds, and community funds—targeted toward the priority key services and infrastructure. This is the typical case in Uganda, Tanzania, and Bangladesh, where there is a huge infusion of donor funds supporting decentralization.

The significance of adopting decentralization policies goes beyond simply having a local government system. It represents a commitment by the government and the intergovernmental system to shift the locus of decisionmaking from the center to local levels. It represents a shift from functional top-down systems to more territory-based bottom-up local development systems. This also rejuvenates existing local governments from simply being administrative and political outposts to becoming "development" agents and seeking to being agents of achieving local development. Many developing countries continue to have local government systems that lack the ability and capacity to deliver development. They lack financial resources, human resources, and the organizational capacities needed to perform a development function. The logic of decentralization policies is to create that capacity, to ensure that the whole public-sector system supports decentralized development.

UNCDF local development programs have promoted a set of innovations to promote more effective infrastructure and service delivery through rural local governments, by twinning innovations in funding with other capacity-development innovations to support improved planning, budgeting, implementation, and overall accountability of local governments.

The financing innovations include allocation of block grants aimed at providing local governments with funds to finance development. Allocation proceeds on the basis of a clear and known formula calibrated to reflect relative poverty and fiscal need; synchronization of the block grants with local government budgeting timetables; a cascading approach allowing the effective utilization of a multitier system to achieve local development; providing local governments with considerable discretion so as to foster accountability and achieve allocative efficiencies; establishment of performance-based funding mechanisms, which encourage local governments to excel; and support to local revenue collection efforts.

Innovations in planning, budgeting, and implementation include effectively linking planning to local government budgeting and promoting cost-effective participatory and inclusive planning methodologies; creating and supporting institutional arrangements that help bridge the gaps between local governments and communities, sector ministries, and the private sector, and inter-local government relationships; and strengthening the local planning process, ensuring adequate technical appraisals, design, and costing.

More specifically, in terms of implementation there is an urgent need to adapt procurement procedures to the local government context, taking into account

the limitations of the rural economies; devise and put in place simplified procedures and formats for competitive tendering, and encourage partnerships between
local governments and the private sector; upgrade contractor and engineering
skills in the private sector, particularly those of informal sector operators and
rural artisans; emphasize operations and maintenance roles of local governments
and the community and provide basic training packages to a range of actors.

Another key area of innovations is that of accountability, that of local governments to the communities and to central government, and their internal
accountability. To accomplish the former, there is a needed to provide local
citizens with access to information about the function of local governments (not
just elections), to acquaint them with the resources of local governments and
decisionmaking procedures and processes. Communities must be able to make
their representative accountable, and local governments, as institutions, must
design systems to promote a culture of accountability. Annual self-assessments
that involve their communities give local governments the opportunity to see
their performance as if reflected in a looking glass. This process should encourage public involvement in planning, budgeting, and monitoring.

For many of the recently decentralizing countries much effort has to be
given to capacity building and development and to develop demand-driven
mechanisms for ensuring that local governments and communities effectively
interact. What is new in decentralization is the strengthening of the demand
side, which tends to be overshadowed by the supply-oriented, top-down-sector
delivery models. The clear delineation of responsibilities coupled with the flow
of the necessary resources to local levels triggers an interest on the part of local
communities in participating in the local development process.

UNCDF's local development programs have had a significant impact because for the first time some locally elected local governments have resources
with a clear budget ceiling, which they can use for local infrastructure and services. The programs have clearly signaled a shift away from "wish-list planning"
to real-time programming. This also allows for the testing of local institutions'
capability, and for their delivery mechanisms to receive attention in terms of
capacity building where they need it. In places where governments are committed to decentralization, this strengthens their resolve, allowing for a much more
concrete delivery of infrastructure and service provision and moving away from
political platitudes.

Tables 14-1 and 14-2 have been extracted from a very comprehensive research report done for the Tax Commission of Zimbabwe in 1986.[4] The tables
are useful to generically illustrate the hierarchical nature of local government
and the distribution of responsibilities within the hierarchy. Delineating and
balancing the nature of the organizational hierarchy is a challenge for all decentralizing countries. Usually the urban municipalities have more responsibilities,
and as agglomerations they require more services. They also generate more

local revenues, which they can invest in service and infrastructure provision. The rural local authorities are much poorer and depend for most of their resources on transfers: table 14-2 shows that the rural district councils are up to 90 percent dependent on transfers from the center.

The experience in many of the least developed nations is that the responsibilities for the different layers of subnational government are defined in legislation, but they fail to make the system work because "resources fail to follow functions." Even some big urban municipalities become dependent on transfers from the center, if their taxing structures give them only marginal and inelastic sources of revenue. The importance of the recent wave of decentralization is that it has been characterized by a greater commitment to transfer resources, whether from national treasuries or from donors. Both sources empower local governments, enabling them to be relevant to local investment processes.

The generic use of the table 14-1 and 14-2 templates in many least developed countries and other African countries would show similar characteristics, although with different configurations of subnational institutions. Indeed, with less-established urban municipalities, which in most countries are small towns and secondary urban centers, one will likely see more dependence on transfers from the center—most likely in the form of conditional grants for specific sectors and services. Experience in Uganda and Ghana, which have undergone major decentralization reforms and reviews, show that the range of increased transfers has been the result of donor support, translated through national budgets under the budget-support modalities.

The different countries vary in the levels of subnational authority that exist, and at times there is real conflict and confusion about attribution of responsibility. These institutional challenges raise fundamental questions concerning the appropriate level of local government and the need to find a balance between creating myriad representative institutions and ensuring their economic and financial viability.

UNCDF experiences in the least developed countries highlight a number of local institutional and accountability challenges.[5]

First, in many countries (Malawi, Lesotho, Uganda, Mali, and Nepal) there are strong links between local governments and traditional authorities, and there is a need to balance democratic legitimacy with local cultural and customary legitimacy. The traditional authorities are still relevant to the local communities, and they perform different functions than local governments, including local land allocation, dispute resolution, and other cultural duties. It is therefore critical that effective and meaningful linkages are created with traditional authorities to ensure effective planning and community resource mobilization.

Second, are the crucial links to nonstate actors—NGOs, community-based organizations (CBOs), church groups, and the private sector. This is the important domain of civil society, which underpins the functioning of local structures and the local economy. The success of local government depends on its ability to leverage the impact of different partners who play key roles in development. In many countries in Africa, church groups play a pivotal role in the provision of health and education facilities. It is also common to find NGOs playing key developmental roles through the funding they receive from international partners. The roles of the different nonstate actors have to be clearly understood in the mapping of decentralized institutions and functioning.

Third, the issue of coprovision, coproduction, and comanagement of services is crucial to gaining an understanding of how the different tiers of subnational authority function. Far too often, emphasis is placed on the local governments, and regional tiers and other lower-level institutions are forgotten. This distorts the advantage that might be achieved by using the full spectrum of institutions. Certain services require significant economies of scale, which a local government cannot provide. The infrastructure or service might also have a major spillover effect that requires a combination of local governments and recognition of the way the different tiers of authority function. Taking these other subnational entities into account also has major implications for accountability—downward, horizontal, and upward.

UNCDF has identified and worked with two generic institutional models prevailing in Africa. The first model is the prefecture-commune model, which has two levels: elected commune councils with jurisdiction over a relatively small area, one or two employees, and a narrow range of functions; and line departments deployed at a higher (departmental) level, under the preeminent political authority of the appointed prefect (governor or district commissioner) who supervises these departments, which are assigned the principal service provision functions and budgets. This model clearly combines some devolution of authority with deconcentration of power through the prefect.

The second model is the district model, in which district councils, whose members are elected, have jurisdiction over a relatively large and populous area. The councils have full supervision authority over their own departments, whose range of powers varies according to their functions and resource base. These district councils also have partial supervisory authority over the activities of national-sector ministries, whom they are mandated to coordinate and work with. It is still a major challenge in many countries to achieve the necessary coordination between the territorial units and the sector ministries.

We can conclude this section on institutions by observing that effective infrastructure and service delivery will depend on clearly mapping the various institutions, understanding their functions, and creating the necessary capacity for them to "deliver the goods." This is an ongoing challenge that governments must meet, taking into account the many institutional and political dynamics at play in their country.

The Resources Framework—Funding Decentralized Infrastructure and Service Delivery

Once the institutional-policy framework for decentralization has been agreed on, the next important challenge is to identify who funds what functions, and who is accountable to whom for the resources and the intended outputs.

The institution of local government is as old as the state itself, and it has evolved over the years as a reflection of the political priorities determined nationally and locally concerning its powers and responsibilities. The dynamics of the relationships between the center and local government continuously change, although the financing of local governments falls within the realm of public finance and is part of the broader functions of government.

The three key functions of government, according to R. A. Musgrave and P. B. Musgrave, are

—The allocative function of providing public goods and services
—The distributive function of sharing of wealth and income
—The economic stabilization function.[6]

Local governments have an important role to play in the allocative function, and this is reinforced when participatory mechanisms are developed and communities are effectively empowered.

Local government financing depends on three key sources: own-source revenues (*la fiscalitè locale*), central government transfers (conditional, unconditional, and equalization grants), and loans and other donor transfers. Own-source revenues include local taxes, nontax revenues, levies, community contributions, and service fees. In many countries, this source is significant for urban and municipal authorities, who have power and jurisdiction over land and property taxes, but very limited for the rural authorities, with limited local economies and lacking the cadastres that form the basis for land and property registers.

Central government transfers are generated from tax revenues (income taxes, company taxes, and so forth), which central governments collect, and form the basis of the public expenditure budgets. Local governments receive grants annually: conditional grants are targeted to specific public services and block grants may be used at the discretion of local governments. Central governments also provide equalization grants to redress inequalities and ensure that there is geographical equity. The experience in most countries suggests that the major urban and metropolitan centers are relatively self-sufficient, as a result of the own-source revenues they generate, and depend only in a limited way on grants from the center. Indeed, this autonomy has sometimes threatened central governments, particularly if the opposition party or parties gain control of the local government; this can result in conflict and the institution of measures to undermine the autonomy of local governments. The experience of rural local authorities is usually the opposite, in that over 90 percent of their development needs are satisfied by transfers, including donor funding coming through common basket funds for the government and through other mechanisms such as SWAPs. Whereas the proportion of local government revenue in total government revenue is very small (less than 10 percent), the proportion of central government transfers as a percentage of local government receipts is very significant—more than 50 percent (table 14-2). The model of local government in many of the least-developed nations is going to continue to depend primarily on transfers, except in the large urban centers.

The role of nonstate resources is growing significantly in all the countries. The poor local authorities found in the predominantly rural economies of the least developed countries are going to depend on government and donor transfers in the foreseeable future. Indeed, dependence on government transfers might be the norm until these countries' economies fully transform to generate local revenues. Depending on their credit ratings, the large metropolitan areas have access to private-sector borrowing, and the experience in southern and east Africa is that they are increasingly turning to the private capital markets for funding to create public goods and services. The activities of NGOs and other such organizations in local and national economic development is also intensifying.

The effective function of local governments depends on the implementation of several key principles of center-local fiscal transfer:[7]

—Providing adequate resources to balance national priorities and local autonomy

—Ensuring fair allocation of resources and giving priority to disadvantaged areas

—Providing transfers in a predictable manner and ensuring that the agreed allocation formulas remain predictable and fair

—Promoting simple and transparent formulas that are understandable to local officials and local communities

—Eliminating negative incentives for local revenue mobilization

—Reducing or removing conditionalities, which create administrative problems and lead to micro-management of local governments.

In practice, several approaches have been adopted by donors and other funding partners to support the transfer of resources to local levels. The social funds have been a very popular mechanism to support local service and infrastructure development.[8] Such funding has not been channeled directly through existing government channels (treasury or local government). Instead, new institutional arrangements for distributing monies have been developed: national social fund agencies in Malawi, Uganda, and Zambia and a deconcentrated field presence at local levels directly funding and monitoring projects. Over the years there have been modifications to this approach, involving a greater recognition of local governments and other deconcentrated central government agencies. The new generation of social funds (community-driven development) has shifted from an exclusive preoccupation with community groups to a much more integrated approach involving local governments.

Another commonly utilized mechanism is the sectorwide approach (SWAP), in which like-minded donors pool their resources to support a specific sector, such as health, education, or water supply. The sectorwide approach is based on commonly agreed funding, implementing, and reporting arrangements and allows government to take the policy lead. In practice, SWAP programs have not integrated local governments and thus have reinforced the sector-based model as opposed to the territorial model. It has also reinforced the top-down technical approach to development as opposed to the more participatory bottom-up approach. The UNCDF local development approach has focused on supporting local governments and building the necessary systems and procedures to promote decentralization. Through the local development funds (provided by UNCDF and other development partners), local governments have been supported to test an integrated model of local development that promotes intersectoral area planning, with local government undertaking budgeting and implementation. The emphasis has been on providing hard budget ceilings to the different operational levels of local government and on allowing them to do real-time planning and make choices for use of the resources that they have. The major limitation has been inadequate funding for pilot programs and a lack of necessary leverage for upscaling.

In the end these approaches can be integrated under the local development umbrella when power is shifted to localities, which then become the focal point for making institutional reforms, achieving local investments, and providing pro-poor infrastructure and services. The concept of local development is not, however, exclusive to local governments, because a variety of other local institutional actors are active development agents, and this is even more significant for the provision of services and infrastructure.

Planning for Infrastructure and Service Delivery

Although infrastructure and services are critical for development, many countries and international agencies have shied away from providing them, and have preferred to concentrate on "software" issues—training and capacity building—and not the actual provision of "hardware." Donors have felt that infrastructure had little implication for poverty reduction, given the tendency in many countries to go for large prestigious projects such as airports and large dams. Nevertheless, the negative consequences for poor people of some large projects were always given significant coverage—the flooding of their homes, their displacement, and environmental damage.

With hindsight, everybody now recognizes that no matter how much public-sector capacity is built and governance is improved, there is no substitute for hard infrastructure investments that stimulate economic development and investments. The most important issue is to strike a balance and recognize the linkage between infrastructure and poverty reduction—it is important to make infrastructure work for the poor.

Infrastructure consists of various types of physical assets and services and varies by size, purpose, usage, and target consumers. The diversity of infrastructure cuts across geographical boundaries, administrative jurisdictions, rural and urban spaces, and public-private domains. It is clear that each level and jurisdiction has its own comparative advantage and that different sorts of infrastructure and services require different levels of design, planning, and implementation capacities.

At the lowest local levels, we are dealing with small-scale and community-based infrastructure and services: small feeder roads, community tube wells, small irrigation schemes. Such infrastructure is very different from national highways, major hospitals, power stations, and airports, whose increased levels of complexity require commensurately complex management. Decentralized provision of infrastructure and services requires a clear mapping of the capabilities and comparative advantage of the different institutions and also community involvement. It also calls for a greater understanding of the critical thematic linkages: capabilities linkage, education linkage, health linkage, empowerment linkage, food security linkage, and vulnerability linkage.[9]

It has been argued that because of its nature, location, design, and implementation process, the development of small-scale infrastructure may have more direct positive impacts on the lives of poor people than large-scale national projects. Small irrigation schemes bring tangible benefits to local farmers through improved productivity; rural feeder roads improve mobility of local communities and reduce transport costs, which have an impact on economic activities; rural public works programs create jobs and improve the overall productivity of the local economy through construction and maintenance of local roads, water supply systems, and small bridges.

Decentralization backed by adequate resources and capacities has the potential to increase both productive and allocative efficiencies through increased participation, better prioritization of projects, and better utilization of local resources. In practice, however, structural bottlenecks and inefficiencies make it difficult to achieve the ideal. The next section presents the results of decentralized development implemented by local development programs that have been piloted by UNCDF in up to thirty countries in the last two decades.

The African Experience

Africa has undergone significant transformations since the attainment of independence of many African countries in the early 1960s. Decentralization has come in waves and has had mixed results. This chapter generally draws on decentralization and local development experiences primarily in Uganda, and more generally Malawi, Zambia, Tanzania, Senegal, Mali, and Ethiopia.

From this overview five points emerge. First, although it is important to recognize that country experiences tend to be historically unique and therefore one must be cautious about sweeping conclusions, some of the key lessons highlighted from a synthesis of four studies (Uganda, Mali, Senegal, and Ethiopia) show that rural local governments, if capacitated, can and do "deliver the goods."[10] Second, local governments will continue to operate side by side with sector ministries, and there are variations in the way that they collaborate—sometimes in a fairly integrated way (Uganda) and in others in an unintergrated manner (Mali). Third, in terms of financing, it is clear that predetermined capital budget allocations make the local planning and development process meaningful, and that the discretion of local governments over prioritizing and spending is critical to local infrastructure and services provision. Fourth, in terms of implementation, there is a need to focus on flexible procurement arrangements that allow the local private sector to participate and provide opportunities to train local contractors. Finally, accountability by the local authorities to the local communities (downward accountability), to central government (upward accountability), and to other local authorities (horizontal accountability) grows as resources become more linked to local development.

Uganda, in the last twenty years, has moved from the bitter civil war in the 1980s to the triumph of the National Resistance Movement (NRM) in 1986 under the leadership of President Yoweri Museveni. Decentralization has been implemented with strong political will from the central government and has also been closely linked to a vision of an effective and efficient public sector system in which the subnational governments play a critical role, such that the country can be singled out as an example of best practice in this area.

The democratic principle adopted in the Uganda constitution is that "the State shall be guided by the principle of decentralization and devolution of government functions and powers to the people at appropriate levels where they can best manage and direct their own affairs."[11] The intention is to transfer real power to the local councils; bring political and administrative control over services to the point where they are actually delivered, thereby improving accountability and effectiveness; give local managers discretionary power and accountability; and improve the capacity of local councils to plan, finance, and manage delivery of services. Uganda's decentralization policy is guided by principles of subsidiarity and integration with nonsubordination.

In Uganda there are five levels of local government in both the rural and urban sectors. In the rural areas there are 56 districts and 856 subcounties, and 78 urban councils (13 municipalities and 65 town or municipal divisions and city divisions). In terms of infrastructure and service delivery, two aspects, provision and production of services, are key to understanding both territorial and sectoral decentralization. Provision involves decisions generally associated with "governing"—what service to provide, the quantity and quality of services, and their financing. Production is the process of converting inputs into outputs, for example, building of schools, health centers, district feeder roads. The strength of the emerging Uganda model rests on the central government's emphasis on the transfer of powers and responsibilities to local governments and its strongly encouraging the central government sector ministries to focus on policy. The provision and production mix at the local levels is manifest through the fiscal mechanisms of conditional and unconditional grants. Through conditional grants, which are the dominant form of transfer, central government sector ministries continue to play an important policy, provision, and production role in education, health, water supply, and agricultural services. This also creates a confluence of devolution to local governments and deconcentration through sector ministries. The major source for financing infrastructure and service delivery in local governments is the sector conditional grant. In financial year 2002–03, conditional sources of revenue accounted for up to 80 percent of the transfer, which has a major bearing on the nature and delivery mechanisms of infrastructure and services. The unconditional sources, including some direct nongovernmental transfers, accounted for 15 percent; the own-source revenue was insignificant. The biggest challenge, in the case of Uganda and other decentralizing countries, is to demonstrate the effectiveness of the local governments' delivery mechanisms, and ensure that there are pro-poor outcomes. The District Development Program piloted by UNCDF starting in 1997 focused on the investment role of local governments and the development of their core competencies to achieve local development.

The key innovation was making discretionary development budget support available to rural local governments and targeting infrastructure and services. The five key sectors targeted were health, education, roads and drainage, water and sanitation, and agriculture. Through participatory planning mechanisms, communities identified, prioritized, and implemented 741 projects in education, 322 projects in roads and drainage, 476 projects in water and sanitation, 169 projects in health, and 117 projects in agriculture. The importance of the project portfolio is that it reflects closely the real community needs and priorities, and effectively connects the democratic subnational institutions in local development. The challenge is to measure the pro-poor nature of the interventions and their impact on poverty reduction. In the five pilot administrative districts participation levels have been very high—up to 80 percent of the total population at parish and village levels have been involved—and there were significant cash and in-kind community contributions to the projects. Analysis of the type of investments reveals three results: the sector allocation by the local governments was consistent with the poverty eradication action plan of the central government; investments targeted well-defined beneficiary groups, most of whom are poor; and the costs of the investments were lowered by the active participation of the beneficiary groups. Local labor represented 19 percent of the total project costs, thus directly putting 2.5 billion Uganda shillings in the pockets of low-income households.[12]

The Uganda case clearly shows that decentralization is a means to an end and not an end in itself. The powers and responsibilities given to rural local governments must be translated into concrete outcomes, the most critical being infrastructure and service delivery. The experience in all the other countries testifies to this growing conviction in the new development paradigm based on clear planning and resource allocation to local governments and clear identification of their roles, responsibilities, and complementarities with other actors (private sector and other nongovernmental entities).

The Asian Developing Country Experience

The Asian experience described has largely been generated from UNCDF's support work in Bangladesh, Nepal, and Cambodia. Although Asia is rapidly urbanizing and industrializing, the bulk of the population in south and southeast Asia is still rural and poverty is still a significant phenomenon. (In 2003, the percentage of the population that was rural was 75 percent in Bangladesh, 82 percent in Cambodia, and 86 percent in Nepal; the average percentage of the population below the poverty line in the three countries is 40 percent, and the levels of service and infrastructure provision are very poor.)

Government policies in Bangladesh, Nepal, and Cambodia have shifted toward decentralization, resulting in their adoption of major new reforms, amendments, and legislation. The logic has been to strengthen the capacities of subnational governments and to refocus them toward a more developmental agenda to achieve the UN's Millennium Development Goals. UNCDF, together with the other key development partners, has supported decentralization programs helping to translate the reform agenda into concrete infrastructure and service delivery options for local governments.

A key innovation—the "trademark" of the local development programs—is the provision of unconditional block grants to local governments, which allows them to engage in real-time planning and dialogue with "hard" budgets available for implementation. The result in all the countries has been a clear focus on local development priorities—the choices made by local communities—with more accountability and transparency.

In terms of outcomes, there has been better targeting of poverty: in Bangladesh, 33 percent of all implemented schemes have been planned by and targeted to women's groups, and in Nepal there is a 30 percent dedicated window of funding for the lower castes and disadvantaged groups. The matching contributions also reflect the programs' success among the lower-income groups and the enthusiasm they feel for it because their priorities are being taken more seriously.

The types of investments supported in Asia included rural roads, education, health, water and sanitation, and agriculture, and the local investment menus were determined through local participatory planning processes. These types of investments are typical also in the African continent, where the local rural communities' needs and their levels of poverty are similar.

In Bangladesh, one of the world's poorest countries, 80 percent live in poverty. The economy is largely rural and dependent on agriculture, the sector in which 74 percent of the population works. The system of local government, though well established, is weak, and many of the local councils have limited resources and little revenue-raising authority and are dependent on local government for funds. All the key basic services—education, health, nutrition, family planning, irrigation, agricultural services, and roads—are managed directly by central government. Local government's share of total public expenditure is below 2 percent.

Four primary pieces of legislation define the powers of rural local government: Local Government Ordinance, 1983; Upazila Act, 1988; the Zila Parishad Act, 1988; and the Hill District Local Government Parishad Act, 1989 (*parishad* means "council"). This legislation provides for a mixture of devolution and deconcentration. At the level of both the 64 *zilas*, or districts, and the 460 *upazilas*, or subdistricts, there is no direct political representation and the line ministries play a central and dominant role. But at the level of the 4,500 union parishads, the lowest local administrative tier, there are twelve elected members (one for each ward and three women members, each representing three wards), and the union parishads have powers to collect taxes and powers to provide small-scale infrastructure.

The problem in Bangladesh is that the subnational levels of development have been dominated by the sector and line ministries, leaving very little room to the elected local governments. This has promoted corruption and very strong rent-seeking behavior by government officials. There has been strong resistance by the center to empower union parishads, which have been overshadowed in local development. After years of supporting local projects, the government of Bangladesh, in 2000, agreed to sign into law the Sirajganj Local Governance Development Fund Project, focusing on poverty reduction and service delivery and paving the way for real support to flow to local government.

The United Nations Development Program and UNCDF have jointly funded the project, whose main objective is the provision of block grants directly to union parishads, the locally elected authority, to give them power to plan, implement, and empower local communities. Based on a clear formula, all participating unions have received grants; to allocate funds fairly, grants are weighted for population, land area, and backwardness. These grants are not subject to the manipulation of the higher bodies and they are announced to the local communities in advance of the planning process. The participating union parishads are judged on their performance annually, allowing them to draw a bonus of 15 percent on the performance grant in the coming year. Both the transparency to the community and the performance grant make the elected members accountable.

Although the union parishads work closely with other levels of government, they remain in control of both the funds and the power to determine the investment priorities within their mandate. The grants are not used for ongoing funding, so collaboration with the sector and line agencies—to ensure that funding is maintained—is very critical to the creation of new infrastructure and services. There has been significant capacity building in planning, budgeting, and implementation, and the participation of local communities, particularly the inclusion of women and marginal groups, has also been strengthened. Planning processes have been systematically designed and implemented to allow maximum community participation and involvement, in contrast to the top-down processes of sector ministries.

While recognizing the "project effect"(that is, that a project creates artificial conditions that are difficult to sustain without it) of the Sirajganj Local Governance Development Fund Project, there is no doubt of the significant improvements in terms of changing attitudes toward participation, increased accountability captured through the participatory review process, improved production and implementation of infrastructure and service delivery, and adoption by government as a model for nationwide replication.[13] The project has reinforced the importance of union parishads as a key subnational level of government and of elected and participatory forums in local development. Indeed, in 2006 the government of Bangladesh has approved with the support of all the key donors a replication of the main features piloted in the project.

It is important to recognize the continued importance of sector ministries, districts, and subdistricts in the provision and implementation of infrastructure and that the union parishads are likely to have an impact only on creation and maintenance of small-scale infrastructure. The hope is that the good practices identified at the union parishad level can be incorporated into overall public sector practice.

Conclusion

While decentralization is not a panacea for achieving effective and efficient service delivery, it certainly adds several positive features that are usually lacking in traditional top-down delivery approaches. It raises the bar on local participation and participatory approaches to planning and implementation and

draws communities closer to the local development process. Elected local officials become more aware and vigilant on behalf of the communities they represent, and the latter are more empowered to act and ask critical questions on
the local development agenda.

In both the African and Asian experiences, the intensifying decentralization
experience is still driven by the support and funding of donors and other development partners. This creates an "artificial factor," one that will eventually dis-
appear as fiscal transfers are put in place and as local governments begin to bring
their own local sources of revenue onstream. Meanwhile, the role of donors in
development finance is critical in most of the least-developed nations, and there
are many evolving mechanisms that support local and national development.
These include "budget support" to the national exchequer whereby funding is
earmarked for local development and local governments; sectorwide approaches
whereby funding is pooled for specific sector activities; and direct project and
area support targeted at specific territorial areas. It has been observed that these
mechanisms should not be allowed to bloat local revenue generation and local
funding, which are key to long-term sustainability.

The importance of direct block grants for local governments has been demonstrated in all the pilot schemes that have been supported by the UNCDF local
development pilot programs, and are being replicated by governments and
other major multilateral and bilateral agencies. Direct block grants are a key
mechanism for promoting local development and empowering local authorities and local communities. They must be packaged with capacity building in
all aspects of the planning and development cycle. In all cases, however, local
contributions are an important "local ownership trigger" and ensure that the
initiatives are not just "gifts" from donors.

Decentralization requires local organization; consequently there is always a
need to "dynamize" local governments and create ad hoc organizational arrangements to support and enhance participatory planning and implementation and
ensure long-term maintenance. At higher levels of local government the staff
that officials hire (planners and engineers, for example) become responsible for
monitoring overall performance and reporting progress and problems to elected
bodies. At the level of small rural local authorities this is not possible, so communities need to play a more active role.

The actual production of infrastructure and service delivery is a complex
affair and it ranges from very small schemes such as culverts, labor-based feeder
roads, and water points to very complex ones such as highways and power systems. The common problem is the lack of qualified and experienced staff to
manage contractors and provide local governments with budgeted and practical plans. There are no quick fixes to the problem; local governments need to
build their capacity and their ability to hire and retain their own staff. This is a
major challenge for small rural local governments, who depend for all their

resources on transfers from the center and have to rely for technical support on staff detailed to them by central ministries.

Ultimately the success of decentralization will depend on a holistic vision of the system in which the different levels of national and subnational government function together in a complementary way, hence the need to put decentralization at the center of public sector restructuring of the state and not limit it to isolated territorial experiments. This is reflected in current initiatives to set up national decentralization and local development programs.

Notes

1. United Nations Capital Development Fund, Local Government Initiative, *Pro-Poor Infrastructure and Service Delivery in Rural Sub-Sahara Africa—A Synthesis of Case Studies from Uganda, Mali, Senegal and Ethiopia* (2004).

2. Ibid.

3. United Nations Capital Development Fund, *Delivering the Goods—Building Local Government Capacity to Achieve the Millennium Development Goals* (2006).

4. Government of Zimbabwe, *Tax Commission Report,* 1986.

5. Ibid.

6. R. A. Musgrave and P. B. Musgrave, *Public Finance in Theory and Practice* (New York: McGraw-Hill, 1984).

7. Jameson Boex and Jorge Martinez-Vazquez, "Local Government Reform in Tanzania: Considerations for the Development of a System of Formula-Based Grants," Working Paper 03-05, Georgia State University, 2003.

8. World Bank, *World Development Report 2004: Making Services Work for the Poor* (Oxford University Press, 2004).

9. United Nations Development Program and United Nations Capital Development Fund, *Governance for the Future—Democracy and Development in the Least Developed Countries* (2006).

10. United Nations Capital Development Fund, *Delivering the Goods.*

11. Constitution of Uganda, 1995 (preamble).

12. Onyach-Olaa Martin, "Lessons from Experiences in Decentralizing Infrastructure and Service Delivery in Uganda," United Nations Capital Development Fund, 2003.

13. United Nations Capital Development Fund, "Empowering the Poor—Local Governance for Poverty Reduction" (2003).

15

Designing Decentralized Coastal Management Programs

KEM LOWRY

O ne of the most sobering realities about contemporary natural resource management and environmental protection is how difficult it is to translate environmental goals into effective action. The result is what might be called an "implementation gap." This implementation gap refers to inconsistencies between policy goals conceived at one level or branch of government and the translation of those goals into specific resource management activities at another level or by other agencies.[1] It also refers to the gap between management actions at all levels of government and actual improvement in environmental conditions.

These implementation gaps are not a new concern, but they have not figured prominently in international deliberations on environmental management. At the major international conferences on the environment—Stockholm in 1972, Rio in 1992, and Johannesburg in 2002—the emphasis was on raising awareness of global environmental issues and mobilizing governments to take action to reduce poverty, change unsustainable patterns of consumption and production, protect the natural resource base, and improve environmental conditions. The list of laudable goals in the *Johannesburg Plan of Implementation* is impressive, but the report offers little guidance about creating the institutional structures to achieve these goals. Local governments, in particular, receive scant attention save this mention toward the end of the 48-page plan:

Enhance the role and capacity of local authorities as well as stakeholders in implementing Agenda 21 and the outcomes of the Summit and in strengthening the continuing support for local Agenda 21 programmes and associated initiatives and partnerships, and encourage, in particular, partnerships among and between local authorities and other levels of government and stakeholders to advance sustainable development.[2]

One of the practical political and administrative realities is that successful implementation of natural resource and environmental management programs requires coordinated actions among a number of agencies, both at the same and at different levels of government. Hence intergovernmental relations are a core consideration in addressing the implementation gap. Although national governments can undertake some environmental management efforts, the practical reality of multitier governmental systems is that effective management requires mechanisms for shared governance responsibility. Designing intergovernmental systems requires allocating responsibility, creating understanding and agreement about management roles and responsibilities, ensuring adequate resources for management at all levels, creating required skills and capacities among implementing officials, and creating systems for monitoring agency performance and ensuring accountability.

Many of the tasks associated with designing intergovernmental systems of environmental management have to do with allocating some authority and responsibility to central government agencies and some to provincial and local agencies. "Decentralization" has become a convenient way of characterizing this process. It has also come to be regarded as a key governmental reform. According to a recent World Bank study, "Out of 75 developing and transitional countries with populations greater than 5 million, all but 12 claim to have embarked on some form of transfer of power to local units of government."[3]

A careful examination of the decentralization experiences in these seventy-five countries would show that decentralization has multiple meanings and practices and is undertaken for a wide variety of motives.[4] Attempts to decentralize may be comprehensive, involving a wide range of services or activities narrowly focused on a specific governmental activity. Relationships between central government and local authorities may range from coercive to cooperative. Authority and responsibility may also be distributed in a variety of ways. Availability of resources for management, technical assistance, and administrative support can vary enormously in different decentralized relationships. Moreover, there is a dynamic quality to efforts to decentralize that is often not reflected in textbook treatments of the process. Central government agencies (or officials) may decide to recapture authority transferred to subordinate units, such that over time authority may ebb and flow among agencies and between levels of government.

This paper addresses some of the conceptual and practical issues associated . with decentralization generally and efforts to decentralize coastal management, in particular. "Coastal management" refers broadly to the governance of human uses and activities affecting coastal resources. It includes everything from decisions about the conditions under which coastal hotels, homes, power and sewage disposal plants (and other infrastructure), off-shore drilling for oil, and other activities can be located and operated in relatively narrowly defined coastal zones in some countries. It also refers to activities intended to inhibit the conversion of mangroves or protect reefs or other biologically productive habitats in tropical countries as well as those designed to prevent oil spills, reduce shipping discharge and marine debris, and protect rare and endangered species such as dugong. Minimizing exposure of public and private property in near-shore areas to flooding and other hazards and facilitating some coast-dependent development activities also fall within the orbit of coastal management. Historically, legal authority for aspects of coastal management such as fisheries, harbor development, near-shore land-use management, and pollution control has been divided among a wide variety of sectoral agencies at the same and different levels of government, each operating somewhat independently. In the last two decades there have been efforts to design strategies to increase the coordination of coastal agencies across jurisdictional boundaries. "Integrated coastal management" (ICM) describes these efforts to coordinate management among agencies and across levels of government. Integrated coastal management

> is designed to overcome the fragmentation inherent in both the sectoral management approach and the splits in jurisdiction among levels of government at the land-water interface. This is done by ensuring that the decisions of all sectors (e.g. fisheries, oil and gas production, water quality) and all levels of government are harmonized and consistent with the coastal policies of the nation in question. A key part of ICM is the design of institutional processes to accomplish this harmonization in a politically acceptable manner.[5]

Reducing the "implementation gap" in coastal management has taken many forms, among which developing new institutional arrangements among levels of government has been one of the primary approaches.

Multiple Meanings of Decentralization

The concept of decentralization describes a variety of legal, administrative, political, and fiscal relationships between central government agencies and subnational or local government authorities.[6] Typologies of decentralization continue to evolve, but in this volume four types are emphasized: administrative, political, fiscal, and economic decentralization. The primary emphasis in this chapter is on administrative decentralization. Administrative decentralization of environmental governance is a means of redistributing some authority for the management of human uses and activities affecting resources from central government authorities to subordinate units of government or semiautonomous public authorities, corporations, or functional authorities. Three major types of decentralization are usually distinguished: deconcentration (shifting some management authority for central government ministries to subnational units of the same ministry); delegation (the transfer of some authority to semi-autonomous subnational agencies); and devolution (transfer of authority to local units with substantial autonomy). These general types of administrative decentralization provide a starting point for a more detailed elaboration of central-local governmental relationships.

Practical Dilemmas of Decentralization

The transfer of environmental management authority from central authorities to local agencies proceeds under the assumption that the new implementing agencies possess or can develop the requisite technical knowledge, management capacities, resources, local support, political will, and other individual or collective perquisites to be effective. Making these assumptions about necessary requirements explicit and determining their centrality to effective management has proved to be difficult.[7] Indeed, as one author notes, "If all these [administrative] requirements were perquisites, no developing country would ever be able to decentralize."[8] Rather than specify a set of necessary conditions for effective decentralized agencies, we can identify some practical dilemmas in the design of decentralized administrative relationships. We can identify specific dimensions or administrative variables, such as accountability or administrative capacity, that we associate with effective decentralization and then analyze how they are addressed in the context of specific experiments in decentralized environmental management. Five specific design dilemmas are reviewed in this section:

—What management authority has been decentralized? Is authority sufficient to engage in effective management? What management authority has been retained in the national level of government?

—To what extent do decentralized agencies have sufficient capacity to manage effectively? To what extent are there capacity deficits? What arrangements have been made to identify and address capacity issues? How effective are they?

—What resources (such as personnel or equipment) are required for effective decentralized management? To what extent are local resources sufficient? What is being done by central and decentralized agencies to deal with resources issues?

—How committed are local officials to effective management? How committed are national officials? What, if anything, has been done to induce or coerce commitment? How effective are those measures? To whom are decentralized agencies accountable? What mechanisms for accountability have been established?

Ensuring Adequate Management Authority

Effective natural resource management requires that agencies have sufficient authority to engage in the developmental, regulatory, revenue-generating, and other activities associated with effective management.[9] "Authority" as used here refers primarily to the legal authority derived from constitutional powers, statutes, or administrative guidelines. Authority is also related to political legitimacy—the degree to which citizens regard laws, guidelines, or other authoritative mandates governing resource uses and activities as valid expressions of government power.[10] In practice, national authorities tend to devolve or delegate resource-management authority for some resources or resource-use activities, such as mangrove protection, but retain some national management authority over resource-use activities such as fishing.

Management Capacity

One of the most frequently cited reasons for not implementing policies through subordinate units of government at provincial and local levels is that they lack the "capacity" to carry out the required tasks.[11] "Capacity," in this context, usually refers to technical capacity. If implementing a policy or plan requires a particular technical skill, the organization will need personnel with that skill or the means to train people to develop it. Providing that training is the narrowest and most obvious meaning of capacity building.

Technical capacity—and the personnel training and education required to develop it—is just one dimension of local capacity. A second important dimension is organizational strengthening, which refers to strategies to strengthen management systems in ways that improve performance of specific tasks. Strategies for strengthening organizations include "improving recruitment and utilization of staff, introducing better management practices, restructuring work and authority relationships, improving information and communication flows, upgrading physical resources, and decentralizing and opening decision-making processes."[12] Organizational strengthening may also include job enrichment and enlargement.

A third dimension of capacity building is institutional reform. Institutional reform means altering the rules by which organizations make decisions and carry out activities.[13] Institutional reform may include legal reform or development of new accountability systems. In natural resource management, a greater emphasis on collective self-management by user groups and the development of locally developed "rules" to govern resource users is an example of institutional reform.

An organization's effectiveness is obviously shaped by the types of personnel it can attract, the resources it can command, and its leadership. It is also molded in more subtle ways by its institutional heritage and organizational "culture." Over time organizations develop linkages with the people and organizations with whom they interact. Decentralizing new responsibilities to subordinate agencies that require it to change its relationships with the people with whom it interacts may be resisted. Fishing ministry staff who have a history of administering small loans to encourage the development of a fishing industry may resist mandates to impose gear regulations or other requirements that impose limits on fishing.

In addition, patterns of personnel recruitment shape the professional culture of the organization. Civil engineers who have been trained to design large, capital-intensive projects may find it professionally demeaning to shift their work to labor-intensive, low-technology sanitation projects needed by the poor. The professional norms and expectations of professional staff affect their orientation toward policy mandates from central government agencies in ways that can undermine or enhance policy implementation.

Designing intergovernmental arrangements for implementing policies requires both an assessment of the technical capacities for implementing mandates and the ways in which organizational culture, leadership, and professional norms of the staff subvert or reinforce the implementation activities subordinate agencies are expected to assume.

Resources for Management

One obvious dimension of local "capacity" that deserves special mention is the adequacy of resources available to managers.[14] Local officials need the funds to hire skilled personnel and train existing staff, and purchase or lease computers and software and other material. They also need access to vehicles and boats for site inspections. Some management initiatives, such as improved means of sewage treatment and disposal, also require capital expenditures. Ensuring the availability of resources for management requires financial transfers from the national government or an enlarged local revenue stream from taxes or fees—as well as effective ways to establish priorities among competing resource demands.

Commitment to Effective Management

Research focusing on factors affecting the implementation of plans and programs has consistently identified the level of commitment of implementing officials as a key factor in determining successful implementation.[15] Research also indicates that acquiring and maintaining commitment from lower-level officials in a decentralized system is a major issue. Reflecting on this analysis of efforts to decentralize in Florida, New South Wales, and New Zealand, Peter May and Ray Burby report that variability in local government efforts either to manage development in hazard-prone areas or otherwise to deal with risks posed by natural hazards is "a serious problem that results in half-hearted efforts and, in some instances, outright failure to comply with higher level mandates. In either case, lack of such commitment serves as a key obstacle to achieving sustainability with respect to natural hazards."[16]

Of course what is perceived as "lack of commitment" by central government authorities may be viewed as strategic political resistance by some local officials.[17] Political resistance accounts for some of the variability in responses by local officials to central government mandates. Local political resistance has several possible sources. One is bureaucratic: local administrators may not understand the need for programs mandated by central government or, to the extent that they understand them, may assign them lower priority relative to other local government activities. Getting local government assistance in enforcing coastal building setback requirements is a continuing problem in some countries, in part because some local officials regard coastal erosion resulting from improperly located coastal structures to be a minor problem unrelated to coastal regulation.

A second source of resistance on the part of local officials is to the means of program implementation. Local government officials may recognize the need for improved management of mangroves, for example, but object to administering a permit system or other regulatory program that imposes significant development restrictions on local residents. Finally, the political influence of local resource user groups or political coalitions, such as aquaculture interests, may inhibit local government officials from implementing environmental management initiatives. The authority of central government officials may not be sufficient to overcome the resistance of the local coalitions.

Local commitment is also shaped by several practical considerations such as adequacy of local implementation skills, technical and financial resources, and technical needs. Some central government mandates are not accompanied by sufficient resources for carrying out the required tasks effectively. Other environmental management responsibilities may require cartographic or data management tasks requiring access to advanced computer equipment or software. Lacking hardware, software, or qualified staff to use them, local officials may decide to ignore program implementation requirements.

If the implementation gap between central government goals and decentralized action is to be narrowed, clearly, finding ways to deal with limited commitment (or political resistance) of local authorities is a key issue to be addressed. Failure to comply with national mandates can be punished by fines, reduced funding for local implementation, national preemption of management authority, and a variety of other means.[18] Such coercive initiatives sometimes reduce political resistance in the short run, but the assumption is that they are unlikely to be sustainable, both because monitoring and coercion are difficult to maintain and because local resistance may increase.

Although coercion may be regarded as an option, most strategies aimed at increasing commitment focus on more positive strategies. Three main types of strategies are most prominent: creating greater awareness and understanding of central government objectives, building stronger local constituencies, and developing collaborative planning and management strategies involving staff at all levels. Implementation research suggests that implementation is enhanced to the extent that staff understand and agree with the aims of policy.[19] Workshops and training courses can be an effective way of helping local officials understand both the environmental issues as seen from the perspective of central government and the strategies that have been developed to address these issues. Of course, merely explaining central government perspectives is not likely to increase local government commitment unless a persuasive case is made about what the issue is and how government has chosen to deal with it.

Constituency-building strategies are based on the recognition that local government authorities are subject to political influence from local resource user groups and other interest groups. Increasing local commitment involves changing local politics. Central government can help bolster local commitment by helping to organize political support for environmental initiatives at the local level. Public-awareness campaigns organized by central government aimed at, for example, mangrove protection or reef conservation can help mobilize local user groups and community-based organizations to assist in conservation strategies.

Finally, genuine collaborative planning among agencies at different levels of government can help bolster local commitment. When local officials, who are likely to be deeply involved in identifying key environmental management problems, are involved in the design of strategies to deal with these issues, their understanding of and commitment to the implementation of those strategies is likely to be strengthened.[20]

The commitment of local administrative officials is a key factor in effective decentralized approaches to environmental management. Once developed, local commitment is not necessarily constant. Effective decentralized approaches to management require strategies for building and reinforcing local commitment.

Accountability Issues

Reallocating authority and responsibility from central government ministries to local ministry officials or local authorities carries with it the assumption that those to whom responsibility is transferred will somehow be held accountable for their administrative actions. Hence, in its narrowest conception, accountability refers to procedures for officials in central government to scrutinize the management activities of local authorities. This concept of accountability also implies that "errors" or instances of "noncompliance" by local officials will be identified and "remedied" in some fashion.

Designing procedures for assessing administrative accountability requires answering several questions:

—For what activities and decisions or behaviors will local authorities be held accountable?

—What information about program milestones, program activities, or coastal conditions is needed?

—What procedures are required for gathering, storing, and retrieving monitoring information?[21]

—How will judgments be made about the appropriateness of administrative behavior?

—How will instances of noncompliance or inappropriate subordinate behavior be handled?

Florida legislation requiring preparation of local plans provides an example of upward administrative accountability.[22] State government officials prescribed the content of local plans, procedures for preparing them, and preparation timetables. Local plans were submitted to state officials and reviewed for compliance. Instances of perceived noncompliance were punished. Five cities had financial sanctions imposed for late submission of the comprehensive plans and two counties were sanctioned because they did not comply with state planning standards.[23]

Designing systems for administrative and fiscal accountability poses a number of practical and political dilemmas. Beyond the sometimes difficult practical questions of how to provide for continual monitoring of local agencies, there are political issues as well. Administrative monitoring is often seen by subordinate agencies as a labor-intensive and intrusive process that doesn't adequately gauge either the level of effort or the quality of what they do. Local officials often regard the indicators of effectiveness used by central government agencies as invalid, incomplete, or irrelevant. Questions about the validity of an accountability process can turn into a more general critique of the legitimacy of central government scrutiny—and of local government resistance to continued scrutiny by central government officials.

Though administrative accountability is important, most contemporary observers regard it as just one dimension of a more inclusive system of accountability.[24] Beyond formal legal conceptions of accountability, public officials, nongovernmental organizations, community user groups, and others with authority to implement environmental programs generally and coastal management programs in particular should also be held accountable. This suggests a broader conception of political accountability. But to whom should implementing officials be accountable? And what are the means of achieving such accountability?

The most obvious form of political accountability is scrutiny by elected officials at all levels. Legislative bodies hold hearings, review reports, and consider new legislation. Legislative forums are an opportunity to identify problems, including those related to intergovernmental structures or processes. The notion of political accountability is based on the assumption that administrative officials are responsible not just to elected and appointed officials but to the multitude of stakeholders whose lives are affected by the implementation of environmental programs. A broader conception of political accountability raises several questions:

—How open are agency planning and decisionmaking processes?

—What opportunities for community or interest group participation does the agency offer?

—How much authority does the agency share?

Transparency of agency planning and management activities is one obvious dimension of political accountability. Many agencies hold occasional public hearings and publish annual reports, which provide a limited basis for public scrutiny. Others publish newsletters, establish procedures for assessing information systems, make maps readily available, and maintain sophisticated websites that provide detailed information about what the agency is doing.

Creating opportunities for community consultation is another mechanism that has the potential for increasing accountability. Some agencies maintain advisory groups composed of resource users, government officials, and representatives of NGOs. Agencies also consult with community groups on a regular basis to get assistance in identifying resource-use problems in specific areas and management issues or in reviewing agency actions or plans.

In community consultation a key question about the degree of political accountability is how much authority agencies share with the community groups or advisory groups with which they meet. Some agencies organize processes in which public groups are encouraged to set priorities for management issues to be addressed, select criteria for evaluating planning proposals, or identify problems. In most such cases it is understood that such assistance is advisory to the agency. (It is not uncommon, however, for advisory groups to regard their advice to the agency as definitive and to seek to ensure that the agency follows their advice.) In a few cases, citizen groups have the legal right to hold management officials legally accountable. Hawaii's coastal management law, for example, has a "cause of action" provision that allows individuals affected by a coastal regulatory decision to bring legal action against the regulatory authority if the decision is perceived to have violated one or more of the state's coastal management guidelines.[25]

Types of Decentralized Administrative Arrangements for Coastal Management

Many of the prominent examples of decentralized approaches to environmental management involve coastal management. The U.S. coastal management program in particular is based on a key assumption that the wide variety of natural coastal conditions, management issues, and administrative and legal contexts requires carefully developed state programs. A review of the international experience with coastal management suggests that there are at least five general types of national-local relationships:

—Classic deconcentration

—Coercive devolution

—Cooperative devolution

—Devolved experimentation

—Local entrepreneurship.

Each of these types is briefly explained and an example is provided.

Classic Deconcentration

In the classic deconcentration model of intergovernmental relations, implementation authority is vested in the local or provincial officers of central government ministries. Technically, these officers are part of the same organization as the central government officers from whom they receive directions.

Coastal wetland management in the United States provides one prominent example of classic deconcentration. Coastal wetlands are important as a buffer against the erosive forces of moving water; as a natural means of flood control; as habitats for many wildlife, fish, and aquatic organisms; as recreational sites; and as open space and the locus of other natural values. Over half of all U.S. coastal wetlands have been filled, substantially altered, or converted to other uses.[26] Of course natural forces such as floods can alter or destroy wetlands, but human uses and activities are the primary source of change. Filling wetlands to create sites for warehouses, housing developments, agriculture, and highways and other infrastructure or channelizing them to create canals are among the many uses to which wetlands have been converted.

In the United States, responsibility for wetland management is shared among national, state, and local authorities, but the primary responsibility for coastal wetlands is the U.S. Army Corps of Engineers, which governs wetland uses under section 404 of the Federal Water Pollution Control Act of 1972, amendments of which in 1977 are commonly referred to as the Clean Water Act.

Anyone seeking to convert coastal wetlands to other uses must get a permit from the Army Corps. The Army Corps has standard national application procedures, but the permit review and decisionmaking process is delegated to the office of the district engineer in the district in which the wetland is located. The staff of the district engineer reviews the permit application, receives public testimony, and makes a recommendation.

The Army Corps regulations set forth extensive procedures for the permit process.[27] The application form must describe the purpose, scope, and need for the proposed activity; its location; and the names and address of adjoining property owners. It is Army Corps practice to consult with potential applicants prior to submission of an application for wetland conversion. Following submission of a permit application for activity in a wetland area, Army Corps staff must decide whether to grant the permit and, if granted, whether any conditions should be placed on the permit. In evaluating a permit application, the Corps is required to consider the recommendations of the U.S. Fish and Wildlife Service and the National Marine Fisheries Service. Comments and objections from certain state agencies, including the Coastal Zone Management Program, must also be considered. For the most recent year for which data are available, about 1 percent of all permit applications were denied and 5 percent were withdrawn. It is not clear what proportion of all applications had conditions attached before they were submitted.[28]

Developing and maintaining commitment of staff to whom management responsibility has been assigned is one of the key challenges in classic deconcentration. Local representatives of national agencies are likely to be generally responsive to the same incentives and sanctions that shape the behavior of professionals in large organizations. They are likely to behave in ways intended to elicit the esteem of colleagues and superiors (especially superiors), to seek to further their chances for promotion and assignment to more desirable posts, and to avoid, if possible, acting in ways that depart from perceived organizational norms. In general, if there is a perceived conflict between the organization and the task, commitment is to the organization. Commitment is often difficult to develop. As one study of a different federal agency found, "Regional and field office personnel generally believe they are in the most maligned of positions: between a 'rock and a hard place.' Agency staff feel that they have tough job assignments. Their burden is guaranteeing programmatic performance—but they often shoulder the responsibility for on-the-ground results with inadequate funding and lack of perceived empathy from the national office, and without [a] strong political base of support for their work from state or national actors."[29]

Coercive Devolution

In the coercive devolution model of decentralization, provisional or local governments are treated as regulatory agents of central government. They are expected to comply with regulatory and procedural requirements imposed by central government ministries. Laws or administrative rules spell out detailed standards and procedures for achieving policy objectives, which reduces the discretion of local authorities.[30] Failure to follow these standards or procedures may result in sanctions such as fines, loss of funding for local projects, or other penalties. The coercive devolution model assumes that local units of government lack the political will, capacity, or sufficient understanding of the management issue to achieve the agency's goals.

Florida's approach to environmental management and comprehensive planning exemplifies coercive devolution. The Florida approach prescribes the content of local land-use plans. It also establishes standards for review of local plans for consistency with state standards and imposes potentially rigorous sanctions for local governments that fail to comply with the substantive or procedural standards.

Florida's 1985 Local Government Comprehensive Planning and Land Development Regulation Act, also known as the Growth Management Act, mandated new local comprehensive plans and required that they be consistent with the goals of the state plan, the comprehensive regional policy plans, and other applicable statutes.[31] The state law requires that all 467 communities, 67 counties, and 11 regional planning councils prepare plans.[32] It authorized the state to establish minimum criteria for local plans, which the Department of Community Affairs subsequently acted on through rules in the Florida Administrative Code. The vertical consistency is complemented by the requirement for horizontal and internal consistency. Each local plan must include an intergovernmental element so that all local plans in a region are compatible with each other, a requirement that is important for coastal hazard mitigation, since hurricane evacuation routes can be protected from overdevelopment by the requirement that the traffic circulation, coastal regulation, and future land-use elements of local plans be coordinated with each other.

Administrative rules set minimum standards for judging the adequacy of local plans for state approval. Element by element, the rules list the types of data, issues, and goals and objectives that must be addressed by local governments in order to meet state goals. Administrative rules also establish an enforceable schedule of completion dates for all local plans. Amendments to adopted plans cannot occur more frequently than twice per year and each amendment is subject to review by the state for consistency with state policy. Another critical aspect of Florida's program is its "concurrency" requirement, which allows local governments to approve development only when there are plans for adequate public facilities to support it.

The Florida legislature authorized sanctions for local governments that did not submit plans on time and for plans found not to be in compliance with the Growth Management Act.[33] The state can withhold 1/365 of the state revenue-sharing funds for each day a local government's plan is late or held not to be in compliance. In addition to authorizing sanctions to induce compliance, the Florida Growth Management Act contains incentives to build the capacity of local governments to plan for and manage development.

In pure coercive devolution, accountability is upward to central government authorities. Central government authorities, such as Florida's Department of Community Affairs, design detailed reporting requirements, which usually include procedural requirements such as dates for completing specific plan elements and substantive requirements such as how the plan addresses floodplain standards.

In addition to these formal accountability requirements, there may be broader political accountability issues. Local elected or administrative officials may feel that the central government's procedural standards are unrealistic or they may regard substantive standards as too restrictive or inappropriate for local officials. Their formal accountability responsibilities may conflict with the interests of some local constituents. Local political accountability may be a source of resistance to central government standards.

In Florida, some local resistance—and resistance by special interest groups such as the development industry—has led to calls for a more focused, less top-down approach. A task force on growth management, the Growth Management Study Commission, appointed by Governor Jeb Bush in 2000, recommended a less centralized, less coercive approach to intergovernmental relations: "The Commission believes that the state's regulatory oversight of local government is too broad and, therefore, threatens the state's effectiveness in focusing on priorities of compelling statewide interest."[34]

Cooperative Devolution

The "cooperative devolution" approach to intergovernmental structures treats states, provinces, and local units of government as partners, albeit junior ones, with national government. It assumes that there is substantial agreement among national and subnational agency staff about the substance of policy or, lacking such agreement, that sufficient incentives can be provided to lower-level officials to encourage their commitment.

Coastal management in the Philippines provides one example of cooperative devolution. It has evolved from when central government agencies made most resource management decisions during most of the 1900s to the current situation in which many day-to-day management decisions and some policy decisions are made by local governments and communities.[35]

This model of intergovernmental relations assumes that local officials have the full range of planning, design, and implementation skills or can acquire them. In practice, however, the relevant capacities are often lacking or are underdeveloped. In the Philippines, capacity building included both skill building and institutional reform. National agencies, international donor projects, academic institutions, and NGOs organized and implemented training programs for local government staff, focusing on key coastal management issues, management frameworks, and specific skills. The relative newness of the notion of coastal management created some uncertainty at all government levels about how most effectively to integrate new management practices into existing management regimes.[36] This was—and is—particularly true for fisheries management and shoreline management. Capacity building is proving to be a long-term endeavor.

Devolved Experimentation

The devolved experimentation model of intergovernmental relations refers to situations in which central authorities identify general goals and objectives and mandate or encourage subnational units (such as provinces or local governments) to develop projects to pursue these general goals. The devolved experimentation model is based on the premise that subnational units have more knowledge about local resource issues and are therefore better able to design projects to address those issues. This model also assumes that local governments have or can acquire the capacity and resources to develop experimental or pilot projects that tailor national objectives to local conditions.

Sri Lanka's special area management (SAM) plans are an example of devolved experimentation. The two pilot projects, initiated in 1994, are part of a comprehensive approach to coastal management that had been evolving since the early 1980s. The Coast Conservation Act, enacted in 1981, was both a response to severe problems of coastal erosion and recognition that a broader approach to coastal management was needed that included measures to deal with habitat degradation and depletion, reduction of conflicts among uses and users, and other problems. The act established a three-hundred-meter coastal zone within which each development was to be regulated by permit, required a variety of coastal planning studies; and mandated the preparation of a coastal plan. A review of the Sri Lanka program in the early 1990s led to consideration of a "bottom-up" community-level strategy that would allow for intensive, comprehensive management of coastal resources in a well-defined geographic setting.[37] The strategy was tested at two pilot sites.

The two basic premises of the special area management plan process are that it is possible to organize local communities to manage their natural resources and that they will continue to do so if they perceive that they derive tangible benefits from better management.[38] Planners, planning agencies, and nongovernmental organizations play a catalytic role in organizing the local community by providing technical and financial support for the local community's management effort. Hence, the planning agency takes the role of facilitator, rather than that of superior authority imposing its will on the local community. An important aspect of such facilitation is that it ensures that technical analysis provides a sound scientific understanding of the nature, scope, and potential for sustainable resource use activities and financial support for project activities.

Community participation is possible in SAM planning and implementation to a degree not possible in broader area planning. Whether SAM planning is initiated by an outside national or local government agency or a private organization, it necessarily involves the people who live within the special area: the planning and management process includes the total ecosystem, including residents. Successful management of natural resources within the context of a SAM site requires local responsibility for implementation and monitoring.

Developing a special area management plan as practiced in the Sri Lanka context involves several steps: developing agreement on the need for a SAM process at the national level, compiling an environmental profile of the area, mobilizing the community with full-time professional facilitators and community organizers, and developing a local plan through extensive local participation.

Collective self-management is central to most local experiments. For example, local fishers may join together to impose fishing restrictions of various kinds on themselves in order to restore the local fishery. Developing and maintaining self-sacrifice requires continuing commitment on the part of participants. That commitment can be created through coercive measures, such as various forms of punishment to those who do not comply, or by earning their support and commitment through education and incentives of various sorts. Many community-level collaborations are organized to create benefits, such as a new pier, early in the project, which can help persuade participants that continuing communal efforts will have benefits sufficient to make participation worthwhile.

Devolved experimentation projects are designed to be accountable upward to the central authorities that encouraged them. Pilot projects are experiments designed to test local management initiatives and the potential of local self-management. Project designers are usually expected to be accountable for describing project activities and outcomes. They are also expected to provide judgments about the degree to which pilot project strategies are likely to be successful in other, similar, contexts.

Participation in project-level coordinating committees meeting regularly over months (or years) may result in real but less formal accountability expectations. The plans developed by the Sri Lanka SAM plan coordinating committees contained scores of specific actions to be undertaken by specific government agencies, user groups, or nongovernmental organizations. For some committee members, these initiatives reflect no more than their hopes about what the agencies they represent might be able to accomplish under ideal conditions. For others, the identification of specific actions in the plan represents an implicit contract for which specific agencies are accountable. Sri Lanka's initial experience with SAM planning has been positive. Indeed, the most recent national plan calls for the replication of SAM planning at twenty-three sites.[39]

Local Entrepreneurship

The "local entrepreneurship" approach to intergovernmental relations recognizes that resource management projects do not necessarily depend on central government mandates or encouragement. Local governments—and even communities—may respond to local resource-use issues by organizing and implementing management initiatives. Purely local projects may be established outside existing legal and administrative frameworks or in cooperation with local governments. They may be organized by community leaders, by staff of nongovernmental organizations or by other community organizers, including university extension agents.

Over the past two decades there has been phenomenal international growth in the designation of marine protected areas. Although some of them are designated by national or provincial government agencies as nature reserves, parks, national monuments, or habitat protection areas, a substantial number are small, well-defined areas where resource use and access is restricted.[40] In tropical areas of Asia, in particular, these marine-protected areas tend to consist primarily of coral reefs, mangroves, or other natural habitats. Community-level coastal resource management projects are being organized at a rapid rate for a variety of purposes, including fishing area rehabilitation, food security, reduction of user conflicts, and development of small-scale tourism enterprises.[41] Many community-based marine-protected areas are developed and managed as a cooperative effort between local communities and local government, and they often require a high degree of collective self-management. Although the development and implementation of local restrictions on resource users can cause community tensions, research indicates that community-level marine-protected areas can be successful in providing ecological, social, and economic benefits.[42]

In the Philippines, one of the first of more than four hundred community-managed marine protected areas worldwide was established in the early 1980s at Apo Island, a 74-hectare (185-acre) volcanic island located about five miles off the southern coast of Negros Oriental, a province on a larger island in the middle of the Mindanao Sea. The island is approximately 25 kilometers (about 15 miles) south of Dumaguete City, the provincial capital, and has about 250 households; it is part of the municipality of Daiun, on the main island. Its most significant coastal resource is its beautiful and abundant fringe of coastal reef.[43] In the late seventies fishing was the principal source of income for more than 75 percent of the households. At that time illegal fishing techniques such dynamite fishing and *muro-ami* (a form of net fishing that devastates coral reefs) were observed.[44]

Because of the beauty and richness of the reef and the apparent increases in illegal and destructive fishing practices, Apo Island began to attract the attention of extension workers at Silliman University, located in Dumaguete

City. Between 1979 and 1980, they conducted informal marine conservation and educational programs with the Apo Island residents. In 1982, an agreement was reached between the island village, Silliman University, and the Dauin municipal council regarding the establishment of a marine sanctuary and guidelines for use of the sanctuary.

In 1984, the Marine Conservation and Development Program of Silliman University, in collaboration with the residents and the local government unit, implemented the creation of a comprehensive marine reserve in the island's waters encompassing the entire marine habitat surrounding Apo Island to 500 meters (about 550 yards) offshore. The marine sanctuary was established on the southeast side of the island and covers an area of 11.2 hectares (28 acres)

In 1985, the community education center, which provided a venue for community meetings, workshops, seminars, and lectures and also functions as a tourist and visitor center, was established. A core group of community residents formed a marine management committee to assume responsibility for the enforcement and maintenance of the community-organized marine reserve. In 1986, a consumer's cooperative was started.[45]

The Apo Island experience was one of the earliest coastal management initiatives in the Philippines that used a community-based approach. Originally, Silliman University extension service representatives intended to conduct academic research at the site, but their involvement in the island's management of its resources eventually took a different turn. They initiated a basic information campaign that eventually paved the way for the establishment of a marine reserve. By developing relationships and strengthening local institutions, they built trust in the community, introduced new ideas, and increased the capacity of the people to make management decisions.[46]

Between 1985 and 1995, conditions of the reefs in the sanctuary significantly improved, from a total coral cover of 68 percent in 1983 to 78 percent in 1995. From 1992 to 1995, cover of hard corals increased from 41.3 percent to 53 percent.

The Apo Island experience is one of hundreds of community-level marine protected area efforts; as such it illustrates many of the intergovernmental issues involved in community-level management.

Some of the key features of each of the five approaches to decentralization are summarized in table 15-1.

Implications for Decentralized Coastal Management

What are the implications of these decentralized approaches for designing new management structures for coastal management? What lessons can be drawn about how to create more effective intergovernmental relationships to support coastal management? Several general lessons can be derived.

Table 15-1. *Models of Decentralization: Some Key Assumptions*

Management challenge	Classic deconcentration	Coercive devolution	Cooperative devolution	Devolved experimentation	Local entrepreneurship
Distribution of authority among levels of government	Local implementing officials are local staff of national agencies. Primary implementation authority remains in the national office. Local officials have minimal discretion in planning and implementation.	Local officials implement (plan, regulate, allocate, and so forth) but central government officials review local actions for consistency with national guidelines. Potential for constant tension between national officials and local officials about who is in charge.	General policy directives are set by national agencies, but local officials work out implementation details. Local officials are in substantial agreement with policy goals. National agencies may review local plans or implementation strategies for consistency with national policy goals.	National agencies set general policy agenda, but leave implementation details to local government. Implementation authority is primarily at local level. Local officials have authority to design and test implementation strategies tailored to local conditions.	Local officials design and implement management strategies. National officials may or may not be aware of local efforts.
Planning and management capacity	Implementation requires knowledge of national guidelines and expectations and the skill to apply them in specific cases.	Implementation requires knowledge of national guidelines and expectations and the skill to tailor them to local conditions if possible.	Local officials have the full range of planning, design, and implementation skills or can acquire them through staff development programs.	Local officials have detailed knowledge of local conditions (or access to people who do), strong leadership skills, specific skills in both community and	Local officials have detailed knowledge of local conditions (or access to people who do), strong leadership skills, specific skills in both community and

				resource appraisal and analysis, and planning and program design skills.	resource appraisal and analysis, and planning and program design skills. Local officials have the political skills to take local initiatives.
Commitment	Commitment of local officials to national direction is high because local officials are agents of national ministries.	Commitment of local officials has to be gained through education and incentives or penalties for non-compliance or both.	Commitment of local officials is gained through frequent interaction and negotiation.	Commitment is from central authorities to local officials.	Intergovernmental commitment is not an issue. Agency commitment is to local resource users and residents.
Accountability	Accountability is upward to national ministry superiors. It is accomplished through routine reporting.	National officials review local plans and regulatory decisions for compliance with national guidelines. National agencies reward local consistency and punish noncompliance.	National agencies are accountable to local agencies and local agencies are accountable upward.	Local agencies are expected to report on strengths and weaknesses of local resource management "experiments."	Local managers are accountable to local resource users and community residents.

Source: Author.

Tailor Administrative Approaches

Administrative approaches to decentralized natural resource management should be tailored to specific resource management issues, administrative and political conditions, and management capacities. The global experience of natural resource management generally and coastal management in particular is that decentralized approaches are more likely to be appropriate when

—The types and intensity of coastal management issues vary from place to place in the country.

—Resource degradation and depletion are the cumulative effect of the actions of many resource users, rather than of a few key users.

—There is a tradition of local management.

—Management capacity, in its many forms, is already adequate or can be developed where it is needed at the local level.

A key challenge in designing an intergovernmental approach to management is to determine what sorts of resource uses account for patterns of resource degradation and depletion. In situations in which the primary threats to coastal resources are associated with a few key uses, such as heavy manufacturing, a more centralized regulatory approach to management is likely to be more efficient and effective. A few key staff can do the analytic work required for identifying potential impacts, analyzing potential mitigation strategies, and making regulatory recommendations. In countries in which coastal problems are more local and involve multiple resource users, however, a more decentralized approach tailored to local conditions and the people who understand those conditions is likely to be preferable. Overfishing, conversion of mangroves to other uses, and other forms of habitat destruction are all general coastal issues, but they may be caused by different resource uses (and users) in different areas.

A second key consideration is the number and types of resource users whose behavior is to be managed. Centralized management works best when the number of users is small. When resource degradation and depletion is the cumulative result of the activities of numerous fishermen, coral miners, or other users, a more decentralized approach based on a detailed understanding of local conditions is likely to be more effective.

Management traditions are also important. Decentralized approaches work better when there is a tradition of local autonomy or where local institutions are already in place. In settings in which there is a history of local collective self-management, as in Sri Lanka and parts of Indonesia and the Philippines, these traditions can often be effectively revived and strengthened for contemporary management needs.

Find Solutions to Practical Dilemmas

Crafting decentralized natural coastal management programs requires resolving a number of practical legal, administrative, and political dilemmas.

Decentralization of coastal management involves more than just a general transfer of responsibility for management. Effective decentralization requires a specification of what resource management issues are to be addressed and a determination of what specific management tasks subordinate units of government are expected to perform. Will they be expected to design comprehensive planning processes? Regulate specific resource uses? Implement education programs? Establishing decentralized management tasks can be mandated by central authorities or negotiated among staff at different levels of government. Sometimes central government authorities provide general task guidance to subordinate units of government and encourage (or coerce) these agencies into preparing detailed plans indicating what management tasks will be performed by whom.

The allocation of authority among levels of government is the central focus of most decentralization efforts, but authority is only one of several issues that have to be addressed for decentralization to be effective. What, if anything, will have to be done to enhance the management skills and knowledge of officials assuming new responsibilities? What equipment, outside expertise, and other resources will they need? How will these resources be acquired? What should be done to ensure that local officials understand—and are committed to—the purposes of their new or enhanced responsibilities? To whom will local officials be accountable? How are they accountable? The types of decentralization sketched above are a reminder that the design of decentralized management presents the designer with a sort of multisided Rubik's Cube with which key institutional dimensions can be combined in a wide variety of ways.

Develop and Nurture Local Commitment

Developing and nurturing local commitment to management goals is a central challenge of decentralized management initiatives. Effective management requires the understanding and support of those charged with implementing management tasks. Implementing officials need to understand such issues as the biological importance of coral reefs and the ways habitat destruction depletes fish stocks and disposing of dredged material can degrade resources. Management officials at every level are more likely to be supportive if they have participated in developing management strategies rather than just carrying out tasks delegated from above. Such involvement can occur in a variety of ways. Participation in identifying key management issues, identifying and evaluating management options, or developing the details of local management plans are a few examples.

The ongoing management of coastal uses and activities occurs in a larger socioeconomic and political context. Converting mangroves, filling wetlands, discharging untreated wastes in coastal lagoons, and mining sand may degrade or deplete coastal resources, but they also generate jobs and income for some coastal residents. Seeking to manage these activities, to prohibit them outright, or impose conditions that mitigate them in significant ways may result in political resistance in some parts of the community.

In the politically charged arena of local resource management, local managers need psychological, political, and financial incentives to maintain a high level of effort. Some of the incentives are obvious: resources are needed to hire staff, organize training, conduct analysis, and engage in all the other tasks associated with developing local management capacity. Intergovernmental grants to support management functions can be a substantial incentive. Political support from national and local political elites in the form of building awareness and support for the management of uses affecting local resources is important. In addition, recognition accruing to local officials in the form of professional awards and acknowledgment can be a powerful incentive to support good management.

Transfer More than Skills

Developing local government capacity involves more than just transferring skills. Each of the five types of decentralized coastal management is based on different assumptions about the necessary skills and knowledge necessary for effective management. In the classic "deconcentration" and "coercive devolution" models of decentralization, effective management is treated as a matter of following detailed instructions for developing plans or projects, reviewing permit applications, and other implementation activities. In practice, effective use of these top-down models of decentralization requires development of some skills among local officials. Analysis of the "cooperative devolution" and "devolved experimentation" models reveals that the greater the management authority and discretion granted to local authorities, the greater the need for organizational strengthening as well as skill development.

Develop a System of Accountability

Developing a system of accountability is essential for effective decentralized management. Accountability systems can take a variety of forms. The conventional emphasis is on systems of upward organizational reporting. Formal systems of upward accountability include central government review of local plans or compliance with national guidelines, regular reports on the extent to which local governments have met national "benchmarks," and periodic program audits. Such accountability mechanisms are often imposed from above according to national guidelines, but they may also be negotiated among levels of government, as is the case of the U.S. coastal management program.

Ideally, accountability should also be downward as well. National government agencies should be accountable to local governments to provide the legal authority and management resources necessary for effective management. As a practical matter, local government agencies are also accountable in a variety of ways to local constituencies. Local officials know that they may be accountable to friends, colleagues, kin, and local citizens. The subtle—and not so subtle—demands and expectations of local constituencies can shape their management behavior. In short, local officials operate in a web of formal and informal expectations about how and to whom they will be accountable. The conventional emphasis in accountability systems is on ensuring bureaucratic or political compliance, but a truly ideal system is one that generates information that contributes to organizational learning, evaluation, and adaptation.

Notes

1. Kem Lowry, "Assessing the Implementation of Federal Coastal Policy," *American Planning Association Journal* 51, no. 3 (1985): 288–98.

2. UN Department of Economic and Social Affairs, Division for Sustainable Development, *Johannesburg Plan of Implementation* 2002, chapter 11, section H, paragraph 167, available at www.un.org/esa/sustdev/documents/WSSD_POI_PD/English/POIchapter11.htm.

3. Arun Agrawal and Jesse Ribot, "Accountability in Decentralization: A Framework with South Asian and West African Cases," *Journal of Developing Areas* 33 (1999): 473–502.

4. Richard Crook and James Manor, *Democracy and Decentralization in Southeast Asia and West Africa: Participation, Accountability and Performance* (Cambridge University Press, 1998); Agrawal and Ribot, "Accountability in Decentralization: A Framework with South Asian an West African Cases"; World Bank, *Entering the 21st Century: World Development Report 1999/2000* (Oxford University Press, 2000); Jesse Ribot, "Democratic Decentralization of Natural Resources: Institutional Choice and Discretionary Power Transfers in Sub-Saharan Africa," *Public Administration and Development* 23 (2003): 53–65; Paul Smoke, "Decentralization in Africa: Goals, Myths and Challenges," *Public Administration and Development* 23 (2003): 7–16.

5. Biliana Cicin-Sain and Robert Knecht, *Integrated Coastal and Ocean Management: Concepts and Practices* (Washington, D.C.: Island Press, 1998), p. 39.

6. G. Shabbir Cheema and Dennis A. Rondinelli, *Decentralization and Development* (Beverly Hills: Sage, 1983); Dennis A. Rondinelli and others, *Decentralization in Developing Countries: A Review of Recent Experience,* Staff Working Paper 581 (Washington, D.C.: World Bank, 1984); Diane Conyers, "Decentralization and Development: A Review of the Literature," *Public Administration and Development* 4, no. 2(1984): 187–97; Richard Crook and Alf Jerve, eds., *Government and Participation: Institutional Development, Decentralization and Democracy in the Third World* (Bergen, Norway: Chr. Michelsen Institute, 1991); Jeni Klugman, *Decentralization: A Survey of the Literature from a Human Development Perspective,* Occasional Paper 13, United Nations, Human Development Report Office, 1994; Joel Barkan and others, *Decentralization and Democratization in Africa,* Report on Decentralization and Democratization in Africa (New York: Ford Foundation, 1997); Mark Turner and David Hulme, *Governance, Administration and Development: Making the State Work* (Houndsmills, England: Palgrave, 1997); and John Cohen and Stephen Peterson, *Administrative Decentralization: Strategies for Developing Countries* (West Hartford, Conn.: Kumarian Press, 1999).

7. Cohen and Peterson, *Administrative Decentralization;* Smoke, "Decentralization in Africa."

8. Ibid.

9. Paul Sabatier and Daniel Mazmanian, "Policy Implementation," in *Encyclopedia of Policy Sciences,* edited by Stuart Nagel (New York: Marcel Dekker, 1983); Peter May, "Can Cooperation Be Mandated? Implementing Intergovernmental Environmental Management in New South Wales and New Zealand," *Publius* 25, no. 1(1993): 89–112; Peter May and Ray Burby, "Coercive versus Cooperative Policies: Comparing Intergovernmental Mandate Performance," *Journal of Policy Analysis and Management* 15, no. 2 (1996): 171–201; Kem Lowry and others, "National and Local Roles in Integrated Coastal Management in the Philippines," *Ocean and Coastal Management* 48 (2005): 314–35.

10. Robert Kay and Jackie Alder, *Coastal Planning and Management* (London: E and FN Spon, 1999).

11. Turner and Hulme, *Governance, Administration and Development;* Cohen and Peterson, *Administrative Decentralization;* Lowry and others, "National and Local Roles in Integrated Coastal Management in the Philippines."

12. Merilee Grindle, *Getting Good Government: Capacity Building in the Public Sectors of Developing Countries* (Harvard University Press, 1997).

13. Ibid.

14. Sabatier and Mazmanian, "Policy Implementation"; Cohen and Peterson, *Administrative Decentralization.*

15. Sabatier and Mazmanian, "Policy Implementation"; May, "Can Cooperation Be Mandated?"; Agrawal and Ribot, "Accountability in Decentralization."

16. May and Burby, "Coercive versus Cooperative Policies."

17. Lowry and others, "National and Local Roles in Integrated Coastal Management in the Philippines."

18. Ibid.

19. Sabatier and Mazmanian, "Policy Implementation."

20. Richard Margerum, "Collaborative Planning: Building Consensus and Building a Distinct Model for Practice," *Journal of Planning Education and Research* 21 (2002): 237–54.

21. Stephen Olsen and others, *A Manual for Assessing Progress in Coastal Management,* Coastal Management Report #2211 (University of Rhode Island, Coastal Resources Center, 1999), p. 46.

22. May and Burby, "Coercive versus Cooperative Policies."

23. Ibid.

24. Agrawal and Ribot, "Accountability in Decentralization"; Turner and Hulme, *Governance, Administration and Development.*

25. State of Hawaii, Revised Statutes Sec. 205A.

26. Tim Beatley and others, *An Introduction to Coastal Zone Management* (Washington, D.C.: Island Press, 2002).

27. U.S. Army Corps of Engineers, Jacksonville (Florida) District, "Regulations and Policy" (www.saj.usace.army.mil/permit/regulations/regulations.htm).

28. Ibid.

29. Denise Scheberle, *Federalism and Environmental Policy: Trust and the Politics of Implementation* (Georgetown University Press, 2004).

30. May and Burby, "Coercive versus Cooperative Policies."

31. Ibid.

32. State of Florida, Growth Management Study Commission, "Background" (www.dca.state.fl.us/growth).

33. May and Burby, "Coercive versus Cooperative Policies."

34. State of Florida, Growth Management Study Commission, "Background."

35. Lowry and others, "National and Local Roles in Integrated Coastal Management in the Philippines."

36. Ibid.

37. Stephen Olsen and others, eds., "Coastal 2000: Recommendations for a Resources Management Strategy for Sri Lanka's Coastal Regions," vols. 1 and 2, Technical Report 2033 (Colombo, Sri Lanka: Coastal Resources Center, Coast Conservation Department, 1992).

38. Alan White and J. Jayampathy Samarakoon, "Special Area Management for Coastal Resources: A First for Sri Lanka," *Coastal Management in Tropical Asia* 2 (1994): 20–24.

39. Coastal Resources Center, Coast Conservation Department, "Revised Coastal Zone Management Plan, Sri Lanka" (Colombo, Sri Lanka: 2004).

40. Rodney Salm and others, *Marine and Coastal Protected Areas: A Guide for Planners and Managers* (Washington, D.C.: IUCN [World Conservation Union], 2000).

41. Graeme Kelleher and others, "Guidelines for Marine Protected Areas" (Gland, Switzerland, and Cambridge, England: IUCN, 1999).

42. Richard Pollnac and others, "Discovering Factors Influencing the Success of Community-Based Marine Protected Areas in the Visayas, Philippines," *Ocean and Coastal Management* 44 (2001): 683–710; Richard Pollnac and others, "Factors Influencing the Sustainability of Integrated Coastal Management Projects in the Philippines," *Silliman Journal* 44, no. 1 (2003): 37–74; Richard Pollnac and Robert Pomeroy, "Factors Influencing the Sustainability of Integrated Coastal Management Projects in the Philippines and Indonesia," *Ocean and Coastal Management* 48 (2005): 233–51.

43. Antonio La Vina, "Management of Fisheries, Coastal Resources and the Coastal Environment in the Philippines: Policy, Legal and Institutional Framework," PIRAP-ICLARM Working Paper Series 5 (Manila, 1999).

44. Ibid.

45. Ibid.

46. Ibid.

16

Issues and Best Practices in the Decentralization of Natural Resource Control in Developing Countries

WILLIAM ASCHER

Many national governments wrested control over natural resources away from former resource exploiters at various times during the twentieth century, but are now in the process of considering or implementing the devolution of control to private individuals, community groups, or subnational governments.[1] The outcomes of these initiatives are often crucial not only because of the wealth generated from the resources but also to the well-being of the local populations, the health of the ecosystems, and even the levels of armed conflict within these countries. This chapter reviews the issues and best practices regarding the decentralization of natural resource control, covering both renewable and nonrenewable resources. The focus is on developing countries, because, despite recent efforts of some developed countries to devolve natural resource user rights,[2] this has been a much more common phenomenon in developing nations, and some of the challenges for developing countries are quite distinctive.

Evaluating the optimal decentralization of government services related to natural resource exploitation is a refreshing approach to assessing the issue of natural resource control. This perspective permits a more refined analysis of how to allocate the multiplicity of services, which are often ignored in the conventional analysis of ownership and property rights. The concepts of ownership and property are too crude to accommodate the fact that government should retain some responsibilities, facilitate but not dominate the exercise of user rights by others, and desist from involvement in yet other aspects of natural resource exploitation.

A few definitions and conceptual clarifications are necessary before getting into the concrete issues of natural resource control. First, "natural resource exploitation" (without the negative connotation sometimes associated with the term "exploitation") consists of

—development of natural-resource assets or infrastructure (for example, planting trees, building a dam, developing a mine, exploring for petroleum).

—extraction of natural resources (removal of ore, lifting of petroleum, harvesting timber).

—processing of extracted natural resources (ore or petroleum refining, wood processing of timber to lumber).

—sale of natural resources or processed products (sale of minerals or processed metals, of raw petroleum or petroleum products such as gasoline, or logs or processed wood products).

—transfer of user rights to natural resources (sale of land, transfer of land or exploitation rights owing to default of loans secured by the land or the rights).

Second, relying on Rondinelli's distinctions, we can differentiate among deconcentration, through which central government personnel are assigned to localities away from the governmental center; delegation, through which control is granted to state enterprises, lower-level governmental actors, or nongovernmental actors, but the higher-level authorities retain the discretion to reassert their control; and devolution, through which higher-level authorities grant or recognize the formal permanent control by lower-level governmental or nongovernmental actors.[3]

The issues, in almost all contexts, are whether to proceed with delegation or devolution, to whom, and how. The line between delegation and devolution is often fuzzy, because sometimes governments renege on devolving control, asserting that the rights holders have not complied with the terms of the transfer. Therefore the distinction between *granting* and *recognizing* the devolution of control is important, in that "granting" control, even if intended and initially understood as devolution, may come to be construed as delegation, if the government claims (perhaps in the face of political and legal challenges) that its authority to grant control implies the authority to take it back.

Devolution can entail privatization (if control is transferred to individuals, families, or corporations), or it can entail transfer of control to communities, which are then required to engage in collective resource governance. One of the auxiliary benefits of transferring control to local communities is that it provides a basis for participation and collective action, especially in regard to resources, such as water and forests, that are best managed on a larger scale. This has become a very common pattern.

Yet the transfer of control for collective management raises crucial issues regarding the definition of *community*. Although it is common to use the term *community* to mean all who live within certain geographical confines, community resource management usually entails control by a subset of people who have enough common background, identifications, and interests so as to legitimize their control and provide the potential for cooperation. Typically this entails related families that had exploited the resources under customary rights. Governance of resource exploitation by such a community is not the same as governance by the authorities over the geographical area (that is, government as conventionally defined). Within the community as defined by prior holders of customary rights, the possibility of fairly equal participation by all is typically much greater than in the case of a geographically defined *community* such as a commune, district, municipality, and so forth. Within many such jurisdictions, what looks to outsiders rather like equally shared poverty is in fact a sharply perceived hierarchy in which the very poor have limited standing in influencing local government.[4]

Background and Current Context

Any assessment of the decentralization of natural resource control must take into account the current context that has given rise to many of the initiatives to restore control to local populations, whether to families or to communities. Much of the context can be summarized in three points:

First, the most important factor is that governments have often moved to relinquish control over land and other resources only after the ecosystem and economic productivity of the area have been badly degraded. In many cases, the degradation had become an embarrassment for the government, especially where the government took over control by invoking conservation goals and the government's supposedly superior capacity to maintain the ecosystem. When control is devolved after such degradation has occurred, it is often an uphill battle for the new controllers to stop or reverse it.

Second, in many cases, natural resource decentralization initiatives are also driven by strong international pressure to devolve resource control to local communities. International conservation and human-rights organizations, official international organizations, and bilateral foreign assistance agencies have relied, rightly or wrongly, on the promise of community resource control to serve both environmental and developmental ends. Therefore initiatives to restore control over renewable resources to local communities are often magnets for foreign assistance. Yet when highly valuable renewable resources are at issue, publicized devolution initiatives are often coupled with less-publicized efforts to capture the resource rents by monopolizing the purchase and resale of the raw materials, taxing the resource profits in excess of prevailing tax rates, or otherwise appropriating the profits of resource exploitation. Moreover, the lure of receiving foreign assistance sometimes provokes insincere efforts at decentralization.

Third, environmental protection, beyond the considerations of sound management of natural resources as economic assets, has obviously become a much more important priority, both within countries and internationally. This entails raised expectations and additional burdens on resource exploiters, ranging from minimizing the contamination of air, water, and soil to the preservation of biological diversity.

Key Challenges

Four major challenges face governments seeking to control natural resources.

Conflict among Rivals for Resource Control

The struggles between people living in the vicinity of exploitable resources are often highly contentious. From Nigeria's Biafran civil war and the country's current conflicts over oil to the armed confrontations over Honduran forests, resource control issues often entail acute conflict far beyond what is typical for most questions of decentralization. For nonrenewable, subsoil resources such as minerals and oil, the conflicts are often regional, whereas for renewable resources such as water and forests the conflict is more likely to be among local contestants for control.

Adding to the potential for conflict, the prospects and effectiveness of resource control decentralization are often jeopardized by the jurisdictional competition among the various government agencies that have some involvement in natural resource exploitation or the initiatives that influence resource exploitation. Forestry departments, land reform agencies, agriculture ministries, irrigation authorities, and so on, are often in competition to control the regulatory processes, even if various user rights are devolved to subnational governments or to local communities. Multiple government entities issue conflicting land-use regulations, offer user rights to different individuals or groups, and create general uncertainty about the prospects of making a profit from exploiting resources responsibly.

Deterioration of the Capacity to Manage the Resources

The period of government resource control per se also poses serious problems for the restoration of user rights to former resource exploiters, especially when efforts to restore user rights to prior rights holders come many decades after the government appropriated control. In many cases the former rights holders or their descendants are too numerous or too physically separated from the resource site for all to reclaim their rights and maintain the resource endowment with sufficient sustainability. The degraded status of much of the land being handed back to earlier rights holders exacerbates the problem, insofar as the degradation has reduced the carrying capacity of the land.

The capacity of community groups to manage natural resources responsibly is challenged by conflict over definition of membership in the community, encroachment by people from outside the rights-holding community, the inability of the community to impose discipline on its own members, and weaknesses in managerial and technical expertise (which is not to say that central or subnational governments are typically highly capable). The community may not have the capital to finance the inputs needed to extract profitably without engaging in excessive extraction. These problems often set the stage for insufficient development and inefficient extraction.

Moreover, for a host of reasons it is rare that resource exploiters with restored user rights will initially practice sound management. Because they are often poor, and lack the social safety nets of access to insurance, inexpensive health care, or nonusurious credit, these resource exploiters often have short time horizons, made even shorter by whatever residual uncertainty they have about whether their rights will be honored in the future.[5] They may have lost the knowledge and skills of their forebears needed for sound resource exploitation, and the period without resource control and out-migration may have eroded the social cohesion needed for intracommunity discipline.

Corruption

Both direct government exploitation of natural resources and governmental regulation of private resource extraction often entail high levels of corruption. Natural resources are frequently exploited in remote areas, far from prying eyes, and government concession grants can greatly benefit concessionaires who pay less than the value of resources they extract. For resource exploitation undertaken by local communities under some degree of governmental regulation, the opportunity for low-level corruption by forest guards, tax collectors, and so on is very difficult to eliminate.[6] Yet the operations of state enterprises, in particular, have been notorious as vehicles for resource-based corruption, although it is often government officials, rather than the executives of the state enterprises, who direct the corrupt activities.[7]

Externalities

Finally, natural resource exploitation, whether of renewable or nonrenewable resources, often damages others without incurring any costs to the exploiters. For example, mining pollutes both air and water; excessive irrigation not only denies water to others but may also lead to salinization of aquifers; and oil spills can contaminate shores and soils. Without externally imposed penalties, these negative externalities are typically ignored by the resource-exploiting community or by the subnational government if the harm is done to other jurisdictions. Only an entity that has authority over the relevant ecosystem boundaries can be expected to address these externalities. By the same token, those who might otherwise be encouraged to maintain forests and marshlands that provide positive externalities in preserving habitat, reducing soil erosion, and conferring other benefits to the broader society lack the incentive to do so unless they can be compensated with some share of the benefits; again, the government is one of the major potential sources for such compensation. Nongovernmental organizations are another potential source.

Best Practices

Best practices considerations can be broken down into two areas: Which services and functions ought to be decentralized? And, when decentralization is advisable, what means and conditions of decentralizing those services and functions should be employed? The logic of dealing with renewable versus nonrenewable resources is different enough for the two categories to be treated separately.

Renewable Resources

As mentioned earlier, the major option for decentralizing renewable resources is to restore some degree of resource control to individual families or to local communities. In some circumstances, depending on the nature of the resource, the choice between transfers to a community or to families will be obvious. For example, control over irrigation systems serving the fields of several families will require communal control. Considerable success has been achieved in providing user-group control over irrigation in countries, such as Mexico, that suffered from very inefficient and deteriorating irrigation systems when the government controlled water distribution.[8]

With respect to control over land per se, however, deciding whether families or communities should be given control is difficult, because individual rights holding can undermine the economic viability of small holdings and exacerbate the problem of negative externalities, while community control may not be viable unless rather stringent conditions are present or can be created. Such conditions include
—Clearly defined boundaries
—Proportional equivalence between benefits and costs
—Effective and accepting collective choice mechanisms
—Capacity for monitoring compliance
—The capacity to formulate and implement graduated sanctions for violating restraint
—The capacity to resolve conflicts within the community
—Recognition by government

—Capacity to make connections with parallel and higher levels of organization, to provide political protection and access to expertise.[9]

These capabilities can be viewed as design principles for the community organizations and the government to follow in order to strengthen "common pool resource" management, but they also point to the difficulties of maintaining viable resource management if some of the capabilities are absent. The specific context has to be assessed from the point of view of the viability of individual versus communal resource control, using the criteria listed earlier.

If the former rights holders or their descendants can be easily identified and are not too numerous to manage the resources soundly, the following functions or rights ought to be devolved to them:

—Determining the use of the resources, as long as its exploitation does not create new negative externalities. However, their rights to liquidate the resources per se should not be constrained. Rather than considering such liquidation as a negative externality, it should be viewed as the withdrawal of a positive externality. If the government wishes to reduce the depletion of the resource, it should compensate the rights holders.

—Controlling the processing of the outputs, again, as long as these activities do not create new negative externalities. Resource exploiters ought to be able to determine whether they should process raw outputs themselves or sell them to downstream processors. Government-granted monopolies to state or private processors can easily squeeze the profits out of resource extraction, discouraging reasonable extraction and often creating smuggling and black markets.

—Controlling the sale of legal outputs of resource extraction, limited by the generic prohibitions against monopoly and oligopoly, and the transfer of user rights to the natural resources themselves. Government restrictions on the sale of outputs (such as requiring sale to a state purchasing organ) typically result in squeezing the producers as the government extracts too much of the potential profit, and often results in corruption. Prohibitions against relinquishing user rights, through either direct sale or using the rights as collateral, frequently leave low-income rights holders with an insufficient basis to secure capital by selling some portion of their assets or by borrowing. A dramatic case in point was the chronic impoverishment of the Mexican *ejidos* (communal lands established largely in the wake of the Mexican Revolution), which were the inalienable property of the *ejido* community members until the system was dismantled in the early 1990s.[10] The sale of output, whether domestic or exported, should be subject to the standard taxes for any product, so that exploitation is neither favored nor disfavored, and the temptation to fill the coffers with excessive taxes is averted. There are numerous cases in which excessive taxes undermine resource exploitation that is crucial for the nation's prosperity, ranging from the decline of cocoa production in Africa to the periodic reduction in Argentine beef exports.

For individual or community resource management to be viable, the government's devolution must be thorough. With reference to forest resources, Fisher notes:

> Very few countries have devolved any real level of authority for decision making over forest resources to communities[,] and tenurial rights, where present, are usually heavily restricted. Even where the legal provision exists for devolution of authority, real devolution has been restricted, either because of lack of commitment on the part of forest authorities to let go [of] their power, because subtle (and sometimes unsubtle) restrictions remain in force, because the resources necessary for effective devolution are limited, or due to some combination of these factors.[11]

In this circumstance, individuals or communities may liquidate the resource hastily in order to lay a stronger claim to tenurial rights.[12]

This devolution by no means implies that the government should withdraw completely, no matter how tempting it might be for the government to reduce its accountability and costs. Indeed, the abandonment of governmental responsibilities can easily undermine the reestablishment of sound community-based resource management. The appropriate government roles, derived largely from the preceding list of eight conditions, or design principles, for the community's effective resource management, are to

—uphold appropriate boundaries and the user rights of the community, making it clear that the government is recognizing user rights rather than granting such rights; this includes reducing the corruption committed by government officials at all levels, corruption that is tantamount to confiscating the fundamental user right of enjoying the profits of resource use.

—enforce rules against spillover damage (that is, negative externalities) when communities cannot resolve these problems.

—increase the availability of (market-rate) credit, whether through state institutions or by stimulating the emergence of private credit markets.

—support research and development; provide technical assistance and training; provide market information to stimulate greater yields, less wasteful resource extraction, better marketing, and so forth.

—aid diversification by reducing the bureaucratic obstacles to entering into new activities or markets.

—assist in the rehabilitation of highly degraded systems—which can be justified as compensation for prior expropriation.

—enter into joint ventures with communities that lack sufficient internal resources.

—undertake general poverty-alleviation programs and create social safety nets to encourage more farsighted resource management.

Another, obviously more difficult, situation prevails when, over the course of time, potential rights holders have proliferated beyond the carrying capacity of the resource base, or they have been so separated from their families' much earlier resource exploitation that they lack the interest to resume resource exploitation, or they lack the competence to do so soundly. In these cases, the government has to be more assertive in assigning user rights. The best way to do this is to establish a commission of respected experts and judges to consider claims and make the difficult decisions as to which of the claimants have not only the strongest claims but also the potential for sound resource management.[13] Nevertheless, the government must make it clear that the assignment of user rights is not rescindable.

When decentralization of aspects of resource management entails transfer of responsibilities to subnational governments, a key requirement is for the national government to ensure that the financial resources to carry out these functions continue to be provided. For example, when environmental regulation is delegated or devolved to provincial or local levels, the monitoring and enforcement capacities will deteriorate unless the national government directly allocates funds or enables the subnational governments to share in tax revenues

Another best practice consideration for delegating or devolving environmental-protection responsibilities is that the nested nature of ecosystems requires a parallel nesting of ecosystem management agencies at the various national and subnational levels. Complete abandonment of environmental-protection responsibilities by the national government would result in conflicts among subnational units regarding pollution.

It must be recognized that neither individual nor communal resource management is likely to be sound overnight. Governments must show great patience in considering whether, ultimately, to rescind user rights, and indeed to ask whether governmental control would in fact be better in any event. Governments must recognize that capacities often need to be built up over time, in terms of expertise, financial capacity, networking, governance capacity, and so on.

Nonrenewable Resources—Decentralization to State Enterprises

In virtually all countries, with the notable exception of the United States, subsoil resource rights are the property of the state. The key administrative and management issue is whether to decentralize control to state enterprises; the key distributional and political issue is whether to earmark control over some of the revenues to subnational governments.

The most important administrative criterion in determining whether to delegate to a state enterprise is the competence of the government to manage the collection of the resource rent from those who extract the resources. It is extremely rare that a state enterprise in the crucial nonrenewable resource sectors of oil, gas, and mining actually monopolizes resource extraction, even in countries that have gone through highly politicized and publicized nationalizations (Mexico and Venezuela in oil; Chile and Zambia in copper). International companies play a surprisingly major role, whether or not the state enterprise is directly engaged in development and extraction. As numerous developed countries demonstrate, a government ministry or department is sufficient for interactions with private domestic or international oil and mining companies.[14] For a developing country, the financial risks to scarce national income are too great to risk on oil or mineral exploration, when international firms can more easily take the risks because of their multicountry diversification. Therefore state financial resources should not be exposed to this risk, and there is no economic or technical reason why a state-owned company should be involved in exploration, extraction, or processing.

The question, then, is whether the government oil or mining ministry has the capacity to arrange fair auctions, negotiate fair contracts, and oversee the activities of the multinational companies to secure the appropriate royalties. Only if civil service regulations do not permit the employment of highly skilled experts who can accomplish these tasks would it be worthwhile to set up separate state oil or mining enterprises. The existence of these enterprises typically reduces the transparency of revenue capture and allocation, creates an off-budget source of finance that top government leaders are tempted to use for political gain, and engenders waste unless the fiscal arrangements between the government and the enterprise charge royalties as if the state enterprise were a private concern. Such fiscal arrangements are rare indeed.[15]

Despite the problematic nature of state enterprises involved in nonrenewable resource exploitation, the reality is that for reasons of national pride and politics, very few are likely to be fully dismantled. Therefore some guidelines on how governments should interact with their state resource enterprises are in order:

—Royalties. The state resource enterprise ought to be charged for the in-ground value of the resource (the "resource rent") as it is extracted, with the rent calculated by deducting the industry-standard operating costs from the sale value of the extracted resources. Unless the enterprise is charged for the rent in this way, meaningful profitability and efficiency cannot be determined. A state enterprise that does not pay the full royalty may appear to be profitable even if the resource wealth is reduced through excessive spending and inefficient extraction or processing. Charging a royalty based on the actual costs rather than industry-standard costs would only mask the inefficiency of the enterprise. This fiscal arrangement will also greatly reduce the scope of the state enterprise to serve as the nontransparent, "off-budget" funder of projects that government leaders wish to finance outside the central budget process. Such projects often do not stand up to careful economic scrutiny (which is frequently why leaders are tempted to fund them off-budget), and the projects are often beyond the scope of the state enterprise's competency. Aside from royalties, state enterprises should be subject to the same profits taxes as private firms.[16]

—Investment budget approval. In some cases the investment budget of the state resource enterprise is so large vis-à-vis that of the national economy that it may have macroeconomic impacts of concern to the nation's economic ministries. Moreover, the state enterprise managers typically wish to expand the operations of their enterprises, despite the risk of wasting investment on a depleting nonrenewable resource base. As the major (and often sole) shareholder of the state enterprise, the government has discretion over the investment budget, yet it must exercise restraint in its handling of macroeconomic issues. Several state enterprises crucial for their countries' export revenues, including Mexico's oil company PEMEX and Chile's copper company Codelco, have at various times been undercapitalized relative to the investments required to maintain efficient operations and to take advantage of strong world prices.[17]

—Social services. State resource enterprises should not be burdened with responsibilities to provide social and community services beyond those expected by private firms in their service to employees and their families. Government agencies have the responsibility, and typically greater competence, to perform these functions. Undertaking these activities without compensation from relevant ministries would also undermine the assessment of the profitability of the enterprise. When the remoteness of resource-extraction locations makes it difficult for government agencies to provide on-site services, the relevant government agencies should pay the enterprise to provide the services.

—Incentives for efficient operation. In keeping with the efficiency rationale of establishing state enterprises rather than simply relying on government agencies, managers of state enterprises must have incentives to pursue efficient operations. Beyond the crucial step of gauging true profitability by charging for the resource rent, and the employee performance bonuses prevalent in the private sector, the government can provide incentives for state-enterprise managers through performance contracts between the relevant government agencies to provide more assured access to foreign exchange; more freedom from government authorizations for importing, exporting, and other operations; greater certainty in future investment budgets; and so on. However, unless performance contracts have meaningful performance metrics and the relevant government agencies are committed to the arrangements, the contracts will not be effective.[18] Partial privatization of state resource enterprises is often helpful for increasing the transparency and available expertise

—Decentralization of control over nonrenewable resource revenues. The difficulty of the issue of decentralizing control over some portion of the revenues from nonrenewable resource exploitation reflects the fact that there are neither technical nor normatively optimal formulae for dividing subsoil wealth between regional residents and the rest of the nation. At a minimum, local residents should be compensated for any disruption in their lives and environmental degradation that the exploitation of subsoil resources entails. Beyond that, the question becomes normative and political: How much of the resource ought to go to the resource-producing region to address poverty in that region—if in fact it is greater than other regions—and how much is necessary to reduce the political backlash when local people realize that "their" wealth is being transferred to other regions? The political disruptions in southern Nigeria, the Democratic Republic of the Congo (formerly Zaire), Amazonian Ecuador, and many other oil- or mineral-dependent countries reflect the dissatisfaction with the low levels of these transfers. However, the recently formulated proposals to Ecuador's Shuar group to open up Shuar lands to oil exploration show that mutually acceptable arrangements may be devised. Whatever volume of fiscal resources is transferred to the resource-bearing regions should be allocated through a process involving communal organizations, if they exist, as in the case of the Shuar, or through government-led public participation, perhaps akin to the poverty reduction strategy process that the International Monetary Fund and the World Bank have required countries seeking debt relief to undertake in order to provide meaningful input from the poorest segments of the population.[19]

Conclusion

Despite the myriad difficulties facing the decentralization of both renewable and nonrenewable natural resource exploitation in developing countries, successful cases of each are not uncommon, and various approaches for overcoming the obstacles have been developed and applied so that governments can learn from these experiences. The prospects for sound management of renewable resources are greatly enhanced if the national government continues to provide facilitative services, reflecting a genuine commitment to transfer control for the sake of the environment and the local residents rather than a convenient abandonment of the national government's responsibility. Viable transfers of management control over major nonrenewable resources, which should be delegated to state enterprises only if relevant expertise cannot be secured within government agencies, face pitfalls that have technical solutions but are politically difficult to overcome. Transfers of control over the proceeds from non-renewable resource exploitation, which must be calibrated according to political considerations as well as considerations of poverty alleviation and to compensate for disruption to livelihoods, should be allocated through processes involving public participation.

Notes

1. There have been many variants on this expropriation. For example, Indonesia's 1946 constitution assigns all property rights in natural forests to the national government; Honduras nationalized all forests under the control of a state enterprise in 1974.

2. In Australia and New Zealand, the issue is restoring land to aboriginal peoples; in the United States, it has largely focused on restoring land to native Hawaiians.

3. Dennis A. Rondinelli, "Government Decentralization in Comparative Perspective: Theory and Practice in Developing Countries," *International Review of Administrative Sciences* 42, no. 2 (1981): 133–45; Dennis A. Rondinelli, "Decentralizing Public Services in Developing Countries: Issues and Opportunities," *Journal of Social, Political and Economic Studies* 14, no. 1 (1989): 77–98.

4. James C. Scott, *Weapons of the Weak: Everyday Forms of Peasant Resistance* (Yale University Press, 1985).

5. It is important to keep in mind that forests are typically found where agriculture is less productive, and generally has low economic yields per unit of area; the "tail-enders" of irrigation systems are often without water during droughts, and the land being restored is often of low quality.

6. Paul Robbins, "The Rotten Institution: Corruption in Natural Resource Management," *Political Geography* 19 (1999): 423–43.

7. Cases of top government officials manipulating the revenues of state resource enterprises are documented in William Ascher, *Why Governments Waste Natural Resources* (Johns Hopkins University Press, 1999); Richard M. Auty, *Resource-Based Industrialization: Sowing the Oil in Eight Developing Countries* (Clarendon/Oxford University Press, 1990); Terry Karl, *The Paradox of Plenty: Oil Booms and Petro-States* (University of California Press, 1997).

8. Cecilia Gorriz and others, "Irrigation Management Transfer in Mexico," World Bank Technical Paper 292 (Washington, D.C.: World Bank, 1995).

9. Elinor Ostrom, "Design Principles and Threats to Sustainable Organizations That Manage Commons," Working Paper W99-6 (Indiana University, Workshop in Political Theory and Policy Analysis, 1999).

10. William Ascher, "Community Natural Resource Management Policies in Colombia and Mexico," in *Great Policies: Strategic Innovations in Asia and the Pacific Basin,* edited by John D. Montgomery and Dennis A. Rondinelli (Westport, Conn.: Praeger 1995): 199–221.

11. R. Fisher, "Innovations, Persistence and Change: Reflections on the State of Community Forestry," in *Community Forestry: Current Innovations and Experiences* (Bangkok: Regional Community Forestry Training Center and Food and Agricultural Organization of the United Nations, 2003): 16–29.

12. For example, R. K. Godoy, K. Kirby, and D. Wilkie, "Tenure Security, Private Time Preference, and Use of Natural Resources among Lowland Bolivian Amerindians," *Ecological Economics* 38 (2001): 105–18, find that among lowland Amerindians in Bolivia, felling trees is regarded as a farsighted action if the forest users believe that "clearing" will strengthen their land claims.

13. The South African Land Claims Court is a good example of a thoughtful, orderly process, though it does not precisely fit the definition because most of the claims brought in it are for restoration of farms under private control by white farmers, not for recognition and restoration of indigenous people's claims.

14. The United States has no government-owned oil or mining enterprise; the formerly state-owned oil companies of the United Kingdom (British Petroleum), and Italy (ENI) are

now fully or largely privately owned. France's Total and Royal Dutch Shell were both formed at the instigation or with the support of the respective governments, but were privately owned from the outset.

15. Yair Aharoni and William Ascher, "Restructuring the Arrangements between Government and State Enterprises in the Oil and Mining Sectors," *Natural Resources Forum* 22 (1998): 201–13.

16. The fiscal arrangements between governments and state enterprises are discussed in Jeffrey Davis and others, eds., *Fiscal Policy Formulation and Implementation in Oil-Producing Countries* (Washington, D.C.: International Monetary Fund, 2003).

17. Ascher, *Why Governments Waste Natural Resources,* pp. 153–65.

18. For example, India's Hindustan Copper Limited had performance contracts with the government of India's Ministry of Mining, but the ministries determining access to foreign currency and relieving approval processes were not bound by the contracts. For a more general treatment, see Mary Shirley, "Why Performance Contracts for State-Owned Enterprises Have Not Worked," Public Policy for the Private Sector Note 150 (Washington, D.C.: World Bank, 1998).

19. The poverty reduction strategy process is described as follows: "Poverty Reduction Strategy Papers (PRSPs) are prepared by governments in low-income countries through a participatory process involving domestic stakeholders and external development partners, including the IMF and the World Bank. A PRSP describes the macroeconomic, structural and social policies and programs that a country will pursue over several years to promote broad-based growth and reduce poverty, as well as external financing needs and the associated sources of financing" (for more information, see the website of the International Monetary Fund, www.imf.org/external/np/exr/facts/prsp.htm).

Contributors

WILLIAM ASCHER is the Donald C. McKenna Professor of Government and Economics at Claremont McKenna College. Previously, as professor of public policy and political science, he directed Duke University's Center for International Development Research (1985–2000). He studies policymaking in developing countries, natural resource policy, Latin American and Asian political economy, political psychology, and forecasting methods and has written *Forecasting: An Appraisal for Policymakers and Planners; Scheming for the Poor: The Politics of Redistribution in Latin America; Natural Resource Policymaking in Developing Countries; Communities and Sustainable Forestry in Developing Countries;* and *Why Governments Waste Natural Resources.*

GUIDO BERTUCCI is director of the Division for Public Administration and Development Management, Department of Economic and Social Affairs, United Nations. He has served the United Nations in a number of capacities for twenty-five years in the areas of human resources, financial management, and administration. From 1971 to 1974 he was associate professor of comparative constitutionalism at the Catholic University of Milan. From 1992 to 1993 he was an associate professor of public administration at New York University, Robert F. Wagner Graduate School of Public Service.

PETER BLUNT is program manager of the AusAID-funded Timor-Leste Public Sector Capacity Development Program. In the 1990s he worked with the United Nations Development Program. His experience encompasses more than fifteen years as a senior consultant specializing in governance and public sector management in developing countries and eight years of small business management in the private sector. His consulting experience has entailed capacity and institution building, policy analysis and development, strategic planning, and major evaluations. He has held professorships at universities in Britain, Australia, and Norway and has published ten books and more than fifty refereed journal articles.

DERICK W. BRINKERHOFF is senior fellow in International Public Management with Research Triangle Institute (RTI International) and has a faculty associate appointment at George Washington University's School of Public Policy and Public Administration. Dr. Brinkerhoff has published extensively, including seven books and numerous articles and book chapters. His research interests focus on democracy and governance, postconflict reconstruction, decentralization, citizen participation, policy management, and capacity building. He holds a doctorate in administration, planning, and social policy from Harvard University.

JENNIFER M. BRINKERHOFF is an associate professor of public administration and international affairs at George Washington University. Her research interests include interorganizational relations and networks, development management, evaluation, civil society associations, failed states, governance, and diasporas. Dr. Brinkerhoff has published numerous articles and book chapters as well as a book on topics related to governance. She holds a Ph.D. in public administration from the University of Southern California, Los Angeles.

ENRIQUE CABRERO is a professor and researcher with the Public Administration Division of the Center for Teaching and Research in Economics (CIDE) in Mexico City and has been its general director since 2004. He has coordinated research and dissemination projects on local governance and innovation, including research on municipal government and financial management trends. Dr. Cabrero's publications include *Los Dilemas de la Modernización Municipal; Políticas Descentralizadoras en México (1983–1993); Políticas Públicas Municipales;* and *Acción Pública y Desarrollo Local.* He is founder of the academic journal *Gestión y Política Pública* and of the *Innovation in Local Government Award* in Mexico. He holds a Ph.D. from HEC in France.

LEDIVINA V. CARIÑO holds the rank of university professor at the University of the Philippines. She has served as dean of the UP National College of Public Administration and Governance and was the director of what is now the Center for Local and Regional Governance. She is a member of the International Advisory Committee of the Ash Institute for Democratic Governance and Innovation, JFK School of Government, Harvard University.

G. Shabbir Cheema is principal adviser on governance, Division for Public Administration and Development Management, United Nations. He is also visiting fellow at the Ash Institute for Democratic Governance and Innovation, Harvard University. Previously he was director of the Management Development and Governance Division of the United Nations Development Program. From 1980 to 1988 he worked as development administration planner at the United Nations Center for Regional Development, Nagoya, Japan. He has taught at Universiti Sains Malaysia, University of Hawaii, and New York University. Dr. Cheema's books include *Decentralization and Development, Building Democratic Institutions: Governance Reform in Developing Countries,* and *Reinventing Government for the Twenty-First Century.*

Merilee S. Grindle is Edward S. Mason Professor of International Development, John F. Kennedy School of Government, Harvard University, and faculty chair of the master's in public administration program. In July 2006 she was named the director of the David Rockefeller Center for Latin American Studies at Harvard University. She is a specialist on the comparative analysis of policy-making, implementation, and public management in developing countries, with particular reference to Latin America. Dr. Grindle is the author of several books, including *State and Countryside: Development Policy and Agrarian Politics in Latin America; Challenging the State; Audacious Reforms: Institutional Invention and Democracy in Latin America;* and *Despite the Odds: The Contentious Politics of Education Reform.*

Goran Hyden is distinguished professor in the Department of Political Science, University of Florida, Gainesville. He has written extensively on politics, administration, and development, especially about Africa. His most recent publications include *Making Sense of Governance* and *African Politics in Comparative Perspective.* He has served as consultant to several multilateral and bilateral agencies as well as governments and other organizations in Africa.

John-Mary Kauzya is chief of the Governance and Public Administration Branch, Division for Public Administration and Development Management, United Nations Department of Economic and Social Affairs. He has also served in the same branch as adviser on governance systems and institutions. The Governance and Public Administration Branch spearheads programs and activities of governance and public administration capacity building in various countries. Dr. Kauzya has lectured at Makerere University and at the Uganda Management Institute, where he worked as assistant lecturer, as head of a division, and then as deputy director.

Kem Lowry is professor and former chair, Department of Urban and Regional Planning, and director of the Program on Conflict Resolution, University of

Hawaii. He has published articles on planning and environmental management, ocean and coastal management, conflict resolution, and evaluation in such journals as *American Planning Association Journal, Urban Law Annual, Publius, Environmental Impact Assessment Review, Policy Studies Review, Ocean Yearbook,* and *Research and Coastal Management Journal.* He has served as a consultant on ocean and coastal management projects in Hawaii, Sri Lanka, Indonesia, Thailand, and the Philippines.

STEPHANIE MCNULTY is a senior program officer at the Academy for Educational Development. She has a Ph.D. in Political Science from George Washington University. As a Fulbright Scholar in Peru she evaluated citizen efforts to oversee and participate in regional governments. She has lived and worked in Chile, Honduras, and Peru, where for ten years she designed, managed, and researched programs to strengthen civil society. Dr. McNulty has written articles and monographs on civil society, accountability mechanisms, and foreign policy.

DENNIS A. RONDINELLI was senior research scholar at the Duke Center for International Development at the Terry Sanford Institute of Public Policy, Duke University; director of the Pacific Basin Research Center, Soka University of America, Aliso Viejo, California; and Glaxo Distinguished International Professor of Management at the University of North Carolina–Chapel Hill. His research and teaching focused on international development policy, globalization, decentralization, privatization and public-private partnerships, and private enterprise development. He wrote or edited eighteen books and published several hundred book chapters and articles in scholarly and professional journals. In addition, he served as an adviser, consultant, or expert to the U.S. State Department's Agency for International Development, the World Bank, the Asian Development Bank, the Canadian International Development Agency, the International Labour Office, the United Nations Development Program, and private corporations. In 2002 Dr. Rondinelli was appointed, and reappointed in 2006, to the United Nations Committee of Experts on Public Administration.

MARIA STEFANIA SENESE is a consultant at the Division for Public Administration and Development Management, Department of Economic and Social Affairs, United Nations. She holds a Ph.D. in public administration from the University of Rome Tor Vergata. She was assistant professor of public management at the university in 2000–04, where she was involved in the coordination of several projects in the field of institution building and public administration reform. As a consultant, she has developed an annotated literature review and issue papers on governance challenges in crisis and postcrisis situations as well as on issues related to trust in government. She has written a book on the role of quality and benchmarking in local administration and several book chapters and journal articles on public management.

NARESH SINGH is the executive director of the Commission on Legal Empowerment of the Poor, the first global initiative for making legal rights work for the poor. Before joining the commission, he served as director general of governance and social development at the Canadian International Development Agency; worked at the United Nations Development Program as principal adviser on poverty and sustainable livelihoods; and was director of the Poverty and Empowerment Program at the International Institute for Sustainable Development in Winnipeg, Manitoba. He is an adjunct professor at Boston University, School of Public Health, and a visiting scholar at Global Equity Initiative, Harvard University. He has been an adviser to several organizations and is an honorary fellow of the Centre for International Sustainable Development Law at McGill University.

PAUL SMOKE is professor of public finance and planning and director of international programs, Robert F. Wagner Graduate School of Public Service, New York University. His main research and policy interests include public sector decentralization and urban development, with a particular focus on East Africa, Southern Africa, and Southeast Asia. He previously taught at the Massachusetts Institute of Technology and worked with the Harvard Institute for International Development. Dr. Smoke has written or edited several books and published in numerous journals, including *World Development, Public Administration and Development, International Journal of Public Administration,* and *Third World Planning Review.*

MARK TURNER is currently professor of development policy and management in the School of Business and Government, University of Canberra. He has considerable experience in public administration reform, especially decentralization, in many countries of the Asia-Pacific region. He has worked as a short-term consultant for a number of bilateral and multilateral agencies, including the Asian Development Bank, the United Nations Development Program, the World Bank, and AusAID. Dr. Turner's books include *Challenging Global Inequality* (with A. Greig and D. Hulme); *Trends and Challenges in Public Administration Reform in Asia and the Pacific; Decentralisation in Indonesia: Redesigning the State* (with Owen Podger); and *Central-Local Relations in Asia-Pacific: Convergence or Divergence?*

KADMIEL H. WEKWETE is director of local development practice, UN Capital Development Fund, which supports programs in the least developed countries. He was previously senior technical adviser in the UN Habitat and the Urban Management Program. He is a leading African urban and regional planner. He has taught at the University of Zimbabwe and has published extensively on Africa, including *Planning Urban Economies in Southern and East Africa* and *Decentralizing for Participatory Planning: Comparative Experience of Zimbabwe and Other Anglophone Countries in East and Southern Africa.*

Index

Abra (Philippines), 182

Accountability: administrative accountability, 274; community consultation and, 275; concepts and issues of, 191, 274–75; democratic decentralization and, 117, 234; development funds and, 224–25; devolution and, 170–87, 279, 281; elections and, 104; innovations and, 251, 252; at the local level, 174–86, 252, 273–74; participatory budgeting and auditing, 181–82, 197–99, 207, 208; political issues of, 43, 274, 275, 279; service delivery and, 115; systems for, 274. *See also* Corruption

Accountability—*individual countries*: in Mexico, 69; in Peru, 197–99, 208; in the Philippines, 100, 105, 107, 108; in Scandinavia, 212

Action Nord-Sud, 33

Administration: decentralized development administration, 22, 24–26, 34–40; externally established administrative structures, 26–29; Internet and, 45, 49–50; parallel and partnership approaches to, 24–34, 35–39; postconflict reforms, 23, 24, 25

Afghanistan: administration and government in, 26, 124, 125–27; build-operate-transfer arrangements in, 29–30; decentralization in, 125, 126; international assistance in, 27, 125, 126; joint ventures in, 32–33; poverty alleviation in, 127; service delivery in, 126, 127; strategic importance of, 125. *See also* Communications issues—*individual countries*

Afghanistan Reconstruction Trust Fund (ARTF), 27–28

Afghan Wireless Telecommunications Company, 32

Africa: centralization in, 214, 215; church groups in, 254; communication technology in, 50; corruption and crime in, 216, 219; decentralization in, 4, 16, 75–76, 77, 118, 213, 215–20, 225–26, 258–61, 264; development in, 214–15, 216–17; economic issues in, 218, 219, 256; educational issues in, 248; foreign aid and development funds for, 216–17, 219, 220, 221–27; governments in, 8–9, 219, 224–25, 247–51; history of, 214, 218; institutional models in, 254; least devel-